Spiritual Elders

Spiritual Elders

Charisma and Tradition in Russian Orthodoxy

Irina Paert

NORTHERN ILLINOIS UNIVERSITY PRESS

DeKalb

Published by the Northern Illinois University Press, DeKalb, Illinois 60115
Manufactured in the United States using postconsumer-recycled, acid-free paper.

Design by Shaun Allshouse

Library of Congress Cataloging-in-Publication Data
Paert, Irina.
Spiritual elders: charisma and tradition in Russian Orthodoxy / Irina Paert.
p. cm.
Includes bibliographical references (p.   ) and index.
ISBN 978-0-87580-429-3 (clothbound: alk. paper)
1. Spiritual directors—Russia—History. 2. Spiritual directors—Soviet Union—History. 3. Spiritual life—Russkaia pravoslavnaia tserkov'—History. 4. Russkaia pravoslavnaia tserkov'-History. 5. Russia—Church history—18th century. 6. Russia—Church history—1801–1917. 7. Soviet Union—Church history. I. Title.
BX382.5.P24 2010
253.5088'281947—dc22
2010014129

Frontispiece: Elders of Valaam.
Source: Rossiiskii gosudarstvennyi arkhiv kinofotodokumentov.
Courtesy of the Russian Archives of Documentary Films and Photographs

To my mother, Tatiana,
and to my husband, Immanuel

Contents

List of Illustrations

Acknowledgments

The writing of this book has taken a long time and has been interrupted by the births of children and moving to a new country. At some point, writing this book became the only thing that was not changing, a token of stability. This is why I feel I must express gratitude to the subjects of my book, the Russian elders, who kept me interested, motivated, and continuously entertained in the process of researching and writing.

I was looking for a new project after the publication of my book on Russian Old Believers. Accidentally, I attended a talk on Bishop Ignatii Brianchaninov, a nobleman who abandoned what had promised to be an illustrious career in the court of Tsar Nicholas I and turned to monasticism under the influence of Elder Leonid Nagolkin. I was fascinated by the relationship between Elder Leonid, the commoner, and the nobleman turned humble novice, and I thought that the subject of elders would allow me to research interactions between the official church and popular culture. I am grateful to the participants of three seminars on spiritual and religious themes in Russian culture, which I co-organized with Anat Vernitsky, and which became an ideal environment in which to discuss the ideas that later took shape as the project on Russian elders. The Gregynog Colloquia Support Fund and the University of Wales, Bangor, were essential for making two of these seminars materialize. My thinking about Russian elders benefitted from the response to research papers I have given at the research seminars at the London School of Slavonic Studies, the Centre for Russian and East European Studies at Birmingham, and the History Department of the University of Wales, Swansea. I am also grateful for the hospitality of the Monastero di Bose in Italy, which organized inspirational conferences on aspects of Orthodox spirituality. I have found three of these especially useful for my project: the conferences on Nicodemus of the Holy Mountain and the *Philokalia* (2000), on Optina pustyn' (2002), and on the Jesus prayer (2004).

Research grants from the British Academy enabled me to carry out research in Russia in 2003–2007, while the study leave in 2004 jointly supported by the Arts and Humanities Research Council and the University of Wales, Bangor allowed me to take time off teaching to write this book. While the book was in its early stages, the central resource for historians of Imperial Russia, the Russian State Historical Archive, lost its home in the center of St. Petersburg and closed its doors to researchers for several years. As an alternative, I decided to survey provincial archives in search of evidence on Russian *starchestvo*. I found the staff at the National Archive of Mordovia in Saransk and in National Archive of Tatarstan in Kazan particularly helpful and friendly. In Moscow, the Manuscript Department of Russian State Library (Leninka), home to the magnificent library and archive of Optina pustyn', served as an endless source of discoveries. I thank the Russian Archives of Documentary Films and Photographs in Krasnogorsk for their assistance in locating the photographs for the book. Larisa Petina of the Estonian National Library went to great lengths helping me with bibliographical searches and illustrative material. I also thank Vladimir Ivanovich Petrov, Maksim Antipiov, and Nikita Andrejev for providing photographs for this book. There were many individuals who made my research trips memorable and efficient. I thank Marina Mogilner and Il'ia Gerasimov for their hospitality, assistance, and intellectual stimulation during my visit to Kazan. In Moscow I enjoyed the hospitality of Aleksei Beglov and Lidia Chakovskaia, Elena Smilianskaia, N. N. Lisovoi, and Margarita Korzo; in St. Petersburg that of Boris and Alla Kordochkiny, Sergei Shtyrkov, and Jeanne Kormina.

When I started to think about the book I found a good many people who were fascinated by the subject of Russian spiritual elders and who provided inspiration and help for my research. The late Archimandrite Simeon (Brüschweiler) shared many insights about spiritual guidance based on his own experience, as well as his memories of Father Sofronii (Sakharov). Conversations with Aleksei Beglov, Krstu Banev, Liviu Barbu, Dr. Stephen Thomas, and Fr. Petr Mangilev about the role and status of elders in the Orthodox Church provided me with new ideas. Nikolai Nikolaevich Lisovoi and Gelian Mikhailovich Prokhorov offered their expertise and advice in guiding my research. Steve Smith, William Wagner, Jeanne Kormina, Faith Wigzell, Aleksei Beglov, and Stephen Thomas read various parts of the book and offered their invaluable comments. I am grateful to Jim English, who has not only skillfully edited the manuscript but also provided criticism and comments on its style and argument.

This book would not have been written without the valuable research assistance of Maksim Antipov, who helped me with bibliographical work and archival research. I also thank Aleksei Beglov and Oksana Filicheva who rendered their help in archives at the earlier stages of research. Margarita Korzo, a dear friend and a colleague, helped to arrange letters to Russian archives and also endured hours of my deliberations on the subject of eldership.

I thank my colleagues at the History and English Departments of the University of Wales, Bangor for their support and encouragement in my pursuits in the field of religious history. I am especially grateful to Ceri Sullivan, Tony Claydon, Wil Griffith, and Hugh Price for sharing their insights into English and Welsh ecclesiastical history and religious poetry. I express special gratitude to Peter Gatrell whose advice and friendship were essential to the success of this project. At Northern Illinois University Press I thank Mary Lincoln who encouraged me to submit the manuscript before she retired from the press, and Amy Farranto, the commissioning editor for Russian Studies, for her support and enthusiasm. Special thanks to Susan Bean and Julia Fauci for their efficient work on the manuscript.

During the writing of this book I had to learn the art of sharing my professional life with my family. My two sons, Matteus and Daniel, were sources of solace during the frustrating struggle to bring the book to its completion, while my husband Immanuel Pärt was unfailingly supportive and encouraging. He spent hours formatting the text and making sure that all drafts of the book were properly archived. I am eternally in debt to my mother Tatiana who helped me to find time for revising the book by taking care of the children and the household. I also thank Arvo and Nora Pärt for giving me insight into the aesthetic side of spiritual life, as well as their love, support, and inspiration.

Spiritual Elders

Introduction

If you see a young monk climbing up to heaven by his own will, grasp him by the feet and throw him down, for this is to his profit. . . . If a person places his faith in someone else and surrenders himself to the other in full submission, he has no need to attend to the commandment of God, but he needs only to entrust his entire will into the hands of his father. Then he will be blameless before God, for God requires nothing from beginners so much as self-stripping through obedience.

—*Apophegmata Patrum*[1]

So, what is a *starets*? A *starets* is the one who takes your soul, your will into his soul and his will . . . .

—Dostoevsky, *Brothers Karamazov*

December is one of the darkest and coldest months in Finland. I am in Heinävesi, 400 kilometers north of Helsinki, sitting in a cozy guest room in Valamo (New Valaam) monastery. I came here to do research on Russian spiritual elders. In 1940, during the Winter War against the Soviet Union, 205 Russian monks took refuge here, bringing with them hundreds of holy books and icons. The monks, the youngest of whom were in their 50s and 60s, had to evacuate their fifteenth-century monastery, which was situated on a group of islands on Lake Ladoga. After the Bolshevik Revolution in 1917, Valaam became part of autonomous Finland. During the 1920s–1930s, it was popular with Russian pilgrims from neighboring Latvia and Estonia as well as tourists from Finland, Sweden, and other countries. The Valaam monks had an established reputation as spiritual elders, or *startsy*, who answered people's spiritual questions and helped to heal the wounds of the soul. One visitor, in an account of his experience at Valaam, wrote that even a brief interaction with an elder would teach one to reevaluate many things in life including one's own self, thus achieving the ideal of Socrates' maxim, "Know thyself."[2] Another recalled the feeling of profound awe when, during a discussion with one of Valaam's elders, he realized that the elder had responded to many of his unspoken thoughts.[3]

The task engaged in here is to capture and recount the story of the Russian elders in order to make clear their historical and cultural significance, not least in the Russian context. Although the term *starets* has various connotations (such as an old person, a person of authority in medieval monasticism or in the Russian South, a blind beggar), in this book I have approached elders as persons of exceptional spiritual insight who often (but not necessarily) provided religious directorship to neophytes. Even though many of the elders were priests or monks, or both, being an elder was not a church office, but rather an informal ministry. Individual supplicants engaged with spiritual elders sometimes with, or sometimes without, the sanction of the institutional church. The reputation of an elder was established "from below" by ordinary believers and an elder's disciples. Hence, within the Orthodox Church, eldership may be regarded as a more democratic, nonhierarchical form of religious authority, which, until now, has not received sufficient analysis.

The main focus of this book concerns a period of Russian history that was characterized by modernizing tendencies and by Russia's unprecedented and profound involvement in the cultural life of Europe. By the beginning of the eighteenth century, spiritual guidance had become an obscure and marginal practice surviving only among a few religious dissenters. The attempts to introduce eldership into some Russian monasteries during the Enlightenment caused conflict and resistance. However, eldership experienced a resurgence in the nineteenth century and survived the ruptures and political changes of the twentieth. In the Soviet Union, the institution and practice of spiritual guidance persisted through informal channels, and it was an important factor in the religious revival of the post-Soviet era. Today eldership is widely recognized as a specific form of ministry within the Russian Orthodox Church. This book is an exposition and analysis of how the practice of spiritual eldership, with its origins in early Christian ascetic communities and fourteenth-century monasticism, became a distinctive characteristic of modern Russian Orthodoxy. It also addresses the manner in which elders responded and adapted to specific aspects of modern life and religious practice.

The number of active spiritual elders during any one period was never large. Even during the "Golden Age" (in the nineteenth century), only a handful of monasteries and parish priests turned to the practice of spiritual guidance. However, when assessing the significance of elders we cannot rely on the data produced by the institutional church, which had authority to legitimize certain religious practices and delegitimize others. For example, there were about 30 elders canonized by the Russian Orthodox Church between 1988 and 2000, but many more were venerated as saints. A number of charismatic leaders who were regarded by the laity as spiritual directors and elders are known to us from popular hagiographical accounts.[4] Many of them had an uneasy relationship with the institutional church. The significance of elders can best be measured by their popularity: the canonization of Serafim of Sarov in 1903 brought about 300,000 visitors, including the royal court, to the obscure provincial town of Sarov.[5] This suggests that the influence of individual spiritual elders was disproportionate to their relatively small number.

Startsy and Tradition

Elders represent a unique characteristic of Russian Orthodoxy, a symbol of Russian spirtitual and cultural tradition.[6] The Latin roots of the word "tradition" (Russian *traditsiia*) suggest the act of passing on, or "giving across."[7] The word itself signifies continuity with the past and unchangeability. It is not surprising that in the periods of historical change that involve the transformation of social and cultural forms, as for example in post-Soviet Russia, there is much emphasis on tradition and traditional values. Keeping in mind that during the modern period many "traditions" have been invented for ideological purposes, the emphasis on "traditionality" of certain cultural forms has to be treated with caution.[8] Despite this caveat, in this book tradition is understood as collective memory. Conceptualizing tradition as a form of collective memory allows the scholar to "emphasize its ability to establish connections and constitute identity."[9] Religious traditions can be interpreted as acts of remembrance of those moments during which transcendent reality interrupts the dominant reality of everyday life. Religious experience of the sacred, however, can be potentially dangerous because it relativizes, if not devalues, the everyday cares of human life. One of the social functions of collective memory is to tame the destructive potential of religious experience by institutionalizing it.[10] Religious collective memory is essentially a reconstruction of the past.[11] It is not unified and coherent; in the case of Christianity, there are always competing claims to the more truthful "remembrance" of Christ's teaching, and there is a tension between "dogmatics," who are preoccupied with making the past conform to the teaching of the church, and "mystics," who claim that they "relive" the past, as in the act of the imitation of Jesus Christ. While the project of mystics in the evocation of the past complements the memory of the church, their experience and claims cannot be totally assimilated by the church, and often cause friction.[12]

Elders need to be understood in the context of ascetic tradition. Even though not all ascetics could be elders, the majority of elders practiced asceticism to various degrees. Asceticism (from *askesis*, exercise, discipline) stands for a specific set of attitudes and practices that aim at combating vices and developing virtues. In Christianity, including Orthodoxy, renunciation of sexual relations, the abandonment of home and property, and extreme forms of fasting and self-withdrawal were widespread expressions of asceticism.[13] Ascetic traditions can be interpreted as forms of "collective memory enacted in the body." Every detail in ascetic traditions, such as the monastic rules, the control of the body, and dietary restriction, relates to performance of the memory of tradition, linking the individual self and the cosmos.[14]

Approaching tradition as collective memory may help explain why certain traditions need to be recovered from obscurity, revived, and apparently "invented." Throughout the modern period there were bursts of interest in ancient theological heritage, including the Desert Fathers and patristic literature.[15] Educated church reformers in nineteenth-century England actively rediscovered pre-Reformation tradition as a way to renew the liturgical and spiritual practice of the Anglican Church.[16] It was not unusual for religious reformers to appeal to the authority of tradition that needed to be recovered and renewed in order to stimulate a profound spiritual revival.

The Russian elders saw themselves not simply as the recipients and transmitters of the Eastern Christian tradition, but as active contributors to the renewal of tradition, which they believed had been distorted and interrupted during the period that followed the fall of Constantinople in 1453. The Ukrainian-Moldavian monastic reformer Paisii Velichkovskii (1722–1794) and his followers were in the vanguard of the contemplative revival that self-consciously appealed to premodern Christian sources. The copying, translation, publication, and dissemination of "forgotten" ancient and medieval texts by monastic reformers like Paisii was accompanied by the introduction of "forgotten" forms of spiritual guidance. This project was in sharp contrast to the dominant discourse of theological schooling and mainstream religious life. The deliberate archaicization of the language (Greek texts were translated into Church Slavonic rather than Russian), the use of medieval liturgy, and the revival of antiquated forms of worship were part and parcel of the elders' project.

Scholars have traditionally interpreted the Russian spiritual revival of the nineteenth century as a recovery of the Byzantine-Bulgarian hesychasm of the fourteenth century.[17] Hesychasm (from the Greek *hesychia*, silence), which refers to a movement in the fourteenth-century Byzantine Empire, serves here as a shorthand term for a set of texts and practices that came to Russia via the South Slavs in the 1300s–1400s, which essentially focused on the nature of mystical experience and its place in the Orthodox tradition.[18] In the eighteenth and nineteenth centuries, this "neo-hesychast" revival was epitomized in the *Philokalia* (known in Russian as the *Dobrotoliubie*), a collection of texts by Early Christian and Byzantine authors on the subject of mystical prayer and practical guidance. What may appear today as a triumphant rediscovery of Orthodox spiritual roots was not perceived as such at the time.[19] Within the mainstream Synodal culture, hesychasm and the writings of the Philokalic Fathers were treated with suspicion. Elders suffered occasionally from accusations of distorting tradition and deviating from Orthodoxy. Ultimately, however, the elders were instrumental in preserving and advancing Orthodox spiritual discipline, including both written and oral traditions, and they played a key role in establishing Orthodox religious identity in the modern period.

Interpreting Elders
Charisma and the Holy Man

Although *startsy* did appeal to the authority of tradition, they could exercise power by virtue of their personal charisma, which endowed them with an aura of exceptional powers and qualities.[20] That *startsy* were charismatic and prophetic figures is not disputed among the theological commentators.[21] While in a theological sense charisma refers to a gift of the Holy Spirit and does not permit social or psychological explanations, in this book the analysis of the social impact of the *startsy* is significantly influenced by sociological theories of charisma, and by Weber's work in particular.

Weber, just like Nietzsche, imagined charismatic individuals as more emotionally charged and more vivid than ordinary humans.[22] In contrast to bureaucratic and traditional types of authority, charisma was personal and had its source of power in itself. The charisma of a prophet, according to Weber, distinguished him from a priest, a magician, and a teacher of ethics, since the prophet exercised his power not only through miraculous acts but also through his claims to divine revelation.[23] Essentially charisma is anti-structural and revolutionary, and usually emerges in times of crisis. However, despite its transformative nature, charisma is essentially unstable and prone to routinization and depersonalization.[24] It is this potential of charismatic leadership to be turned into an institution (which perpetuates itself through office, legal regulation, tradition, and education) that underpins Weber's deep pessimism about the possibility of individual action.[25]

Subsequent studies of charisma paid attention, not to charismatic leadership as such, but to the conditions in which it arose and the social networks it produced. For example, situations in which there was a social need for charismatic leadership (the so-called "charismatic demand"), and the interaction between the leader and his followers were deemed to be of equal or greater importance than were the individual qualities of the charismatic leaders.[26] Charisma was no longer perceived as a personality attribute, but "a successful claim to power by virtue of supernatural ordination."[27] To understand charisma, anthropologists argued, one must decipher the cultural ontologies, the symbolic order on which the charismatic relationship was built.[28] Scholars also became more skeptical about the revolutionary power of charisma, since "individuals who set their personal authority over and against established text, norms, and customs [had] already begun to 'perpetuate' themselves in the form of a re-textualization, a re-normalization."[29]

In addition to the sociological concept of charisma, the understanding of *startsy* in this book owes much to Peter Brown's insights about the holy man in early Christian society and to the debates that these insights provoked. Just like the holy men and women in the world of late antiquity, the Russian *startsy*, who were not formally canonized as saints and were largely interstitial figures, performed a mediatory role in a socially divided society and exploited the symbolic capital of their spiritual authority. The holy man was an influential outsider who—by virtue of his peripheral position—was able to perform the role of a patron, or a "hinge-man," in the rural world of late antiquity.[30] According to Brown, even though the rise of the holy man marked a specific phase of religious history, one could speak of certain continuities and parallels between the world of early Christianity and that of eighteenth- and nineteenth-century Russia, traceable at least in the forms of religious behavior. In Russia, the spiritual authority of *startsy* rested on the perceived holiness of their persons and coexisted with other loci of sacred power, such as icon, temple, and the relics of saints.

Startsy and the Russian Orthodox Church
Problems of Status and Identity

This book was conceived with an aim to reevaluate our understanding of certain aspects of the Russian Church by focusing on the status and role of the *starets* within the Orthodox community. There has been a persistent tendency to treat the Russian Church in the modern era as an over-governed, impersonal institution that, due to its assimilation with the state apparatus, had lost its initiative and social influence.[31] Even though the Church's dependence on and subservience to the state has never been as absolute as historians sometimes believed, there is no doubt that following the reforms of Peter the Great, the Church increasingly became a bureaucratically rationalized institution that operated through formal procedures and restricted spontaneous expressions of popular piety. How then do we explain the extraordinary role that elders came to play during the Synodal era, given that their authority and popularity derived not from a formal position within the Church but from personal holiness? Here elders are presented as an example of the internal incongruities and tensions within Russian Orthodoxy. One cannot simply contrast the noninstitutionalized authority of a *starets* with the formal-instrumental rationality of the Holy Synod, or to put it in Weber's terms, charisma against bureaucracy.[32] Formal office and charisma were not mutually exclusive in the Russian Orthodox Church; many nineteenth-century spiritual elders combined the reputation of a prophet with the position of a priest, abbot, or even bishop.[33] Although the conflicts between *startsy* and church administrators often revealed differences between these forms of power, some bishops had a high regard for *startsy* and respected them as holy men.[34]

While the tension between the centralizing tendencies of the Synod and the centrifugal and sometimes anarchic forces of eldership was to be expected, it did not signify that elders had a dissenting and antistructural nature. Charismatic authority was a legitimate and sanctioned element of the Church's theology and practice. Yet it should be noted that the elders' unique position within Russian Orthodoxy demonstrates more often than not an extraordinary autonomy exercised by individual bearers of charisma vis-à-vis church hierarchs. Brown remarked on this paradoxical feature of the Eastern branch of Christianity—that power came not from a single source but from multiple sources, as was the case with the holy men of late antiquity.[35] This feature of Orthodoxy acounted for Father Sergii Bulgakov's comment that the absence of church discipline would break the unity of the church in periods of crisis.[36]

The uncertainty of the elders' status partly derived from the lack of uniformity and consensus within Russian theological discourse. Bishop Makarii Bulgakov's scholastic view of the Church as a hierarchy of ordained clergy with Christ as its founder and the laity as a subordinate "class" was a typical expression of the official theology of post-Petrine Russia.[37] In this vision of the Church the charismatic elders could only be regarded as bona fide religious leaders if they had a proper place within the church structure—being ordained as priests or tonsured as monks. This view was opposed by the Slavophiles' understanding of the Church as a living organism, thus shifting the emphasis from the established hierarchy to interior principles that expressed the "agreement and unity of spirit and life of all the members who acknowledge it."[38] Khomiakov emphasized that the catholicity (*sobornost'*) of the Church was an expression of the presence of the Holy Spirit that guaranteed its inner unity, understood not as a mechanical combination of all parts and members, but as a mystical and spiritual communion with God among all of the members of the Church.[39] This vision shifted the emphasis from the ordained hierarchy to the community of saints who "reign with Christ."[40] Khomiakov's interpretation was extended through the discussions of the Circle of Enthusiasts of Spiritual Enlightenment, founded in the early 1900s by the ex-Tolstoyan intellectual, Mikhail Novoselov.[41] Although the group included members of the clergy, its affiliates were critical of the Synod, which was presented as a force alien to true Orthodox *sobornost'*.[42] Pavel Florenskii, the most distinguished theologian in the circle, argued that the essence of Orthodox ecclesiality (*tserkovnost'*) had to be defined not in legal or historical language, but in aesthetic terms. For Florenskii, beauty was the criterion of the authenticity of spiritual life, and elders were the experts in the beauty of the spirit and masters of the ascetic "art of arts." Thus, elders served as an example of the existential and practical character of Orthodox ecclesiology as well as the precursors of the new millennium.[43] Another member of the Circle, Sergei Mansurov (1890–1929), included spiritual elders in his ambitious project of rewriting Christian history, which was now presented as a succession of men and women, including apostles, martyrs, ascetic saints, and spiritual elders, who were guided by the Holy

Spirit. This succession did not exclude priests and bishops, as long as they were true witnesses of Christ; they were not included merely by virtue of their ordination.[44]

Although the institution of eldership did not originate in Russia, elders became central to Russians' understanding of their own religion and culture. The ways in which eldership was defined (in accordance with the view that the Holy Spirit was the essence of Christian life) made the national church appear unique and spiritually superior to other Christian traditions. However, the elevation of eldership could lead to theological distortion, such as the view that salvation comes via an individual elder rather than through the sacraments of the Church or the commandments of Christ.

According to some scholars, the Orthodox Church, presented as one of the pillars of the Old Regime, failed to capitalize on popular support in the revolutionary era.[45] This thesis, too, requires modification. While in the past, the degree of the Church's popularity was evaluated by means of estimates of church attendance, performance of sacraments, and the lure of sects, the study of elders allows us to assess the more intimate and subjective aspects of religious belief as evidenced in the relationship between individuals and charismatic religious leaders. While the study of *startsy*-focused spirituality addresses only one aspect of popular religion, it provides a more nuanced assessment of the ways in which the Church was gaining or losing popular authority across the prerevolutionary and postrevolutionary period.

Popular Religion

Two aspects of our subject, the social impact of elders who had some rank or position within the institutional church, and the possibility for the laity to exercise charismatic authority that gave them the status of elders, lead us to the problem of popular culture, or, more specifically, popular religion. During the late 1960s–1980s, the scholarly interest of medieval and early modern historians in the field of popular beliefs and cultural practices resulted in a fascinating body of research that has influenced other sections of the historical profession.[46] The debates that were inspired by this research cannot be avoided by the student of Russian culture and religion. Challenging such a persistent stereotype of Russian popular culture as the "dual faith" or "double belief" (*dvoeverie*), which implied that the Russian masses retained their pagan beliefs under a "thin coat" of Christianity, allowed scholars to write critical and more nuanced histories of Russian religion and culture and respond to the debate among European historians about "the two-tier model," which constructs "popular" and "elite" culture as analytically distinct categories for the purposes of investigation.[47] The key areas of the debate—to summarize roughly—were firstly, whether the concept of popular culture continued to have any heuristic value; secondly, whether it was possible for a historian to access the domain of popular culture through historical sources that may reveal nothing more than "forms of downward mediation by educational or literary elites"; thirdly, if popular culture was no longer understood as autonomous, how should a historian approach the relationship between the various levels within any particular culture; and, finally, how could the study of culture deal with problems of power and hegemony?[48]

Russian elders have been conceptualized as those who "straddle[d] the boundary between the church and the world," as the mediators between the Church's "high culture," on the one hand, and the laity, including the Russian peasantry, on the other.[49] If we adopt this view of spiritual elders as mediators, we have to deal with the following questions: in what ways did they play the role of mediators; how can this view help us to understand the relationship between the different domains of Russian religious culture; and, does it allow us (at least indirectly) to access the realm of the beliefs and practices of ordinary people? Here we apply what Peter Burke called the "oblique approach" to the study of brokers or mediators between learned and popular culture.[50] The mediators, who in Burke's view possessed a second culture, that of the uneducated popular classes, in addition to their own, could act as transmitters of popular culture to the learned, thus producing a "two-way flow."[51]

Elders could embody the different aspects and ramifications of cultural processes: they often adopted the language and values of a subordinate culture, which made them more successful in accessing the moral communities of the peasantry.[52] This form of *starchestvo* is usually associated with Optina pustyn'. Other *startsy* were the representatives of a subordinate culture that adopted some of the values of the hegemonic culture, subverting it from within, as was the case in the "Name of God" (*imiaslavtsy*) spiritual movement.

Heterodoxy

For a long time the study of Russian religious history was influenced by a distinction between mainstream Orthodoxy and religious sectarianism in Russia (the distinction produced by the polemical exchange between these religious camps and from there transported to the minds of scholars). This was constructed using the familiar dichotomies "high" and "low" and dominant and alternative cultures. In fact, however, there were more influential exchanges between the Orthodox Church and dissenting Old Believers than scholars generally assumed.[53]

What the Orthodox Church and various dissenting groups had in common was a set of shared ideas and practices which were legitimized by tradition, personal experience, and miracles—what Engelstein called "a variation on a common theme."[54] The themes that the dissenters and mainstream Orthodoxy held in common were hesychast spirituality, which influenced various mystical sects, and asceticism. Nineteenth-century hesychasm was not an exact copy of the fourteenth-century Byzantine monastic movement, but a loose set of texts and oral traditions that were shared by semiliterate peasants and high-born aristocrats, by sectarian Old Believers, or skoptsy, and Orthodox bishops.[55] It was the pervasiveness of hesychast teaching in the Russian culture of the seventeenth and eighteenth centuries that, according to Clay and Panchenko, played a principal role in the formation of ecstatic spiritual practice and ideology among Russian mystical sects such as the *Khristovshchina* and the Skoptsy.[56] The parallels in the practices and beliefs of "pernicious" sectarians on the one hand, and Orthodox elders on the other, such as prophecy, asexuality, and the tendency toward self-sacralization, suggest that there was a greater exchange and more interaction between these different layers of religious culture than has hitherto been assumed.

Apart from the transmission of these shared values and beliefs, there were also direct exchanges between Orthodoxy and "heterodoxy" in Russia that found expression in conversions, direct borrowings (texts, liturgical and monastic practices), and missionary contacts. Spiritual elders' encounters and associations with Old Believers, sectarians, and non-Orthodox confessions (so frequently mentioned in their biographies), were central rather than incidental to their function and religious identity. Several prominent *startsy* in the nineteenth century had backgrounds in Old Belief or in *edinoverie* (the official form of union between Old Believers and the Orthodox Church), while others were involved in proselytizing work among Old Believers. The combination of the elders' charismatic authority and their ability to form nonauthorized associations often made them the targets of accusations of sectarianism. Thus, the elders not only bridged a gap between the Church's "high culture" and the religion of the Russian peasant, but also traversed the camps of the Synodal church and that of its apostates.[57]

Sources

To a certain extent, availability of sources has dictated the parameters of this work. It is based on a synthesis of, firstly, archival sources deriving from both local and central archives, and secondly, diverse materials relating to biographies and works of individual elders including memoirs, correspondence, and edificatory texts. As a rule, archival sources for church history provide only a limited insight into the practices and methods of spiritual elders, as their focus is primarily on the economic aspects, organization, and building projects of particular monastic establishments, and on the conflicts between individual elders and church hierarchs. Occasionally, the archives of particular monastic communities, such as Optina or Sarov pustyn', or Valaam monastery, contain rich material reflecting the ways in which eldership was practiced, received, and promoted within monasteries and beyond them. While elders in Imperial Russia are the main focus of the book, in the last chapter we trace their fortunes in the world transformed by the revolution. While not aiming to present an exhaustive analysis of elders in Soviet Russia (that subject merits a separate book), attention is drawn to the persistence of Orthodox tradition and changing concepts of *starchestvo* in the twentieth century. Since the Perestroika era, many formerly classified archives of the Soviet period have become accessible to historians. Yet there is a fundamental problem with these sources, compared to those of the prerevolutionary period: religious institutions, the clergy, and the facts of their biographies are usually presented in a distorted way, through the prism of ideology. To compensate for this shortfall, published sources, memoirs, and biographies, in particular, have been used, as well as secondary material.

Sources that originate from within the elders' circles provide a valuable insight into the practices of spiritual guidance, yet have their limitations: in particular, the popular genre of spiritual biographies (*zhizneopisanie*), or accounts of the life of specific revered men and women who were not yet canonized as saints. In G. Fedotov's words, "The sources of the saint's life . . . are documents of unequal value as historical evidence: some of them are testimonies of the first order, others belong to the category of legend."[58] In comparison with medieval hagiographies, however, an eighteenth- and, especially, nineteenth-century *vita* is better grounded in historical and biographical details, and expresses more interest in individuality, rather than conforming to a specific hagiographical model.[59] The writer Konstantin Leont'ev, for example, praised the spiritual biographies of Elder Leonid of Optina and Hegumen Antonii (Medvedev) of Trinity-

Sergius Lavra, authored by Klement Zendergol'm, for surpassing works of the same genre in their attention to the subjects' individuality.[60] Even though published biographies had to conform to the specific requirements of the genre and of censorship, many *zhizneopisaniia* reflect the struggle for an elder's legacy among his disciples, and provide rich background for assessing a saint's life.

THIS BOOK HAS SIX CHAPTERS. Chapter One provides a historical background of the phenomenon of *starchestvo*, tracing its history from the desert monastic communities of the early Christian era, through medieval Byzantium and the Latin West, its evolution in the world of Eastern Orthodox Slavs, and to its revival in the eighteenth century. The focus of Chapter Two is the revival of spiritual guidance in the period of the secularization and Westernization of Russian society and the Orthodox Church. The connection between Russian elders and the rediscovery of hesychast writings in the Balkans is examined, while the path of the Balkan monastic émigrés who were instrumental in introducing the discourse and practices of eldership to Russia is traced. The invention of tradition is assessed in the context of the policies of secularization, religious competition, imperial expansion, and the Enlightenment. In this chapter, the engagement between "institutional" authority and the charismatic elders is analyzed through a focus on the patronage of elders by the "enlightened" bishops and local gentry. Intolerance toward elders on the part of the Synodal system and the police is also addressed.

The reconstruction of eldership in the era of Romantic nationalism is the subject of Chapter Three. In this period, the Church coordinated a backlash against the rationalist and modernist ideological currents associated with the French Revolution. The search for more "authentic" forms of spirituality, and the rediscovery of hesychast writings and medieval mysticism, brought recognition of the institution of spiritual guidance from prelates and philosophers. The chapter analyzes the recognition of the institution of spiritual guidance by a section of the Orthodox establishment. The substantial argument of this chapter is that despite the ideological support for eldership from some conservative philosophers and open-minded prelates, the most striking feature of this period was the endemic tension between charismatic elders and the church dignitaries.

The changes and continuities in eldership in the context of modernization and social reform following the emancipation of the serfs in 1861 are explored in Chapter Four. The focus of this chapter is on the ways in which elders came to symbolize social integration in an increasingly divided society. However, the attempts by the Synod to incorporate elders into the institutional structure revealed the limits of the official conception of charismatic elders, while the literary image of the elder that emerged in the works of the major Russian writers reflected an idealized image of an Orthodox religious leader. A parallel process is discussed in Chapter Five: the appropriation of the charismatic power of Russian elders by both the political elites and the lower classes. Despite the attempts of the Synod to institutionalize the "tame" version of eldership, it ultimately failed to gain control over the popular appropriation of charismatic authority. The reasons for the association between "eldership" (as an invented tradition and a monastic institution) and "popular religion" by the end of the nineteenth century are examined, as are the ways in which lay supporters, or imitators of elders coming from lower classes, understood and practiced spiritual models produced by educated elites in a particular way, and how accurately the literary representations of elders reflected the ideas and teachings of their protagonists.

The legacy of the elders of the Imperial period following the revolutions of 1917 is the subject of Chapter Six. Elders in both the Soviet and post-Soviet periods and in the Russian diaspora are discussed, and the role of elders in clandestine religious activities, the appropriation of eldership by parish priesthood and the laity, and the repression of some of the leaders in the 1930s–1950s are assessed. The status of religion in the Soviet Union affected the official church leaders' attitude to informal spiritual guidance, which was perceived as harmful for the Church's already weak status within the state. Social and political shifts in the Soviet Union resulted in the extension of the tradition of spiritual guidance beyond its traditional geographical loci. The fragmentation of national Orthodoxies made an ecclesiological model of eldership popular among the Orthodox and non-Orthodox communities in the Russian diaspora. The return of the "spiritual father" figure following the breakdown of the Soviet Union in 1992 had legacies in both Soviet Russia and "Russia abroad." The attitude of the institutional church to elders has remained ambivalent: while some popular spiritual leaders have been officially recognized as genuine spiritual elders, others have been accused of sectarianism and abuse of pastoral power. The revival of eldership in present day Russia points to the limits of the secularization that allegedly took place in society during the Soviet period, and shows that the "erosion of the supernatural" was certainly not typical for twentieth-century Russia.

There are a number of terms pertaining to Orthodox monastic culture that require a certain qualification. Eremitic (from Greek *eremia*, desert) monasticism, associated with its founder St. Antony, was the model for both the lavra (a Greek word meaning pathway or passage) and skete (from the name of the valley in Nitria in Egyptian desert), both of which were colonies of hermits who lived around a church where they gathered for the weekly celebration of mass. The communal or cenobitic (from the Greek word *koinos* meaning "common") type of monastery is associated with St. Pachomius (c. 292–346), whose monastic establishment in the region of Egyptian Thebes included several hundred monks and nuns who gathered daily for collective prayer and meals. While groups of these ascetics could have their own spiritual father, all of the members of community had to live in obedience to the superior. St. Basil the Great developed a further the communal model: in his monastery monks constituted a spiritual family who lived under one roof. The term idiorrythmic (that is, separate living) was applied (often as a criticism) to those monastic establishments whose members were allowed to possess property and retain considerable autonomy. Despite the efforts of the church authorities to introduce communal living in monasteries at various stages of church history, noncommunal forms of monastic life persevered.

CHAPTER ONE

Spiritual Guidance, *Pneumatikos Patir*, and the Mystical Prayer

Lost and Found

A discussion of spiritual eldership in Russia would be incomplete without a consideration of the influence of early Christian desert monasticism on the practices and ideas of the Russian monastic *startsy*. Drawing upon texts that originated in the communities of the desert ascetics, the Russian *startsy* forged an imaginary link with ancient monastic customs, thereby creating a sense of continuity across time. Hence, it is important to discuss the function and purpose of spiritual guidance in early Christian asceticism.

The elder (*geron*, *apa* or *abba*, not infrequently, *amma*, or mother) was a familiar figure in late Roman society, in the villages, cities, and deserts of Egypt, Palestine, Syria, and Asia Minor.[1] In those days monasticism was less remote from society than it appears in the heroic lives of the Desert Fathers.[2] The first monks, who preceded the desert ascetics, were the so-called *apotaktikoi* (renouncers) who broke with domestic ties, yet remained in the proximity of their homes. The threefold scheme of monasticism that distinguished between solitary living, skete, and coenobium (community) was developed in later writings on the subject and thus should not be applied to the earlier period.[3] The early Christian monks had a wide choice of ascetic life-styles: some lived in small clusters in the city, others dwelled alone as anchorites, some formed communities (cenobitic monasticism)[4] and yet others formed small groups around their spiritual *abbas* in the desert.[5] There were "Stylites" who lived for long periods on the top of a pillar and, at the opposite end of the spectrum, there were educated theologians and bishops like Eustathius of Sebaste (c. 300–c. 377) and his follower Basil of Caesarea (330–370), who organized communal monasteries, hospices, and hospitals in Cappadocia.[6]

Within the monastic milieu the elder had a very specific function—to direct and instruct novices in ascetic practices and contemplative prayer (*oratio mentalis*). In this sense the elder was a *paidagogos*, a guide and instructor of neophytes. He was rarely ordained[7] and was not a scholar; his instruction was based on personal experience, not on knowledge acquired from books. One of the terms used in the early Christian sources to describe the relationship between the novice and the elder was *aleiptis*, an athlete's instructor, literally the one who anointed the athlete's body with oil.[8]

The relationship between the master and his disciple was the main expression of power in ascetic society.[9] Generally speaking, the relationship embodied a holistic experience; the disciple had to learn to imitate his teacher in his entire way of life and thought. This relationship was voluntary and based upon the unconditional trust of the pupil. Obviously, the institution of discipleship as a key instrument for the transmission of knowledge and wisdom was not unique to Christianity. It had analogues in classical antiquity, in Talmudic Judaism, Buddhism, and Taoism, where it facilitated the spiritual or intellectual progress of the disciple through the transmission of meditation techniques and ascetic precepts alongside coaching in the interpretation of holy books or philosophical systems.[10]

Although many desert *abbas* and *ammas* were educated and of noble origin, it was not unknown for a spiritual instructor to have had little formal schooling or even to be illiterate. An emphasis on the esteemed illiteracy of some spiritual teachers suggests that the institution of spiritual guidance reflected one of the "dominant characteristics of the eastern monastic mentality," which was the distinction between two types of knowledge, one based on formal learning, the other received directly from God.[11] Discernment of spirits (*diacrisis*)—a spiritual rather than an intellectual gift—was the "most precious asset" among the resources of the spiritual instructor.[12]

Ephrem the Syrian and Theodore the Studite explained the relationship between the master and his disciple using the images of family and kinship. In contrast to biological parents, the spiritual father (*pneumatikos patir*) or mother (*mitir pneumatiki*) begot their "children" in spirit.[13] The early

Christian *abbas* were not spiritual directors in the later Western sense but parents to the children whom they begot in Christ.[14] Simeon the New Theologian wrote to his spiritual father: "You are my father and my mother[,] the instructor of my good deeds, my guide toward the kingdom of God . . . ."[15] The symbolic relationship that bestowed paternity upon Christian ascetics replaced the primacy of kinship in late Roman society and became the basis for a new religious structure that had only a loose association with the institutional church.

The obedience of the novice was the essence of spiritual paternity.[16] Sometimes novices who shared a cell with their elders voluntarily performed the role of a servant. Byzantine texts provide numerous examples of "obedience-heroes"—monks who risked their life and sanity keeping their promise to their elders, whose authority was equated with that of God. The story of John the Dwarf, who on the order of his *abba* daily watered a piece of firewood until it apparently became a blossoming tree, emphasized the moral and spiritual benefits of the virtue of obedience.[17] Byzantine authors emphasized the necessity of obedience and its centrality to salvation through recounting the accomplishments of ascetics: "by virtue of obedience the ascetics could perform various miracles, cross crocodile-infested rivers, stand in prayer for weeks, and other feats."[18] Obedience and the renunciation of personal will were believed to liberate ascetics from the necessity of making decisions about their own lives, thereby allowing them to pursue ascetic virtues and the contemplative ideal. By virtue of obedience a novice could also share and inherit the charismatic gifts of his elder.[19]

The ultimate goal of spiritual guidance was theosis, the transformation of human nature through union with the divine.[20] Guidance in the perpetual consciousness of God's presence, imageless prayer, and spiritual combat facilitated the achievement of that goal. A discourse on the mystical union with God emerged under the influence of Origen and Dionysius the Areopagite and developed in parallel with the institution of eldership. According to Lossky, Origen was a master of ascetic life as well as its theoretician.[21] Evagrius Ponticus synthesized the theology and practice of early Christian desert monasticism,[22] but was condemned by the Fifth Ecumenical Council, which accused him of Neoplatonism and Origenism. The censure of Evagrius did not prevent his becoming one of the most popular authors in the Byzantine Empire, and later, in the Greek and Slavic world (where he was known under the name of Nilus of Sinai).[23]

The central instrument of instruction in spiritual guidance, as summarized by Evagrius, was the practice of *exagoreusis*, the "disclosure of thoughts."[24] The notion of *logismoi*, discursive thoughts that lead to sin, discussed by Evagrius and later by St. Maximus the Confessor, were of central importance in confession to the spiritual father, who "[p]ossessing the fullness of knowledge of both the demonic ruses and the weaknesses of the soul . . . is able to provide the weapon against the demonic attacks and a remedy for spiritual sickness."[25] This form of monastic confession had developed independently from the church administration of penance. The relationship between the elder and his disciple differed from that between the penitent and the confessor; confession as a sacrament had different aims from the "disclosure of thoughts." A penitent made a public or private confession of sins (usually understood as actions rather than thoughts) in order to receive healing penance and absolution. In the context of the relationship between the elder and his spiritual child, a neophyte had to open up his heart in order to "receive advice and guidance on how to withstand the attacks of the enemy."[26] In response to criticism by church authorities, the elders pointed out that "disclosure of thoughts" was part of ascetic discipline, not a sacrament.

It would be wrong, however, to reduce the relationship between elders and their spiritual children to confession, whether as sacrament or *exagoreusis*. Elders received visitors in person and in groups, or performed symbolic acts in public; their actions were later interpreted by witnesses as responses to their own particular problems. Many visitors came to elders asking for a "word"; others benefited from miraculous healings and exorcisms.

Who could become an elder? Ideally, an elder was someone reputed for their virtues (especially humility), their deep love of God, and their knowledge of scripture.[27] Virtue and asceticism were not sufficient qualifications alone; the elder needed to be endowed with spiritual gifts by God (charisma) such as discernment of spirits, revelation, power over demons, prognostication, healing, and prophecy.[28] In addition, the performance of miracles demonstrated the enormous power that the holy man possessed.[29] Although some of these qualities were associated with Montanism, an apocalyptic dissenting movement that deployed ecstatic prophecy, ascetic elders , while displaying charismatic fervor, remained in the church fold.[30]

The elder was an intercessor before God on behalf of the people.[31] He or she was an influential outsider, the mediator, who relieved the existential anxieties of people in late antiquity and arbitrated social disputes. Although the majority of the elders' lay admirers could not enjoy directly the spiritual benefits of the elder-novice bond, they gained from elders' advice and intercessory prayer.

Eldership (*starchestvo*) was not a hierarchical stage in the church, but a particular type of holiness that could belong to anybody regardless of gender or social status.[32] The early Christian elders certainly represented a prophetic type of authority. The social role of these nonordained monks, who were regarded as holy men, became particularly important during times of crisis, for example, during the Iconoclastic Controversy (c. 725–842). Monks had real power based on their spiritual authority.[33] Hence, monastic elders represented a more democratic form of authority that could pose a challenge to the institutional church.

The Legacy of the Desert Fathers

Although the Desert Fathers' teachings were familiar in Western Christendom, spiritual eldership had no significant role to play in the West. The ideals of the desert ascetics became known through the writings and activities of John Cassian (c. 360–c. 430), who lived in the Egyptian desert and was influenced by Evagrius Ponticus. However, in the early Middle Ages the doctrine of obedience was used to strengthen the authority of the abbot, who in the Rule of St. Benedict was described as occupying the place of Christ in the monastery.[34] The functions and attributes of the desert spiritual fathers, such as the direction of souls (*animas regere*), spiritual paternity, and the unchallengeable, almost absolute power over the monks' will, were now transferred to the abbot.[35] The spiritual and administrative power combined in the hands of abbots was compared to that of pope, king, general, or Roman paterfamilias.[36] The spiritual friendship that existed within medieval monastic communities, on the one hand, and between monks and lay men and women, on the other, was also quite remote from the ancient ideal of spiritual direction.[37] "Disclosure of thoughts," as practiced in Benedictine communities, gradually lost its significance and was replaced by sacramental confession made to a priest.[38] The Gregorian Reform brought several amendments to rules governing the authority of the abbot and the doctrine of obedience. Apart from the more solicitous image of the abbot, a number of restrictions were placed on his authority. The early doctrine of obedience, which emphasized abnegation of the will by the individual monk, was replaced in the twelfth century by the principles of "individual responsibility and independence of judgment."[39]

In the Christian East, eldership persisted as a parallel pastoral structure within the church due to decentralized monasticism and frequent heterodox movements that split the loyalties of the religious communities and the laity. During the fourth and fifth centuries, informal groups of monks in the Byzantine Empire, where spiritual guidance was practiced, formed private religious communities, whose internal order and practices were out of the reach of bishops and presbyters.[40] The rise of the Monophysite movement in the sixth century led to growing concerns about monastic discipline among church hierarchs.[41] During the iconoclastic period (eighth and ninth centuries) some monasteries became hotbeds of resistance against official policies. It is during this period that icon-worshipping members of the church, both lay and religious, turned away from the iconoclastic bishops and priests to embrace nonordained monastic *abbas* who were perceived as the defenders of Orthodoxy.[42] Probably as a result of popular distrust towards church hierarchy, monastic confession triumphed over "official" penitential practices.[43] Under the dynasty of Comneni in the eleventh and twelfth centuries, monastic founders emphasized the role of the abbot, who was presented as a spiritual instructor and confessor of the brethren.[44]

Despite the hierarchical elevation of abbots, the authority of spiritual fathers did not decline within the Byzantine Empire. Under the influence of St. Simeon the New Theologian (949–1022) there was a renewed emphasis on the spiritual guidance of elders. Simeon was born to a wealthy Byzantine provincial aristocratic family in Paphlagonia, Asia Minor, and was destined for a political career; this was seriously disrupted when he lost his uncle's patronage following the palace coup in 963.[45] Simeon combined his political duties with spiritual exercises under the guidance of a nonordained monk—Simeon the Studite (Eulabos)—and he believed that he experienced a vision of uncreated light. Simeon's passionate veneration of his spiritual father brought him into conflict with the ecclesiastical authorities of Constantinople, which resulted in his expulsion from the monastery of St. Mamas. In his writings Simeon described the spiritual father as having five roles: doctor, advisor, intercessor, mediator, and sponsor.[46] In Simeon's model, spiritual fatherhood was not a hierarchical institution, but a form of spiritual fraternity: for example, he always addressed his spiritual children as "children and brothers." For Simeon, the aim of spiritual guidance was not to create a paternalistic relationship of dependence, but to engage in a process of education through which the novice could reach spiritual maturity and eventually spiritual freedom.[47] Yet Simeon's model of spiritual fatherhood did not advocate a more egalitarian and decentralized monastic community. On the contrary, Simeon's reclamation of the old monastic tradition of spiritual fatherhood served to support his own authority as abbot of St. Mamas.[48]

The practice of spiritual guidance owes much to the Athonite monasticism that originated during the ninth century. The reputation of Athos as a school of Christian asceticism attracted novices from Georgia, Italy, Armenia, and the Slavic lands. During the tenth century, Athos accommodated three thousand monks under the authority of abbots, and cenobitic monasticism became the predominant form of organization there. However, the leaders of small groups of anchorites and idiorrythmic monks had an equal vote with the abbots of large communal monasteries due to the canons of self-government.[49]

A condition of the acceptance of newcomers to Mount Athos was that they had to find a spiritual mentor and follow his guidance for at least a year.[50] The model of spiritual fatherhood practiced by eremitic monks, whose disciples performed the role of servant to their elder, was typical for the Athonite solitaries of the tenth century. Besides, during this period the abbots of large cenobitic monasteries began to utilize the forms of obedience that were standard for eremitic monasticism.[51] Monastic rules described the authority of the abbot as analogous with that of a spiritual father: the abbot was expected to be humble, a good shepherd, and a healer of the souls of his brethren. The abbot also could practice the nonsacramental "disclosure of thoughts," or appoint his deputies to exercise this ascetic practice.[52]

The Hesychast movement of the thirteenth and fourteenth centuries, which revived the Evagrian Neoplatonism that had survived in monastic circles, was beneficial for the institution of eldership. The teaching of Gregory Palamas on the possibility of experiencing and participating in divine energies, perceived as uncreated light, was central to hesychasm, and it provided a theological background for what had already been part of monastic spiritual life.[53] According to Palamas, the goal of theology was not simply knowledge of God, but a union with God.[54] The Hesychast movement had two aspects: a monastic one (primarily in Mount Athos) that "was expressed in a profound spirituality and extreme otherworldliness," and a political one, since many of the players in wider ecclesiastical politics were hesychasts.[55] Hesychasts recognized the great value of eldership. Nicephorus Hesychast (thirteenth century) wrote that every neophyte required an instructor in the process of learning mental prayer.[56] Palamas and hesychasm had no influence on Western monasticism and remained exclusively defining characteristics of the Orthodox tradition.

Spiritual Guidance, Hesychasm, and Pre-Modern Russia

Not much is known about the practice of eldership in medieval Russia. Monasteries served as the agents of Christianization and often engaged in the dissemination of ascetic practices and writings. The collections of the lives and sayings of the Desert Fathers were among the earliest translations in Kievan Rus.[57] However, even the account of the lives of monastic founders (such as Antonii and Feodosii of Kievo-Pecherskii monastery in the eleventh to thirteenth centuries) shed no light on the actual practices of spiritual guidance. It seems that in Kievo-Pecherskii monastery the authority of the abbot was more important than the relationship between a neophyte and a spiritual elder. For example, on his deathbed Abbot Feodosii instructed his monks: "This is your new abbot elected by you, regard him as your spiritual father, respect him, fear him, and do everything according to his will."[58] According to Fedotov it was at this time, and particularly during the leadership of Feodosii, that the Kievo-Pecherskii monastery started the "humanization of the ascetic ideal," which made it akin to Palestine monasticism. In contrast to the heroic asceticism of the Syriac and Egyptian Fathers, the Palestinian ascetics developed a model of monasticism that was characterized by moderation and prudence in spiritual life and attention to the world. These qualities would later be attributed to nineteenth-century Russian eldership, especially that of Optina pustyn'.[59]

Since hesychast practices were closely linked with the tradition of spiritual guidance, it would be logical to look for the traces of this institution in post-Mongol Rus. A connection with hesychasm (through links with Athos and Bulgaria) boosted the Russian religious revival of the thirteenth and fourteenth centuries, which culminated in the activities of St. Sergius of Radonezh. St. Sergius was the spiritual guide to a group of ascetic disciples and was regarded as a holy man by many lay people who sought his advice. During this period, interest in ascetic and contemplative writings among the Muscovite monks was at its peak, as demonstrated by the popularity of *The Ladder* by St. John Climacus, a treatise on spiritual perfection, which was one of the most popular texts copied by monks.[60] During the fourteenth century, the books of Abba Dorotheus, Isaac the Syrian, Simeon the New Theologian, and Gregory the Sinaite were translated into Slavonic for the first time. These texts explicated the theory and practice of ascetic exercises and contemplative prayer. Yet the acquisition by Russian monks and hermits of hesychast texts and techniques had a spontaneous character and, although monks and laity in the thirteenth and fourteenth centuries could practice hesychastic prayer, it is unlikely that they received any instruction.[61]

While Nil Sorskii (1433–1508) certainly was (in George Maloney's words) the "first serious hesychast writer in Russia," there is no indication of the practice of *starchestvo* in his hermitage. Rather than exercising the authority of a spiritual father in regard to his disciples, he seemed "to allow great freedom to the individual workings of grace and personal temperament."[62] One reason for the allowance of such a greater degree of freedom could be that his community on the river Sora consisted of literate, experienced monks who had already passed the "elementary school" of communal monasticism and were already equipped for more advanced training.[63]

The dual questions of maintaining discipline and strengthening the role of the abbot were key issues for communal monasteries in the fourteenth and fifteenth centuries. Monastic obedience was a central theme of several compilations of the Fathers produced in this period.[64] One of the advocates of monastic obedience, Joseph of Volokolamsk, was the leader of the monastic movement (known as Josephites) that defended the communal model of monasticism. In this model, the economic welfare of the monastery depended on the acquisition of land and serfs. To achieve this, it was believed that there needed to be a centralized administration where power was concentrated in the hands of the abbot. The Rule of Kirill of Belozersk followed the Josephite model and emphasized the necessity for unconditional obedience of monks to the abbot.[65] In a similar vein, the Rule of Efrosin of Pskov in the fifteenth century stated that a monk should renounce his will to the abbot and accept the latter's instructions as if they had been given by God. The abbot was expected to be a teacher and pastor for those in his charge and was compared to Christ in that he was responsible for his monks on Judgment Day.[66] As in the earlier communal monasteries on Mount Athos, expectations of the relationship between the spiritual father and his disciples were used to strengthen the authority of the abbot. The Rule of Joseph of Volokolamsk contained a long section on the relationship between the hegumen and his subordinates, which was supported by references to the Desert Fathers and John Climacus. It asserted that the hegumen who received his power from Christ "should be meek and furious, humble and high and mighty."[67] The hegumen could delegate his power to senior monks who aided in the education of brethren, which was primarily focused on discipline and subordination. The Rule encouraged monks to denounce one other, either openly or in secret; this was meant to represent "perfect love." The elder brethren were expected to maintain discipline and order partly through the imposition of punishments on the disobedient. There is a paucity of evidence related to spiritual guidance within the large monasteries in premodern Russia, and a passing reference to "elders" from the fifteenth century by Archbishop Simeon of Novgorod (as part of a criticism of Snetogorskii monks)[68] can be discounted as it refers to older, experienced monks who occupied leading administrative roles (*sobornye startsy*), but who did not act as "spiritual guides."

There is no firm evidence suggesting that spiritual guidance was an established practice within Russian monasticism before the eighteenth century. However, some traces of the eldership ideal existed within eremitic monasticism. Late fifteenth- and sixteenth-century hagiographers provide some evidence of the relationship between the elder and disciple constructed on the model of the Desert Fathers. Martirii Zelenetskii (d. 1603), the founder of Trinity monastery, lived with his teacher, the hermit Bogolep, in one cell. Their spiritual bond continued even after Martirii became a hermit; Bogolep continued to guide the life of the young monk, communicating with his pupil by letter.[69] Similar hagiographical accounts influenced Ivan Kontsevich's claim that the tradition of eldership had been widely practiced in Russian monasteries.[70] In his consideration of the lives of ascetics and monks and their interaction with lay men and women between the tenth and seventeenth centuries, Kontsevich presented selected episodes with a common theme related to the ideal of the contemplative life.[71] The accounts of the lives of the saints also suggest that lay men and women in medieval and early modern Russia were attracted to monasteries and hermitages that had reputable holy men in residence, and that to a large extent lay people were responsible for the creation of the reputations of the living saints. Lay devotees came in search of miracles, healing, or prognostications, and they were not disappointed.[72]

In contrast to the spontaneity that characterized the relationship between lay people and monks, the closest to the early Christian ideal of spiritual father (*pneumatikos patir*) for the laity was, according to Smirnov, the relationship between a parish priest and his penitential family (*pokaial'naia sem'ia*).[73] The penitential family was based on a relationship of moral and social support between the confessor and his spiritual children.[74] Yet this tradition was indebted to monasticism, and to the practice of spiritual guidance of the first centuries CE. Even in the sixteenth and seventeenth centuries the declining penitential family continued to compete with the new organizational unit of church life, the parish.[75] After the church reforms of the second half of the seventeenth century, however, the medieval penitential family was preserved among religious dissenters only.[76]

In the sixteenth century, the decline of the spiritual significance of monasticism resulting from the strengthening of episcopal and priestly authority is exemplified by the decline in monastic saints after 1550.[77] Furthermore, the Church saw a reorientation of spirituality from monks to laity. In reaction to the threat of dissent, in the 1660s–1670s the Church strengthened the bishop's control over diocesan life and gave parish priests substantial powers over matters concerning parish life.[78]

The centralization of the state and ecclesiastical autocephaly led to developments similar to those in the West, including the strengthening of the position of the abbot, the institutionalization of the parish, and the reinforcement of the role of parish priests. Within communal monasticism, monks were expected to live in obedience to the abbot (as a spiritual father) and his closest representatives. However, cenobitic monasticism did not prevail in Russia, which allowed a variety of idiorrhythmic monastic configurations to survive. Although Eastern monasticism experienced similar developments to its Western counterpart (i.e., strengthening of the abbot's role), overall there was less centralization and less political involvement. Besides, hesychast influence, treated as heresy in the West, became widespread within Russia via its South Slav neighbors. In theory, contemplative prayer should not have been used without the guidance of an experienced *abba*, yet in practice, it was learned by many without any supervision, on the basis of written texts.

The appropriation of monastic practices by parish priests (known also as "white" clergy in contrast to monastic "black" clergy), who played the role of spiritual fathers to numerous spiritual children (not necessarily members of one parish), may have been a practice specific to Russia. The influence of spiritual fathers on the social and religious life of Muscovites was considerable: their names were frequently placed on wills and economic contracts. Although these "white" spiritual fathers had wives and offspring, they operated with monastic notions of discipline and piety, especially emphasizing obedience.[79] While monastic authority among the laity, hesychast spirituality, and penitential families were marginalized in the sixteenth and seventeenth centuries, they survived as a form of collective memory and subculture.[80] This may explain how these institutions and practices could be revived among religious dissenters in the late seventeenth century.

The Balkan Revival in the Eighteenth Century

Following the Turkish capture of Constantinople in 1453 and reconciliation with Rome, theological life in the Orthodox East came to a standstill. While monasteries continued to exist, by and large, hesychast practices and spiritual guidance fell into disuse, so that they had to be rediscovered in the eighteenth century, when the religious life of the Orthodox Slavs, Greeks, and Romanians in the Ottoman Empire began to show signs of revival. Following centuries of theological dormancy, a succession of religious writers, translators, and monastic reformers came to the fore and self-consciously tried to revive the Orthodox tradition by going back to patristic and hesychast sources. The Greek Church took the lead in this movement. The influence of the European Enlightenment was important among Greek intellectuals, a majority of whom were, paradoxically, members of the clergy.[81] Some members of this Western-oriented group of clerics, who were as a rule also champions of national liberation from the Turks, proposed church reform; they advocated limitations on fasting and lengthy church services, as well as the abolition of both a celibate episcopate and monasticism.[82] Opponents of the "Westernizers" accused the Western Church of breaking its historical link with the Church Fathers, which had resulted in a loss of faith and piety. They attacked the ideas that inspired the French Revolution, which they understood as a distortion of the ideals of the early Christian community. In particular, they challenged the idea of *liberté*. They argued that freedom in the Christian sense of the word was not opposed to obedience, while the secular idea of freedom made man a slave of his passions.[83]

This criticism of the European Enlightenment is often associated with the movement of the *Kollyvades* that began in mid-eighteenth-century Greece and was concerned with the reformation of religious life. Yet, in common with the enlightened members of the Greek clergy, the anti-Western *Kollyvades* were also driven by the spirit of renewal and reform, which they thought should come about not through the adoption of secularization and a new philosophy, but via a return to patristic roots and a recovery of Orthodox tradition. The name of the movement, deriving from *koleva*, the name for the ritual meal in remembrance of the dead, refers to the fact that the *Kollyvades* refused to celebrate memorial services for the dead on Sundays, arguing that it was inappropriate on the day of Christ's Resurrection. Although they were correct from a canonical point of view, their proposals were at odds with the widespread custom throughout Greece, including at Mount Athos, of commemorating the dead on a Sunday. In 1754, the refusal of the *Kollyvades* on Athos to conform provoked a bitter conflict with the Great Lavra and with the Patriarch of Constantinople Cyril V, who at the time lived in a monastery on Athos. As a result, the *Kollyvades* were expelled from their monasteries and sketes, and some of them were accused of being Freemasons and were forced to leave Athos after condemnation by the council in 1774.[84]

Contrary to its reputation, the movement was concerned less with the details of ritual and more with the reformation of spiritual life.[85] The key members of the movement, Makarii of Notara (1731–1805), Afanasii Parios (1721–1813), and Nicodemus the Hagiorite (1748–1809), all educated and well-connected members of the Greek Church, believed that the revival of spiritual life was not possible without a recovery of the authentic sources of spirituality from the earlier centuries. They rescued early Christian and

Byzantine authors from obscurity, including many works of the third to the fourteenth centuries, which were preserved in the monastic libraries in Athos, Chios, and Patmos. In 1782, an edited compilation of the collected manuscripts was published in Venice under the title *Philokalia*. This impressive anthology ran to over one thousand pages. The title was borrowed from the fourth-century anthology of Origen's writings compiled by Gregory the Theologian, and literally meant "love of beauty."[86] Makarii's assistant, Nicodemus the Hagiorite, contributed biographical details of the authors, who included Greek and Syriac ascetic and mystical writers such as Evagrius Ponticus, John Cassian, Diadochus of Photike, Hesychius of Alexandria, Maximus the Confessor, Simeon the New Theologian, Petr of Damascus, and Gregory of Sinai. There is no evidence that the *Kollyvades* tried to cultivate spiritual guidance. However, the texts that they recovered from obscurity provided inspiration to those Christians who wanted to pursue a contemplative life. The writings of the Greek and Syriac ascetic authors emphasized the centrality of spiritual guidance on the road of mystical prayer.

The emergence of neo-Byzantinism in the eighteenth century, which was linked with the wealthy Greek Phanariots, created a climate favorable for the *Kollyvades* projects. It is a paradox that this neo-Byzantine revival, often presented as a "traditionalist" reaction against "Occidentalism," incorporated elements of Western spirituality. Nicodemus the Hagiorite's insistence on frequent communion was influenced by the ideas of the Spanish Quietist Miguel de Molinos, the author of *The Spiritual Guide*, an instruction on the prayer of quietude.[87] Nicodemus also introduced the Orthodox public to the works of the Italian Jesuit Lorenzo Scupoli.[88] In particular, Scupoli's book on spiritual warfare appealed to the Greek reformers. Scupoli insisted that for a Christian to achieve spiritual perfection it was not sufficient merely to perform rituals and other "external" forms of devotion (no matter how diligently), but it was also necessary to focus on the struggle with the passions and inordinate affections.

The efforts of the *Kollyvades* movement to regenerate Orthodoxy cannot be described as anti-Enlightenment; this is too narrow an interpretation.[89] Superficial "external" religion was also challenged by some Enlightenment thinkers who favored the dismantling of superstition and advocated a return to the wisdom of ancient philosophy. While some members of the *Kollyvades* were opposed to Western civilization, others freely borrowed Western texts and ideas when they found these to be applicable to their project. In common with the French Jansenists who wanted to return the Church to its "primitive, Augustinian purity,"[90] *Kollyvades* tried to bring back the spirit of early Christian community. This reformist ethos and probably the *Kollyvades'* flirtation with Western Enlightenment thought led to conflict with the church authorities.

The influence of the *Kollyvades* movement on Greek Orthodoxy is not conclusive and must be assessed using a wide view. Their impact upon Greek monasticism is negligible because they were expelled from Athos and there is no evidence that spiritual paternity as a practice and theory was of any importance to their teaching. Nevertheless, the *Kollyvades*, in recovering patristic and hesychast writings, recruited supporters among Orthodox Slavs and Romanians who formed the so-called "Philokalic movement," which was quite crucial in the process of spreading hesychast writings and ideas in monastic communities.[91]

Paisii Velichkovskii

The religious revival in thirteenth- and fourteenth-century Russia was indebted to South Slav influence, and the eighteenth- and nineteenth-century Russian spiritual renaissance was also influenced from the South. This time it came from Moldavia, where a thriving religious center was established under the leadership of the Ukrainian-born monk and religious writer Paisii Velichkovskii (1722–1794). Paisii (Petr) Velichkovskii was born in 1722 in Poltava to the family of a priest. His mother Irina came from a family of Jewish traders, some of whom had converted to Christianity, probably at the time of the Khmel'nitskii uprising in 1648.[92] Paisii's grandmother was the abbess of the Sviato-Pokrovskii convent in the vicinity of Poltava and his aunt was a nun at the same monastery. It is possible that Paisii's attraction to monastic life was influenced by his Jewish-Christian relatives. In order to secure for her son the position of a priest in the Poltava Cathedral (a position formerly held by Paisii's father), Paisii's mother presented the twelve-year-old boy to the archbishop of Kiev, Rafail (Zaborovskii). The bishop liked the boy's flamboyant recitation of a poem and gave him permission to join the Kiev theological seminary. During his three years of study, however, Velichkovskii became frustrated with the seminary's teaching program, which involved the memorization of Latin verses and a study of the ancient philosophers.[93] The young man sought a deeper spiritual commitment and protested against the learning of "pagan philosophers." Despite his mother's objection, Paisii left the seminary and wandered from monastery to monastery in Kiev and Lubech until finally, in 1743, he traveled to Moldavia.[94]

After spending three years in Moldavia, Paisii moved to Athos where he lived in the skete of St. Elisha, rummaging through the monastic libraries in search of ancient manuscripts. St. Elisha skete was under the influence of the *Kollyvades*, whose forceful challenge to the authoritative Athonites might have been a possible reason for Paisii's departure in 1763 when, accompanied by 64 disciples, he left Athos for Moldavia.[95] The Danube Principalities attracted monks because the Princes of Wallachia and Moldavia generously supported the Orthodox Church in the manner of the Byzantine caesars.[96] It is also possible that the rulers of Moldavia encouraged Paisii in the hope of strengthening Orthodoxy in their region, which was a target of the Habsburgs in their attempts to impose Catholicism in the Balkans.[97]

In 1763, Paisii settled with his disciples in the beautiful and remote Dragomirna monastery in Bukovina, but he had to move to Sekul in 1775 because Bukovina became part of the Catholic Austro-Hungarian Empire. Sekul was a desirable location, but in 1779 on the orders of Moldavian Prince Joan Konstanine Moruz, Paisii unwillingly relocated a section of his growing community to Neamt monastery. Neamt was one of the oldest religious establishments in Romania and kept an important collection of manuscripts as well as being home to a wonderworking icon of the Mother of God.[98] Despite this move, Paisii as abbot continued to guide both communities, in Neamt and Sekul.

Paisii's community in Moldavia became a magnet both for émigrés from the Russian Empire who wanted to escape the rigidity of antimonastic policy, and the young men of Bulgarian, Ukrainian, Wallachian, and Moldavian origin from other Slav countries who searched for spiritual leadership and learning.[99] The community in Neamt monastery numbered about one thousand monks and novices—approximately one third of them came from the Russian Empire. To accommodate his international community, Paisii introduced bilingualism: services and sermons were performed in both the Slavonic and Romanian languages, a practice that had no precedent in either Russian or Romanian monasteries.[100]

In 1789, during the Second Turkish War (1787–1791) the Russian army occupied Moldavia and the community at Neamt drew attention from the Russian authorities. The newly appointed *locum tenens* of Moldavia and Wallachia, Amvrosii (Serebrennukov) (1745–1792), who was also the translator of Milton's *Paradise Lost*, was impressed by the "Moldavian elder" and had him ordained as an archimandrite, a title given only to graduates of theological academies. The attention paid to Paisii by the Russian authorities in combination with the loss of sovereignty by Moldavia in the

1.1. St. Paisii Velichkovskii.
Source: Zhitie i pisaniia moldavskogo startsa Paisiia Velichkovskago. Moscow, 1847

Russo-Turkish wars exacerbated ethnic tensions among Paisii's community and weakened his pan-Orthodox spiritual ideal.[101]

Paisii and the "Philokalic Movement"

Paisii was an author of original works; he wrote his autobiography, letters, and several treatises on the Jesus prayer and monastic obedience. His main contribution to the revival of Byzantine Orthodoxy, however, was his discovery and translation of the Greek patristic and medieval texts (altogether more than 20 authors who wrote between the fourth and fourteenth centuries), including Evagrius Ponticus, Isaac the Syriac, Barsonuphius of Gaza, and Simeon the New Theologian.

Prior to his enrollment in the Kiev Academy, Paisii developed an ardent interest in ascetic literature. As a child he read the monastic authors Ephrem the Syrian and Abba Doropheus, whose books he found in the library of the Poltava Cathedral.[102] As a novice in the Lubech monastery, he hand-copied *The Ladder* by St. John Climacus, the sixth-century monastic writer in Sinai. He continued his search for ancient manuscripts, exploring monastic libraries in Moldavia and Mount Athos, ordering copies and transcribing books by hand. Because Paisii was dissatisfied with the inaccurate Slavonic translations of the Desert Fathers, he started to collect the original manuscripts in Greek and their Romanian translations. Despite the reputation of Athos as a cradle of hesychasm in the fourteenth century, by the eighteenth century the discipline of mental prayer had been long forgotten there. Almost by chance, Paisii discovered manuscripts that contained patristic writings on prayer in the skete of Basil the Great.[103] It is difficult to imagine today what a mammoth task Paisii took on; first he tried to correct the Slavonic patristic translations using different editions of the same text; when he realized the futility of this task he turned to the Greek originals. Handicapped by a shortage of dictionaries and lacking training in Greek, he initially used the Romanian translations; only later was he able to translate from the Greek. His precision was sometimes excessive: when he could not find the word for a Greek term in Slavonic, he had to invent one.[104] In Moldavia, in his efforts to produce high-quality translations, Paisii appointed some members of his multicultural community to study Greek and theology in Bucharest. The monks in his monastery were trained to copy manuscripts by hand before the establishment of the printing house in Neamt in 1807.

Paisii's desire to bring Orthodoxy back to its roots was, perhaps, a reaction against scholastic theology, which dominated the main center of theological learning in the Russian Empire. The Kiev Mogila Academy's curriculum was heavily influenced by Roman-Catholic medieval and post-Tridentine (1545–1563) authors, such as Thomas Aquinas, Albertus Magnus, Duns Scotus, Robert Bellarmine, Francisco Suárez, Tirso Gonzáles, and Tomasz Młodzianowski.[105] Despite their merits, the imitation of Western methods of teaching (a predominance of Latin and a focus on rational argument and Aristotelian schemes), led to what Florovsky called the "pseudomorphosis of Orthodox thought," an unnatural state where theological thought is separated from religious practice. Paisii's rediscovery of patristic writings, primarily the writings of the Philokalic Fathers, symbolized the retrieval of an authentic Orthodox identity that, according to him, was inseparable from the Greek-Byzantine legacy.[106] Paisii's self-conceived task was to bring Orthodox theology back to its sources and bridge the gap between practice and theory.[107]

Paisii's translation of the Fathers' writings was independent of the work of the *Kollyvades* movement and he had begun his labors earlier than the Greek reformers. He was aware of the ongoing Greek project and regarded his own translations inferior by comparison.[108] Yet the merits of Paisii's translations were recognized by Moscow publishers, who used these alongside Makarius' printed edition for the publication of the Slavonic *Philokalia*.[109]

Paisii's bibliographical and translation work in monastic libraries had a practical implication. Paisii's intention was to reintroduce the practices of hesychastic prayer into monastic life. In his understanding of mental prayer Paisii followed his teacher, the Russian émigré schema-monk Vasilii of Poiana Marului (1692–1767). Vasilii was one of the most authoritative commentators on canon law and scripture as well as the author of a treatise on the Jesus prayer, which consisted, with some variations, of the words "Lord Jesus Christ, son of God, have mercy on me, a sinner." According to Vasilii, the Jesus prayer was not a divine gift given to saints, but rather the means to achieve sainthood. It was egalitarian and thus could be practiced not only by hermits, but also by all Christians. He supported his argument by drawing on the examples of the patriarchs John Chrysostom, Photius, and Kallist: hesychasts who lived not in the desert, but in cities among the people. According to Vasilii, the ethical and mystical aspects of the Jesus prayer existed in harmony; practicing the Jesus prayer with caution could help a Christian develop humility and love for one's neighbor. Vasilii contrasted the Jesus prayer with external worship and private (*keleinaia*) prayer. "External" worship (i.e., church services) was likened to the law of the Old Testament whose aim was to direct people to Jesus.[110]

In response to critics of the mystical prayer, Paisii argued that the evocation of the name of Jesus purified the believer from sinful passions and bestowed grace. He believed that the reason people rejected this form of prayer was through lack of trust in the experience and writings of the Fathers and their own unforgivable ignorance.[111] Nevertheless, both Paisii and Vasilii warned of the dangers involved in imprudent practice of the Jesus prayer. A Christian ascetic had to practice it "with fear and trembling, with repentance and humility," always consulting scripture and taking advice from like-minded and more experienced brethren. Vasilii warned that one had to be cautious and critical of one's own reason and avoid attempts to interpret various physical and spiritual experiences during the contemplative exercise, as individual interpretation of these physical and spiritual experiences could result in demonic delusion and depravity.[112]

Paisii and Spiritual Guidance

During his wanderings in Ukraine, Moldavia, and Athos, Paisii did not have a formal spiritual mentor, but he learned from a number of people who were more experienced in monastic life. Abbot Nikifor of Lubech monastery was an example of a good abbot who patiently and lovingly dealt with human weakness. He was the opposite of Abbot German (Zagorovsky), the former archbishop of Chernigov, who once struck the young Paisii in the face for serving the wrong variety of cabbage for the abbot's meal.[113] Paisii also mentioned the elders from the Kievo-Pecherskii monastery who provided him with books and advice. One monk called Pavel, a former priest who used to be a missionary in China, gave him lessons in virtue. Sometimes these lessons could be unorthodox, such as on the occasion when the young Paisii was astonished to find that Pavel was preparing to hit him. Pavel revealed that his threat of violence was just pretence, enacted in order to make his lesson on meekness and turning the other cheek more memorable.[114] Paisii learned the value of a good sermon through listening to spiritual talks delivered by Elder Mikhail of Treisteny, who used to gather the brethren of his skete for spiritual discourses, which took place after meals or in moonlight during festivals.[115]

Yet despite his meetings with experienced ascetics, Paisii saw himself as a spiritual orphan and he lamented the absence of a respectable elder in his life to whom he could become a disciple. He declined an offer to join Vasilii of Poiana Maruli, who could have become his spiritual mentor. A union between the two did not emerge partly because of Vasilii's insistence that Paisii be ordained as a priest.[116] In Athos Paisii searched in vain among the hermits for a spiritual mentor who was well-read in scripture and patristic writings, but he received no instruction from a senior monk even when he had taken monastic vows. A week after Paisii's monastic tonsure in 1750, his sponsor Vasilii left the monastery offering Paisii the profound valediction, "You, brother, are literate. Live by God's advice."[117] Failing to find a spiritual elder, Paisii decided to follow advice taken from the patristic books.[118]

After taking his vows, twenty-eight-year-old Paisii became the spiritual focus for a group of monks who regarded him as their *starets*. These circumstances were in keeping with Paisii's aim to revive hesychast spirituality. Paisii's successful adoption of the role and authority of a spiritual father was as much a consequence of his charismatic personality as it was the result of his knowledge of the hesychast writings. Hagiographers were very careful to emphasize the role of circumstance and necessity when describing the transition of Paisii (a relatively young monk) to spiritual fatherhood. Paisii's biographer (Mitrofan) insisted that although the monk was reluctant to take on the role of spiritual father, his motivation to do so stemmed from pragmatic concerns about the scarcity of virtuous spiritual fathers who were free from passions. In such times, Paisii thought one had to learn from books and seek advice from like-minded people. Paisii's disciples were attracted by his wisdom and lack of interest in power. In response to the request of monk Vissarion from Wallachia, who asked Paisii to become his spiritual mentor, Paisii suggested that the two of them should live together as spiritual friends; they should try to follow the will of God, practice mutual obedience, and share all material cares. Yet even in this egalitarian relationship, Paisii's authority was prominent, and young monks and novices continued to flock to St. Elisha skete in the hope of becoming Paisii's disciples. During the 1750s, twelve monks of Slavic and Romanian origin insisted that their teacher be ordained as a priest so that he could act as their confessor. In a way, Paisii became a hostage of his disciples, who proclaimed his superiority in relation to other spiritual leaders.[119] Mitrofan's narrative shows a reversal of the relationship between a *starets* and a "disciple": the unwilling elder, who regarded himself unworthy of priesthood, had to obey his "children."

Paisii was a skillful teacher who treated each of his monks in accordance with their character and disposition; while one could be reformed through a strong hand, another needed gentler methods. In order to keep an eye on the community in Moldavia (which had about 350 members in 1775), Paisii monitored the lives and spiritual development of the brethren with the aid of a team of spiritual fathers. Consultations with the fathers allowed Paisii to better prepare for his one-to-one meetings with novices. The doors of his cell were open all day to brethren who sought his advice.[120]

Paisii's model of "spiritual fatherhood" was based on the theology of obedience (*poslushanie*). He argued that there were two kinds of obedience—a blessed and a cursed one—which existed in three different loci: heaven, hell, and earth. In heaven, all celestial powers and prelapsarian man were obedient to God the Creator, while the fallen angels, who lived according to their own will, obeyed the devil. Paisii played with the words "listen" (*slushat'*) and "obey" (*slushat'sia*); holy obedience meant the ability to listen to both the voice and the will of God. Jesus was the ultimate example of such obedience: he came to fulfill the will of the Father, not his own.[121] While Jesus' disciples followed the example of holy obedience on earth, Judas, who listened to the voice of the devil, was the model of "evil obedience."[122]

The hermitage had traditionally been regarded as the ideal monastic arrangement for practicing hesychast prayer under the guidance of a wise spiritual father. Contrary to this ideal, we know that Paisii's community was populated by hundreds of monks who had common meals and shared property. The novices learned to read, translate, and copy patristic texts. This type of organization responded more favorably to the ideal of the monastery as a school of prayer and obedience.[123] Paisii was not solely responsible for spiritual guidance of the brethren, but he retained the role of the arbiter and spiritual father for the entire community. The experience of Paisii's community inspired monastic reformers in Russia.

THE INSTITUTION OF SPIRITUAL guidance that emerged in the context of early Christian monasticism and colonized the main institutions of ancient society, such as school and kinship, functioned as a component of religious memory that facilitated the transmission of religious experience from one generation to the next. The monastic milieus in which spiritual guidance was practiced served also as schools of asceticism, where scripture was interpreted in a mystical sense and radical forms of religious renunciation were practiced. During times of theological disputes and religious reforms, ascetics advocated more conservative methods for the preservation of tradition and drew supporters among the laity, especially among the lower classes, who eagerly embraced the antihierarchical appeal of the nonordained charismatic spiritual leaders.

With the institutional development of the church, the emergence of formal religious education, the growth of monastic wealth, and an alliance between the secular and religious authorities, the practice of spiritual guidance suffered a gradual decline. The authority of the charismatic holy man, a mediator between the elites and the people, and between people and God, waned in the Middle Ages both in the East and the West, while in monasteries the authority of the abbot replaced that of the spiritual father. In medieval and early modern Russia, parish priesthood retained some characteristics of the ancient *pneumatikos patir*, but also declined with the emergence of the territorialized parish system and bureaucratic state.

The Hesychast movement in the late Byzantine Empire, which revived the institution of the spiritual father, had some repercussions in the Slavic world. Nevertheless, even though hesychastic prayer was known to hermits and even to lay people, no instruction was available to its practitioners. Following the contemporary Athonite tradition, hesychastic practices in Russia became associated with the idiorrythmic rule and eremitic monasticism. In contrast, the strict cenobitic rule of Joseph of Volokolamsk, with its emphasis on discipline and obedience, was usually dismissed by commentators as alien to the spirit of the Desert Fathers and Byzantine hesychasm. Yet in the eighteenth century there was a revival of interest in hesychastic practices and the institution of spiritual guidance, which was connected with the renewal of cenobitic monasticism.

Following Russia's colonization of the Balkan Orthodox lands, tensions in this region, which was economically backward and situated in the midst of the geopolitical interests of three empires (Ottoman, Austrian, and Russian), created the background for an Orthodox revival. In their search for an authentic Orthodox spiritual identity, educated Greek monks rediscovered ascetic-mystical theology, which was deemed to be the essence of Orthodox spirituality. The revival of the hesychast tradition in the Balkans was concerned with the restoration of a symbolic link with the Byzantine Empire prior to the Ottoman conquest. The Greek *Kollyvades* did not intend to emphasize the mystical aspects of Orthodox theology, but merely wanted to challenge the contemporary moral theology influenced by scholasticism and the post-Tridentine approach to spiritual life.

Paisii Velichkovskii and the Greek reformers seemingly had much in common. They recovered, published, and translated the early ascetic texts, which aimed to rescue the ancient roots of patristic theology from obscurity. Both *Kollyvades* and the Ukrainian-Moldavian monastic reformer believed that the return to the early Fathers was an antidote to moralistic, Westernized academic and popular theology. Like the Pietist movement in Europe, the Balkan revival placed spiritual life at the center of religious reform. In contrast to a moralistic approach to salvation, as expressed in an outward piety and conformity with the demands of religious institutions, the revivalists advocated the mystical way of communion with God.

The difference between Paisii and the Greek reformers lies in their targeted audiences. The Greek reformers were concerned with the revival of popular piety, not specifically monasticism. In addition to the *Philokalia*, they published anthologies on the benefits of frequent Holy Communion and on canon law—compilations that were intended for parish priests and the laity. In contrast to his Greek counterparts, Paisii was primarily concerned with monasticism. In fact, he was wary about the spread of mystical prayer outside monasteries and expressed concern that the publication of his translations would make mystical prayer subject to misuse if practiced without an experienced instructor. The translation, reading, and copying of the Philokalic Fathers served to fulfill the spiritual needs of Paisii's community.[124] Paisii had no sympathy for the enlightened principles that justified monasticism by its social usefulness, and he resisted the attempts of the church authorities to get him or his community involved in projects associated with these principles. For example, he turned down a request from the Russian and Moldavian authorities to spare some monks from the Neamt monastery to work as school teachers. He begged the enlightened prelates to leave the monks alone to cry for their sins, rather than apply themselves in the field of education.[125] Contrary to the expectations and intentions of Paisii, the Slavonic *Dobrotoliubie* enjoyed more popularity and had a wider circulation than its Greek counterpart: it was published in six editions within 60 years and was translated into Russian in 1877. The Greek anthology of the Hesychast Fathers, however, has been reprinted only once (in 1893) and was translated into Modern Greek only as late as 1957–1963.[126]

Father Georges Florovsky believed that Paisii Velichkovskii continued the interrupted project of Nil Sorskii that aimed to introduce the gems of Byzantine theology to the Slavs.[127] By and large, even in comparison with the *Kollyvades*, Paisii appears traditionalistic and conservative in his attempt to revive the ancient and medieval forms of monasticism, which focused on the attainment of spiritual goals, rather than service to society. Paisii and other monastic émigrés in Moldavia, like Vasilii of Poiana Marului, revived the ancient form of spiritual guidance that cultivated discipleship and obedience to a master. Yet unlike ancient forms, this practice was revived in the context of cenobitic community, where hundreds of monks followed a strict rule under the supervision of their spiritual fathers. While Paisii's teaching and monastic reforms certainly challenged some of his contemporaries, his activities were supported by the church and secular elites in Moldavia and Russia, where the enlightened prelates encouraged Paisii's disciples to inject the Moldavian model into Russian monastic culture. Despite its disengagement from Enlightenment projects and its anachronistic orientation toward the "obscurantist world of Byzantine monasticism,"[128] the Balkan revival, and in particular the Moldavian experiment, played a significant role in the spiritual revival in Russia during the eighteenth and nineteenth centuries.

CHAPTER TWO

Monasticism and Elders between Reform and Revival, 1721–1801

The reemergence of spiritual eldership—in a period marked by anti-monastic reforms, secularization, and rationalism—is a paradox that requires an explanation. Monasticism as a way of life and an institution had a weak currency in the cultural and political system forged by eighteenth-century Russian rulers. Due to the efforts of the enlightened monarchs, the monasteries began to lose their former privileges, social prestige, and economic autonomy. Nevertheless, toward the end of the century Russian monasticism had entered a new cycle of regeneration that expressed itself in the growth of (predominantly female) celibate communities, the adoption of new organizational forms, and an intensified interest in contemplative spirituality.[1] In this context, spiritual elders took on multiple roles as monastic reformers, organizers of new religious communities, spiritual mentors to the laity and clergy, and vigorous critics of religious laxity and social and moral evils. In the period between the Petrine revolution and the reforms of Catherine II, elders formed part of an antireform opposition, and in the second half of the eighteenth century they began to actively assert their value within institutional monasticism.

Peter I and his successors shaped a consistent model for integrating monasteries into the centralized system of church administration and for giving them some socially useful roles such as caring for war invalids and mental patients, or teaching children. The reformers announced their commitment to eradicate parasitism and prevent the spread of "superstitions" and "heresies."[2] They attacked monasteries for their encouragement of popular "superstitions" such as putting on display dubious relics of saints and wonderworking icons, or selling holy oil and holy honey. Under the pretext of bringing monasticism back to its ancient ideals of nonpossession and asceticism, the state intended to limit all possibilities for its organic development.[3]

Monks were one of the three major groups (the other two were peasant insurrectionaries and Old Believers) who defended the old order by opposing Peter's reforms.[4] While some monasteries like Solovki took up arms in protest against reformed Orthodox rites, other groups of monks and nuns surreptitiously joined the opposition to the reformers.[5] Even monks who remained loyal to mainstream Orthodoxy expressed disagreement with Peter I and often portrayed him as the Antichrist. They criticized the religious reforms of Peter and his successors and circulated pamphlets in which they advocated a return to pre-Petrine ways.[6]

The state responded to monastic dissent by curtailing the autonomy of the monasteries and limiting freedom of movement for individual monks and nuns. The law prevented monks from keeping ink and paper in their cells so that they did not write incendiary letters and leaflets.[7] According to a decree of 1732, every monastery had to keep a register of its members, copies of which were to be sent to the Synod and Bishops' Chancellery.[8] Under the threat of legal prosecution, monks were not allowed to leave their monasteries, even temporarily, without the permission of the consistory and the Synod.[9] Those monks and nuns who were caught outside the monastery wearing lay dress were subject to a life sentence of labor in the mines.[10] Such limitations on their freedom of movement relegated monks to the status of other nonprivileged groups in the empire, including serfs.

The Ecclesiastical Regulation (1721) and the subsequent decrees published between 1721 and 1742 consistently undermined monastic autonomy. The state aimed to centralize the monasteries: smaller monasteries were abolished, and their monks were transferred to larger ones. All decisions about accepting novices and the ordination of new monks had to be made in the Synod. The law also imposed restrictions on the minimum age for monks, 30 for men and 50–60 for women. Joining a monastery became more difficult; freeborn men and women had to apply for formal leave from their estates (*soslovie*) and the State Chancery (*Kazennaia Palata*), while serfs had to have permission from their owners. But even if the application was successful, there was no guarantee that an aspirant could find a place in a monastery. Due to the introduction of official quotas on the number of monks (*shtaty*), the number of available places in the monasteries became limited.[11]

The Ecclesiastical Regulation did mention monastic elders but ascribed them primarily a disciplinarian role: they were expected to supervise the behavior of novices and prevent violations of the rules prescribed by the legislation. Although under Elizabeth (1742–1762) there was a relaxation of laws concerning monasticism, the Ecclesiastical Regulation continued to provide the legal basis for the official treatment of monks and nuns.[12] Thus the state tried to incorporate monks into the bureaucratic Synodal system and make them agents of its program of social disciplining.[13] The roots of the tension between the forms of spiritual life advocated by *startsy*, on the one hand, and by the Synodal system, on the other, were implanted in the age of the Enlightenment.

The Russian secularization reform carried out by Peter III and his wife Catherine II followed the model of Austrian and French rulers who shut down hundreds of monasteries and dissolved several religious orders. As a result of the secularization, the Russian Church lost a total of 8.5 million desiatins (22.95 million acres) of land and 910,886 male serfs,[14] while the number of monasteries was reduced by 53–60 percent and convents by 64–67 percent, and the monastic population fell from 11,000 to 5,450 monks and nuns.[15] The surviving monastic institutions retained meadows, arable land, and vegetable gardens. Part of the revenue from the former monastic serfs, who now were the property of the state, was used to subsidize monasteries. However, these subsidies were derisory and not all monasteries were entitled to them.

Apparently, Catherine's reforms reflected quite a moderate position. According to Catherine's lover and advisor Prince Potemkin, Russian monasteries were nothing less than "assemblies of parasites and drunkards that cause disgrace to the reputation of the church." He believed that the number of monasteries should be reduced to just three, which he identified as the Sofronieva, the Nilova, and the Sarov hermitages. The rest of them, announced Potemkin, should be closed or turned into schools, hospitals, and almshouses.[16]

The reforms had a far-reaching effect on monasticism. Between 1764 and 1769 postulants could not take vows before the so-called *shtaty* (the officially approved fixed number of monks or nuns in any particular monastery who received a small stipend from the state) were established.[17] Even after the removal of the ban on tonsure, in many areas monasteries and convents experienced a distinct shortage of postulants who were willing to take vows within *shtatnye* monasteries.[18] In 1769 monasteries in Russia (excluding Ukraine) had 250 unfilled vacancies. In 1777 this number had increased to 433.[19] In 1773, Bishop Antonii of Olonets delivered a report to the Synod about the lack of hieromonks (monks who were ordained as priests) in the monasteries due to a dearth of worthy and willing candidates, either from novices or from the widowed clergy.[20] The convents, too, lacked postulants: convents in Novgorod diocese, for example, had a shortage of about 48 nuns in the 1770s.[21]

There were several reasons for this decline of interest in the monastic vocation. On the one hand, the loss of monastic wealth and the requirement that members provide their own food and clothes (under the prevalent idiorrythmic form of monasticism) could not be compensated for by the meager state stipend.[22] It was also the case that the prestige of the "officially funded" monasteries and convents had fallen considerably. The social prestige of monasticism, too, declined during the eighteenth century. Monasteries functioned as lunatic asylums, almshouses for soldiers and widowed clergy, and prisons for fugitive serfs and dissenters. The presence in the monasteries of a disparate crowd comprised of both sexes, which had nothing to do with the monastic vocation, could hardly help monks pursue their spiritual goals.[23] Discipline was weak and spiritual life was not a priority. In the early eighteenth century, Bishop Dimitrii of Rostov complained that monasteries had been corrupted: "there are grouses, misery, and moaning [among monks]."[24] Abbots often abused their power: in one of the Rostov monasteries, the abbot flogged his spiritual father.[25] The majority of monks and nuns were illiterate. Drinking was often the only activity that monks pursued with a devout fervor.[26] Furthermore, members of the black clergy were often charged with accusations of "witchcraft" and blasphemy.[27]

Although many of the reforms remained on paper, and monasticism proved very difficult to discipline, overall the eighteenth century legislation was detrimental to spiritual life in the monasteries and impeded the development of *starchestvo*. Religious reformers of the eighteenth century stripped monasticism of dignity, social prestige, and possessions. These traumatic developments meant that official monasticism was an unlikely place to launch a religious revival. This is why the spiritual renaissance came to Russia from the margins of the Empire, through religious dissent, unofficial hermitages, and from abroad. Unofficial female communities, too, proved central to the revival of *starchestvo*.[28]

Religious Dissent and Startsy

The religious schism of the second half of the seventeenth century produced the most dramatic of ecclesiastical conflicts in Russia. The state-sponsored religious reform in Alexis' reign (1645–1676) amended the texts of liturgical books using the contemporary Greek practice. The opponents of the reforms, known as Old Believers, considered reformed Orthodoxy to be heretical and anti-Christian. In the years that followed, various groups in society signaled their opposition to the social, political, and cultural reforms of the Russian rulers and thereby intensified the schism within the church. Apart from Old Believers, a number of mystical sects including Christ-Faith (*Khristovshchina*) believers sprung up in the late seventeenth century.

The religious crisis that marked Russia's entry into the modern era had an impact on the popular understanding of spiritual authority. Compliance of priests and bishops with the unpopular reform and violent persecutions of those who opposed it made ordinary believers wonder whether the established church had any moral ground. Spiritual leaders of religious dissent, including women, came from a variety of social backgrounds and included noblemen, the lower clergy (sacristans), monks and nuns, tradesmen, peasants, soldiers, and Cossacks.[29] They interpreted scripture, criticized the church authorities, performed sacraments, and often preached that the end was at hand. Hesychastic practices such as the Jesus prayer were popular among both Old Believers and mystical sects.[30] Old Believers had a vested interest in the legacy of the Desert Fathers, collecting and reproducing their writings and modeling their communities on the sketes and hermitages of Egypt and the Middle East.[31] The writings of Syriac authors such as Abba Dorotheus, Isaac, and Ephrem appealed to Old Believers because of their mystical interpretation of church sacraments.

Old Believers used ascetic rules and monastic spirituality to organize their daily life. In the eighteenth century, the Old Believer monastic and semimonastic institutions (sketes, hermitages, and large communities) in Arkhangel'sk and Nizhnii Novgorod provinces, the Urals, Siberia, and outside Russia (which combined both cenobitic and idiorrythmic forms), functioned as centers of learning, propaganda, and missionary activities.[32] Even though Old Believers lacked priests to perform important sacraments, they had no deficit of monks.[33] Old Believer *startsy* (fem. *staritsy*)—as both official documents and Old Believer sources named them—organized new institutions, recruited new followers, and participated in public disputes with the Orthodox clergy. Persecutions and the challenge of official missionaries forced these Old Believer elders to concentrate on survival and religious polemic rather than spiritual contemplation, which meant that their lives were far from the contemplative ideal of Nil Sorskii.

During the era of religious reforms, the boundary separating religious dissent from mainstream Orthodoxy was still quite permeable. Contact between Orthodox monks and dissenters was not rare. One of the founders of Sarov monastery, Isaakii (Ioann Stefanov, b. 1670), was well known among the Old Believers of Kerzhenets (on the Volga). Although church historians have praised Isaakii for his missionary work among religious dissenters, it appears that these exchanges can be described in a more ambivalent way. The Kerzhenets Old Believers visited Sarov to discuss matters of faith, took part in monastic services, and invited the most respected monks to visit their communities. The Orthodox monks, on the other hand, borrowed Old Believer books and introduced elements of pre-Petrine religious ritual into their communities (among 46 manuscripts confiscated in 1734 from Sarov monastery were prayers of Isaac the Syrian and Makarii of Egypt, lives of Athanasius the Sinaite and Makrida, and a number of monastic rules).[34] Serapion, the founder of the Beloberezhskaia hermitage in Briansk province, collected old printed books in order to satisfy his interest in the Old Believer sign of the cross. This curiosity cost him arrest and imprisonment in 1726.[35] Exchanges between Old Belief and Orthodox monasticism continued in the late eighteenth century. According to some evidence, Serafim of Sarov (Prokhor Moshnin), a quintessential Russian elder, came from a family that practiced Old Believer ritual at home while formally belonging to the Orthodox Church. He joined the Sarov monastery, which was known for its Old-Believer–inspired liturgical music and Old Believer rosaries (*lestovka*). A Kineshma merchant, Aleksei (a member of the community of the charismatic Fedor of Sanaksar) became popular among Old Believers for his ascetic life.[36] These exchanges between Old Belief and the Synodal church were also facilitated by relatively favorable legislation that allowed religious dissenters to transition smoothly from Old Believer to Orthodox monasticism.[37]

The tolerant religious policies of Peter III and Catherine II and the return of large groups of Old Believers from Poland meant that Old Belief became a robust and thriving competitor of the Orthodox Church. Toleration made possible the union between Old Belief and Orthodoxy (*edinoverie*) but it also made Orthodox bishops more apprehensive about the appeal of religious dissent. Following the efforts of eighteenth-century rulers to ascribe some social function to monasticism, monks and archimandrites became actively involved in the polemic against religious dissent,[38] and monasteries began to be used as prisons for religious dissenters.[39] The enlightened bishops enticed elders to their dioceses, trying to raise the prestige of Orthodoxy in dissent-ridden areas. For example, the Simonov monastery in Moscow in the Rogozhsk district was restored shortly after the 1771 epidemic of plague as a counterweight to the center of priestly Old Believers in the Rogozhsk cemetery. Popular elder Adrian (Blinskii) was invited to Simonov monastery with his disciples, perhaps in the hope that he would divert local folk from falling into "heresy." Both Optina pustyn' and the Sarov monasteries were established in areas densely populated by dissenters. From the point of view of the hierarchs, reformed monasteries could become the grass-roots institutions of the church that promoted Orthodoxy on the ground. Therefore, the introduction of communal rule and the strengthening of internal discipline were deemed essential in bringing about a monasticism for the new era, and fostering what Gregory Freeze called the "re-Christianization" of Russian society.

Unlike the enlightened hierarchs, hermits, monastic reformers, and elders did not believe that the conversion of dissenters should be their primary aim. They had a much more ambivalent relationship with Old Believers, which was characterized by the exchange of books, religious objects, practices, and individuals. Both Old Believers and Orthodox monks found inspiration in the same sources of ascetic literature, and both were indebted to the sixteenth-century monastic reformers, Joseph of Volokolamsk and Nil Sorskii. This common heritage often meant that there were more similarities than differences between the two groups.

"Forest Elders" and Monastic Dissent

The treatise on ascetic life, *The Ladder* by St. John Climacus, distinguished between three forms of monasticism: anchoritic life, sketes, and the cenobitic community.[40] A monk could choose one of these forms in accordance with his spiritual experience. The younger monks were as a rule discouraged from practicing anchoritic life. In Russia, hermitage was usually associated with nonpossessors, whose proponent Nil Sorskii compiled the first Russian rule of hermitic life.[41] New hermitages in pre-Petrine Russia would often emerge around *startsy* who had left their "mother" monastery in a search of a more radical form of withdrawal from the world. *Startsy* were followed by their disciples, who formed new monastic communities.

Peter I's reforms threatened the survival of hermitages. Feofan Prokopovich, the religious legislator of Peter's era, argued that Russia lacked the intellectual and natural resources of the Middle East and Byzantium that could justify eremitic life. He also warned about the spiritual dangers of the eremitic way of life: "[the hermit] deprives himself of great benefit for his soul since he has no one around to ask spiritual advice about dubious thoughts and lapses of conscience; [neither] does he have role models for ascetic exploits."[42] Despite references to ascetic literature, the law itself implied that hermits were dangerous, as they could potentially become leaders of dissent and opposition.

Despite the repeated decrees prohibiting the building of hermitages and sketes, unsanctioned or semilegal monastic establishments kept appearing throughout the eighteenth century. In some cases, this unauthorized monastic development was a protest against the authoritarian actions of the civil and church authorities. For example, in 1706 during the war with Sweden, the Russian military destroyed several churches and monasteries in order to strengthen the defense of the city of Briansk. The monks of the demolished Pesotskii monastery were transferred to Petropavlovskii monastery, with the exception of sixteen monks who refused to join the new monastery and founded their own community on the river Snezhet'. The community, which became known later as the Beloberezhskaia hermitage (a spiritual home to several elders), had to defend its autonomy against the Petropavlovskii monastery.[43]

It is impossible to calculate the number or discern the identity of the hermits who lived in eighteenth-century Russia: while some of them were monks who spent between several months and several years in a hermitage and then returned to their main monastic base or founded new communities, others pursued ascetic life without any formal association with official monasticism. During the reign of Elizabeth, nobleman Ivan Ushakov abandoned his regiment and hid for four years in a forest hermitage near the Dvina River in the north. When he was arrested by the police, the dashing officer had metamorphosized into a thin, pale, bearded man. Only through special permission from the Empress (who was the chief of the Preobrazhenskii Guards, where the runaway officer had served) did Ivan receive pardon and the opportunity to become a monk in Aleksandr Nevskii Lavra.

Hermits sometimes settled on land that belonged to gentry or state peasants. Around 1775, the hieromonk Adrian (Vasilii Blinskii, d. 1812), accompanied by the monk Ioann and two novices, left the Ploshchanskaia pustyn' to live as hermits in a particularly wild and remote part of Orel province. They received permission from the local landowner to stay in his forest and he also supplied them with a guide. The hermits settled near a source of water and hired peasants to build log houses for them.[44] From

Adrian's biography we also learn about another hermit named Varnava, a neighbor of Adrian, who was so annoyed by the growing number of monks around Adrian that he had to move about 100 kilometers further into the forest. During a time of famine, however, Varnava returned to Adrian's hermitage because he was not able to feed himself.[45] The eremitic way of life was also popular among Sarov monks: the log cabins of monks Mark and Serafim (1754/59–1833, a hermit from 1794) were hidden so deep in the forest of Tambov province that one needed to follow elaborate instructions to get there from Sarov.[46]

The aim of all hermits was to minimize their dependence on the world. In addition to their exposure to a harsh climate and mosquitoes, hermits existed on a limited diet; most hermits were strict vegans. Once, at Easter, a local landowner sent eggs and milk to Adrian's community. Despite the solicitations of the hungry monks, Adrian was reluctant to accept the gift and returned the food to the sender. He argued that if they consumed the eggs and milk, the benefactors would bring more, thus making the monks more dependent on the world.[47] As a rule, hermits survived by growing root vegetables and picking mushrooms and berries; sometimes they accepted bread from visitors. Vasilisk managed to survive for several years eating only potatoes, which he grew in his vegetable patch. Serafim of Sarov claimed that during three years of his solitude he fed only on *snit'*, a wild plant that could be eaten fresh in summer and dried in winter.[48] The plant was known to local peasants who used it to survive during periods of famine.

The life of a hermit was precarious: wild animals, hunger, and the elements threatened survival. Yet hagiographers used the stories of encounters with wild beasts as an additional indication of holiness. This traditional hagiographic motif emphasized the holiness of an ascetic who no longer antagonized nature. The vita of Serafim of Sarov tells of his friendship with a wild bear. This motif was used in the illustrations for the ascetic's biography produced in the 1850s, and was subsequently copied in numerous primitive icons of the saint. The story of taming wild animals could also be found in the life of Amfilokhii of Troitse-Rekonskaia pustyn'.[49]

Hermits could also fall victim to robbers (usually local peasants), who believed that monks possessed money and treasure. "People visit you and give you money," robbers said to Serafim, and battered the monk until he was unconscious. Adrian's hermitage was attacked by robbers who had already mutilated some other monks and beaten the monk Varnava to death. The robbers mistakenly believed that hermits took a fee for confession from their visitors.

On the other hand, there is also evidence of the respect and awe that local populations had toward forest elders. The Chuvash peasants, on whose land several hermits settled, paid special respect to Elder Vasilisk (d. 1824) and brought food to his threshold, covering it with crosses made of twigs. They believed they had a special blessing from the elder if he took their food. The "forest elders" also enjoyed the patronage of the gentry, who provided access to woodland on their estates and promised protection. An aristocratic woman from Roslavl' (Smolensk province), Nadezhda Bronevskaia, remembered that when she was a child in the 1780s–1790s, there were about 40 monks living in the forest on her family's estate who came to celebrate church services in the home chapel of her parents.[50]

Hermits were prosecuted as vagrants, runaway serfs, and dissenters (and many of them probably were). Bishop Tikhon of Sevsk and Briansk launched an expedition for finding runaway monks in his diocese in the 1760s. In 1765, a regiment of soldiers led by a clerk of the Bishop's Chancellery, Vasilii Alekseev, arrested a hermit called Ioasaf, a former abbot of Ploshchanskaia pustyn' (between 1741 and 1746), who had lived for twenty years in a well-hidden hermitage with several of his followers. Oblivious to state prohibitions, he ordained some of his disciples as monks.[51] The seventy-two year old abbot was put in chains and escorted to the bishopric's seat in Sevsk. Local legend maintains that the bishop was so touched by the saintly appearance of the forest ascetic in chains that he allowed him to return to his former monastery, Ploshchanskaia pustyn', where he died in 1766.[52]

Elder Aleksei (Blinskii) and his pupils, too, faced charges of religious dissent made by the Smolensk ecclesiastical authorities in the late 1780s. Despite the protection of the Smolensk vice-governor, I. G. Khrapovitskii, on whose land they settled, they were not left in peace. A local priest reported the hermits to the police. Following police interrogations and an interview with Bishop Parfenii, the hermits had to leave Smolensk diocese and move to St. Petersburg diocese under the protection of Bishop Gavriil (Petrov).[53]

In 1800, hermit Ippolit applied to the Sevskaia Spiritual Consistory for a place in the Makhrishchskii monastery. He had become a monk in 1775 in the Beloberezhskaia hermitage and had subsequently moved to the Afanas'evskii monastery in Iaroslavl' province, where he had spent five years. He left the monastery and came to live in a forest near Beloberezhskaia, spending seven years there altogether. It is possible that Ippolit was one of the disciples of Elder Adrian. He was denied a place in the monastery because the local consistory deemed his living in the forest illegal.[54] Thus, it is possible that the last hermits in the Briansk forests left around the late eighteenth to early nineteenth century.

Monastic Emigration

In addition to hermitic movement, emigration represented another form of protest against the religious and cultural reforms of the eighteenth century. Some Russian seekers of monastic vocation aspired to live an unconstrained ascetic life in Mount Athos or Moldavia. Paisii Velichkovskii's community beguiled young men from Russia and Ukraine, who numbered up to one third of the population in his monastery at Neamt. Among them were former officers, merchants, and family members of the clergy.

Fedor Pol'zikov (1756–1822) from Karachev (Orel province) was one such typical émigré. The son of a merchant and a priest's daughter, Fedor was educated in Church Slavonic by his grandfather. His widowed mother wanted the youth to follow in his father's footsteps and become a merchant, but Fedor aspired to become a monk. He made an unsuccessful attempt to secretly escape from home to a nearby monastery: his mother discovered his location and brought the young novice back home.[55] Unable to resist the family pressure, Fedor married a merchant's daughter. The young couple was unhappy and their two daughters died in infancy. Pursuing the dream of his youth, Fedor absconded from home, crossed the border with Moldavia, and joined Paisii's community. Apparently, the citizens of Karachev did not condemn their neighbor for desertion, but respected him. There were several Karachev dwellers who dedicated themselves to monastic life.[56] Leonid Nagolkin, 12 years Fedor's junior, from the same village, became Fedor's spiritual son. "In my thoughts I was prepared to prostrate myself in front of him," he said later. Some sources suggest that Fedor's wife agreed that she would never marry again, so that she would not be treated as a bigamist.[57] In Paisii's community, Fedor worked in the kitchen, baking bread for hundreds of brethren and visitors, and he also supervised an apiary. Fedor's experience of living in Poliana Vorona hermitage under the guidance of two aged elders, Onufrii and Nikolai, both born in Chernigov province, taught him not to rely on physical exploits only, but rather to focus on his heart.[58]

Some members of Paisii's community began to return to Russia from Moldavia as early as the 1770s–1790s. In 1779, a member of Paisii's community, monk Feodosii, returned to Russia with his pupils at the request of Prince Potemkin to head Sofronieva pustyn', in the new province of Tavrida. Potemkin, who had advised Catherine to close all but three monasteries, was obsessed with everything Greek and supported the learned monks who translated the Byzantine authors into Slavonic. Perhaps his patronage of Paisii's disciples had something to do with the ideology of the

"Greek project" that aimed at the restoration of the Byzantine Empire with the Russian monarch as its emperor.[59] After Paisii's death in 1794, another 70 disciples returned to Russia and resettled in Russian monasteries.

Many of the émigrés returned to Russia en masse in Alexander I's reign, after state policy toward monasticism changed and émigrés were allowed to keep their monastic and priestly status. In 1801, Fedor joined a group of monks leaving Moldavia for Russia. He returned to his native Orel province and joined the Cholnskii monastery, and later came to the Beloberezhskaia hermitage where he met his compatriot Leonid, who became Fedor's spiritual son and the founder of *starchestvo* at Optina pustyn'.

Monastic emigration, which was followed by the repatriation of the Russian clergy from the Balkans, had an important effect on Russian monasticism: it promoted the legacy of Paisii's theology and endorsed practices of spiritual guidance in Russia. Firstly, it revived and strengthened interest in the patristic Byzantine roots of Russian Orthodoxy. Secondly, Paisii's disciples contributed to the reform of monasticism, strengthening the authority of the spiritual elder whose position did not overlap with the administrative role of the abbot, as was the case in Paisii's community.

Elders within the Russian Church

Bishop St. Tikhon of Zadonsk, a luminary of the Russian Church, wrote that bishops and priests were called pastors because they looked after Christ's flock. This duty required uncompromised motivation and high personal moral standards from the pastor so that he could truthfully preach the word of God.[60] In reality, however, the low moral standards of the parish clergy in Russia were the subject of criticism by the authorities and visiting foreigners. The Frenchman Charles Masson criticized the illiteracy, drunkenness, and rowdy behavior of these "servants of Christ":

> Priests in Russia are greatly despised. Many of them are illiterate, and their depravity and crude ignorance provoke social contempt. There are, of course, seminaries for clerical education, but one could become a priest without studying. A father could pass his parish, church, and parishioners to his son, as long as the landlord agrees. The latter seeks the bishop's approval. The son, like his father, is regarded an expert as soon as he can read a tiny bit of Church Slavonic and know the liturgy and vespers. As soon as he becomes a priest, he begins drinking and fighting with his parishioners. The latter come to receive his blessing and kiss his hand even after the fight. On the streets of Moscow

> and St. Petersburg you can often see drunken priests and monks who are singing, swearing, talking rubbish, and harassing women.[61]

The clergy, weakened by the eighteenth-century reforms, had little moral and social control over the lives of their parishioners, especially those of noble origin.[62] "[W]ith their special garb, old norms of conduct . . . and alien Latinism . . . [the clergy] formed an identifiable group distinctly separate from lay society."[63] Some parish priests showed disrespect to the Orthodox religion in public, which included blasphemy, jokes, and swearing.[64] Despite the Synodal attempts to raise the moral standards of the priests, the clergy's immoral behavior, drinking, and neglectful attitude to their duties continued to call forth frequent complaints from peasants.[65]

According to St. John Chrysostom, a priest had to be a philosopher, who in contrast to a monk had no need of "external devices" for his success (by which St. John, perhaps, meant ascetic exploits) but had "all his art in his soul."[66] In Russia, however, even though the married "white" clergy certainly had shared experience of family and economic life with their parishioners, they hardly were "philosophers" in accordance with Chrysostom's ideal. The Russian "little fathers" were oppressed by the official regulation of consistories, shackled by a total economic dependency on their parish, and made weak by their impoverishment.

Yet by the eighteenth century, the model for a good pastor could already be found among the monks rather than the priests. *Startsy* presented a pastoral ideal that was in contrast with the prevailing norms of clerical behavior. The less authority that the *starets* derived from official sources, the more favorable was the contrast. Ascetic monks appealed to the laity: unburdened by families, these single men, who preached ideals of non-possession, were less dependent on their pockets than the fecund and often drunken village priests. In addition, the educated and refined *startsy* attracted the local nobility through their ability to hold a conversation and speak the language uncontaminated by the Latinisms and Church-Slavicisms of the seminary-educated priests.

The popularity of ascetic *startsy* presented a challenge to parish priests, who sometimes out of envy reported "suspicious" forest hermits to the authorities. Yet occasionally, collaboration between monastic elders and parish priests stimulated religious revival in parish life. Elder Fedor of Sanaksar supported the missionary zeal of his spiritual son Mikhail Nikiforov, the deacon of the village Bol'shaia Talinka of Tambov district, who helped to eradicate alcoholism and introduced mutual aid and charitable initiatives among the villagers. Following a denunciation that Mikhail was the leader of an Old Believer sect, he and a group of peasants were arrested. But having examined the books confiscated from Mikhail and his flock, Bishop Feodosii remarked that if all his diocesan clergy had religious inclinations similar to Mikhail's, their prayers alone would be enough to save them![67]

Regardless of the degree of respect shown toward a charismatic monastic elder, his authority was restrained by the Ecclesiastical Regulation that subordinated monastic leadership to the authority of bishops and the Synod. In some cases, however, when abbots or elders came from the nobility and enjoyed the patronage of the royal court, they tried to reassert their status and prevent the intervention of church authorities into the internal affairs of monasteries. Fedor of Sanaksar's life illustrates the tensions between a charismatic monastic leader and the church hierarchy. Fedor had a reputation as a strict and rigorous monastic leader. In 1768 he punished two members of his community for disobedience, assigning them heavy physical work and banning them from celebrating the liturgy. The monks ran away from the monastery to seek justice from the bishop. Bishop Pavel of Vladimir took the side of the runaway monks, accusing Fedor of cruel treatment, and sent the monks to the Florishcheva pustyn' for one year as a punishment. Fedor disagreed with the bishop and argued that it was the duty of the abbot to impose an appropriate penance on the wrongdoers.[68] The exchange of letters between Fedor and the bishop demonstrated the difference in the interpretation of canon law between the two. The bishop argued that, according to the canons of the Church, only a bishop could ban a priest from celebrating liturgy. Fedor, however, insisted that canon and civil law stipulated obedience only to those righteous pastors who kept the Lord's commandments and judged righteously (implying by this the bishop's lack of righteousness). According to Fedor, the bishop's decision was against the law of God, since it endorsed the self-will of the guilty monks.[69]

We have no evidence that tells us whether monastic elders had more to say about the social injustices of serfdom than parish priests, who were as a rule passive and silent. Yet there is evidence that some of them enjoyed a reputation for being protectors of peasants and challengers of the powerful authorities. The Sanaksar monastery, where Fedor (Ushakov) was abbot, was the only monastery spared by the peasant war in 1783, which ravished all the estates and churches in the area. The reason for this special treatment was Fedor's reputation as a man of the people. In 1773, he engaged in a public dispute with the governor of Temnikov, accusing him of corruption and the mistreatment of peasants. Predictably, the investigation by the Voronezh chancellery failed to find any of the governor's alleged crimes. Fedor paid with his freedom: he was defrocked and imprisoned in

Solovetskii monastery.[70] These events led to the emergence of the popular myth of Elder Fedor as a protector of the peasants against the unrighteous hierarchy and corrupt bureaucrats. It is possible that Fedor cultivated this image of a patriarchal leader who believed that he could rule his community without the intervention of the church authorities.

"New Monasticism"

Nikolai Lisovoi pointed out that the age of the decline of traditional monasticism was also the age of the revival of ascetic life and spirituality.[71] We can speak about the emergence of "new monasticism" from about the 1770s–1780s, the roots of which could be found in the eremitic movement and the Balkan spiritual revival. This process coincided with the erosion of the official ideology of the Enlightenment and the rise of interest among the church hierarchs in traditional sources of Orthodox piety.[72] The new generation of monks was brought up in the period of Catherine II's reforms and they were encouraged by the enlightened hierarchs to become the reformers of Russian monasticism.

The bishops Gavriil (Petrov), Dosifei (Il'in), and Platon (Levshin) invested much effort in the revival of monasticism. They were part of a new generation of educated prelates who were ethnically Russian (in contrast to the Ukrainian clergy that dominated the profession in the first half of the century). These men were well-versed in theology, philosophy, and languages. They could compose their sermons in verse and charm their aristocratic patrons with wit and intelligence. Bishop Dosifei of Orel, a friend of the Russian freemason Ivan Lopukhin and Platon of Moscow, and an admirer of the French abbot Fenelon, dazzled the court with his inspiring and well-versed sermons. The dissemination of *starchestvo* and Philokalic spirituality, the encouragement of cenobitic rule, and the strengthening of monastic discipline was a result of the efforts of these bishops.

Bishop Gavriil (Petrov) (1730–1801) was perhaps the first Russian prelate to recognize the promise of *startsy*. He was one of Catherine II's entourage, valued by the empress as a "sharp and reasonable" advisor, whose statue was placed in the newly built Cathedral of the Aleksandr Nevskii Lavra. Gavriil was chosen by the empress to offer a version of Orthodoxy that would fit into the discourse of the Enlightenment. Yet the bishop was also known for his support of ascetic spirituality. The apparent contrast between these two sides of Gavriil's personality has been explained by Zhivov, who argued that "Gavriil the Philosopher" was nothing but an element of scenery in the grandiose theatre of Catherine's empire, which served to hide, not to reveal, the true nature of the actors.[73] This is evident from Gavriil's moralistic sermons at court, which—designed in accordance with the rhetorical canons of the era—show little indication of the spirituality he sought to encourage.

Gavriil believed elders would carry out the reform of monasticism. He changed the practice of appointing the graduates of theological seminaries to positions as abbots and archimandrites. Despite his respect for knowledge and learnedness, he believed that true leadership did not depend on the education of the abbot, but on his experience and spirituality. For example, he appointed Elder Nazarii from Sarov monastery as abbot of Valaam on Ladoga Lake in 1782.[74] Abbot Pachomius of Sarov monastery was surprised by the bishop's choice and, unwilling to let Nazarii go, presented the elder as a simpleton (apparently, Nazarii could not write). According to Gavriil's biographer, the bishop replied: "I have plenty of smart alecks (*umniki*) here, send me your idiot."[75] Nazarii introduced the communal rule in Valaam and developed a set of instructions on monastic behavior.[76] Gavriil was impressed by Nazarii's achievements and appointed him as a monastic supervisor, whose role was to visit monasteries in St. Petersburg diocese and report to the bishop on how to improve monastic order and discipline.[77]

Gavriil protected hermits and monks who were in conflict with church or civil authorities. For example, he was supportive of the monastic "school" of the controversial Elder Fedor of Sanaksar. According to the author of *Fedor's Life*, Bishop Gavriil petitioned the empress, appealing for the release of the troublesome monk from Solovki monastery.[78] One of Fedor's disciples, Feofan (Sokolov), had become an attendant (*keleinik*) to the bishop in 1782.[79] Another elder, Adrian, came to Bishop Gavriil after his expulsion from Smolensk diocese by Bishop Parfenii in 1790. The bishop offered the elder and his disciples a choice of several monasteries in his diocese where they could relocate (Adrian selected Konevets monastery on Ladoga Lake).[80] Gavriil also tried to entice the retired Bishop Tikhon of Zadonsk to come to his diocese, promising to appoint him as abbot of the Iverskii monastery in Valdai.[81] Gavriil encouraged the publication of the Russian *Dobrotoliubie*, the book that had become the essence of the "new monasticism" and new spirituality. Paisii's translations together with the Greek originals were examined by the teachers of Greek from the Aleksandr-Nevskii Academy and the Trinity-Sergius Lavra.[82] The print run of the first edition was 2,400 copies. If the publication of the Greek *Philokalia* required the support of the Mavrodikis family of Phanariot merchants, in Russia, the book was published with the support of the state.

2.1. Bishop Gavriil (Petrov).
Source: Russkie deiateli v portretakh izdannykh redaktsieiu istoricheskogo zhurnala Russkaia Starina. Sobr. 1-e. St. Petersburg, 1886

With the support of the *startsy*, Gavriil managed to introduce communal rule in twelve monasteries in his diocese. According to Gavriil, the abandonment of the ancient tradition of communal living had resulted in the decline of morality among the religious and loss of monastic prestige among the laity.[83] The principles of communal living were meticulously stipulated. Gavriil's main emphasis was on discipline and obedience to the monastic hierarchy, and his instructions primarily addressed the issues of discipline (drinking, denunciations, wandering, and insubordination). Surprisingly, Gavriil's instructions did not mention elders. Was this because Gavriil did not want to reveal his true intentions and had to show conformity with the Ecclesiastical Regulation?[84]

Bishops Dosifei (Il'in) of Orel (1751–1827), Feofil (Raev) of Tambov (1737–1811) and—to some extent—Platon (Levshin) of Moscow (1737–1812) belonged to the younger generation of church hierarchs who came to power during the reign of Paul I and in the early years of Alexander I's reign. In their attitude to monasticism they resembled Gavriil, and, perhaps, tried to imitate him. They strove to restore monastic order, to promote "new spirituality," and to encourage the social mission of monasticism. Dosifei appointed Elder Vasilii (Kishkin)—a monk who had lived in Mount Athos—as abbot of Belobrezhskaia pustyn'. Under Elder Vasilii, the number of monks and novices grew, and included several repatriates from Moldavia.[85] As Bishop of Moscow and Kaluga, Platon supported the restoration of Optina pustyn' and appointed a new abbot, Avraamii from Peshnoshesk monastery.[86] The impoverished monastery had no official status and received no state subsidies prior to 1797. Under the new abbot, and due to the patronage of Platon, the monastery gradually restored its financial affairs, and recruited 18 novices in 1800.[87]

Although according to the Ecclesiastical Regulation, abbots could only be appointed from theology graduates, Gavriil and Platon often circumvented this rule by appointing pious *startsy*, who did not study in seminaries and academies, as leaders of monastic institutions. There was an apparent contradiction in the policies of the bishops Platon and Gavriil, who promoted education on the one hand and appointed semiliterate monks as heads of monastic communities on the other. This contradiction could be explained by the traditional emphasis on virtue and morality as the principal criterion for an ideal leader, whether political or religious, while learnedness was regarded as secondary.[88] In their emphasis on virtue, Russian thinkers had more in common with the European political thought of the sixteenth and seventeenth century than with the French Enlightenment.

It seems that the monks often regarded the reforming efforts of the bishops as burdensome. Elder Vasilii (Kishkin) had to use illness as a pretext to resign from his duties as abbot in Belobrezhskaia pustyn'. Monks in the Optina monastery resented the newly introduced church services that lasted for several hours. They appealed to Bishop Platon to let them retire to another monastery.[89]

Elders as Reformers

To understand why Gavriil and like-minded bishops supported elders, one has to look closer at the elders' reforming efforts. As if in response to highly placed critics of monasticism like Potemkin, elders focused their efforts on the reform of monastic internal order. Guided by the models of Athonite and Moldavian monasteries, *startsy* introduced the communal rule, banned alcohol, and organized orderly church services. Fedor (Ushakov) tried to revive monastic rigor among the monks of Sanaksar monastery in Tambov diocese by expanding the length of church services, which could last between six and twelve hours.[90] Poverty and asceticism were considered to be important virtues. The monks in Sanaksar monastery had to wear old, coarse clothes and peasant bast shoes.[91] Abbot Nazarii used the same pair of boots for six years. Industriousness was another supposed virtue. Filaret of Glinskaia compared sweaty labor to the blood of martyrs.[92] External discipline was to be complemented by internal discipline. *Startsy* encouraged brethren to systematically monitor their conscience, which found expression in the so-called "disclosure of thoughts" that some communities practiced daily. The reformers also laid emphasis on individual prayer, which was believed to be more important than the formal observance of church rituals. In order to support their practices with authoritative texts, *startsy* encouraged the learning, copying, and publication of translations of patristic texts.

The preference of *startsy* for the communal principles of monastic life was in seeming contrast with the idiorrythmic tradition of the nonpossessors, who defended the right of monks to have personal property and support themselves by their own labors, but opposed accumulation of monastic wealth. At the same time, elders had a natural affinity with the opponents of Joseph of Volokolamsk in that they had no interest in defending the right of monasteries to landownership.[93] According to them, spiritual life was the only domain of the monk, not land and personal possessions. This position seemed like acquiescence with the state policy of confiscation of monastic property. Rather than challenging the regime in the style of the vociferous critic of Catherine II, Bishop Arsenii (Matsievich), the elders and the bishops who supported them tried to find a legitimate space within the political and religious order that came into being as a result of Peter I's and Catherine II's reforms.[94]

The Social Profile of Elders

While the social composition of monasteries was dominated by the clerical estate, a typical spiritual elder in the eighteenth century was anything but a clergyman. Two social groups of origin, particularly prominent among elders, were the nobility and the merchants. Despite legislation that tried to prevent noblemen of an age eligible for military service from entering a monastery, there was no lack of young men of aristocratic birth seeking a monastic vocation either in Russia or abroad.[95] According to one sample of 1805, 12 percent of monks were of noble origin whereas later in the mid-nineteenth century they comprised only 3.5–3.9 percent of the total.[96] What brought a Russian nobleman to a monastery? Many noblemen had a traditional upbringing, where a home chapel served as a focus of spiritual and social life.[97] The transition of a noble youth from the family estate with its traditionalist values to public service accompanied by an immersion into Western, rationalist culture could result in a spiritual crisis.[98]

Military service, in particular, presented the nobleman with a world of "new" cultural values and unfamiliar modes of behavior. Although hagiographical evidence must be treated with caution, it is useful in providing insight into the challenges and dilemmas that pious noblemen encountered during army service. In the 1740s, Ivan Ushakov (the future Elder Fedor, 1719–1791) joined the elite Preobrazhenskii regiment, which was notorious for its lavish banquets and moral laxity. Shaken by the sudden death of one of his fellow officers during an orgy of drinking, Ushakov experienced the reawakening of his Christian faith. He secretly left his regiment for a hidden hermitage in the forests near Archangel'sk to pursue a life of prayer.[99] Vasilii Blinskii (Elder Adrian) served 24 years in the army and achieved the rank of captain as the conductor of his regiment's orchestra. His regiment served both in the military campaigns in Prussia and during Pugachev's rebellion in the Urals.[100] During the regiment's placement in the provincial town of Bolkhov, Vasilii lost interest in the merriments of the officer's life and preferred to spend his spare time fishing, rather than participating in the lavish banquets organized by the colonel. Vasilii's disdain for the rules of society caused a conflict with the colonel. The norms of behavior that were accepted within officers' corps were in evident contrast with the traditional Christian morality that governed the households of many Russian noble families. Zakharia Verkhovskii (Elder Zosima, 1768–1833), served in the St. Petersburg Guards, joining in 1782 at the age of 15. He was distressed about cardplaying and gambling in his regiment, and his younger brothers became the victims of both vices.[101] Nobles who broke with the norms and culture of their environment and became monks often attracted other members of their class. The community of Fedor of Sanaksar, for example, included several demobilized officers.[102]

While there is no doubt that pious young men from the provinces could be diverted from the military lifestyle, the army could also stimulate their interest in religion and mysticism. Each regiment had its own church and priests, who ensured that the officers and soldiers took sacraments regularly. Life in a regiment was not dissimilar to a monastic one: both were communities of men that brought together the elite and the lower classes, both forged a spirit of brotherhood and of a closely-knit family. Campaigns abroad could bring officers into contact with Pietism and other mystical movements.

The second largest group among *startsy* and their followers were the representatives of urban commercial classes, including merchants and *meshchane* (petty tradesmen). Just like the noblemen, they had difficulties in trying to break the conventions of their social milieu. The expectations of their families and the legal constraints that obliged other merchants to pay taxes for those members of their class who wanted to join monasteries created obstacles for those young men who were attracted to the ascetic life. Nevertheless, three brothers of the Putilov merchant family from Serpukhov successfully pursued a monastic vocation. The five male heirs of Putilov's family had joint ownership of the family's capital, but when the elder brother Timofei decided to become a monk, his father and First Guild merchant Samgin agreed to pay taxes for him. Two other brothers, Aleksandr and Iona, followed the lead of Timofei and eventually became abbots in major Russian monasteries.[103] *Startsy* who came from the trading classes were propertied, literate, and well-traveled. Lev (Leonid) Nagolkin (1772–1841), from the trading town Karachev in Orel province, was the son of a *meshchanin* (a petty tradesman) and a merchant's daughter. He worked in the hemp trade as an assistant to merchant Sokol'nikov from Bolkhov. In 1797, however, this successful tradesman joined the Optina pustyn' as a novice and in 1801 took vows in Beloberezhskaia pustyn'. Lev became a monk in the same year and in the same monastery as the son of his former boss, Maksim Sokol'nikov.[104] This was not a coincidence. These two young men, one the heir to a fortune and the other a promising entrepreneur, had probably influenced one another in their decision to follow a monastic vocation. The Russian trading classes had a reputation for displays of piety and the patronage of churches.[105] For example, Isidor and Agaf'ia Mashnin, parents of Serafim of Sarov, supervised the building of a new stone church in Kursk dedicated to the Kazan Mother of God and St. Sergius of Radonezh (completed in 1778). The risks and perils of the trading profession, the insecurity of individual fortunes, and the high value of trust within the social group are all factors that helped shape a specific profile of merchant religiosity. Experience of traveling to different places and meeting different people could provide merchants with invaluable insights into human psychology.[106] Democratic behavior, the use of folk idioms and jokes, lack of sentimentality, and a typical merchant shrewdness distinguished Leonid from the elders of noble origin. While today Leonid is venerated as the founder of the succession of Optina eldership, during his lifetime he struggled for recognition. The ecclesiastical authorities regarded Leonid's spiritual guidance of nuns and lay women as inappropriate, while some fellow monks accused Leonid of heresy. Some visitors, provoked by Leonid's style, criticized him for his lack of asceticism.[107]

In contrast to the privileged social groups among *startsy* during the era of Enlightenment, peasants were less prominent. Elder Vasilisk, the mentor of Zosima (Verkhovskii), was quite exceptional. This semiliterate peasant was one of the genuine mystical authors in Russia. To some extent he represents a model for the peasant elders in the nineteenth century and bears resemblance to the renowned peasant saint of the twentieth century Siluan the Athonite. Vasilisk (Vasilii, d. 1824) came from the impoverished family of a state peasant from Tver province who had fallen victim to robbery. Three brothers, who lost their mother very early, had to earn a living by begging. As a poor peasant, Vasilisk moved to the household of his father-in-law after his marriage. Yet unsatisfied with his life in the world, Vasilisk left his wife and lived initially in Kaliazin, near the monastery of St. Makarii, with his elder brother Koz'ma, from whom he had learned reading and writing. Koz'ma, a cripple and a reputed holy man, lived off alms from the local gentry and townspeople. He attracted popular interest as the owner of the miraculous icon of Mother of God, "The Salvation of the Damned," given to him by the Mother Superior of the Sviato-Dukhov convent in Novgorod. The icon's reputation for healing and other miracles attracted visitors to Koz'ma's house and provided the owner of the icon with his livelihood.[108]

In contrast to his brother, Vasilisk sought the silence and solitude of eremitic life.[109] Having become a hermit, he practiced mental prayer and meditated on God's creation. While Koz'ma was a man of the people and a putative miracle-maker, Vasilisk was an introverted dreamer (as a child he made himself wings in order to imitate the angels painted on icons). These two brothers exemplified different expressions of peasant spirituality. While Koz'ma enjoyed his popularity as the owner of the miracle-working icon, his brother renounced his dependency on the world.

Vasilisk's experience as a beggar and wanderer brought him in contact with a monastic culture that attracted him by its asceticism and promise of holiness. The monks of Vvedenskii monastery near Moscow (where Vasilisk applied to become a novice) tested the young peasant, ordering him to run on the thin ice over a recently frozen lake. They were amazed when Vasilisk duly obeyed and nearly drowned. "You will make a good monk if you are always so obedient to your spiritual fathers," they told him. [110] Unfortunately, as a state peasant Vasilisk could not be accepted into any monastery without permission from his village commune. He had to regularly renew his passport, which was issued to him only for a limited period. The Vvedenskii monks advised Vasilisk to become a hermit even though it was not in line with the existing laws. It seems that unofficial hermitages served as outlets for those who failed to find a place within established monasticism.

During his life in the forests in the Chuvash lands (northeast of the Volga heights), Vasilisk mortified his body with all-night vigils and ascetic exploits. He shared a forest cabin with two monks, the "wise, ascetic, and well-read" Pavel, and blind, illiterate, and humble Ioann. Vasilisk learned very soon that erudition could not prevent even experienced monks from grave mistakes in spiritual life. One night, after struggling in vain against a sinful passion, Pavel cut off his own arm with an axe. While self-mutilation for religious reasons not unheard of, and was practiced among the sectarian Skoptsy, who interpreted literally the quotation from the Gospel "there be eunuchs which have made themselves eunuchs for the kingdom of heaven's sake"(Matt 19:2), Vasilisk intuitively knew that self-mutilating physical asceticism was not the answer to his spiritual quest.[111] Nevertheless, he did not find an alternative until his meeting with elder Adrian.

Adrian (who made Vasilisk a monk) introduced Vasilii to the hesychast prayer in the forests of Roslavl'. Inheriting Elder Adrian's forest cabin after the elder moved to Konevets, Vasilii began to record the mystical visions and revelations he experienced during his practice of the Jesus prayer. The result of these exercises and meditations was an original treatise on the Jesus prayer that described in detail the psychosomatic changes that a practitioner experienced at various stages of his spiritual progress.[112] This treatise influenced the author of the religious bestseller of the late nineteenth century, known in English as *The Way of a Pilgrim*.[113] Vasilisk's faithful disciple and biographer, former officer Zosima (Zakhariia Verkhovskii), followed his teacher from the forests of Konevets Island to the Siberian taiga where the two ascetics helped to found a women's community. Spiritual friendship between a representative of the Russian educated classes and a semiliterate peasant was the prototype for several similar unions in the nineteenth and twentieth centuries.

One social group that was strikingly absent among elders in this period was the clergy. As mentioned above, there was a gap between the spirituality promoted by the elders and the prevailing culture of the theological seminary that was dominated by the Latin language and scholasticism. In the eighteenth century, few of the spiritual elders whose lives we have considered in this chapter came through a theological seminary. Paisii Velichkovskii, a descendant of Ukrainian priests and a student in at the Kiev-Mogila Academy, was a notable exception. Although the monasteries that survived secularization attempts were staffed by members of the clerical estate, which included widowed clergy and their offspring, this group was underrepresented among the spiritual elders.[114] This was partly due to their reputation: monks who came from the clerical estate were known for drinking. Abbot Nifont of Sarov, for example, made it a rule not to accept representatives of the clerical estate into his monastery so that their behavior did not tempt other brethren.[115]

Female Elders and Founders of Communities

In theory, the role of a spiritual guide that was not connected with the authority of office could be performed by either gender. In practice, however, we know of very few women who achieved official recognition. Only a small number of women were officially canonized by the Russian Church (out of 386 Russian saints only 10 were women) by the end of the nineteenth century, while there were a large number of female ascetics and recluses who were venerated as saints by Orthodox believers.[116] The majority of these women gained their reputation by their ascetic deeds and pious life, but not all of them had an affiliation with officially recognized monastic communities. The careers of many male elders were associated with the founding of women's religious communities, which raises important questions about the gender aspects of the elders' pastoral work. Collaboration between male clerics and religious women was a widespread phenomenon within medieval and modern Catholicism. In eighteenth-century Russia, the majority of new female monastic communities emerged with the assistance of monks and spiritual elders.[117] This collaboration revealed not the structured hierarchy of power, but a complex interplay of spiritual friendship, patronage, and mutual dependence. It is possible that specific aspects of the elders' spirituality (sentimentalism, the emphasis on the human nature of Christ, cultivation of the virtues of love and humility) particularly resonated with women.

Institutionalized female monasticism prior to the nineteenth century was numerically smaller and economically weaker than its male counterpart. The legislation of Peter and his successors imposed new restrictions on female religious vocation. The supplement to the Ecclesiastical Regulation in 1722 stipulated a minimum age for nuns of between 50 and 60 years old. In 1764, the number of female convents was reduced from 185–203 to 67; this represented a reduction that was on a larger scale than that of their male equivalents.[118] Historians, however, have argued that such restrictions did not deter, but rather stimulated the revival of female ascetic life.[119] Numerous unofficial female communities were founded either on the sites of former convents or as entirely new institutions.[120] Because funding from the state was not available, these communities only existed as private initiatives, benefiting from the material support of the local population.

Setting up a new female community required various means of legitimation. Pious women who had material and personal resources for organizing a new religious institution often resorted to the authority of visions and miracles. Agafiia Mel'gunova (neè Belokopytova, born c. 1723), a rich widow who inherited land and about 700 serfs, was the founder of the women's community in Diveevo. In the late 1750s, following the death of her husband, Colonel Mel'gunov, Agafiia stayed in the Florovskii convent in Kiev. She claimed that she had a vision of the Holy Virgin, who instructed the widow to be her mediator in establishing the "fourth domain" on earth. Agafiia appeared to be familiar with the legend that the Kievo-Pecherskaia Lavra was the "third domain" of the Virgin. According to the legend, Mary and the apostles cast lots to determine which countries they would evangelize. Mary's lot was Georgia, considered by legend as the first domain. Mary claimed that divine intervention (in the form of a warning from an angel) delayed her visit to Georgia, but during a journey to Cyprus, the wind forced her boat to Mount Athos, where she converted the pagans, thus making the holy mountain her second domain. In the eleventh century, an Athonite monk, Antonii from Chernigov, was instructed by Mary to return to his homeland and establish the Kievo-Pecherskii monastery.[121]

Nevertheless, the visionary experience of Agafiia Mel'gunova, which was congruent with the foundation legend of the Kievo-Pecherskaia Lavra, had to be approved by spiritual authorities. In her case, the Kievo-Pecherskaia monks deemed that Agafiia's apparition was of a divine, not evil, source, judging that the devil could not adopt the appearance of Mary, who was the "plague of demons."[122] In addition to the Kievo-Pecherskaia Lavra monks, Agafiia also secured the blessing of the monks in one of the most prestigious monasteries in Russia, the Sarov monastery. The choice of location for the new community, while framed in the hagiographical motif of a repeated vision and divine sign, was not accidental. Agafiia's family had for a long time owned land in the area, which became the site of the new women's community (about 13 kilometers from the Sarov monastery).

In the origins of Serafimo-Diveevo community one can discern a recurrent pattern. The female founders of new celibate communities consulted monks rather than bishops regarding the organization of spiritual life in the community. The authority of elders like Abbot Pakhomii, Fedor (Ushakov), Feofan (Novoezerskii), or Paisii Velichkovskii meant more to these women than Synodal decrees. Sarov's abbot Pakhomii and other Sarov monks including Serafim (Moshnin) were supportive of the rich widow's initiative, and acted as confessors and spiritual advisors to the religious women. Serafim (Moshnin) later became a spiritual leader of the female community and he adapted the Sarov Rule to meet its needs.

Agafiia Mel'gunova's experience suggests that wealthy women (who enjoyed legal privileges concerning their property) had the means and authority to establish new religious communities in the period when state policy was generally unfavorable to monastic development.[123] Despite their relative autonomy and wealth, these pious noblewomen still had to legitimize their actions by appealing to mystical visions and by seeking the support of male ascetics, including monks and abbots. To use the argument of C. B. Walker, "ambivalence about wealth and authority" allowed male ascetics to encourage the efforts of mystical women.[124] This ambivalence made them more accommodating to female charismatic authority, as it was an alternative to clerical authority.

It was not unusual for male spiritual elders to delegate their authority to female leaders of women's communities. For example, noblewoman Mariia Protas'eva (1760–1813), became Mother Superior of Arzamas Alekseevskaia community. Initially she was instructed by Elder Fedor of Sanaksar, one of the founders of Arzamas community, but eventually she became a spiritual advisor of the sisters in her community (and other women), in her own right. Mariia Protas'eva developed a taste for monasticism from an early age, having been brought up by her pious grandmother. As a teenager she made an unsuccessful attempt to escape from home disguised as a poor pilgrim.[125] Her father, the governor of Rostov, was eventually persuaded by his daughter's determination and let her join a convent in Kostroma where she spent four years.

Under the influence of the ascetic tales recited by her grandmother, Mariia was determined to find a spiritual guide. She learned about Elder Fedor (Ushakov) and visited him in his exile in Solovki between 1774 and 1783, becoming his spiritual daughter. Paisii Velichkovskii, who corresponded with Mariia, described her relationship with Elder Fedor as an example of perfect obedience. Inspired by Fedor, the young woman joined the Arzamas Alekseevskaia community, which at the time had about 150 sisters. On his return from exile Elder Fedor supervised every aspect of the community's life, visiting it frequently and introducing "disclosure of thoughts" among the sisters.[126]

Around 1786 Fedor appointed twenty-six-year-old Mariia as the spiritual director of the Arzamas community. She initially objected to her spiritual father's decision. In due course, however, Mariia got used to her new role, imagining that she was simply a vehicle through which her beloved *starets* Fedor continued to guide the community. Yet perhaps having developed her own style of leadership, Mariia became more cautious and critical of her mentor.[127] Following Fedor's death, she regretted bitterly this loss of trust, which bothered her so much that she decided to share her anxieties with the renowned Paisii Velichkovskii. The Moldavian Elder interpreted Mariia's spiritual disposition as a "temptation" and a fruit of disobedience; he advised her to repent and learn from her mistakes.[128] Paisii also instructed Mariia in the art of good pastorship. The abbess, he believed, was to give a personal example of virtue, mercy, and patience, motivate sisters with prayer and tears, and instruct them in the virtues of obedience and humility. In this respect, it seems that Paisii did not make a distinction between male and female spiritual leadership. Nuns, like monks, had to perfect themselves in the art of mental prayer, following the teaching of the Fathers.[129] Mother Mariia's disenchantment with her first mentor did not mean that she subsequently relied only on herself and on advice from books. She sought spiritual guidance elsewhere, writing to monk Amfilokhii of Rostov monastery and to Paisii Velichkovskii.[130] She was planning a visit to Moldavia, but was deterred from it following Paisii's death in 1795.

Despite her relatively young age and initial lack of confidence, Mother Mariia asserted her role as an experienced spiritual guide. She kept the records of Elder Fedor's councils for use in her community. Her letter to young noblewoman O. V. Strigaleva (the future nun Olimpiada), in which she justified the superiority of ascetic way of life, while not original in argument, was one of a very few theological writings produced by a Russian woman. The letter suggests that Mother Mariia corresponded with several women who wanted to dedicate themselves to celibate life. Her advice to them was candid. "What is better, a corruptible and sometimes debauched man, or most sweet Jesus who so loved us that he poured his most pure blood for our salvation?"[131] Mariia tried to inspire the young woman with the examples of the great *ammas* (female, pl. from *abba*, or father) of the heroic age of early Christianity: Evpraksiia, Apollinariia, Evfrosiniia, and Ksenia the Wanderer, as well as the learned and pious Russian princess Evfrosiniia of Polotsk. The advice was gratefully received. Olga Strigaleva ran away from home to join the community founded by Fedor Ushakov, and after the death of Mariia Protas'eva became the leader of the community.[132]

Mariia's ambitious spiritual aspirations found support among the heirs of Paisii. She was not satisfied with four volumes of the *Philokalia* and, after Paisii's death, requested that Abbot Sofronii of Neamt monastery send her a copy of the book by the Gaza ascetic St. Barsonuphius (d. 563), which contained advice on how to direct a monastic community.[133] The abbot ordered Barsonuphius' book to be copied for the female community as a matter of priority, which angered some of the brethren who themselves had not yet found an opportunity to read it.[134]

The male ascetics treated the abbess of the Arzamas community as their equal, comparing her to a good shepherd. In addition to the traditional role of mother superior, she also became a spiritual guide, a role based on the hesychast spirituality influenced by the Philokalic movement. It is noteworthy that, following Fedor's advice, women in the Arzamas community did not take monastic vows, even though the community could have been granted the status of a convent. This set them apart from other convents where distinctions existed between novices, nuns, and schema-nuns.[135] Although the male mentors to whom Mariia appealed in times of difficulty preached to her about obedience, there is no evidence that they treated her any differently because she was a woman.

Collaboration between spiritual elders and religious women tells a story of interdependence and exchange. It was often the case that women lent stronger support to the ideas and reforms that the elders sought to implement than did their fellow monks. On the other hand, female communities, which had no formal approval and institutional support from the Synod, benefited from the contribution of elders to the social, liturgical, and spiritual organization of their day-to-day life.

THE SCHOLARLY EMPHASIS on the defeat of religion by the forces of the Enlightenment and secularization often obscures the potential for reorganization and revival within the traditional churches of the Old Regime. The reinvention of the ancient institution of spiritual guidance within institutionalized monasticism in eighteenth-century Russia can be seen as a paradox or antinomy. Indeed, there is no doubt that monasticism was a casualty of the reformist efforts of eighteenth-century rulers who, at best, tried to give it a more utilitarian purpose and, at worst, to abolish it altogether. Yet the outcomes were different from the intentions, and contemplative monasticism persisted, albeit with a greater emphasis on discipline and communal living.

Four major sources contributed to the revival of *starchestvo* in the eighteenth century: the anchoritic movement, religious dissent, the return of the monastic émigrés to the Balkans, and last but not least, the rise of women's communities. These developments help to explain why the end of the eighteenth century was very different from its beginning: "The eighteenth century has ended with a monastic revival and unmistakably intensive invigoration of spiritual life."[136] Their small number notwithstanding, spiritual elders played a leading role in the monastic revival.

The factors that account for this revival were paradoxically the same as those that led to monastic protest at the beginning of the century. The state's final suppression of monastic economic and administrative autonomy stimulated the development of a new model of monasticism, which in a peculiar way combined the Josephite denial of the right of personal property for monks with Nil Sorskii's contemplative life.

Startsy and their supporters presented themselves as the renovators and guardians of the Orthodox tradition. In this respect they had much in common with Old Believers, who rejected the Westernization of the Russian Church and culture. Like Old Believers, monastic reformers appealed to the authority of the past to legitimize their innovations. The legacy of Byzantine spirituality was revived by Paisii Velichkovskii and the communal forms of monastic life were presented as a "forgotten" ancient tradition.

The proponents of the tradition of spiritual guidance posited themselves in opposition to the existing forms of pastorship and church hierarchy, placing personal virtues and spiritual experience above education and position in the social hierarchy. Using the Weberian distinction between traditional and charismatic authority, elders fell under the category of "charismatic" leaders, despite their claims to the traditional and scriptural origins of their position. Thus, the authority of the *starets* was from the beginning potentially subversive to the church hierarchy. Nevertheless, different forms of cooperation existed between the charismatic elders and the church hierarchs. One reason for some bishops' encouragement of elders was a growing religious diversity, which increased with the expansion of the Russian Empire and with the policies of religious toleration. Attempts by the enlightened prelates to guard the hegemony of the established church and lead the re-Christianization of society were not necessarily shared by elders, who saw their foremost task as the redefinition of monasticism, which they believed was the most direct path to spiritual transformation. On the whole, however, the number of bishops who had a broader social and political vision of Orthodoxy, and of the *startsy* who aimed at the reformation of Christian life remained exceptionally small in eighteenth-century Russia.

CHAPTER THREE

The Institutionalization of Spiritual Guidance, 1810–1860

Achievements and Tensions

Although Alexander I's policies were firmly based upon the rationalist philosophy of the Enlightenment, mysticism continued to permeate the official ideology that influenced all aspects of Russian religious politics. "Mystical universalism" was expressed in the official promotion of the Bible Society and the state's support of missionary activities. It was an essential element of the growth of Masonic lodges and the development of foreign Christian groups within Russian cultural life. "Mystical universalism" underpinned the creation of the Dual Ministry of Spiritual Affairs and Education in 1817, chaired by Prince Alexander Golitsyn, who shared the ecumenical inclinations of the emperor and was a patron of the Bible Society.[1]

The impact of these developments on *starchestvo* is difficult to overestimate. In the atmosphere of religious liberalization, the disciples of Paisii Velichkovskii and the members of various forest hermitages experienced unprecedented freedom and received official support in organizing their communities and spreading their teaching among monks and lay people. Furthermore, in 1801, Alexander I granted amnesty to all Russian émigrés should they wish to return to the Russian Empire.[2] Although Alexander's decree did not specifically mention émigré-monks, the authorities often treated them in a similar way as other repatriates. For example, in 1801 the government granted 20 monks from the Neamt monastery in Moldavia permission to return to Russia and allowed them to retain their monastic and priestly status. Alexander I personally instructed the minister of justice to ensure that in similar cases repatriate-monks were to be accepted as Russian citizens and referred to bishops who, having confirmed the "authenticity" of their monastic vows, would allocate them to various monasteries in their diocese.[3] Monastic emigration to the Balkans continued in the nineteenth century, but the Russian government became less lenient toward those who wanted to come back. It was believed that some émigrés simply wanted to hasten their progress to holy orders or priesthood and avoid the long probation period and age restrictions stipulated by Russian law. Hence, in the 1820s, Alexander I decreed that Russian pilgrims going abroad were not to take vows in foreign monasteries unless they intended to remain there permanently.[4]

Spiritual elders enjoyed the patronage of the mystics in power. Minister Golitsyn personally intervened when the elders Fedor and Leonid had troubles with the abbot of the Valaam monastery,[5] and in 1821 Golitsyn approved the petition of the monk Zosima (Verkhovskii) for the establishment of a female community in the Siberian town of Turinsk that emerged under the spiritual direction of Elder Vasilisk, the author of the mystical treatise on the Jesus prayer. Golitsyn appears to have known the peasant-mystic personally and had great respect for him.

The attention of the ruling elites to spiritual elders, some of whom, like Vasilisk, came from the lower classes, was in the spirit of the ideology of "mystical universalism," which did not distinguish between "elite" and "popular" religion. Alexander sympathized with popular expressions of piety, even if these were at odds with the official religion. In 1818, both Golitsyn and Alexander I intervened in the investigation of an unsanctioned pilgrimage in the Cossack Don region. The pilgrims had flocked to a cave dug by Mariia Sherstiugova into a chalk mountain above the River Don. The ecclesiastical authorities condemned the pilgrimage as a form of superstition and accused Mariia (who had the reputation of an ascetic and prophetess) of spiritual pride and avarice. They demanded that the civil authorities stop the flow of pilgrims by destroying the cave. Alexander I, however, interpreted Sherstiugova's endeavor as "an intention to imitate the ancient ascetics, inspired by Christian zeal," and proposed that the local consistory assist in the building of an Orthodox church inside the cave at the treasury's expense.[6]

These liberal, pro-Western, evangelical, and mystical tendencies were opposed by the "archaists," some of whom founded the literary society of the Lovers of Russian Language (1811–1815).[7] The "archaists" defended the purity of the Russian language, and tried to protect it against contamination by foreign influences. On the eve of the war with Napoleon, the patriotic sentiment of the archaists received official encouragement from Admiral A. S. Shishkov, who had become a member of the Cabinet of Ministers in 1814.[8] Shishkov opposed the translation of the Bible and lamented the dominance of the French language among the Russian nobility.

The archaists joined forces with the "Orthodox opposition" to Golitsyn's ministry, which included the archconservative bishops Mikhail (Desnitskii), Innokentii (Smirnov), Serafim (Glagolevskii), and Archimandrite Fotii (Spasskii). Metropolitan Filaret (Drozdov), too, was for a period a member of the opposition, although he did not condone the methods used by the "archaists." The opposition staged a "revolt" against Golitsyn in 1824, which resulted in the downfall of the liberal minister, the dissolution of the Dual Ministry, the closing down of the Bible society, and the appointment of the archconservative Shishkov as the head of the Ministry of Education.

The Orthodox conservatives did not oppose mysticism as such, but tried to purify it of alien, heterodox tendencies. The conservative Orthodox critics of Alexandrine eclectic spirituality were not averse to seeking advantage through the use of emotionalism, eschatological prophecies, and visions—religious practices more commonly associated with mystical sects. Fotii (Spasskii) (1792–1838) attacked the ecumenism, evangelicalism, and pro-Western mysticism of the Alexandrine era. A protégé of Bishop Mikhail (Desnitskii) and a graduate of St. Petersburg Spiritual Academy, Fotii became known as a "young elder." His fiery sermons at Kazan Cathedral, in which the twenty-eight-year-old monk condemned the anti-Christian character of "inner Christianity," earned him popularity among the merchants and lower classes of St. Petersburg.[9] Initially Fotii made an impression on Golitsyn, who believed the young preacher was the new St. John Chrysostom.[10] Yet before long Fotii's attacks on the ecumenism of the court led to his exile to the Novgorod Iur'evskii monastery, where he was appointed as abbot.[11]

The conflicting cultural developments of Alexander I's era provided a context for the revival of spiritual eldership in Russian monasticism and beyond it. The interest in mysticism among the elites was paralleled by spiritual searching among the lower classes. The spiritual experiment that Paisii's disciples carried out in Russian monasteries and the growth of popular cults around prophets and holy men could not have taken place in a more favorable political climate. The victory of the "Orthodox opposition" over Golitsyn's mystical universalism was also advantageous for the elders, because they represented an Orthodox alternative to the ecumenical and universalist tendencies of the Holy Union.[12] The elders and their patrons in the Synod, including Metropolitan Filaret Drozdov, were not opposed to mysticism as such but were eager to distinguish between "good" and "bad" mysticism, expanding and at the same time restricting the boundaries of the Orthodox faith.

Elders and Monasticism

Even though spiritual guidance continued to remain a marginal practice, in the nineteenth century it experienced a routinization, a gradual process in which "basically two antagonistic forces of charisma and tradition . . . merge with one another."[13] In the eras of Alexander I and Nicholas I, the reversal of official policies towards monasticism and the rise of interest in mystical theology allowed spiritual elders to find a niche within monastic institutions. In several monasteries, eldership—which fulfilled important functions in monastic life—was turned into a perennial institution.

Following the death of Catherine II, the development of monasticism was characterized by two contradictory tendencies. On the one hand, the Synod continued to abide by the Ecclesiastical Regulation, which deprived monks of economic and social rights (while at the same time trying to utilize monasticism for social purposes). On the other hand, there was a reversal of secularization policies and of the extreme anti-monastic aspects of eighteenth-century legislation. Between 1808 and 1861 the number of monasteries, convents, and religious communities in Russia increased by 22 percent, while the number of monks, nuns, and novices grew by 77 percent.[14] These trends were influenced by Catherine II's successors, who generously provided monasteries with land.[15] The state also provided monasteries with laborers recruited from state peasants who were obliged to serve for 25 years, thus replacing the monastery's freed servitors.[16]

Monasticism, however, did not fully recover from the eighteenth-century secularization efforts: it remained constrained by the rules and regulations concerning every aspect of its internal life. Decisions concerning tonsure, transfer of monks and novices between monasteries, and monks' mobility required special permission of the Synod. The centralization of control, coupled with a shortage of experienced spiritual leaders, exacerbated problems of discipline within monasteries.

The introduction of eldership in Russian monasteries, as previously discussed, owed a great deal to the Balkan religious revival and particularly to the activity of Paisii Velichkovskii. While some members of Paisii's community had already returned to Russia by the 1790s, the 1801 amnesty brought about a mass repatriation of monastic émigrés from the Balkans in the early 1800s. The impact of the monastic migrants was twofold. Firstly, they revived and strengthened interest in the patristic Byzantine roots of Russian Orthodoxy. Secondly, Paisii's disciples contributed to the reform of monasticism by strengthening the authority of spiritual elders. According to estimates made by Father Sergei Chetverikov, Paisii's disciples made an impact on 107 Russian monasteries.[17]

"The Moldavians" introduced spiritual and ascetic practices, such as mental prayer and the "disclosure of thoughts," which were either unknown or had fallen into desuetude within Russian monasteries. The repatriates and their followers passionately sought to improve monastic discipline and reform spiritual life by confronting lax monks. For example, Fedor Pol'zikov, a former member of the Neamt monastery, encouraged his brethren to read the Gospel every day and clear their cells of books with unorthodox content.

Of those 107 monasteries where the legacy of Paisii Velichkovskii was preserved through his disciples, the most distinguished was the Ioanno-Predtechenskii skete, which was affiliated with Optina pustyn'.[18] This monastery was founded in the fifteenth century and fell into decline during the 1700s, but was transformed in 1797 by the efforts of Bishop Platon (Levshin) of Moscow, who improved its financial and legal status and introduced the communal rule. In the 1820s, with the support of Bishop Filaret (Amfiteatrov) a group of hermits from the Roslavl' forests (Smolensk province) relocated to Kaluga province and formed a hermitage under the auspices of Optina pustyn'. Like his contemporary Bishop Filaret (Drozdov) of Moscow, the Kaluga bishop believed the revival of monasticism would benefit the Orthodox Church as a whole.

Filaret, who was a son of priest, pursued a career in church administration; he graduated the Orel Seminary in 1797 and took holy orders soon after. A typical representative of "learned monasticism," he taught poetry and Greek to theology students and held appointments as abbot to various monasteries before he became a rector of Moscow theological academy in 1814. A busy administrator, the bishop liked to spend several weeks a year in Optina as a spiritual retreat. In Optina—one of the most beautiful monasteries of Kaluga province—Filaret wanted to cultivate the hesychast spirit of Nil Sorskii and his hermitage.

Optina pustyn' had a semi-independent position: it was located about 300 meters away from the monastery in a dense pine forest and it had its own rule and separate finances.[19] In 1825, only 12 monks lived in the hermitage. The purpose of the founders was to promote the ascetic and hesychast principles of monastic life: an isolated position, a small number of brethren, moderate regulations concerning the observance of church services, common meals, and the absolute prohibition on entry for women, were all believed to provide better conditions for contemplative life. Five elders from Smolensk province, who had experience of solitary life and possessed a good library of patristic texts, comprised the core of this new community. The appointment in 1826 of monk Moisei (Timofei Putilov), a former hermit from the Roslavl' forests, as the abbot of Optina pustyn' guaranteed that the hesychast spirit would be preserved in the hermitage. Moisei, who supported eldership and encouraged the dissemination of the Paisii Velichkovskii' legacy in Russia, was the founder of the Optina library, which by the 1860s contained more than 4,000 volumes.

The establishment of eldership in the monastery is associated with Leonid (Nagolkin) who arrived with his disciples to Optina in 1829. Unlike the Roslavl' hermits, Leonid had valuable experience in spiritual directorship, which he had practiced in various monastic communities with the support of Paisii's own disciples, elders Fedor and Kleopa. Spiritual guidance was an important part of the monastic vocation; in fact, the route to eldership depended on it, as demonstrated by the rule of the skete, which distinguished between the role of a confessor and that of a spiritual elder, stating that only spiritually experienced monks, who were not necessarily ordained as priests, could become elders.[20] At Optina, the role of elder became institutionalized: an elder trained his successor, while the senior members of the community confirmed the choice of a new elder.

In the 1840s, the hermitage began its publishing activities with the assistance of educated novices Leonid Kavelin, Amvrosii Grenkov, and Iuvelian Polovtsev, and with the active support of the Slavophile Ivan Kireevskii and Bishop Filaret (Drozdov). The aim of the publishers was to introduce the legacy of Paisii Velichkovskii and other works of monastic spirituality to the reading public in Russia. By the turn of the century Optina had published 125 titles (225,000 total print copies), the majority of which were by hesychast authors.[21] The monastery sent their published books to all Russian communal monasteries and to the Russian and Bulgarian monasteries in Athos, as well as to seminary and academic libraries.[22]

The Optina eldership was quite unique in that it forged a link with a section of Russian educated society, which Stanton described as the "Optina intelligentsia."[23] Perhaps due to its special place in the Russian literary imagination, the Optina eldership became the model (applied by the church hierarchy and commentators such as S. Chetverikov and I. Kontsevich) against which all other forms of eldership were assessed. It is nevertheless important to keep in mind that, despite its influence and reputation, the Optina model of eldership was only one among many other styles and forms of spiritual guidance.

Russian "Indigenous" Elders within Monasticism

It has become commonplace to link Russian spiritual eldership with Paisii Velichkovskii's disciples.[24] This interpretation overlooked the heterogeneous character of Russian eldership and underplayed the role of elders who had no association with Paisii. Nevertheless, it must be pointed out that the Optina elders paid homage to these Russian elders and treasured their writings.[25]

While the monastic repatriates from the Balkans represented a distinct group within nineteenth-century Russian monasticism, there were a number of monks who had no direct association with Paisii's legacy, but who nevertheless enjoyed the reputation of elders. They were connected with the Balkan revival through the ideas and practices of the *Dobrotoliubie* and the Jesus prayer. Many of these elders were the successors of eighteenth-century hermits who resisted the spirit and letter of the Ecclesiastical Regulation.

Serafim (Prokhor Moshnin) was one such monk from the provincial Sarov monastery who spent most of his monastic life as a hermit. He was neither a prolific religious preacher and writer, nor a missionary or monastic reformer. The son of a pious merchant from Kursk, Prokhor Moshnin chose a monastic career at the age of 24, joining the community of Sarov, known for its strict rule and the encouragement of an ascetic life. A mystically inclined young monk who despite poor health determinedly pursued ascetic feats, Serafim (ordained as a priest in 1793) claimed he experienced a vision of the Virgin Mary, who supposedly cured him of dropsy. Although he was respected by the monks of Sarov, he avoided taking part in the internal affairs of Sarov and turned down an offer to head the neighboring Sviato-Troitskii monastery in Alatyr' in 1796. In 1799, he left the monastery to live in a wooden log cabin in the Sarov forest, following the example set by other solitary ascetics from Sarov (Mark, Nazarii, and Dorofei). An attack by robbers, which left him crippled, did not deter him from solitary life, and Serafim's detachment from the community politics only strengthened his authority as a spiritual adviser of the Sarov monks and novices. In 1810, after 11 years of solitude, Serafim returned to Sarov on the order of the new abbot, who was concerned about the hermit's withdrawal from Holy Communion. He continued, however, to live as a recluse in his cell for another 15 years, maintaining a vow of silence, and making several attempts to return to eremitic life. The last 18 years of Serafim's life, until his death in 1833, were quite different from his period of seclusion; he opened the doors of his cell to visitors and contributed energetically to the organization of the female community in the village of Diveevo, which became his primary legacy.

The Catholic priest Vsevolod Roshko, a son of refugees from Bolshevik Russia, suggested that although Serafim and Paisii's disciples knew each other, their spiritual experiences diverged. According to Roshko, none of the Moldavian repatriates elected Serafim as their spiritual instructor, Serafim had no experience with Paisii's practice of "disclosure of thoughts," and he never taught the Jesus prayer.[26] Serafim's reputation as an elder was based on his fame as a holy man enlightened by God whose advice was sought because of his foresight. His ascetic achievements and pious life gave him the informal status of a spiritual guide who was able to direct a person on the path to salvation. During his eremitic life in the Sarov forest between 1797 and 1807, Serafim was consulted by lay and monastic visitors.[27] Despite the strict ban on the unsanctioned private use of ink and paper, as stated in the Sarov Rule, novices and monks often scribbled Serafim's teaching on pieces of scrap paper.[28] As soon as Serafim's reputation as a holy man was established, even his blessing was treated as a sign of God's grace.

However, unlike the elders of the Optina pustyn', Serafim did not produce a successor or a community of disciples. Serafim's guidance of the female community in Diveevo and his communication with lay visitors were the major forms of his spiritual directorship. It appears that Serafim's authority was largely informal and not based on any sanctioned structure or hierarchy within or outside Sarov. Novices and monks would often come to Serafim for "blessing" and only subsequently did they consult their confessors in the monastery.

– Zosima

A former army officer, Zosima (Zakharia Verkhovskii) was another elder of non-Paisiian descent. Like Serafim of Sarov he was actively involved in the foundation of women's communities such as the Nikolaevskii convent in Turinsk and Troitse-Odigitrievskaia community in Smolensk province. Zosima composed a rule and a set of instructions for spiritual life; he settled legal issues with the ecclesiastical authorities, found sponsors, and directed women in their spiritual progress. The nuns who followed Zosima's spiritual directorship signed a pledge promising to live in spiritual union with each other and in obedience to their elder.[29] Even though the form of such a pledge was unique to the history of Russian monasticism, it received approval from Bishop Mikhail (Burdukov) of Irkutsk. These pledges reflect Zosima's aspiration to create an ideal community characterized by total renunciation of personal possessions and individualistic impulses.

3.1. St. Serafim of Sarov.
Source: Skazanie o zhizni i podvigakh startsa Serafima, ieromonakha Sarovskoi pustyni i zatvornika. 3-e izd. St. Petersburg, 1851

Charismatic Elders versus Administrators

Giles Constable described three distinct sources of authority in medieval religious communities: "the word of the founder, embodied after his death in a rule, customs, or traditions; personal holiness, as reflected in detachment from secular life and intimacy with God; and the official ranks of ordination and office within the community."[30] Sometimes these sources of authority overlapped, so that the founder could also be regarded as a holy man and father to his disciples.

In post-Catherinian Russia, abbots began to be appointed rather than elected.[31] The Synod either appointed abbots single-handedly or considered two candidacies proposed by the local bishop.[32] The abbots of noncommunal monasteries were chosen by local bishops and authorized by the Synod. The heads of "first-class" monasteries (who usually held the title of archimandrite) enjoyed many privileges; for example, they had the right to accumulate and use private property. Abbots, who were recruited from the pool of the "learned monks" (*uchenye monakhi*) and appointed by the Synod, were separated—culturally and by their lifestyle—from the rest of the monastic community.

Spiritual elders, who advocated the invigoration of monastic life, to some extent filled the growing distance between the rank-and-file monks and the abbot. This led to a transformation of the relationship between charismatic elders and administrators, which usually developed according to one of three scenarios. According to the first, the abbot and elders established a union in which their roles were complementary rather than confrontational. Elders could act as assistants to an abbot in ensuring the discipline and spiritual education of the brethren, especially novices. Abbot Moisiei (Putilov) of Optina, for example, enthusiastically implemented eldership at Optina and recommended it to other monastic administrators. In one of his letters, addressed to the abbot of the Sarov monastery, Isaiia II (Iona Putilov, Moisei's own brother), he suggested that the abbot should not rely on his own reason, but instead accept advice from other more experienced members of the community and select from among them assistants for the spiritual instruction of the brethren. He criticized the internal discipline of the Sarov monastery, where novices were left to their own devices without proper spiritual guidance; as a result, they developed a high opinion of themselves and suffered from delusion and pride.[33] In contrast to the Sarov abbots, Moisei relied on the advice of elders and protected them from abusive administrators. For example, while abbot of the Optina monastery, he managed to have his brother Antonii appointed as the head of the

Predtechev skete. Both brothers rendered assistance and protection to Elder Leonid, who previously had had difficulties with the superiors of the Valaam and St. Aleksandr Svirskii monasteries.[34]

The second scenario was that of a conflict between an abbot and a charismatic elder. In 1817 the abbot of the Valaam monastery, Innokentii (Moruev), complained to Bishop Amvrosii (Podobedov) that elders Fedor and Leonid (who in 1812 came to Valaam together with their disciples) openly disobeyed his authority. He disapproved of the practice of spiritual guidance and resented the popularity of the elders. The reason for the conflict was the weakness of Innokentii's authority and his encouragement of asceticism so severe that it drove some monks to the point of suicide.[35] Monk Evdokim, who was once close to the abbot, experienced spiritual rebirth under the influence of Fedor and Leonid, realizing that severe ascetic practices only made him cold and suicidal. The elders pointed out that only inner prayer and humility could soften his heart and bring evangelical love and joy. The shift of loyalty from Abbot Innokentii to Fedor and Leonid caused tensions between the abbot and the elders. His predecessor, the charismatic abbot Nazarii, characterized Innokentii as a mediocrity, a quarrelsome and ungrateful man who had no respect for Nazarii's own contribution to the welfare of the monastery.[36] Lacking personal power, Innokentii appealed to the local bishop for help. An official investigation revealed that the elders did not practice anything contrary to the spirit of Orthodoxy and helped to clear them of the abbot's accusations.[37] It was often the case that in the monasteries where abbots did not support eldership, the elders unwittingly caused the breakdown of discipline. The loyal disciples, following the example of Peter in Gethsemane, felt obliged to defend their teacher and directed their anger against the legitimate monastic authority. Faced with such unwanted expressions of loyalty, the elders sometimes had to restrain their disciples. In 1822, Leonid discouraged his disciples in Valaam from following him to the Aleksandr-Svirskii monastery. He warned them that disobedience was against Christ's commandments and urged them to show respect and submission to the abbot.[38]

In the third model of the abbot-elder relationship, abbots successfully played the role of elders themselves. This worked well when the abbot in question had a charismatic and strong personality and was not challenged by competition from other spiritual leaders. Abbot Filaret (Danilevskii, 1777–1841) of Glinskaia pustyn' combined the roles of father superior and monastery founder with that of spiritual guide. As a novice in the Kievo-Pecherskaia Lavra and the Sofronieva pustyn', he gained the reputation of a wise spiritual elder at the relatively young age of 35.[39] In 1817, he began the restoration of the rundown Glinskaia pustyn' in Kursk diocese, showing his talents as a capable administrator and monastic reformer. He introduced the Athonite monastic rule, which prescribed lengthy and well-ordered church services, and provided detailed instructions concerning all aspects of monastic life and the behavior of the brethren.[40] The rule had a specific section concerning spiritual guidance in the community, according to which a newcomer was assigned to an experienced elder. Alongside Abbot Filaret, a number of hieromonks, among them the reputable Elder Vasilii (Kishkin), acted as elders, but were subordinate to the position of abbot.[41]

Nevertheless, the combination of the role of an administrator with that of a spiritual guide was more typical for eighteenth-century Russian eldership. In the course of the nineteenth century, as the abbots became more heavily involved in the bureaucratic structure of the Synodal system, the role of the spiritual elder became further removed from that of the monastic administrator. It was not unusual for elders to be reluctant to take the position of superior, although many of them were quite capable of administering monastic communities.[42]

In the nineteenth century, elders were active in founding or cofounding new religious communities, which as a rule were women's communities. Perhaps the reason for this was growing gender disproportionality within Russian monasticism.[43] During Alexander I's reign, the participation of elders in the creation of women's communities often received formal approval. In 1822, the Synod gave monk Zosima (Verkhovskii) the title of benefactor (*popechitel'*) of the Nikolaevskii convent in Turinsk and approved the rule composed by the elder. However, power struggles between ambitious nuns and male benefactors could lead to problems for the elders despite support from other members of the community. In 1826, two members of the Turinsk community founded by Verkhovskii, a mother and daughter, complained to the bishop about abuses of power by the benefactor. The official investigation supported their complaint and removed Zosima from the administration of the convent. As the century progressed, the Synod looked askance at the active involvement of monks in the affairs of religious women.[44]

Elders and the Reinforcement of the Christian Ideal within Monasteries

Hesychast spirituality is traditionally associated with solitude, an emphasis on the interior life, self-examination, and essential otherworldliness. Yet the writings and practices of Russian spiritual elders changed over time in their attitudes toward confessional practice, in the prevalence of intimate spiritual correspondence over other genres of religious writings, and in a shift away from physical asceticism. These changes appear to echo the wider discussions on the "inner church" or "inner Christianity" that flourished in the era of mystical universalism.[45] According to this teaching, influenced by Karl von Eckartshausen, God could be revealed through inner illumination, not through doctrines and rituals. In Russia, the discussion on the "inner church" that began within Freemason circles soon became part of Alexander I's ideology. The authors of *Sionskii Vestnik* (*The Messenger of Zion*), published by Freemason A. Labzin in 1806, declared the priority of the "inner" church over the "external" one, but maintained that membership in the established church was necessary for social stability. Yet even though some parallels can be established between the writings of the advocates of the "inner church" on the one hand, and the elders on the other, hesychast spirituality did not separate sharply the individual from the community, that is, the private religious experience from the collective one.

The primary aim of eldership was the reinforcement of spiritual ideals of Christianity. Monasticism, with its principal vows of poverty, obedience, and celibacy, corresponded ideally to what elders viewed as the "narrow path" to salvation, referring to the words of the Gospel: "For the gate is small, and the way is narrow that leads to life, and few are those that find it" (Matt 7:14). While some of Paisii Velichkovskii's disciples had a rigorous attitude toward observation of medieval canons, their followers in Russia developed a more moderate style. Unlike Greece or Romania, Russia had experience of Old Belief, whose proponents placed excessive emphasis on the observance of the canonical rules, especially regarding diet and ritual. Paisii's Russian followers believed that it was more important to focus on spiritual reform, than on the meticulous observance of the church canons.[46] Optina pustyn' under Leonid introduced more relaxed rules regarding diet and church services, apprehensive that it would be otherwise difficult to recruit novices.

One of the most significant changes that monastic elders brought about was a reevaluation of physical asceticism. It would be wrong to claim that they disapproved of fasting, long hours of prayer, frequent prostrations, and exposure to extreme weather (walking barefoot in winter, for example). Although most elders discussed in this book took vows of celibacy, they also emphasized that mortification of the flesh was not a prerequisite of holiness but often a sign of spiritual pride; according to hesychast theology, the source of sin was not in the flesh but in the mind. In the Optina monastery Monk Vassian, a former serf who practiced severe fasting (during Lent he took food only twice, at Annunciation and Easter) felt challenged by Elder Leonid Nagolkin, who discouraged practices directed at mortification of the flesh.[47]

In popular culture, however, physical asceticism served as a sign of person's saintliness. The word *podvizhnik* served to indicate a person's achievement in the field of ascetic feats (*podvig*).[48] This is why some visitors to the monastic cells of Leonid of Optina and Amfilokhii of Rekon doubted whether these chubby monks could possess any special spiritual gifts.[49] Indeed, Leonid Nagolkin deliberately broke away from the stereotype of a saintly ascetic who looked as if he was about to die of starvation. In the manner of Gargantua and Pantagruel, Leonid challenged his critics and exaggerated his own lack of asceticism. For example, he told the bishop that he had a good appetite for food and wine, to which the bishop supposedly remarked "you are one of us, then."[50]

Vladimir Kotel'nikov pointed out that the elders of Optina advocated "inner asceticism" in opposition to "external asceticism."[51] They favored moderation in spiritual life, and discouraged pious lay men and women from severe ascetic practices. For example, in his letters around 1834 to a married couple, Aleksei Nikolaevich and Varvara Borisovna, who had two children, Leonid Nagolkin advocated the advantages of the "middle way." The pious couple, who aspired to ascetic feats and—ultimately—to monastic life, asked permission from the Optina elder to intensify their private "rule" by adding more prostrations and prayers. Leonid discouraged the couple from their ambition to join a monastery and from their more severe ascetic practices at home.[52] He argued that even if the couple eventually joined a monastery, the devil would try to convince them that the life in the world was more perfect, thus they would never be happy wherever they were. Leonid warned them of the dangers of excessive asceticism by drawing on examples of ascetics who lost God's grace by taking upon immoderate ascetic endeavors. In Leonid's view, the achievement of salvation was a gradual progress that would ultimately result in perfect wisdom (*liubomudrie*).[53] In a similar vein, Serafim of Sarov, an enthusiastic practitioner of self-mortification, did not impose a strict ascetic rule on the Diveevo community of religious women. On the contrary, he adapted the rule of the Sarov monastery, reducing the lengthy services and proposing a new abridged daily rule that consisted of only three prayers.[54]

Filaret (Danilevskii) of Glinskaia, too, advised his spiritual children to be judicious and rely on the advice of those who were more experienced in spiritual life. According to him, keeping one's mind free from vicious thoughts was more important than ascetic feats. Above all, the main criterion of true asceticism for all elders was humility. It was better to break fast in a humble spirit than endure self-torment and feel righteous. Elders demonstrated that humility, denial of one's self in the name of love to one's brother, was truer to the spirit of the Gospel than the ascetic sport of wearing chains and enduring without food for days and weeks.

The reevaluation of the norms of ascetic life by the elders signified the shift towards spirituality that was characterized by self-restraint rather than self-inflicted violence; by control of one's passions and cultivation of the virtues of humility, sacrifice, and love rather than extreme ascetic practices. Elders advocated the interiorization of spiritual life and favored a more personal, even intimate, style of religious communication. That is why the elders did not employ the genre of theological treatise or sermon. Their teaching was transmitted primarily by means of correspondence and oral discourse. The use of letters as a means of instructing and advising in religious matters represented a traditional genre of Christian literature.[55] This form of religious writing was especially important for the Catholic Reformation, as the example of Francis de Sales (who wrote approximately 20,000 letters) shows. He wrote primarily to his "spiritual children," many of whom were lay people like Baroness Jane de Chantal (1572–1641), a widow and mother of four. The model of spirituality developed in the letters was "spirituality for all"—a devotional practice that could be suited to anyone under any circumstances.[56] In published form, spiritual letters became a source of advice for lay and religious readers.[57] Published correspondence between the Russian elders and their spiritual children—despite their personal and specific character—dealt with universal issues and therefore could be utilized by readers who sought in them answers to their own questions. Some nineteenth-century readers used elders' letters for divination purposes, thus giving them the status of Psalter or Bible that traditionally were used in bibliomancy.[58] It was a popular practice to open randomly a volume of Elder Amvrosii of Optina's letters for advice on urgent questions.[59]

Georgii (Mashurin), the Recluse of Zadonsk (1789–1836), was an eminent representative of the epistolary genre in Russian spiritual prose. He was also the first spiritual writer whose letters were an immediate literary success; five editions of his letters were published between the 1830s and 1870.[60] Influenced undoubtedly by the writings of Tikhon of Zadonsk (who was the abbot in the same monastery), Mashurin's style was admired by such prominent ecclesiastical and secular writers as Bishop Ignatii Brianchaninov and Nikolai Gogol. Mashurin was born into a noble family headed by a local government clerk in Vologda, who died in a tragic accident when Georgii was a child. Following 11 years of service in the Lubin Hussar Regiment (including action during the War of 1812), in 1818, Lieutenant Mashurin joined the Zadonsk monastery in Voronezh province.

Living most of his short life as a recluse in a damp and ice-cold private cell, Mashurin corresponded with lay men and women, primarily among the nobility, who sought his advice. These letters were collected and published by his attendant and spiritual son Petr Grigorov, who subsequently joined Optina pustyn' as a monk. The name of Mashurin was so well known in the first half of the nineteenth century that the publishers of Serafim of Sarov's homilies thought it necessary to compare Serafim to Mashurin, who was already familiar to the reading public.[61] Mashurin's style was influenced not only by Tikhon of Zadonsk, but also by the Sentimentalists and in particular, Karamzin. Mashurin used Church Slavicisms sparingly and had a fluid literary style that incorporated obvious liturgical and biblical references.

The Jesus Prayer

The spiritual searches of the Alexandrine era reawakened popular interest in the Jesus prayer. After the publication of the *Dobrotoliubie* (1793), the Jesus prayer was transformed from an esoteric practice passed from master to disciple to a discourse or meta-prayer. A treatise on the Jesus prayer by Elder Vasilisk was circulated in handwritten copies among monks and the laity in Russia in the first half of the nineteenth century. The treatise described 75 physical signs of grace that might be experienced through the prayer (e.g., numbing of the tongue, light pain in the gums, inflammation of the right hand, sending warm waves throughout the whole body).[62] One editor of the text, the monk Arsenii (Troepol'skii), tried to publish the treatise in 1842 under the title "Psychology: The Tale of a Disciple about Elder Vasilisk Who Lived in the Siberian Desert." However, the censor Antonii (Medvedev) found the text unsuitable for publication; he felt that inexperienced lay readers might be misled by the graphic and, probably erroneous, descriptions of the Lord's grace.[63]

Antonii (Medvedev), the spiritual son of elder Leonid, was not alone in his caution about the popularization of hesychastic prayer. The Optina elders were also wary about the unrestrained appropriation of the Jesus prayer. Leonid warned one of his female correspondents, who described her psychosomatic experiences during the practice of the prayer, about the inadvisability of using the prayer without an experienced advisor.[64] He was concerned that his correspondent was practicing the Jesus prayer without prior purification from the vice of irritability. Leonid quoted St. John Climacus, who warned against the untimely exercise of hesychast practices (*bezmolvie*) by persons who were prone to anger, revenge, rage,

3.2. Georgii (Mashurin) the Recluse.
Source: Pis'ma v boze pochivaiushchego zatvornika Zadonskogo Bogoroditskogo monastyria Georgiia. St. Petersburg, 1843

and slyness. These passions, he believed, could only be only cured by living in a community of fellow monks. Leonid pointed out that his correspondent mistakenly interpreted some of her physical symptoms as the signs of grace, which caused her serious psychological problems: anxiety, depression, and insomnia.[65] This did not mean that the elders discouraged people from practicing the Jesus prayer (many lay persons learned the Jesus prayer from the Optina elders).[66] Rather, they warned against premature expectations of mystical illumination: "The time will come and the prayer itself and the Lord's mercy will enlighten your soul."[67] Elder Makarii of Optina, for example, criticized the treatise by Vasilisk. He noted that the author made no references to the writings of the Fathers and described his own subjective experience.[68] Bishop Ignatii (Brianchaninov) also shared the approach of the Optina elders, and he discouraged his lay correspondents from reading the *Dobrotoliubie* so that they would not fall into delusion (*prelest'*).[69]

Delusion was an important subject for the Desert Fathers. Saint Antony said, "I have known many monks who fell away after many labors and lost their mind, for they had put their hope in their own works. In their delusion, they did not obey the commandment that states: 'Ask your father, let him teach you.'"[70] The elders understood *prelest'* to be an ascetic's uncritical acceptance (in combination with pride) of mystical experience. For example, the elders were cautious about claims made by some believers that they had experienced apparitions, levitations, and other supernatural encounters.[71] According to Leonid (Nagolkin), one could become a victim of delusion as a result of intellectual and emotional self-exaltation; a human mind that lost humility was more at risk of delusion.[72]

In the writings of nineteenth-century Russian elders and monastic writers like Ignatii Brianchaninov, the concept of *prelest'* became a discourse that helped to define the boundaries of Orthodoxy more rigidly. It was defined as a kind of spiritual and mental illness "under the influence of evil spirits, resulting in the subject mistakenly imagining himself reaching a higher spiritual state."[73] Brianchaninov believed *prelest'* was a "natural" state of humanity: after the fall of man from paradise, the devil had constant access to the human soul, using lies as his favorite instrument to stimulate human passions. This explanation was somewhat akin to the priestless Old Believers, who believed that the spiritual energies of the Antichrist pervaded the world.[74] Yet unlike Old Believers, Brianchaninov believed that grace could rescue humanity from the pervasiveness of *prelest'*. One could be freed from the attacks of the devil by following the commandments and not trusting one's own will and reason.[75] The use of imagination during spiritual exercises was deemed very harmful. Following the Origenist tradition of non-anthropomorphic prayer, Brianchaninov and the Optina elders discouraged their followers from visualizing the divine subjects on which they meditated.[76]

Delusion often affected worshippers who practiced the mystical prayer without guidance. Brianchaninov told a story about a clerk from St. Petersburg who practiced spiritual exploits and had divine visions; while praying, he had visions of light, smelled a pleasant fragrance spreading from the icons in his room, and had a sweet taste in his mouth.[77] Yet in addition to his heavenly visions, this mystically inclined clerk often thought of drowning himself in the Fontanka River. Having taken both experiences into consideration, the bishop deemed the clerk to be deluded. It was not unusual, wrote the bishop, for deluded mystics to perform ascetic feats, for example walking barefoot in snow or sleeping and eating very little. Yet suicidal or self-harming thoughts and actions were believed to be signs of a spiritual illness. One such "deluded" monk in Ploshchanskaia pustyn', after cutting off his own hand, became convinced it was treasured and venerated as a holy relic in the Moscow Simonov monastery.[78]

It may seem paradoxical that the elders who were immersed in hesychast spirituality felt so guarded about the popular appropriation of the Jesus prayer and its associated mystical experiences. The reason behind this, however, lies in the concept of spiritual sobriety (*trezvenie*), which was also an important part of the *Dobrotoliubie*. The elders were anxious that, because of its apparent simplicity, the mental prayer could be taken out of context and practiced without any attempt to take part in church sacraments or struggle against sinful passions.

To avoid falling into delusion, a novice had to reveal his or her "movements of the heart" (mental struggles and inner promptings) to the elder. It was believed that through revealing their thoughts to the elder, the novices could avoid committing sins that might otherwise develop from such inner impulses.[79] Some elders could point to the sins or thoughts that the novice failed to mention.[80] In contrast to sacramental confession, which monks were expected to attend at least four times a year, "disclosure of thoughts" could be practiced daily.[81] This is why Varlaam, the abbot of the Valaam monastery, criticized formal confession, which in contrast to daily confession failed to account for the frequency of a particular sin.[82] He believed that the roles of spiritual elder and confessor should be complementary; the elder should help penitents to make sense of their own actions and direct them to a confessor for formal confession.[83]

"Disclosure of thoughts" encountered opposition from the official Orthodox culture, especially from the parish clergy educated in theological seminaries.[84] Despite its ancient origin, the elders' practice of "disclosure of thoughts" was criticized as innovation and heresy.[85] One of Leonid Nagolkin's female disciples warned her companion that while making a confession to a parish priest she had to be careful about using the terminology of the *Dobrotoliubie*. Leonid's female disciples were clearly disappointed with the official pastors who misunderstood their spiritual aspirations and ridiculed the language used by the nuns to describe their inner spiritual life.[86] In 1841, the priest of the Belev convent in Kaluga province denounced the practice of "disclosure of thoughts" as unorthodox.[87] When in 1826, Dmitrii Brianchaninov (then a student at the Military Engineers School) made a confession to his college priest using some terms from ascetic literature, he was promptly summoned to the school administrators. The parish priest believed that the pious youth had confessed revolutionary inclinations, while the penitent had attempted to express his inner spiritual struggle. In the atmosphere of suspicion and fear that followed the Decembrist uprising, the priest did not hesitate to report the youth to the school directors.[88] Thus, ascetic language united elders and their followers into a distinct penitential community on the margins of mainstream Orthodoxy.

Elders and Policing the Borders of Russian Orthodoxy

Romanticism provided a new vocabulary for the ideological reconceptualization of the institutions of state, community, and nation, which were imagined as the bearers of some transcendent mission. The Romantic concepts of nation and history that informed conservative European thought in the nineteenth century influenced the political doctrines of Nicholas I's reign and the philosophy of the Slavophiles. Orthodoxy was an essential element in the "theory of official nationality" proposed by Minister of Education Sergei Uvarov, who tried to combine the modern concept of nation with the traditional institutions of the ancien régime: autocracy and the established church.[89] In response to the European revolutions of the 1830s and cholera riots in 1831, the Russian autocracy mobilized the Orthodox moral categories of obedience and humility and presented them as the spiritual qualities of the nation.[90]

The efforts to define the boundaries of Orthodoxy and the nation were even more important in the context of the expanding empire. In the first half of the nineteenth century, the Orthodox Church experienced institutional expansion; it carried out aggressive policies towards the non-Orthodox, including the campaign against the Ukrainian Uniates in 1838–1839, and it established four theological academies as centers for the cultivation of Orthodox doctrine.[91] The Orthodox Church, which was now accepted as an integral element of Russian nationality, attempted to purge itself of internal dissent, heterodoxy, and superstition.[92]

During this period, officialdom's perception of elders changed: they were expected to perform a special role in nation-building, to actively dissociate themselves from accusations of dissent, and to demonstrate their loyalty (*blagonadezhnost'*) to autocracy and Orthodoxy. In 1833, Bishop Nikanor summoned Leonid of Optina, who had been denounced as the leader of an unorthodox sect.[93] The accused elder was required to demonstrate his orthodoxy in front of the bishop. "How would you like me, Master, to profess my faith: in the regular or the Kievan manner?" asked Leonid. "All right, go ahead in the Kievan way," replied the bishop, intrigued by the answer. Leonid began to recite the Nicene Creed in the manner of a deacon chanting the Orthodox liturgy: starting from the lowest pitch possible, raising his voice with every sentence, and finishing at a highest possible pitch. This humorous performance pleased the bishop and supposedly convinced him of Leonid's orthodoxy. Despite this, during 1835–1836 Bishop Nikolai of Kaluga, acting on a denunciation by the monk Vassian, banned the Optina *starets* from receiving female visitors. In 1841, Leonid again became the subject of an official investigation; this time it concerned his involvement with the Belev convent (Tula diocese) in which several nuns followed Leonid's spiritual advice. The consistory insisted that Leonid move his residence further away from the gates of the skete and from visitors, and ordered him to attend daily church services, which the elder had often missed because of his engagement with visitors.[94]

Despite the recurring clashes with the diocesan authorities, *starchestvo* survived with the support of such prelates as Filaret (Drozdov) of Moscow and Filaret (Amfiteatrov) of Kaluga and later, of Kiev. Despite the personal conflict between these two prelates, both encouraged the elders' mission. The flourishing of *starchestvo* in nineteenth-century Russia can be partially attributed to Filaret of Moscow's enormous influence in church politics. He was a pupil of Metropolitan Platon, an active member of the Bible society, an advocate of the translation of the Bible into Russian, and the editor of the Emancipation Manifesto of 1861.[95] From Filaret's point of view, the reformed monasteries could become grass-roots institutions that promoted the Orthodox Church among the peasantry. That is why he supported monastic revival, encouraged cenobitic practices, and promoted eldership in monasteries.[96] He also was instrumental in supporting female communities and convents, many of which relied on spiritual and organizational support from the elders.[97] Filaret's own inclination toward a life of prayer and solitude led him to establish the Gethsemane skete, a hermitage under the general administration of Trinity-Sergius monastery.

Filaret had a conservative view of spiritual elders: he conceived them as "the experienced and reliable (*blagonadezhnye*)" monks and nuns who were responsible for the supervision, instruction, disciplining, and catechization of neophytes.[98] According to this definition, the elders did not need to be priests or have a special charisma. In 1841, in response to violations of discipline in the Belopesotsk monastery in Moscow diocese, Filaret toughened the rules of admission to monasteries and convents. The bishop placed a stronger emphasis on the role of elders in monasteries and female convents: only on the recommendation of a spiritual elder could a novice take monastic vows.[99]

Elders were instrumental in the promotion of the Orthodox vision of spirituality. In the period when Orthodox monasticism faced competition from heterogeneous sources, each claiming a more direct access to mystical experience, the theology of the *Dobrotoliubie* on the control of passions provided the basis for discriminating between true and false spiritual experiences. Despite the urge for a greater spiritual freedom, as expressed in the practices and teaching of the elders, the teaching on *prelest'* was used to curb what was perceived as either "excessive freedom" or the work of dark destructive forces (the way in which Orthodox spiritual teachers interpreted various deviations from orthodoxy). The elder was a gatekeeper of mystical experience, which could liberate the human spirit from the constraints of ritualistic religion. But he was also a spiritual guardian, who protected the neophyte from spiritual pride and attacks by demonic forces, and a doctor who could treat those who suffered from the spiritual illness of delusion.

It was not unusual for bishops and official Synodal inspectors to seek the elders' assistance in the internal reform of monasticism and in cases involving popular piety. For example, in 1838, when completing the complicated inquest into the Valaam monastery, Archimandrite Ignatii Brianchaninov sought assistance from the Optina elders. The inspectors criticized the Valaam monks for factiousness, defective administration, general lack of literacy, and misleading views on spiritual guidance. Varlaam, the former abbot of the monastery, was sent to Optina pustyn' under the supervision of Hieromonk Leonid (Nagolkin).[100]

In 1858, the visionary Anufrii Krainev was subjected to the spiritual elders' surveillance. The twenty-year-old former soldier from Nizhnii Novgorod experienced a series of visions in which an unknown saint, Fedor, appeared to him, urging him to reveal the site of his relics in a desecrated church in

Moscow (the former patriarchal residence in Krutitsy), which in the 1850s was used as a military barracks.[101] Krainev's visions (which he experienced in a lethargic dream, or *obmiranie*) were supported by a popular rumor that the holy relics could indeed be found in the former patriarchal church.[102] Bishop Filaret of Moscow, who personally investigated the Krainev case, suspected that the soldier was inclined to religious dissent and suffered from spiritual delusion.[103] Filaret believed that the popular cult of the unknown Fedor had some connection with Deacon Fedor, the opponent of Patriarch Nikon's reforms, but doubted that the remains of Old Believer martyrs were interred in the church of Krutitsy. Filaret's skeptical attitude is an illustration of Eve Levin's argument that from the mid-seventeenth century, church hierarchs no longer shared with local communities the belief that the relics of unidentified saints could reveal themselves through miracles.[104] In order to discern Krainev's way of thinking and reform his spiritual state, Filaret sent the soldier to the Trinity-Sergius Lavra under the care of Archimandrite Antonii (Medvedev), the disciple of Leonid of Optina. Antonii reported that despite Krainev's apparent piety and peaceful temper, he often acted under the influence of his imagination. Antonii noticed Krainev's critical attitude toward other monks and his inclination to prophesy (he predicted death for some and recovery for others). Filaret and Antonii agreed that Krainev was in a state defined by the Fathers as *prelest'* and resolved to send him to a well-organized secluded monastery, similar to Optina pustyn', in the charge of a skilled spiritual elder. They believed Krainev had to learn how to eschew his own judgment and allow his visions and thoughts to be interpreted by those more experienced in spiritual life.

Although public penance had declined in Russia, monasteries were still used as spiritual clinics for apostates from Orthodoxy or those who were threatening it (such as members of sects, the Uniate clergy, and renegade Orthodox priests).[105] In the 1840s Uniate monk Flavian Lisovskii had to spend three years in Optina pustyn' as part of his public penance.[106] According to Evfimii (Trunov), the chronicler of the monastery, although Flavian had shown outward virtues and piety, in his heart he remained loyal to the Roman pope. Eventually, the Synod ruled to forcibly defrock Flavian with a pension of 100 rubles a year.[107] Similarly, in 1837–1838 the Optina monks tried in vain to reform a former Orthodox priest, Solov'ev, who converted to Old Belief and sought official approval for his activities. Despite the efforts of the monks and elders, Solov'ev refused to take communion and made the sign of the cross with two fingers (the Old Believer style) in public.[108] The hegumen of Optina asked permission to send Solov'ev away from the monastery. These particular cases demonstrate that the utilization of elders for the purpose of policing the borders of Orthodoxy was not always successful.

An analysis of elders that views them through the prism of modern ecumenism would be misleading. They certainly followed in the footsteps of both Nil Sorskii and Joseph of Volokolamsk in their lack of tolerance toward non-Orthodox expressions of faith and other deviations from Orthodoxy.[109] The elders believed that Orthodoxy was the only true path to salvation, yet they were not servants of the state and the Synod. Their response to the policing tasks assigned to them by the imperial state was ambivalent. While the elders addressed problems of spiritual illness among Orthodox believers, they doubted the possibility of successful conversion in respect to apostates and non-Orthodox Christians. Leonid Nagolkin sabotaged the attempts by the Bishop of Kaluga to impose a missionary task on the Optina elders.[110] The "policing" duties also represented an extra burden: monasteries had to provide for those who served public penance, while the elders were distracted from their direct pastoral duties toward members of the community and pilgrims. Moreover, the presence of enthusiastic religious dissidents could have adverse effects on the community. That is why abbots petitioned to the Holy Synod to remove such persons from their monasteries.[111]

Elders and the Laity
Material and Spiritual Exchange

The elders shared the vision of monasticism that prioritized spirituality over social service to society. Yet in many ways they redefined the relationship between the monastery and the world. While novices and fellow monks remained the main objects of their pedagogical and reforming efforts, lay men and women became enmeshed, to an unprecedented degree, in the world of the spiritual elders.[112] Ilana Silber has interpreted the relationship between the laity and spiritual elders as a form of material and symbolical exchange between the monastery and the world. She applied Marcel Mauss' theory of the gift to the study of monasticism in Buddhism and medieval Catholicism. According to Mauss, the gift has a moral power, which puts an obligation on the recipient to return the gift. Mauss posits three essential duties that characterize the dyadic relationship pertaining to "the gift" (to give, to take, and to return), among which the "duty to duly return has an imperative character."[113] The gift relationship underpinned the intricate network of material and symbolic exchanges between monastic virtuosi and laymen.[114] The shift in the material position of the monasteries in the second half of the eighteenth century, without doubt, reinforced the monasteries' material dependence on the world. Yet contrary to the aims of the reforming empress, nineteenth-century monasticism developed dependence, not on the bureaucratic state and its stipends, but on private donors.[115] This especially concerned the monasteries that practiced eldership.

The elders were the key agents through which transactions between donors and the monastic community were carried out. Donations had a personal character. They were often a sign of gratitude from an individual who had experienced a spiritual conversion as a result of meeting with an elder. Two noblemen who owned land in Arzamas province, Nikolai Motovilov and Mikhail Manturov, were healed and instructed by Serafim of Sarov and subsequently helped him create an economic base for the Diveevo women's community.[116] The noble Polugarskie and Kliucharev families of Kaluga generously supported the Optina elders and their associates.[117]

Donors who bequeathed their property to monasteries were not driven solely by religious motivations. As Daniel Kaiser has shown in his compelling analysis of testamentary behavior in early modern Russia, generous donors were often guided by considerations of social prestige.[118] The commemoration of deceased donors and their families in the monastic institution was also a motivation for their charitable acts. In the nineteenth century, donors accompanied their wills with detailed instructions concerning the form and frequency of the commemoration of their names. Many noble families continued to use monasteries as their family burial vaults and continued to patronize the institutions that were associated with several generations of their family.[119]

Although donors were of both genders, female nobles and merchant women were slightly more likely to use religious charity as a means of social influence.[120] In many instances, charitable initiatives were based on a personal relationship between the donor and a religious leader, or else served as the basis for such. Countesses Orlova and A. A. Shakhovskaia and Princesses T. Potemkina and T. Sheremeteva made friendships with the leading monastic figures of their time who also served as their spiritual directors. Having the advantage of legal rights that did not put too many gender-specific restrictions on property ownership, wealthy Russian women mastered the skills of gift-making and this brought them closer to the spiritual ideals to which they were attracted. For example, Countess Orlova-Chesmenskaia, the only daughter of Catherine II's favorite, gave generously to the Iuri'ev monastery in Novgorod province, which was led by the young Elder Fotii (Spasskii). She donated 250,000 rubles for the commemoration of Fotii's relatives. Moreover, according to the testament of the childless countess, her estate was distributed between 340 monasteries in the Russian Empire, so that every monastery received at least five thousand rubles.[121] The relationship of the gift between monks and propertied women surely made male clerics more receptive to specific female spiritual concerns and emotional needs.

The personal character of the gift could potentially raise problems concerning the accountability and financial management of a monastic institution. Elders often reserved the right to dispose of a gift in the ways they found appropriate. Nazarii of Valaam deposited one thousand rubles, which he had personally received from his sponsors, in a bank under the condition that the interest be used for the benefit of the community. This decision caused a conflict between Nazarii and the new abbot, Innokentii. The autonomy of Predtechev skete in Optina monastery was based on a substantial property in land and cash (in 1873 this capital amounted to thirty thousand rubles) kept separately from the Optina treasury.[122] Until the 1870s the Optina abbots protected the right of the elders to keep their finances separately.[123] Abbot Moisei respected the agreement and did not interfere with the property of the skete, even though he needed money to pay the debts of the monastery.[124] In 1861, Mariia Polugarskaia, the widow of a state advisor, complained to Bishop Grigorii of Kaluga that the Optina monastery tried to claim 16,000 rubles, the donation intended specifically for the needs of the Predtechev skete.[125]

Polugarskaia's complaint suggests that it was not unusual for lay patrons to use their gifts to exercise control over the recipients of their charity. Nikolai Motovilov insisted that his donation would remain divided between the two Diveevo communities, regardless of the wish of the women of both communities to be united. In order to achieve his aim, he delayed the transfer of the land rights to the Diveevo sisters for 12 years (1838–1850).[126] Under the influence of profound antipathy to Serafim's self-proclaimed disciple Ioasaf (Ioan Tolstosheev), another donor, Mikhail Manturov, refused to donate a plot of his land to the Diveevo community so as to prevent the merger of the two communities.[127]

Many of the donors were frequent visitors to monasteries, which traditionally served as spiritual retreats for the laity. The presence of skillful spiritual advisors and confessors in the monastery attracted crowds of lay visitors. Optina pustyn' had hostels for pilgrims that could accommodate up to 200 people.[128] Male visitors could stay in the skete itself, but female pilgrims had to reside outside the walls. Visitors came from all levels of society, including nobility, merchants, and peasantry. The Kaluga nobility frequented monasteries during the major feasts and Great Lent.

The elders' contribution to the symbolic and material exchange with the laity consisted of time and emotional investment. They received visitors individually and in groups for conversation or confession. Although the elders had secretaries, correspondence with the laity could occupy long hours.[129] While some letters were spontaneously written, others required a careful formulation and the selection of references from scripture and patristic books.

The letters to elders from their spiritual children provide an insight into the laity's motivation and the relationship they had with the elders. Princess Shakhovskaia shared her everyday worries and concerns with Elders Makarii and Leonid through letters. As a mother of four and foster mother to her orphaned niece, she managed the household and the estate, took part in the lives of her relatives, and supported her passive husband.[130] Her special bond with the Optina elders gave symbolic meaning to her life of daily chores and anxieties. She believed, for example, that the chain of misfortunes that she experienced during Lent in 1841 (the loss of a good governess for her children, misjudged investments and purchases, her sister's marriage breakdown) was divine punishment for upsetting Elder Leonid, her confessor.[131] Perhaps to Shakhovskaia, monasteries represented a retreat where she could escape from her social roles as mother, wife, and the manager of the estate, and concentrate on her private pursuits and spiritual self-development. Her letters reveal that amid her daily chores, she found time to read ascetic books like the *Dobrotoliubie*, *The Ladder*, and the *Lenten Triodion*, all of which she purchased at Optina.

The noble family of Kireevskii, who had an estate near Optina pustyn', developed very close relations with Elder Makarii (Ivanov) of Optina, and introduced him to all aspects of their everyday life. Ivan Kireevskii, the Slavophile philosopher, was involved with the publishing activities of Optina pustyn', but he also shared personal concerns with Makarii, his spiritual father. In particular, Ivan was worried about the lack of positive moral influence on his son Vasilii, a student at the Imperial Lyceum in St. Petersburg, who was frequently reprimanded for his bad behavior.[132] Ivan also disclosed to Makarii his anxiety about his wife's tuberculosis and asked for advice in regard to tobacco smoking.[133] Makarii, who was confessor for both the husband and wife, suggested that Ivan should take more responsibility for the household to help his ailing wife.[134] Ivan, however, proved incapable of managing the family economy. He complained to Makarii about the servants and, on one occasion, said that he suspected them of trying to poison his family.[135] The letters demonstrate the value of the elders' advice, blessings, and prayers to lay correspondents.

Undoubtedly this value had a subjective character and was only valid within a particular system of symbolic exchanges.

Taking into account that a large proportion of elders' spiritual children were serf-owners, one could expect the question of serfdom to be raised in the elders' correspondence. As a matter of fact, elders did not directly criticize serfdom as an institution, yet they were critical of those landowners who exploited their serfs to maintain a luxurious lifestyle.[136] Despite their material dependence on noble patrons, elders nevertheless tried to exercise a moral influence on the Russian elites. For instance, Elder Leonid refused Holy Communion to a local landlord who for many years cohabited with one of his serfs. Despite the complaints of the nobleman to the abbot of the monastery, Leonid remained unbending.[137]

Ordinary people, as well as the Russian elites, valued the elders and flocked to the monasteries where they could receive blessings and advice from these wise men. The reputation of elders as clairvoyants and healers endowed them with specific functions in the eyes of peasants who came with particular needs such as a cure for illness, assistance in finding a good wife or husband, the identification of a thief, punishment of evildoers, or the need to exorcise evil spirits from a "possessed" member of a family. Although the elders objected to their reputation as "wizards" and wise men, they tried to help people and did not criticize them for being superstitious or ignorant.

The elders' moral influence on local peasants took various forms. In some cases, they tried to promote evangelical ideals that could supplant animosity and hostility in communities. A craftsman from Kozel'sk (the nearest town to Optina pustyn') came to Elder Leonid complaining about a thief who had stolen the wheels from his cart. The peasant suspected a Polish soldier who used to lodge in his house. The elder advised the craftsman to treat the theft as without consequence and let God judge. In this way, he advised, God would protect the man in the future. The craftsman subsequently testified that through following Leonid's advice he managed to avert attempted thefts on three other occasions.[138] A peasant woman who felt unfairly treated by her in-laws received advice to pay no attention to insults and say the Jesus prayer silently. As a result—or so the story goes—she changed her disposition, became less sensitive to petty fighting in the household, and eventually gained the respect and love of her in-laws.[139] Although the elders did not believe that ordinary people needed a special mission, they promoted hesychast spiritual ideals among the populus using personal example, advice, and the encouragement of a good Christian life.

Popular Veneration and Popularization of Elders in the First Half of the Nineteenth Century

In his analysis of the cult of saints in the Middle Ages, Peter Brown pointed out that "the tombs of the very special dead were exempt from the facts of death."[140] A belief in the imminence of resurrection, the temporality of death, and the radiance of paradise permeated the veneration of the relics and objects associated with saints. Worshippers began to visit the graves of popular elders soon after their demise. Peasants in Kaluga province collected soil from Leonid of Optina's grave, which they used as a cure for illness.[141] Orthodox Christians believed that performing a memorial service (*panikhida*) at the grave of a holy person would make God more receptive to their requests.[142] Thus, a priest from Shadrinsk in the Urals claimed that he was healed from his fever as soon as he made a promise in his heart to celebrate a *panikhida* at Serafim of Sarov's grave.[143] In 1836, the Synodal authorities became concerned about mass devotion to the grave of Melaniia Pakhomova, a humble nun from the Znamenskii convent in Elets. The abbess of the convent reported to the Synod that, soon after Melaniia's death, people began to venerate her grave and reported miraculous cures from serious ailments like palsy. Melaniia, a simple peasant woman who had lived in the convent as a recluse for 50 years, had gained the popular reputation of a holy woman and an intercessor for the people. The abbess and the diocesan authorities, who had little awareness of the reputedly holy Melaniia, seemed surprised by the growing cult of the dead nun.[144]

Miraculous powers were also attributed to material objects that had belonged to a saint. The women of Diveevo created a shrine behind an altar where they placed different bits of Serafim's clothes, his shoes, axe, hat, mittens, and rosary as well as the pieces of the stone on which he prayed while living in the forest.[145] The monks of Sarov who controlled access to Serafim's grave kept some fragments of his body (nails, hair, teeth).[146] Even before his canonization in 1903, some people treasured Serafim's hair and used it in protective amulets. After Serafim's canonization, the Sarov monastery distributed parts of his relics in response to multiple requests. The fragmentation of the body of the saint, detaching it from the context of physical death, as Brown argued, strengthened the image of the saint as a link between heaven and earth.[147] Serafim's mantle was brought to St. Petersburg by one of the nuns from the Diveevo women's community. It apparently cured the five-year-old daughter of Alexander II of laryngitis in 1860. The same mantle supposedly assisted the empress Alexandra, Nicholas I's widow, to pass into the other world without suffering.[148]

Although in many cases the cult of new saints emerged spontaneously, church elites, male and female disciples of the elders, educated admirers of the holy men, book publishers, and the royal family were all involved, in various ways, in constructing around the graves of new saints "a new structure of the relations between heaven and earth."[149] Bishop Filaret of Moscow, who was deeply impressed with Serafim, was the main engine behind the publication of the first biography of the Sarov monk and his spiritual instructions, only a few years after the saint's death in 1833. Together with Archimandrite Antonii (Medvedev), Filaret edited the text written by Serafim and the vita of the saint by monk Sergii to make them more acceptable to the censors.[150] Prelates such as Filaret, far from making "concessions to 'superstitious' beliefs," regarded the elders as capable of revitalizing the spirituality of the Synodal church.[151] In 1838, the Moscow Censorship Committee remarked that Serafim's vita, as promoted by Filaret, was important because it set a contemporary example of a virtuous ascetic that could strengthen faith and stimulate enthusiasm for pious life.

Serafim's spiritual instructions, edited by Filaret and published in 1839, emphasized humility and obedience. The time of publication coincided with the official backlash that followed the Polish uprising (1831), peasant disturbances, cholera riots, and the government's crackdown on religious dissenters. The promotion of new saints such as Serafim and Mark of Sarov, recluse Georgii of Zadonsk, Leonid of Optina, and many other ordinary monks and mystics, was designed to convince the renegades and competing confessions that Orthodoxy had inner spiritual resources and heavenly protection. In the 1850s, however, the Synod tried to thwart overly enthusiastic attempts to promote the cult of Serafim of Sarov. The Synodal censors expressed skepticism regarding the written accounts of Serafim's visions, prophecies, and miracles.[152]

Literary journals like *Maiak* (*The Lighthouse*) and *Moskovitianin* (*The Muscovite*) capitalized on hesychast spirituality and published the biographies of Paisii Velichkovskii (1845) and Serafim of Sarov (1841). The journal *Maiak* was published by the conservatives Shishkov, Burachek, and Korsakov. It represented a mixture of mysticism and "official nationality," attacked skeptics, liberals, and atheists, and consistently challenged Russian writers such as Pushkin and Lermontov for their lack of patriotism (*narodnost'*) and religious sentiment.[153] The editors of *Moskovitianin*, Pogodin and Kireevskii, however, had a different agenda, which diverged from that of the proponents of "official nationality."[154] Ivan Kireevskii, who converted from a position of pro-European liberalism and joined the camp of the Slavophiles, was instrumental in the publishing activities of Optina pustyn'. He edited, sponsored, and helped to publish Paisii Velichkovskii's translations of Philokalic authors, including Isaac the Syrian, Abba Fallasius, Theodor the Studite, and Barsonuphius ("the Great") of Gaza.[155] His participation in the activities of the Optina elders had personal and ideological importance for Kireevskii. Apart from personal faith, nourished by his friendship with Elders Filaret Puliashkin and Makarii of Optina, Kireevskii believed that the Russian Orthodox Church preserved the traditions of Byzantine Christian culture that were unknown to the West, because the West had adopted the rationalistic thought of pre-Christian antiquity. Elders, in his view, were the representatives of this Byzantine theological tradition that was free from scholasticism and rationalism.[156]

The royal court, too, expressed interest in the new saints, especially Serafim of Sarov. The fascination with Serafim among the members of the royal family can be traced back to 1849 when the monk Ioasaf, a self-proclaimed disciple of Serafim, published his first "Tale of the Life and Ascetic Deeds of Elder Serafim," accompanied by watercolor illustrations. He presented the book, together with his monarchist poems, to the royal family.[157] Ioasaf and the sisters of Diveevo convinced the members of the court that Serafim was a great saint. At that time, Serafim had not been promoted to the status of a national saint, but his charisma had public as well as private significance for the royal family. Grand Duchess Mariia, mother of seven and a widow from 1852, became interested in Serafim. Like other women in the Romanov family, she actively supported Orthodoxy as the bulwark of conservatism and traditionalism. The favorite daughter of Nicholas I, Mariia shared her father's allegiance to the formula of "Orthodoxy, Autocracy, Nationality." Mariia surely regarded Serafim as a divine protector of the royal family and helped Ioasaf to overcome the resistance of the Censorship Committee and publish a new biography of Serafim that, in contrast to the previous ones, contained detailed accounts of the miracles and prophecies of the saint. Mariia also patronized a group of the Diveevo sisters who came to the capital to study icon painting.[158]

DESPITE THEIR APPARENT contrasts, the political and ideological developments during the reigns of Alexander I and Nicholas I produced a legitimate space for elders and endowed them with certain social and ideological roles. Elders fit into the vision of the messianic kingdom anticipated by the mystics of Alexander I's reign and they enjoyed a certain degree of freedom in the atmosphere of religious toleration. The ideological shift from cosmopolitan mysticism to official nationality that followed the Decembrist uprising and the European revolutions of 1830 led to the redefinition of elders' roles; they began to play the role of "spiritual policemen" and the guardians of the borders of Orthodoxy. Zorin maintained that Russian elites adopted potentially subversive European ideas to strengthen the ancien régime.[159] In similar fashion, the potentially subversive mystical spirituality of the *Dobrotoliubie* was used to strengthen the foundations of Russian Orthodoxy. The institutionalization of eldership in monasteries and their semiautonomous position within the Synodal church became possible due to the support of powerful prelates and the economic patronage of the laity.

The conservative Slavophiles used Romantic ideas of the nation to present Russian Orthodoxy as a direct descendant of the Byzantine Church and an upholder of unchanging tradition. The involvement of Ivan Kireevskii with the publishing activities of Optina pustyn' played an important role in the association of the Optina eldership with the Slavophile agenda in the eyes of the educated public. The emergence of a non-official nationalist vision of elders, an essential component of Holy Russia, was different from the pan-Orthodox vision of Paisii Velichkovskii.

The popularity of elders derived from the perception of them as prophets and wonder-workers, an image they did not attempt to dispel. Some representatives of the church hierarchy, together with members of the royal family and conservative intellectuals, encouraged the activities of elders and their cults as alternatives to religious dissent, superstition, and Westernization. After the mid-seventeenth century, church hierarchs no longer cooperated with local communities in promoting the cults of unknown saints that spontaneously emerged around unknown relics discovered by chance. Instead, they sought to promote the saints whose life and teaching corresponded with Orthodox doctrine. However, even these efforts encountered the resistance of the bureaucratic Synod and individual parish priests and prelates.

In the first half of the nineteenth century, charismatic eldership experienced the processes of routinization and institutionalization. In several monasteries, including Optina and Glinskaia, eldership was turned into a perennial institution. Attempts by a section of the elites to utilize eldership and make it part of Russian Orthodox tradition were often confronted by the attacks of the Orthodox establishment that felt threatened by the charismatic elders. This demonstrates that although eldership was assimilated into the ideological and institutional framework of the Russian Church, the tensions between charisma and institution remained unresolved.

CHAPTER FOUR

Elders, Society, and the Russian People in Post-Emancipation Russia, 1860–1890

The era of the Great Reforms under Alexander II (1855–1881) that followed the emancipation in 1861 brought several challenges to the Russian Orthodox Church. Attempts by the state to modernize the church without satisfying the demands of the clergy proved counterproductive. The emergence of two trends, clerical liberalism (a critical attitude toward the ecclesiastical and state authorities) and episcopal conciliarism (a movement to shift control from the Synod to diocese), was the result of the assertion of bishops and the parish clergy as two self-conscious social groups.[1] The awakening of a religious press and journalism in the wake of the relaxation of censorship in the 1860s stimulated debates among theologians and historians about the social roles of the Church and theology. Both secular and religious authors criticized the hegemony of the black clergy, the lack of a social mission in the Church, the passive role of the laity, and the lethargy of parish life.[2] These discussions, calls for reforms, and other liberal tendencies were temporarily suppressed during Pobedonostsev's chief-procuratorship, but were revived again in the revolutionary period of 1900–1917.

The era of the ascendancy of arch-conservative K. D. Pobedonostsev (1880–1905), a professor of law and the educator of Alexander II's children, was characterized by the growth of religious brotherhoods and missionary activities, suppression of liberal reforms, and support of monasticism.[3] Pobedonostsev was by all means a complex figure: a close friend of Dostoevsky, and translator into Russian of "The Imitation of Christ" by Thomas à Kempis, he firmly believed in the political and moral superiority of autocracy and the Russian nation. His activities during Alexander III's reign, including the high-profile celebrations of various religious jubilees (the 500th anniversary of death of St. Sergius of Radonezh, the 1000th anniversary of SS. Cyril and Methodius), the policy of Russification in the national borderlands, and the state-sponsored building of massive Orthodox cathedrals in pseudo-Byzantine or "Muscovite" style underscored attempts to relaunch the ideology of official nationality in which Orthodoxy was intimately linked with autocracy and nationality.

During Pobedonostsev's tenure as chief procurator of the Holy Synod, the number of monasteries grew by 17 percent and the number of monks and nuns by 42 percent (an unprecendented development during the Synodal era).[4] In his support of monasticism Pobedonostsev abided by the letter of the Ecclesiastical Regulation, yet encouraged the missionary and charitable activities of convents and monasteries.[5] During the reign of Alexander III, thousands of new converts to Orthodoxy, mainly from the Lutheran Church in the Baltic, joined the Russian Orthodox Church. For example, between 1881 and 1904, 31,314 former Lutherans in the Baltics adopted the Orthodox faith.[6] Consequently, one of the central official concerns was keeping these new converts within the Orthodox fold. The translation of liturgical books into the native languages of the converts, the financial support of parish life, and catechization were of foremost importance for sustaining Orthodoxy among the converts. However, monastic spirituality and missionary activities by monks also could serve as noncoercive instruments to promote the prestige of Orthodoxy.

In parallel to the attempts to strengthen the appeal of Russian Orthodoxy there was a rising popularity of hesychast theology, which was heralded as the Byzantine legacy and an element of Russian national uniqueness. Theological scholarship challenged the long-embedded prejudice to the Byzantine theologian Gregory Palamas (who argued that God could be known through His uncreated energies perceived as uncreated light), and interpreted his teaching as a defense of Orthodoxy against Western religious and political influences.[7] Even though the elders were numerically too weak to satisfy social demand and the expectations of some sections of the Church, in the changing world of post-Emancipation Russia they were significant in promoting in practice the hesychast teaching, in particular the *Dobrotoliubie* (an anthology of writings on mystical prayer), and many instructed novices and the laity in the technique of mental prayer.

Embracement of hesychast mysticism was the reaction of a section of the clergy who were dissatisfied with or dispossessed by the insufficient outcomes of emancipation, and who realized how little influence they had on the process of the Great Reforms. The tragic example of Father Ivan Belliustin, the parish priest from Tver province, who tried to draw the government's attention to the deplorable state of the parish priesthood and who was silenced and humiliated by the authorities, signified the failure of reformist efforts by the Russian clergy.[8] It was in this period that members of the married clergy abandoned their traditional dismissal of monastic spirituality and either became monks (most notably, Elder Amvrosii of Optina) or introduced monastic spirituality into their pastoral activities (Father John of Kronstadt).

Also, hesychast spirituality, which emphasized the capacity of an ordinary person to achieve a mystical union with God, appealed not only to monks but also to lay Christians. The popularization of hesychasm was an attempt to raise the prestige of Orthodoxy among the Russian folk as well as among new converts to the Russian Church. In the second half of the nineteenth century, the conservative Slavophile thinkers represented elders as the moral and spiritual compass of the nation and true leaders of the Russian people. Despite the claims of the intelligentsia to the role of prophets and spiritual guides of the nation, the elders seemed to be more successful among ordinary people. Nevertheless, the elders' numerical weakness severely limited the impact they were likely to have upon the contested space of spiritual and social morality, even if the combined efforts of the intellectuals and the institutions of the bureaucratic state were unable to satisfactorily fill that void.

Communal Monasticism:
Another Attempt

As in Nicholas I's reign, in the 1860s elders played a vital part in the official attempts to reform monastic discipline and promote communal organization of monastic life. The Synod, which was not in the least interested in the charismatic and mystical appeal of elders, supported eldership as the instrument of discipline and training of novices. Even this somewhat limited understanding of spiritual eldership—in its association with communal monasticism—proved difficult to implement on the ground.

Communal monasticism had some resemblance to the peasant commune, the institution that had economic and fiscal functions and served as an instrument of social control. Like the peasant commune, cenobitic monasticism was self-sufficient. As of 1862 the abbots and abbesses were elected from within, not appointed by the Synod. In contrast to those in idiorrythmic (noncommunal) monasteries, cenobitic monks and nuns did not have an income or individual property; day-to-day tasks and duties (*poslushaniia*) were distributed among the brethren by the superior. The proponents of monastic reform believed that communal monasticism responded better to the ideals of nonpossession, obedience, and renunciation of one's will than did other types of monasticism.[9] The advantage of communal monasticism for the state was that, in theory, it did not rely on state resources for its survival. At the same time, the state hoped that communal rule would ensure a stricter internal discipline.[10] Hence, the role of elders was central. Elders, as experienced, reliable, and pious monks and nuns, were appointed by the abbot or abbess to train and discipline novices. The supervision of elders over novices and monks or nuns was regarded as insurance against such vices of monastic life as sexual abuses and drinking. Elders were expected to instruct novices in moral catechism, to explain the meaning of monastic vows, and to show a good personal example.[11]

Following St. Joseph of Volokolamsk, church hierarchs emphasized the advantages of communal over idiorrhythmic monasticism. In 1799, the Synod ruled that each diocese should have at least one communal monastery, hoping that others would follow. However, before 1861 the efforts to introduce communal monasticism were practically a one-man struggle. Bishop Filaret of Moscow, inspired by the examples of Optina and Sarov, tried to introduce communal monasticism in his diocese, but of ten convents, only one had become communal by 1867.[12] After the death of Chief Procurator Protasov, however, Filaret had the opportunity to use the Synod as the instrument of monastic reform. Both chief procurators of the Synod, Count A. P. Tolstoi (1856–1862) and A. P. Akhmatov (1862–1865), had great respect for Filaret as the man who drafted the text of the Emancipation Manifesto. In 1862, the Synod issued a circular in which it recommended the conversion of all noncommunal monasteries into communal ones.[13] The Synodal decree stated that the practice of spiritual guidance by elders was a sign of well-organized communal monasticism. It also acknowledged that the appointment of superiors from noncommunal monasteries was undesirable, since they would certainly be at odds with the internal communal order.[14] The decree, which limited the powers of bishops in monastic administration, was issued in the aftermath of the Diveevo affair, during which the intervention of a local bishop in the election of the new mother superior in 1861 caused a terrible rift in the community.[15]

The attempts "from above" to convert idiorrythmic into communal monasteries met resistance "from below." In 1869, the Synod repeated its proposal to introduce communal rule and instructed diocesan authorities to collect responses regarding this proposal.[16] As a rule, local monasteries showed little enthusiasm. In Novgorod diocese, Archimandrite Paisii, father superior of Nikolaevskii Viazhitskii monastery, argued that communal monasticism had scarcely any economic and moral advantages over noncommunal, state-funded monastic institutions. He deemed that it was not possible to introduce communal rule in Novgorod diocese owing to the poor financial state of monastic institutions. Even so, although the Novgorod monks rejected communal monasticism, they did not object to eldership. The treasurer of Viazhitskii monastery, the monk Iraklii, argued that in order to improve monastic organization it was necessary to include experienced spiritual elders who would supervise and counsel monks and novices.[17]

Ultimately, the Synodal attempts to encourage eldership in association with communal monasticism reflected two seemingly conflicting tendencies. On the one hand, the authorities tried to modernize the Church by transforming the clerical estate into a professional service class.[18] On the other hand, the State promoted the traditional institution of eldership, which was believed to facilitate the reform of monasteries and ensure discipline. The contradiction was apparent rather than real. In the official view, elders were understood to be a specific group of experts with specific pastoral responsibilities. The state also ignored and played down the potentially subversive aspects of eldership, as present in elders' roles as charismatic and mystical leaders.

To the Synod, elders had a purely instrumental role: to carry out the reform of monasteries and ensure discipline according to the Josephite model.[19] The ecclesiastical authorities, however, did not take into account the position of "professional monks." The latter remained skeptical about the official attempt to create a uniform nonidiorrythmic model for all monasteries. At the same time, they clearly distinguished the institution of eldership from the communal model. Indeed, there was no reason why eldership could not be practiced in noncommunal monasteries. The differences in the understanding of eldership among ordinary monks and the functionaries in the Holy Synod would occasion conflicts in the future.

Elders in a Changing World

The Synodal attempts to utilize spiritual elders for promotion of communal monasticism reflected the improvement of the image of elders in the eyes of the church hierarchy. While in the past elders had suffered from accusations of dissent or heresy, in post-Emancipation Russia they enjoyed support and encouragement from abbots and bishops.[20] The leaders of monastic communities perceived elders as a source of monastic identity and spirituality, and a magnet for visitors, novices, and donors. Bishops were proud if monasteries in their diocese could boast a succession of spiritual elders. In 1861, Bishop Sergii (Liapidevskii) of Kursk diocese reported to the Synod: "Of all monasteries, Glinskaia alone [deserves a special mention]: church services there are more magnificent than in other monasteries and it has more elders who know by experience the power and joy of spiritual life."[21] In 1881 the Bishop of Kaluga chose Optina as his temporary residence during his visitation of the diocese.[22] But while bishops encouraged elders as the heralds of spiritual revival in the region, they would not tolerate elders' interference in the economic and administrative affairs of the monastery. However, episcopal power was limited: Pobedonostsev frequently transferred bishops from one diocese to another and allowed civil authorities to intervene in ecclesiastical affairs.[23]

Monasteries, which represented a natural environment for elders, experienced several changes in post-Emancipation Russia. The monasteries where eldership was practiced continued to recruit new followers. In Glinskaia pustyn', the number of monks doubled between 1861 and 1885.[24] The number of monks and novices also increased in Optina pustyn' and Valaam monastery.[25] The social profile of monasteries changed too. After the emancipation of the serfs, the number of peasants among monks and nuns increased, leading to a "peasantization of monasticism."[26] In Glinskaia pustyn', for example, the presence of the peasantry was felt very strongly. If in 1829 peasants made up less than one tenth of monastic membership, which was dominated by the Cossacks and urban ranks, in 1885 monks of peasant origin represented more than half of the entire monastic community.[27] Optina pustyn', too, became dominated by peasants from 1881.[28] While Valaam had traditionally recruited from the peasantry, in the second half of the nineteenth century it had visibly become what the writer Vasilii Nemirovich-Danchenko called a "peasant kingdom." The growth of the peasant element was also typical for female monasticism, and William Wagner has argued that this new development made rural convents and communities less attractive for urban women.[29]

The average monk had also become younger. In the late 1860s, the average age of an Optina novice was 25.8 years.[30] At Glinskaia in 1885, more than a third of the brethren were 30 or younger. In female communities, the young age of novices and nuns was accepted as the norm. However, whereas the average age for becoming a novice was 30, it was not unusual for convents to admit novices as young as twelve.[31] The novitiate in monasteries lasted between three and five years (though it was often longer in convents), yet it was customary for hieromonks to be ten to twenty years older than the average novice.[32] Spiritual hierarchy in monastic life was organized in accordance with age: younger monks and nuns were subordinated to elder.[33] The importance of age as a factor in the hierarchy of spiritual power is even more evident within female celibate communities, where the absence of ordination made age, experience, and charisma the important criteria for spiritual authority.

Spiritual elders, nevertheless, did not have to be old. A sample of three popular elders, Amvrosii of Optina, Amfilokhii of Glinskaia, and Varnava of Gethsemane, demonstrates that experience of monastic life rather than age led to their promotion to the position of confessors. While Amvrosii and Varnava became novices in their twenties, Amfilokhii joined Glinskaia at the age of 36. Amvrosii and Amfilokhii made relatively quick progress from novices to hieromonks: Amvrosii took vows within two years of his joining the monastery and in four years he was ordained as a priest; Amfilokhii became a priest within six years. Varnava, however, had to wait fifteen years before he could take vows and six years before he could celebrate the liturgy as a priest. However, all three monks became confessors in their communities in their late forties and fifties. On average, it took about twenty years to progress from novitiate to spiritual fatherhood. Two decades of monastic life were deemed to be a minimum for a monk to gain experience of ascetic life and knowledge of the human soul.[34]

In the post-Emancipation period monasteries in which eldership was practiced became active agents in the market economy.[35] Monasteries purchased land, mills, and fishing ponds, practiced new farming methods, and set up profitable works processing agricultural produce. Notwithstanding such endeavors, the largest increase in monastic wealth was due to private donations. Merchants and noble landowners donated their land to monasteries.[36] Generous benefactors also gave money for building and decoration of churches so that their souls would be remembered after their death. Many communities required newcomers to bring a deposit, which was used to provide them with accommodation. In Optina monastery and Anosin convent, the usual sum was 1000 rubles. Well-off novices could contribute even larger sums of money to the monastic treasury, as well as donating other property.[37]

If, according to Joseph of Volokolamsk, the abbot was the spiritual father of his brethren as well as the economic manager, in the second half of the nineteenth century elders appropriated the functions of abbots. They acted as economic agents, in the sense that they took part in monastic finances, received and distributed donations, and actively participated in land transactions. This unusual and often burdensome role was a result of several factors, among which were the weakening of the abbot, who—far from the Josephite ideal—was often a marionette in the hands of the Synodal administration, and dependence of monastic welfare on private charity.

Elders were personally in charge of large sums donated by their admirers. In Optina hermitage, elders had a final say in all economic matters.[38] In his mediatory function the elder was believed to be a better agent of charity distribution than formal institutions. Dostoevsky provides an illustration of this. In *Brothers Karamazov*, a peasant woman brought sixty kopecks to Elder Zosima, asking him to give it to one who was poorer than her.[39] The woman believed that Zosima was a disinterested agent who would be able to dispose of her money justly. Amvrosii of Optina—who, many believed, inspired the character of Zosima—had personal control over the monastic treasury, using large sums of money without accountability for charitable works but, primarily, for the construction of a female convent in neighboring Shamordino, and Gusevskaia community in Saratov province.[40] Varnava of Gethsemane collected donations for the establishment of the Iveron female community in Vyksa, Novgorod diocese.[41]

Understandably, monastic administrators and bishops tried to regulate the elders who exercised an unprecedented financial, spiritual, and administrative autonomy. From the 1870s, bishops often treated monasteries as sources of revenue.[42] The partially successful attempts of Bishops Grigorii and Vitalii of Kaluga in 1890 to impose Synodal regulations on the Optina *startsy* suggest that there was a growing concern among the church hierarchy about the financial freedom exercised by the *startsy*, who single-handedly controlled large sums of money. In 1890, the Synod tried to replace the treasurer at Optina, so that it could better control Amvrosii in his financial dealings.

Max Weber believed that charisma was an anti-economic force. He wrote: "The point is that charisma rejects as undignified all methodical rational acquisition, in fact, all rational economic conduct."[43] The economic activity of elders was not in line with the rationalized system of monastic economy imposed and regulated by the Synod. Elders played the role of disinterested agents of material redistribution. Their charismatic authority legitimized informal economic transactions. The involvement of elders in economic affairs was not necessarily a matter of choice: they felt it their responsibility to provide for the monks and nuns whose welfare depended on the stream of donations from the elders' lay supporters. Russian believers used the term "spiritual nourishment" (*dukhovnoe okormlenie*) to indicate sacraments, confession, and spiritual guidance; it seems that elders not only fed their spiritual children with spiritual food, but also provided them with daily bread.

Modern technology brought disruptions to life of solitude and isolation so much treasured by elders. The modernization of transport and improvement of roads meant that far-off hermitages became more accessible to the public. Following the decree of 1843, which allowed freedom of the waterways to private steamer navigation, the regular paddle steamer *Valaam* brought hundreds of visitors to the remote island in Ladoga Lake populated only by monks. *Valaam* was later replaced by the more advanced *Peter the Great*, which could transport up to four thousand people to the monastery in one trip. The roads built by Abbot Damaskin (d. 1881) allowed visitors to enjoy the rare beauty of the island and become closer to the strange and fascinating world of ascetics and hermits. In the 1860s, steamers also facilitated access to the legendary Mount Athos. Female pilgrims, who were not allowed to put their foot on the holy ground of Athos, could observe from the deck the architecture and natural beauty of the Holy Mountain, and while on deck they could receive blessings at a distance from the monks in St. Panteleimon monastery. The railways, the construction of which boomed in the 1860s–1880s, improved access to provincial monasteries. The influx of visitors prompted monks to build more guest houses and hostels. Optina had four hostels, which were always full, so that one required a special reference to get a place. By the 1860s, Valaam had three hostels, one for Finnish visitors and workers, one for pilgrims, and another for beggars and poor wanderers.[44] Many well-off visitors bought property and built houses near monasteries so that they could avoid using monastic hostels, which were alive with bed bugs. Konstantin Leont'ev, the former Russian consul in the Ottoman Empire, had his own house at Optina where he lived as a layman.[45] While there is no evidence to judge whether elders objected to the surge of visitors to monasteries, it is possible that many of them regretted the lack of time for private prayer and communication with the members of the community. Yet many perceived their role as a missionary service to the people and dedicated themselves to this task.

The Elders of the Holy Mountain
Athos in the Russian Imagination

The flow of pilgrims from Russia to Mount Athos brought Russian Orthodoxy even closer to its Byzantine roots. The spiritual affinity between the Russian elders and Athonite monastic traditions was reinforced in the second half of the nineteenth century through the activities of St. Panteleimon monastery, an exclusively Russian monastery in a predominantly Greek area. Thanks to the activities of St. Panteleimon monks, Athos became a trademark of spirituality that Russian believers associated with profound otherworldliness, timeless beauty, and unrivaled holiness.

In the nineteenth century, after two centuries of Russian indifference, the monastic republic on Mount Athos and its elders began to captivate the imagination of the Russian public.[46] The significance of Athos in the Russian spiritual revival can be explained by several factors: the restoration of Russian monasticism in Mount Athos from the 1830s, the boom in publications about Athos, and the growth of pilgrimage to the Holy Mountain. The revival of Russian monasticism in predominantly Greek surroundings began in the 1830s, when a descendant of one of the most prominent aristocratic families, Prince S.A. (Anikita) Shirinskii-Shikhmatov, became a monk in the St. Elijah hermitage and generously helped to restore the monastery established by Paisii Velichkovskii in 1757. However, the number of Russians in Athos remained very small, not exceeding fifty monks in the 1840s. The period that followed the emancipation of the serfs saw a dramatic rise in the number of Russians who left their motherland for the Holy Mountain. In 1864, the number of monks in St. Panteleimon monastery was about 200 and by 1885 it had risen to 800, while the total number of Russian monks on Athos was perhaps even larger.[47] The joint efforts of popular confessor Father Ieronim (Solomentsev) and Abbot Makarii (Sushkin), the son of a wealthy Tula merchant, improved the welfare of the monastery during these years. Russian travelers to Athos and the monks of St. Panteleimon popularized the Athonite way of life, which was centered on spirituality and nature.

Athos had an ancient tradition of spiritual guidance. In the deserted areas of Karulia and Vatopedy, outside the giant monastic centers like St. Panteleimon and Iveron, lived white-bearded *abbas*, who shared small *kaliva* (huts) with two or three disciples. These hermits, who were regarded by many as exemplary monks, attended church services only once a week and led a life of contemplation and physical work.[48] Traditionally, Athos was a center of mystical prayer, which was practiced in both cenobitic and idiorrythmic monasteries. Mastery of the Jesus prayer consisted of repetition of the words

"Lord Jesus Christ, son of God, have mercy on me, a sinner" and was the ultimate condition of the monk's progress towards mystical union with God. Beginners had to say the words of the prayer either aloud or in their mind and, with time, praying would become as natural as the heartbeat. The most experienced *abbas* were said to be able to keep this prayer going while performing their daily duties, conversing with brethren, and even in their sleep. To become proficient in the art of the Jesus prayer required a master who explained the technique and theology of the prayer and monitored the progress of the learner. This was the role of the elder.

In cenobitic Russian monasteries like St. Panteleimon, the role of spiritual elders was of paramount importance. The Rule of St. Panteleimon distinguished between the roles of confessor (*dukhovnik*) and mentor (*nastavnik*), pointing out that a mentor could be a nonordained monk experienced in spiritual life, who could teach the newly ordained monk how to resist temptation and prepare for penance. Confession as a sacrament, however, was in the hands of ordained priests, including the abbot, who was the chief spiritual father in the community.[49] The Athonite monks treasured the relationship between the elder and the neophyte, for it was regarded as an image of the relationship between Christ and God the Father. Monks were expected to consult their elders on all aspects of monastic life, including private and church prayer, fasting, manual work, Holy Communion, and church discipline. They were also expected to reveal to the elders their secret fantasies, visions, and dreams so they would not fall prey to demons.[50]

The monastic republic of Athos was a citadel of Orthodoxy and tradition, which seemed to remain immune to the social and political turmoil that troubled European nations in the second half of the nineteenth century. Nevertheless, Athonite elders worried about the impact of social turbulence upon Russian Orthodoxy. They regarded the Paris Commune (1871) to be the work of the Antichrist.[51] They worried about the spread of nihilism and socialism, which they regarded as godlessness and disobedience. In the aftermath of the revolutionary events in France, the fathers of St. Panteleimon monastery wrote a proposal to the Holy Synod for improving morality in Russian society. They included such measures as tightening of censorship on imported and domestic literature, the introduction of special liturgies against nihilism, an increase of religious tuition in secular educational establishments, a proscription against graduates of spiritual institutions joining the civil service, and the closure of theaters during Sundays and Great Lent.[52] They believed that the government should be paying more attention to morality, fasting, the observation of Sundays, and religious holidays in the army. They requested that the decision to abolish the observation of Lent in public institutions be reversed. In short, the Athonite monks advocated the desecularization of spheres of public life such as the army, the civil service, and education. They wanted the Church brought back to the center of public life. Some of the reforms implemented during the chief-procuratorship of Pobedonostsev appear to have been influenced by the arch-conservative Athonite monks, but it is doubtful that the voice of the elders on Mount Athos had a serious bearing on Synodal policy.[53] In fact, the Russian monks in Athos were so disappointed in both the Russian and Ottoman authorities, and felt so despondent and besieged, that in the 1870s they contemplated a migration to some desert island in the Pacific Ocean where they could recreate a perfect monastic republic.[54]

The transfer of the Athonite model of eldership and its conservative ideology to Russia took place in a variety of ways. Firstly, the monks in Athos could circulate their ideas through the publications of St. Panteleimon monastery, which included, among others, the works and translations of Bishop Feofan the Recluse and the journal *Dushepoleznyi sobesednik*. Pilgrimage and correspondence brought many pious men and women into personal contact with the spiritual authorities at the Holy Mountain. The frequent visits of Athonite monks to Russia for fundraising helped to cultivate the image of Athos as timeless and free from social turbulence and the perils of the world. This image remained attractive for the hundreds of Russian novices who flocked to the mountains of this unique peninsula, eager to follow in the steps of famous ascetics and hermits. There was also a more prosaic explanation for the popularity of Athonite monasticism: Athos provided novices with much quicker progress to monastic profession and ordination.

Many Russian monks returned home because they were either unable to bear homesickness and the harsh climate or because they realized that Athos, too, had many limitations to ascetic freedom.[55] These returnees, nevertheless, were important in bringing back the experience of Athonite spiritual eldership and the practices of the Jesus prayer. Archimandrite Mikhail (Kozlov), the compiler of the extremely popular publication on Orthodox mental prayer, *The Way of the Pilgrim*, and its first publisher, Abbot Paisii (Erin), spent several years on Mount Athos. Another lesser known monk, Feofil (Golubinskii), a merchant's son, left Athos in the 1870s for the Boriso-Glebskii monastery in Tver diocese. Feofil, who corresponded with dozens of lay men and women in Russia, believed that the grace of God was the reward for obedience to one's elder.[56] It seems that Athos' eminence as a "smithy of holiness" in the eyes of pious Russian men and women enhanced the monks' reputations back in Russia.

The Recluse of Vysha

Bishop Feofan (Govorov) and Theorizing Eldership, 1860s–1890s

Correspondence between monks and the laity provided a medium through which specific religious ideas and methods were communicated. One of the most prolific religious writers in the nineteenth century, Feofan the Recluse (1815–1894) corresponded with hundreds of men and women, sharing with them his experience of spiritual life and mental prayer. Feofan's example shows that eldership was not only a set of practices passed through the master to the disciple; it was based on (or closely connected with) a discourse on mystical prayer and the struggle against passions.

In the second half of the nineteenth century, due to the relaxation of censorship, the publication of the *Dobrotoliubie* in vernacular Russian and of a number of texts that popularized the Jesus prayer and spiritual guidance became possible. The discourse on mystical aspects of Orthodoxy, including spiritual guidance, became part of mainstream Russian religious culture thanks to the writings of Bishop Ignatii Brianchaninov (1807–1867) and Feofan the Recluse. However, while Brianchaninov only saw his writings in print shortly before his death in 1867, Bishop Feofan, his younger counterpart, had the entire publishing house of St. Panteleimon monastery at his disposal, eager to publish his work.

The group of "learned monks" that emerged in the first half of the nineteenth century consisted of bright theology graduates who were encouraged to take vows of celibacy and pursue careers in church administration. As a rule, these "learned monks" were unsympathetic to ascetic theology and the *Dobrotoliubie*. Both Ignatii (Brianchaninov) and Feofan broke this rule, and reintroduced patristic ascetic writers of the fourth and sixth centuries and Byzantine hesychasts to the reading public.[57] For both of them, eldership was inseparable from ancient monasticism. However, while Bishop Ignatii accepted with sad resignation the fact that there was a huge gap between the world of Desert Fathers and that of modernity, and that elders had no place in the modern world, Feofan—whom many regarded as an elder—actively supported eldership as a living practice in the Orthodox Church.

Born to the family of a parish priest in Orel province in 1815, Georgii Govorov was meant to follow in his father's footsteps. As a boy he would help his father to keep parish records, and he enthusiastically pursued his studies in the spiritual seminary of Livny and the Kiev Spiritual Academy. Just before his graduation from the academy, he took monastic vows and the new name of Feofan, which meant "God is revealed." What followed was a typical career for a bright "learned monk": teaching at and administering theological educational institutions, serving in the Russian Mission in Jerusalem, and heading cathedrals in Tambov and Vladimir. In 1866, at the age of 51, Feofan left the world of church politics and took an appointment as an abbot in a monastery of his choice, Vysha hermitage in Tambov province, known for the beauty of its natural environment. Unable to combine the pressures of monastic administration with his studies and ascetic pursuits, in 1872 he shut the doors of his room, and communicated with the world only by letter until his death in 1894. Despite his reputation as a saintly recluse, he presented himself as a scholar who wanted peace and quiet to concentrate on his work. His seclusion resulted in remarkable productivity: translations from Greek (the *Philokalia*, the Homilies of Simeon the New Theologian, the *Miterikon*), exegetical works (commentaries on the Epistles of St. Paul), treatises on spirituality ("Spiritual Life and How to Become Attuned to It," "The Way to Salvation"), and numerous letters. According to Father Georgii Tertyshnikov, Feofan's publications before 1917 amounted to five hundred titles.[58] In his free time, the bishop-monk occupied himself with wood carving, painting, and playing the harmonica.

Bishop Feofan projected the image of a medieval recluse, a contemplative and nonpossessor. He was a craftsman and self-sufficient man, but at the same time, his hobbies and beliefs were in harmony with the spirit of the times: despite his inward-looking mystical vision, Feofan was a believer in science and scholarship; he had a microscope and a telescope in his cell, as well as geographical atlases. He also relied on a printing press to print his work and provide references: he owned 150 volumes of the *Theological Encyclopedia* in French, and all the modern editions of the Church Fathers. Last but not the least, he relied on mail service, complaining when his letters took too long to reach their destination. The bishop's remarkable productivity and his speed of writing earned him the title of the "heavenly patron of the Russian Internet" in 2004.[59]

Was Feofan a *starets*? He did not have a following of faithful disciples either among the brethren of his own monastery, or outside its walls. But in his numerous letters to priests, abbots, monks, and lay people, Feofan offered advice on the organization of spiritual life and pastoral issues. His principal recommendations to the laity concerned the necessity of transformation from the routine, mechanical performance of ritual to the constant memory of God. He stressed living in God's presence and focusing on one's inner discourse with Him rather than thoughtlessly repeating the canonical prayers. As for the priests, he believed that the sacraments of confession and Eucharist had too great an impact on the penitent to be treated lightly. He reminded a priest, who had disclosed a confession to a third person, of the canon law which recommended that the guilty confessor should have his tongue cut out. Likewise, he warned another priest against banning his parishioners from Holy Communion. According to Feofan, since many Russian churchgoers took communion only once a year, depriving them of this sacrament would drive them even further from God.[60]

Feofan encouraged and promoted eldership in Russian monasteries. He corresponded with the elders of Valaam monastery, among them the blind monk Agapii, a friend from the time of Feofan's tenure at the St. Petersburg Spiritual Academy. To him, the bishop explained the difference between confession as church sacrament and confession to an elder. Only confession as a sacrament of the Church could absolve sins. Elders, however, provided guidance, dispelled doubts, explained misunderstandings, and consoled those who sought their direction.[61] The most important qualities of a spiritual elder were, according to Feofan, discernment of thoughts (*razlichenie pomyslov*) and good judgment (*rassuzhdenie*); not every good and experienced monk had the qualities to make a good elder.[62] He believed that eldership was a powerful instrument to improve monastic life and was also convinced that one elder with his disciples was sufficient to transform an area "contaminated" with religious dissent into an exemplary Orthodox community.[63] He referred here to the elders of Optina, for whom he had a great respect.

Many of Feofan's correspondents asked his advice on the Jesus prayer. It seems that although this was one of the simplest meditative practices in the Orthodox Church, not everyone felt confident practicing it without some spiritual advice. Feofan differed from other writers on the Jesus prayer, and debated the topic with Father John of Kronstadt. He objected to excessive attention to the technical aspects of prayer, such as different techniques of breathing, excessive attention to the posture, and focus of the mind on the body.[64] For him, practice of the Jesus prayer was premature for those who had not fully explored the effects of canonical church prayers. He called those practitioners "dolls," who mechanically repeated the words of the prayer with no result.[65]

The Jesus prayer, according to Feofan, was nothing else but the memory of God. Any other short prayer pronounced mentally could substitute for it and, with the right disposition of the practitioner, these prayers could create an emotion of the divine presence. The purest form of *oratio mentalis* was nonverbal communication with God.[66] What Feofan meant was not simply a pious emotional state, but a mystical experience of union with God, theosis—the goal of ascetic life. This higher form of prayer, the "prayer of the heart," was a gift of grace that a believer could receive also through the sacraments of the Church: confession and Eucharist. The main characteristic of mental prayer was its continuous and often nonverbal character.[67] The grace of God could not be attracted by persistence and emphasis on technique. Grace was given to those with pure hearts, a clean conscience, and zealousness in the cultivation of virtues.[68] There is a seemingly simple combination of the ethical, sacramental, ascetic, and mystical aspects of prayer in Feofan's writings: the mystical union with God cannot be achieved by voluntary efforts alone without the Lord's grace; yet grace can only be given to those who make ascetic efforts, take part in church sacraments, and lead a good life. Feofan was distrustful of the physical effects of mental prayer, some of which were described in detail in *The Way of a Pilgrim*, first published in 1881. The bishop, at his own discretion, edited the popular book in order to prevent confusion and misinterpretation of the text by the Orthodox reader.

Bishop Feofan was the remarkable representative of a group of clergy who consciously disengaged themselves from public life and church administration in order to cultivate "mystical discourse" and live a life of contemplation. His disengagement had several motivations: personal disappointment with the Synod, which implemented reforms haltingly and treated bishops as pawns, the growth of sectarianism and secularism, and the failure of religio-political ideals to influence foreign policy. Taking an early retirement from the life of a church functionary, he actively attempted to forge an Orthodox "science" of human psychology based on the teachings of the Fathers, and to provide a manual for contemplative prayer.

Female Spiritual Authority

In contrast to male monasteries, female communities and convents had a more complex system of spiritual authority. Female elders (*staritsy*) were experienced nuns who, by the appointment of the abbess or without it, were responsible for the spiritual guidance of novices or newly professed nuns. In addition to the internal organization of spiritual life and discipline, female communities and convents had officially appointed confessors, often monks from nearby monasteries. For example, the Anosin Boriso-Glebskii convent in Moscow diocese, founded by Princess Meshcherskaia in 1821, traditionally had confessors from Savvinskii monastery in the same diocese. However, nuns could also choose a confidante in the person of another monk or nun who was not part of the official structure. As a rule, only nuns from the educated classes could exercise such freedom.

Despite efforts by Feofan the Recluse to educate the reading public about the correct forms of Orthodox spiritual life, there was no single model or blueprint for the path to union with God. The experience of female communities is of great value because it shows significant diversity and creativity in the choice of religious models. Charismatic authority in female communities was reproduced and routinized in a similar way to male communities. Women religious imitated their own spiritual guides and ascetics, and educated nuns collected evidence about famous holy women in their community. This emulation of ascetic models can be called, in the words of Professor Sven Linnér, "mimesis of virtue."[69] It seems that women were more flexible and eclectic in the choice of their models for imitation: they could choose male as well as female models. They compiled biographies of famous elders and cherished their correspondence.[70] While, as William Wagner perceptively noted, the discourse on domestic and maternal roles of women certainly influenced female monasticism, finding reflection in religious women's educational and social welfare projects, ascetic ideals continued to attract women.[71]

Although in some convents the practice of the elder-novice relationship was well established, elsewhere it remained informal. The autobiography of Mother Arseniia (Sebriakova) provides an illustration. The only child of the chief of the local nobility in the Don Cossack district, Anna Sebriakova joined the provincial Ust'-Medveditsk convent in 1849, when she was only sixteen years old. In 1859, Anna took the veil and a new name, Arseniia. While in charge of the monastic library, she met an older nun, Ardaliona, who came to borrow books. At first, the young noblewoman disliked Ardaliona's plebeian manners, but eventually she discovered a depth of spiritual wisdom in this woman of inferior social status. The fast-developing friendship between the two women, who decided to share the same house, worried the abbess.

Arseniia, who had lost her mother as a child, found someone who became a spiritual mother to her. Ardaliona, a daughter of a parish priest, had no theological education apart from her practical knowledge of parish life. Ardaliona's spiritual guidance aimed at the mortification of the "passions" and breaking of the egocentrism of her spiritual children. Once, Ardaliona shredded Arseniia's favorite rug into pieces, to discourage her pupil from treasuring material things. On another occasion, she confiscated fifty kopecks from a beggar, which had been given as alms by Mother Arseniia, so that this generous donation would not make her spiritual daughter feel self-righteous. Ardaliona believed that virtues could only be achieved through total renunciation of one's own self. Other nuns, however, found this teaching too severe and denounced it as heresy. Arseniia, however, discovered deep theological meaning in the teaching of her spiritual mother and later compared it to Ignatii Brianchaninov's theological vision.[72]

Arseniia, who in 1863, at the age of 31, became the mother superior of the convent, was one of the few Russian religious women who spoke out about her experience and understanding of spiritual life. In the 1870s–1880s, when just in her forties, she enjoyed the role of spiritual mother to many nuns and a few lay men and women. Despite her popularity among the sisters, she limited the number of members in her spiritual family, explaining this decision by her weakness. To help younger nuns with their spiritual progress, she organized collective readings of the *Dobrotoliubie* and commented on some passages. Mother Arseniia combined the duties of abbess and spiritual guide in her community, preparing novices to make their profession and looking after their problems, illnesses, and well-being.

Arseniia's power derived from several sources: she was a noble heiress, a well-educated woman, an abbess, and a friend of bishops. Her role as a spiritual guide was the result of years of attentive reading, self-examination, prayer, and friendship with other experienced nuns. Arseniia's approach was egalitarian and communal. The only hierarchy she recognized was a spiritual one: she would only bow down before those who had progressed further in their efforts towards salvation. This position explains her boldness and self-assurance. The egalitarian image of Christian community is symbolized in a dream she recorded in her autobiography. She dreamed about the Last Supper: men sat at one end of the table, women sat at the other. She could not see Christ anywhere although His presence was felt in the supernatural lighting of her dream. Then she saw two readers of the Gospel, a deacon and a deaconess, standing at the opposite ends of the table. She interpreted this image as the mystery of the Last Supper: all saints—male and female—were partaking in the word of God, all were transformed by it. Even though in Arseniia's dream male and female saints were sitting at the opposite ends of the table, they were semiotically equal. This egalitarianism of saints who become divinized in God without distinctions of sex or rank was, ironically, the vision of a religious woman who followed one of the most conservative Christian denominations in the world.

Arseniia's hope in the saving grace of the Lord derived from her understanding of human weakness. "The way to God lies through our sinfulness," she wrote. In this paradox, theological concepts of incarnation and atonement are translated into moral theology. Just as sinful humanity could not be saved in its incompleteness, so too the human soul could achieve salvation only through awareness of its own sinfulness and weakness.[73] Man should know his limits and not exceed them. She called for self-understanding and acceptance of one's own weakness, which would open the way for the Lord's grace. Weakness was a typical characteristic of womanhood in both religious and secular discourses. If self-realization of weakness was a virtue, then women had an advantage; their weakness could be turned into power.

Cassandra from Diveevo

Holy Fools and Spiritual Guidance

Arseniia's spiritual authority had a rational basis: she appealed to the authority of scripture and the Fathers of the Church as well as to her own mystical visions. However, there was an alternative spiritual model for women, that of the holy fool (*iurodivyi*). *Iurodivye* challenged the wisdom of this world by their provocative and irreverent behavior.[74] They violated moral norms by appearing naked in public, or behaving as drunks and prostitutes.

In 1837, a strange woman was brought to the Diveevo community, which had been founded by Aleksandra Mel'gunova in the late eighteenth century. She was dirty and shoeless; her skull and ribs had been fractured in several places and her hair was infested with lice. She was Pelagiia, the wife of Arzamas merchant Sergei Serebriakov, and she was later acclaimed as a great female elder (*staritsa*) of Diveevo and the true successor of the charismatic Serafim. Her appearance as an idiot, "Mad Palaga," was interpreted by many as holy foolishness (*iurodstvo*), the Byzantine and medieval Russian hagiographical model of a saint who imitated madness in order to hide his or her spiritual gifts and ascetic exploits.

Pelagiia was born to a merchant family in 1809 and married at the age of 17 to Serebriakov; she gave birth to two children, who died in infancy. It is unclear when exactly Pelagiia started to exhibit signs of madness. According to the *Diveevo Chronicles*, Pelagiia's mother was so eager to marry off her daughter that she carefully hid her daughter's disturbing behavior from her suitor. It has also been suggested that Pelagiia began to behave irrationally following the newly wed couple's visit to Diveevo, where they received a blessing from Serafim. Claiming that Serafim put a spell on her, Pelagiia broke all norms of propriety, wearing rugs and making herself a fool in public. She remained indifferent to the birth of her two sons, who might have died due to her negligence. According to the *Chronicles*, she learned the Jesus prayer from another merchant wife and prayed at night in the conservatory. The family drama unfolded: Pelagiia's husband never doubted his wife's sanity and tried to correct her behavior by violent beating and chaining the blameless Pelagiia to a wall. The battered woman would often escape from her sadistic husband and wander half-naked through the city. In 1837, after the death of Serafim, the mother superior of Diveevo made an agreement with Pelagiia's relatives that the abused woman would join her community. There she stayed for 47 years.

It took some time for Pelagiia's reputation as a holy fool and *staritsa* to develop. The woman's irrational behavior challenged the members of the community, many of whom doubted the wisdom of the mother superior. However, soon a growing number of followers believed in Pelagiia's supernatural ability to foresee the future, and they helped to establish her reputation as an ascetic, holy fool, and elder. Pelagiia told strangers the intimate details of their life, foretold death and illness, and sometimes provided a cure by striking the ailing limb or a section of the body affected by the illness. On the other hand, Pelagiia's public behavior challenged the norms of Christian virtue and piety. She was violent to animals and people, ignored church services, and refused to confess or take communion. In order to explain this incongruence with her saintly reputation, her biographers mentioned that Pelagiia communicated spiritually in a company of angels and saints.[75] Her violent and irrational acts were seen as part of great mystery that surrounded her personality.

Although several commentators, including the *Diveevo Chronicles*, insisted that Pelagiia exercised the charisma of a female elder, her experience stands apart from other spiritual guides of the period.[76] In fact, we have only one account from a spiritual child of Pelagiia, the icon painter M. P. Petrov, who came to Diveevo in 1874 to ask the holy fool whether he should marry or become a monk. During his second visit, Pelagiia not only answered Petrov's question but also gave foresight into his future and healed his shoulder ache. From this time on he was in constant communication with Pelagiia, receiving answers to his and other people's questions through short notes or via good friends. Petrov was also a mediator between Pelagiia and other men and women who wanted to receive predictions about their future.[77] Petrov's special spiritual kinship with the holy fool did not follow the Philokalic model practiced in Optina. It was a mystical connection between the saint and the admirer who had great faith in her, so that by invocation of her name he could avert disaster and receive cure.

Historically, desert monasticism and the phenomenon of holy fools were closely connected: like holy fools, the desert *abbas* challenged their visitors with irrational and debauched behavior. In accordance with the Byzantine canon, only those ascetics who developed absolute indifference to the world (*apathea* in Greek or *besstrastie* in Russian) could perform seemingly immoral acts (for example, visit brothels or share a bed with naked persons of opposite sex) without having any effect on their soul or bodies.[78] Elders could adopt the appearance of holy fools in order to avoid popular adoration, so that people would never find out the true virtues of the ascetic behind the appearance of a fool.[79] Serafim of Sarov, too, had conformed to the canon of *iurodstvo*. Once, he gave a rake to a girl whose hands and feet were paralyzed. A member of Diveevo community recollected that once Serafim gave her and her sister two bags of dried bread (his usual gift to visitors), and then started to beat the bag with his stick, much to the amusement of his guests. Only in hindsight did the woman interpret this inexplicable action as a symbolic prediction of her sister's suffering.[80]

Pelagiia's behavior was interpreted in accordance with the Byzantine canon of *iurodstvo*, which was based on the motif of concealed sanctity.[81] The Russian Orthodox believed that holy fools carried out ascetic exploits imitating the desert ascetics of the past, which had to be concealed behind the mask of madness.[82] The Diveevo chroniclers used the testimony of Pelagiia's abusive husband, who never doubted his wife's sanity, as a proof of the woman's concealed spiritual gifts.[83] The *Chronicles* emphasized that while Pelagiia spent most of her day in a ditch full of manure, when she was not violently breaking windows and killing cats she continued to pray and carry out ascetic exploits.[84] Pelagiia was not the only example of the popular association between bizarre behavior and holiness. Another holy fool from Diveevo, a former serf mutilated by her owners, known as Pasha Sarovskaia, reputedly also had a gift of foretelling the future, despite her appearance of being mentally deranged. Visitors interpreted Pasha's nonsensical comments and her childlike behavior, such as playing with dolls, as prophecies. According to the Diveevo nuns, in 1903 Pasha foretold the birth of the male heir to the throne.[85]

Charisma and Popular Demand

Popular interest in elders in post-Emancipation Russia can be explained by several factors. Apart from specific peasant beliefs in charismatic power for healing of the sick, and exorcism as a prophylactic against famine and illness of animals, there were other existential concerns shared by both urban and rural folk. Concerns about illness, death, welfare, and the future are universal. In the period that followed the emancipation and Great

4.1. Pasha Sarovskaia.
Source: Rossiiskii gosudarstvennyi arkhiv kinofotodokumentov. Courtesy of the Russian Archives of Documentary Films and Photographs

Reforms, all social groups were affected by social and economic changes. Industrialization, urbanization, commercialization of agriculture, and migration to the cities led to displacement, insecurity, and the erosion of communal relations. As a result, individuals could no longer rely on the traditional mechanisms that had regulated their lives in the past; yet they did not become rational and self-reliant at once. Elders responded to individual insecurities, anxieties, and alienation. Often, what people sought from elders was not only spiritual healing, but also practical advice, approval of their choices, and encouragement. For example, a noblewoman who decided to build a mill on her estate asked Elder Varnava of Gethsemane to give her his blessing. Varnava did not just give her his approval, but encouraged her to build a more ambitious project that became one of the more profitable enterprises in the area.[86] The son of a peasant from Tula, Varnava (Merkulov) had a practical mind, taking an interest in minute details of the business ventures of his spiritual children, among whom were many merchants and traders from Moscow. Women, in particular, benefited from the elder's advice. Widows with children and poor young women from the village came to him seeking help. Varnava placed some of these women in the Iveron-Vyksa community; others received a place as servants in the households of rich and pious members of Varnava's spiritual family.[87]

The popular appeal of religious virtuosi, including Russian elders, is sometimes explained by their special gift of predicting the future.[88] Popular interest in the future and fortune-telling was ubiquitous in prerevolutionary Russia.[89] Fortune-telling books, dream books, and astrological and oracle books translated from European languages, used in combination with traditional folk methods of divination, became extremely popular after 1750 among literate readers. Divination and prognostication gained currency in traditional society whenever the economic fate of the family and community were threatened.[90] In post-Emancipation Russia, people invested in the future and based their current actions on knowledge of it. Knowledge of the future was especially important during times of transition. Men and women of marriageable age came to consult elders regarding whether they should join a monastery or a convent or marry and have a family.[91] Lay and clerical pilgrims came to ask for elders' blessings before a long journey, especially a pilgrimage. Insecurity and dire conditions of travel often meant that pilgrims could die away from home on their way to a holy site.[92]

An overwhelming number of people came to elders seeking advice on marriage. It seems that as a result of the breakdown of traditional community, the custom of marriage as a contract between family groups with the aid of marriage brokers (*svakha*) declined; therefore, marriage involved higher risks. Varnava was skeptical about the marriage of the daughter of his spiritual son, who lived in St. Petersburg. Despite his advice, the marriage took place but proved to be unhappy: the husband turned out to be an idler who could not provide for his family. In the end, the woman returned to her parents.[93]

Illness, too, was a transitional state, marking the possibility of the journey from the world of the living to the world of the dead. Of course, many sick and ailing people came to holy places in the hope of being cured, but many others came to find out whether they should prepare for death and the afterlife. Knowledge of the outcome, even if negative, was still a consolation to a person and their family, since all necessary arrangements could be made and the individuals in question could come to terms with the inevitable fact. A peasant woman, for example, came to Pelagiia of Diveevo to ask about the future of her twenty-year-old daughter Grusha, who was sick. The Diveevo oracle gave no reply but kept staring at a lilac flower which Pelagiia held in her hands and then uttered "Grusha! Grusha! This flower will be good for God too!" The strange words were interpreted as a prediction of Grusha's death, which followed shortly.[94] This story indicates that existential anxiety and concerns about the afterlife were sometimes stronger than practical considerations or emotional bereavement.

Thus, the popular appeal of elders was not singularly centered upon religious divination, as some interpreters argued.[95] It was, rather, part of a more complex combination of social, religious, and psychological factors that arose after the emancipation, the period that could be called (following the model suggested by Peter Brown) "the crisis of freedom."[96] The breakdown of the structures of serf-landlord relations, peasant commune, closed estate system, and traditional parish network brought the elder into the forefront of Russian spiritual politics. It was not the lack of freedom, but the real possibility of it, and the risk and social insecurity typical of periods of transition, that encouraged many individuals to seek support and advice from the Russian spiritual elders.

The National Elder
Amvrosii of Optina

There is no better illustration of the ways in which elders responded to the "crisis of freedom" than the life of Elder Amvrosii (Grenkov), an obscure monk from a provincial monastery, who gained the symbolic status of the spiritual father of the Russian people, and was often associated with Father Zosima from Dostoevsky's novel *Brothers Karamazov*. It has been argued that although eldership traditionally was aimed at the perpetuation of monastic profession, in Optina, the main emphasis was on the service to the laity. Therefore, the national character (*narodnost'*) of Optina elders, including Amvrosii, derived from their service to the people.[97]

The future Elder Amvrosii (Alexander Grenkov, b. 1812) came from the family of a church sacristan and grew up in a community of church servants. A recent graduate of Tambov spiritual seminary and teacher at the Lipetsk spiritual seminary, Aleksandr Grenkov came to Optina in 1839 and decided to remain in the monastery without yet notifying diocesan authorities. In September 1839, he appealed to the bishop to allow him to stay in the monastery due to his ill health.[98]

Aleksandr became very close with Elder Leonid, who treated him like a typical elder would treat his disciple: he was strict and often unnecessarily fussy, instructing the young novice in the virtue of obedience.[99] Grenkov worked in the monastery kitchen before he was professed as monk with the name Amvrosii (after St. Ambrose, Bishop of Milan) in 1841.[100] Already quite weak in health, Amvrosii damaged his body following a strict monastic routine and taking the wrong medicine. In 1847 he was so weakened by a series of illnesses (neuritis, hemorrhoids, severe indigestion, and so on) that he had to appeal for retirement.

Amvrosii was the third in the line of "great elders" at Optina, succeeding Leonid and Makarii. In the late 1840s–1860s, Amvrosii began to assist Makarii with the publishing activities of the monastery, and helped deal with Makarii's enormous correspondence and the confession of visitors. Sometimes Makarii mockingly complained that Amvrosii was stealing his bread, hinting that Amvrosii's popularity among people exceeded his own. Amvrosii was responsible for receiving and advising some noble and wealthy visitors to the pustyn', like the Kliucharev family, who—father and mother, with an underage son and grandmother—wanted to join a monastery. The transference of Makarii's former spiritual children to Amvrosii suggests that it was the tradition and the spirit of eldership, as well as personal charisma, that attracted people to the younger elder.[101]

The peak of Amvrosii's popularity was in the period of the Great Reforms, the 1860s–1880s, when the Optina monastery became the site of popular pilgrimage. Although the railway to Kozel'sk (the nearest town to Optina) was not built until 1899, the railroads to Kaluga and Tula made the monastery more accessible to visitors, who came from all social classes. Peasants, however, dominated the crowd of pilgrims and flocked at Elder Amvrosii's door; this helped to form Amvrosii's reputation as a moral and spiritual guide of the Russian *narod*.[102]

The era of Amvrosii in Optina signified the emergence of the crowd. People were waiting day and night at the doors of the elder's house, but often had to leave without having an individual meeting with him. Unable to give a personal audience to each member of the crowd, Amvrosii communicated with the public using the skills of a professional performance artist. He exchanged remarks with people in the crowd, cracked jokes, wittily responded to the shouts from the gathered people, used his stick when someone asked him for cure, and poured holy water on the sick and possessed. "Everyone received whatever one expected," wrote one memoirist. Those seeking spiritual wisdom received counsel based on the writings of the Fathers; others, seeking advice in the matters of life, received more practical guidance.[103] An educated but skeptical gentleman who came to Optina out of curiosity was impressed by Amvrosii's civility, charm, and intelligence.[104]

The elder's ability to attune himself to the inner disposition of others was the basis of his gift of *kardiognosis*, the knowledge of the heart. He criticized a correspondent who tried to record his sins in a neat table, marking with ticks the boxes of particular vices he was prone to. Amvrosii advised this person to stop this unorthodox practice. It was wrong because it made his correspondent feel good about himself, especially when he seemingly managed to overcome particular vices. He also noticed that the penitent was not very honest with himself: while finding himself not guilty of avarice (according to the table), he complained that his servants and workers cheated him. What mattered to the elder was a feeling of remorse, not a neat accounting of committed and avoided sins. This is a striking example of the Orthodox understanding of sin, understood not in a computational sense, but as a general sense of one's weakness before God.[105]

Those who sought Amvrosii's advice came from diverse backgrounds. For example, a French Roman Catholic woman, consumed by feelings of guilt and despair, opened her soul to Amvrosii, because she heard he was truly a man of God.[106] Peasants invoked Amvrosii's name along with other saints in times of trouble.[107] Many lay visitors, especially women, were attracted by Amvrosii's reputation as a clairvoyant. In contrast to this popular view, the fellow monks in Optina expressed doubts as to whether Amvrosii had any preternatural gifts apart from the skill of spiritual discernment.[108]

Some members of the royal family, such as Grand Duke Konstantin Konstantinovich, came to Optina as private persons, asking the monastery to keep their visit as secret as possible.[109] Elder Amvrosii made a great impression on the guilt-ridden duke, who all his life struggled in vain against his homosexuality. However, it remains a mystery whether Konstantin discussed his sexual life with the great elder. A lover of letters and art, a poet dilettante and the father of nine, Konstantin Konstantinovich was, until his death in 1915, tormented by remorse for the failure to stop his secret life as a homosexual.[110] It seems that following his visit to Optina in 1887, Konstantin felt that he received absolution and forgiveness through Amvrosii's prayer. He happily reported to the Optina monks news about the birth of his children and asked prayers for his Lutheran wife Elizabeth.[111] In a letter written in 1889, when his wife was expecting her third child, he wrote to Amvrosii that he was at peace with God and happy in his family life, admitting that he did not deserve God's mercy.[112] Konstantin's choice of the provincial Amvrosii as his confidante was unusual. The members of the royal family had their own confessors, ordinarily married parish priests. Perhaps Amvrosii's distance from the capital and his reputation as a holy man made him a better choice for the troubled aristocrat.

According to many accounts, Amvrosii embodied the spirit of the Russian people. His *narodnost'* had many expressions: he liked folk proverbs, peasant wit, and humorous rhymes. The writer Konstantin Leont'ev who lived in Optina found Amvrosii's love of folk wisdom quite distasteful. However, the monk was not patronizing to ordinary people, and he adapted to their beliefs. For example, he never refused to treat members of peasant families who it was believed were "possessed" by the devil.[113] Neither was he angry when a group of Roma women asked him to share the secrets of his divination technique.[114] He was genuinely amused by their suggestion that he was in the same trade as they. Amvrosii always tried to help local peasants materially and spiritually.[115]

Nevertheless, the elder's enthusiasm for the popular forms of Orthodox worship, such as icon veneration—despite, or rather, owing to his success—sometimes brought him into conflict with the ecclesiastical authorities. A few years before his death, Amvrosii ordered a special icon of the Mother of God, the Multiplier of Crops, to be painted in Bolkhov monastery.[116] The nuns of Shamordino and local peasants processed with the icon around the fields, to protect the harvest from drought. They sang a special hymn (*akafist*) composed by Amvrosii in hope that it would rain after the procession. Whether or not it actually helped to protect the harvest, especially during the famine of 1891, the copies of Amvrosii's icon, on which Mary is depicted floating in the air above the field of ripe corn, spread beyond Kaluga province into Moscow, Odessa, and Viatka province.[117] To put an end to the unsanctioned use of the new icon, the bishop of Kaluga confiscated the "Multiplier of Crops" to the treasury of the cathedral in 1892, and the civil authorities confiscated the lithographic copies of the icon that had been produced earlier.[118]

Elder Amvrosii is often seen as a culmination of the Optina model of eldership and as a quintessential *starets* in Paisii Velichkovskii's succession. Amvrosii's example demonstrated that eldership had left the orbit of the "local" and entered the orbit of the "national." Amvrosii demonstrates that although Optina embodied the most evident example of routinization of charisma, it did not lose its "personal foundation and emotional faith."[119] Amvrosii was the third, after Leonid and Makarii, in the succession of spiritual elders of Optina, but he was also the most famous of all three. Amvrosii's death marked the decline of charismatic eldership in Optina. He did not designate a successor, and after his death Optina monastery was torn between rival parties.

Appropriation of Elders by Literary Elites

The literary elite were instrumental in the transition of eldership into a national symbol. Although the Slavophile authors had made Optina their spiritual home as early as the 1840s–1850s, it was in the 1870s and 1880s that a Russian elder became a recognizable character within Russian prose. During the 1860s–1880s the monastery unwittingly became a part of the cultural myth about the union between Russian literary culture and spirituality.[120] It is impossible for an educated Russian to enter a monastery today without the image of Gogol or Dostoevsky coming to mind. Surely, the popularity of the monastery among literary visitors was part of its charm; in the 1940s, Akhmatova mourned the end of this union with a lament: "But to Optina I will never come again."[121]

Literary visitors to the monastery often had the same aims as ordinary pilgrims. Dostoevsky came to Optina to mourn the death of his beloved son. The Tolstoys (whose estate was not very far from Optina) followed the habit of the local gentry, who visited local monasteries as a pastime. They visited friends of the family who lived in the monastery, local gentry, and the elders. Leo Tolstoy, who had little interest in confession and clairvoyance, was amused by his conversation with Amvrosii and made a note in a condescending tone in his diary: "Amvrosii deserves his rank; he is painfully religious. Poor thing."[122]

Writers were essential in the production of the image of the elder as a typical symbol of Russian spirituality and culture. The appropriation of eldership by literary elites suggests that charismatic spiritual guidance no longer belonged to some obscure ascetic tradition that only had relevance for monastic life. Dostoevsky was the first of the Optina literary visitors to choose a monastic elder as the protagonist of a novel: *The Brothers Karamazov* was published shortly after his visit to Optina in 1878, in the company of Vladimir Solov'ev. While the writer was certainly impressed by Elder Amvrosii, it would be an oversimplification to interpret *Starets* Zosima as a literary portrait of Amvrosii. The novel realistically described the location of the Optina skete adorned by autumn flowers (planted by the hand of poetic Elder Makarii), the scarce furnishings of Amvrosii's room, and his physical appearance.[123] Yet Amvrosii was not the only influence on Dostoevsky's protagonist. The literary influences on the novel included Orthodox sources such as the life of Tikhon of Zadonsk and a biography of Elder Leonid written by Klement (Zendergol'm), as well as Karamzin's sentimental novels and Hugo's *Les Misérables*.[124] Even though there were positive portrayals of parish priests and bishops in Russian literature (early Leskov, I. N. Potapenko, A. A. Izmailov, and A. P. Chekhov, among others),[125] Elder Zosima remains one of a few rare representations of monks in Russian literature.[126]

The bond between Elder Zosima and Alesha Karamazov had a key importance for the novel. Dostoevsky's novel illustrates the point made earlier that the relationship between elders and their disciples was constructed on the basis of the family model and was described as spiritual fatherhood (or motherhood). The deep emotional attachment that united Zosima and Alesha served as a contrast to Alesha's relationship with his own father, Fedor Karamazov, a depraved and degenerate aristocrat. In *Karamazov*, Dostoevsky pursued the theme of "fathers and sons" that found a reflection in his novels *A Raw Youth* (1875) and *The Possessed* (1871).[127]

Before and after Dostoevsky, the true Russian *starets* belonged to the people: he was either a folkloric fairy-tale hermit or a sectarian.[128] An elder from Saltykov-Shchedrin's short story *Starets* (c. 1860) is an Old Believer. Saltykov-Shchedrin's character describes himself thus: "I am an elder. I am called an elder, firstly, because I left the sinful vanity of the world for the desert, secondly, because I am more skilled than other Christians in interpreting the holy scripture."[129] The character of this story is based on the Old Believer prototypes that the writer met during his early career as a government servant in Viatka. Like Saltykov-Shchedrin, Tolstoy, too, searched for true eldership among the people. He reworked a medieval legend for his charming short story from the literary series intended for peasants. The story "Three Elders" is about three simple-hearted hermits living on an island in the White Sea. They have little knowledge of theology and church doctrine but pray to God, "Three of you, and three of us, have mercy on us." An Orthodox bishop, who happens to pass the island on a boat, disembarks onto the island and spends hours trying to teach the hermits the Lord's Prayer and the basics of catechism. When he boards his boat he sees the three *startsy* running toward him on the water saying that they have forgotten the words of the prayer the bishop had just taught them. Realizing that the men were saints, the bishop begs them to continue to pray in their own way and makes a deep bow to them.[130] The story suggests that an understanding of church doctrine was not necessary for salvation and saintliness. The elders from Tolstoy's story were "noble savages," the innocent children of God who had an innate sense of God's grace, which substituted for catechism and knowledge of scripture.

Leskov reworks another of Tolstoy's ideas in his fairy tale, "The Hour of God's Will," which shows a tendency toward aestheticization and folklorization of asceticism. The holy men, three brothers called Dubovik,

Polevik, and Vodovik, are sought by the reformist fairy-tale tsar Dobrokhot. One lives on the top of an oak tree, another is buried in earth up to his neck, and the third one lives in a swamp. The tsar, who wants impartial advice on good government, orders the three hermits to be brought to him in baskets. The language of the story imitates traditional fairy tales. The elders, like true hesychasts, either don't speak at all or reply in riddles. Finally, they magically disappear, making the reader wonder about their role in the story.

The elders imagined by these Russian writers lived in harmony with nature: they did not cultivate land and did not depend on civilization. They were at one with their environment: wild beasts did not harm them and the beauty of nature stimulated their religious inspiration.[131] This was a familiar trope not only in the medieval lives of saints and Desert Fathers but also in the philosophy of the Enlightenment (the idea of the noble savage). The literary representation of hermits and *startsy* reinforced the "nature versus culture" dichotomy, projecting onto elders the Enlightenment paradigms of the educated classes. The writers also imagined elders as bearers of authentic spirituality that was uncontaminated or was at odds with the teaching of the institutional church. Even Zosima, who is closest to the monastic ideal, is in conflict with his monastic surroundings.

In his search for true Christianity, Tolstoy paid visits to Optina. In some of these visits, he attempted to abandon all signs of his social distinction and merge with simple folk. In the spring of 1881 he came anonymously to Optina on foot accompanied by a village teacher and his secretary, Arbuzov. All three were dressed as peasants, wearing coarse bast shoes. The monks, who did not recognize the famous writer in disguise, sent him to the hostel for poor pilgrims, where he was tormented all night by bedbugs. The next day Tolstoy met a peasant woman in the monastery bookshop who complained that she could not afford to buy a pricey edition of the Gospel. Tolstoy paid one and a half rubles for the book and told the woman to read it and teach her children to read since "the Gospel brings comfort to our life." After this self-disclosure, Tolstoy was offered a better accommodation and he was invited to visit the Father Superior and Elder Amvrosii.[132] The monastery attracted the great Russian moralist because it allowed him to share the search for truth and holiness with the crowds of simple pilgrims. For Tolstoy, this crowd itself was the representation of the God-fearing people, the Russian *narod*. Although the writer respected the Optina monks' charitable activities, he dismissed the spiritual authority of the elders, who in his eyes were yet another, albeit better, example of the servants of the institutional church that distorted the true Gospel; he also did not like Dostoevsky's *Brothers Karamazov*. At the same time, he was aware of his own role as an elder to many Russians, including admiring readers, younger writers, and the followers of his own teaching, the Tolstoyans. Tolstoy's rejection of personal wealth, embracement of poverty, and, in his late years, denial of sexuality, all suggest that the ideals of monastic asceticism were not so alien to him after all.

The only Russian writer who actually embraced monasticism as a way of life was Konstantin Leont'ev, a former Russian consul in the Ottoman Empire, who lived many years in Athos and from 1886 made Optina his residence. A conservative thinker, one of the late Slavophiles, called by Simeon Frank "a Russian Nietzsche," Leont'ev had a two-story house built for him in Optina where he lived and secretly took monastic vows in 1891.[133] Both Athos and Optina embodied his religious-political ideals. These were the last bastions of Byzantinism that resisted the spirit of modernization, liberalism, and embourgeoisement.

Leont'ev's views on eldership were quite controversial; he condemned Dostoevsky's novel for its failure to convey the essence of Russian eldership. According to him, Zosima was a teacher of morality, not a mystic like the Athonite or Optina monks. Yet Leont'ev was also disappointed by Amvrosii, who was too folkloric for him, not well read, and had little time for intelligent conversation. In Optina, Leont'ev preferred to spend time with Father Klement (Zendergol'm), whose biography he completed in 1879. Yet even though Leont'ev shared similar intellectual tastes with Father Klement, he did not choose him as his spiritual father: Father Klement often gave bad advice and cared too much about his own reputation in the monastery. At the risk of shocking his Orthodox readers, Leont'ev compared the Russian elder to the Roman-Catholic "*directeur de conscience*."[134] According to him, eldership had always been a central element of Russian pastoral practice, but it suffered a decline in later centuries because people began to rely on themselves in spiritual matters, while the parish clergy were too oppressed by social deprivation to provide guidance. Nevertheless, the need for a spiritual advisor was deeply imbedded in the Russian soul. According to Leont'ev, Russians were not satisfied by a regular confession and did not trust their own consciences. In the most critical moments of life, Russians felt the need to confide in a person who was free from passions and worldly turbulences. Even though a *starets* was a mortal man who was subject to human passions and sins, he could provide precious advice once he was approached with faith and unconditional trust.[135] For Leont'ev, the difference between a monk and a layperson was quantitative, not qualitative.[136] *Starchestvo* was more useful to lay people than to monks because the latter had better conditions for their spiritual development, such as daily church services and hearing the word of

God.[137] Thus, for Leont'ev, the elder was not an awe-inspiring saint who was larger than life. He was simply a wiser and more experienced spiritual guide and confessor than other members of the clergy. Leont'ev's views, however, were not typical of other commentators on elders. Being provocative and controversial were important ingredients of his polemical style. In Vasilii Rozanov's view, Leont'ev unintentionally played the role of Father Ferapont in Russian literature and politics.[138] Ferapont was the antithesis of Zosima in *Brothers Karamazov*: a monk who had a reputation for his ascetic exploits and visions of demons everywhere and was an anathematization of Zosima's sermon of universal love.

Elders, for various reasons, fascinated a section of educated society. There were two main camps: one, which had affinity with the Slavophiles, associated elders with national and religious ideals. One spokesman of this camp summarized these ideals: "The Slavs need to break away from a dying, spent Europe and form an Orthodox pan-Slavic federation under the Russian tsar, with Russian as its lingua franca and Constantinople as its capital."[139] There was fragmentation and division among late Slavophile thinkers, many of whom were associated with Optina pustyn'.[140] Debates about Orthodoxy and nation, in Stanton's view, could be interpreted as the division between "heart" and "land."[141] The other camp, represented by non-Slavophile literati like Tolstoy, Leskov, and Saltykov-Shchedrin, also found elders appealing but tended to perceive them as men of the people and possessors of spontaneous spirituality, unspoiled by the doctrine and institutional structures of the church. To both camps, elders were representatives of a unique Russian religious tradition (with the notable exception of Leont'ev, who compared elders to Roman Catholic directors of conscience) and, therefore, an essential component of Russian national identity.

Eldership and the Popularization of Mystical Discourse

The opposition between spontaneous popular religiosity and institutionalized religion was characteristic not only of the Russian literati, but also of spiritual prose produced by members of the Orthodox Church. Eldership and mystical prayer were essential elements that allowed the emergence of a spiritual model that placed an uneducated peasant mystic in the center of the narrative and sent a clear message that holiness was not to be achieved through "piety by the Rule" (*ustavnoe blagochestie*). The publication in 1881, the year of Alexander II's assassination, of an anonymous text with the obscure title "A Sincere Tale Told by a Wanderer to his Spiritual Father . . . ," marked an important stage in the "nationalization" of eldership. The text (which later became known in the West as *The Way of a Pilgrim*) symbolized the meeting of two traditions of mystical Orthodoxy that existed in parallel universes: on the one hand, the tradition of contemplative prayer cultivated by the learned monks and, on the other, the spontaneous ascetic and mystical movement among the lower classes.

The story line of the text was intentionally simple: it was constructed as a first-person narrative by an anonymous wanderer (*strannik*), a crippled peasant from Orel who led a nomadic way of life in search of an explanation of the words of the Apostle Paul: "Pray without ceasing" (1 Thess 5, 17). On his quest, the wanderer met a number of people from all walks of life, including representatives of the Orthodox Church. But neither a parish priest, a bishop, an abbot of a major monastery, a pious squire, nor a learned preacher could satisfy the wanderer's quest. Eventually, he came across a holy elder, living in a hermitage, who instructed him in the Jesus prayer and provided him with a copy of the *Dobrotoliubie*. After the death of his elder, the wanderer (who by then had obtained the gift of incessant prayer) continued his pilgrimage, presenting a panorama of Russian life.

The wanderer symbolized the values of Old Russia which were resisting the "iron cage" of modernity. The wanderer traveled on foot or, occasionally, by coach, at a time when most of the Russian population had converted to travel by "iron road," which brought "the first massive intrusion of mechanical force into the timeless, vegetating world of rural Russia."[142] By ignoring or not being able to afford the comfort of rail travel, the wanderer continued the tradition of the Russian pilgrims, who preferred to walk to holy sites, avoiding other means of transportation.[143] The wanderer was unschooled: he learned from personal contacts with spiritual people who shared their wisdom with him.

The text was a fictionalized treatise on the Jesus prayer that aimed at the popularization of what had hitherto been regarded as essentially a monastic practice. The central character of the story, the poor peasant *strannik* in search of his spiritual ideal, was extremely appealing. The simple-heartedness of the protagonist, who in many ways incarnated the Gospel ideals of non-possession and itinerancy, made him one of the most popular characters of Russian spiritual prose. However, perhaps the main advantage of the text was that it managed to avoid the moralistic, sugary-sentimental, and overtly pious style that was typical for the bulk of Orthodox writings of the era. It did not patronize its reader. It presented a seemingly artless narrative of one person's spiritual journey which the reader could choose to follow or not. Punctuated with sparks of humor, the tale was entertaining and easy to read.

There are several diverse interpretations of the text. Some interpreters perceive it as a genuine autobiographical account by some unknown Russian mystic from the lower classes of society.[144] Boris Vysheslavtsev, a friend of Berdiaev and one of the editors of the religious philosophical almanac *The Way* (published in France during the 1920s–1940s), believed that the Wanderer from *The Way of a Pilgrim* was an expression of the Russian soul and Russian character. Wandering, according to him—despite a number of precedents in world literature—was a typical expression of Russian religious life characterized by disinterestedness in practical everyday matters, voluntary homelessness, union with nature, and cosmopolitanism.[145] This Russian émigré philosopher endowed the peasant protagonist of *The Way of a Pilgrim* with the features of the Russian intelligentsia, who after the revolution found themselves torn from their roots.

This view has been challenged by those literary critics who have noticed in the *The Way of a Pilgrim* the elements of masterfully constructed literary prose. The extensive use of the first person, imitation of oral speech, and other elements conformed to the narrative device called *skaz*, used by professional writers such as Leskov and Gogol.[146] These literary critics also have noticed the striking resemblance of the Russian text to the classic tale of pilgrimage by John Bunyan.[147] The Russian *strannik*, like the seventeenth-century Pilgrim, left his house with nothing but a copy of the Gospel. The allegorical types that Bunyan's Pilgrim meets on his way, Mr. Worldly Wiseman, Formalist and Hypocrisy, Piety and Prudence, are turned into realistic characters that inhabited the Russian spiritual and social landscape.

While the literary elements and influences of Western spiritual prose on *The Way of a Pilgrim* cannot be denied, the text needs to be evaluated within the religious context of post-Reform Russia. The recent discoveries of the manuscript version of the book in the papers of Archimandrite Mikhail Kozlov has led to the theory of Kozlov's authorship of the first four books of *The Way of a Pilgrim*.[148] An Old Believer convert to Orthodoxy, Mikhail Kozlov (born 1826) was initiated into ascetic life at Mount Athos and in the 1870s–1880s he used his knowledge of religious dissent to carry out missionary work among Old Believers in Kazan and Irkutsk provinces. Old Believer traditions of the Jesus prayer, on the one hand, and the familiarity of educated middle-class Old Believers with Western spiritual literature, on the other, all make Father Mikhail a very probable candidate for authorship of the book. His career as a missionary indicates a possible target group of readers—religious dissenters—with whom Kozlov proposed to engage not through the means of polemical theology and force, but by offering tales of spiritual conversion.

This vision of missionary work was shared by the first publisher of *The Way of a Pilgrim*, Abbot Paisii, who had a lot in common with the protagonist of Mikhail Kozlov's story. Paisii had been a former serf, named Petr Erin, who had married and been widowed, and finally had freed himself from serfdom and become a monk in Sarov monastery.[149] Like the wanderer from *The Way of a Pilgrim*, Petr actively traveled: to Kiev and Trinity-Sergius Lavra, Jerusalem, and Mount Athos. He also had a deep attachment to his spiritual father, a parish priest from Pavlovo, Avraamii Nikitin. Like Father Mikhail Kozlov, Paisii was involved in missionary work. In 1872, he received an appointment as abbot of the Mikhail-Arkhangel'skii Cheremiskii monastery in Kazan diocese, which was founded as a result of the ascetic movement among the Mari peasants in the 1850s. These indigenous ascetics lived a life of prayer, imitating the ascetic deeds of the Byzantine saints, about whom they had learned from the Russian *Menaion*.[150] Despite conflicts with the police, this indigenous ascetic movement received encouragement from the Russian ecclesiastical authorities, who helped to establish the Mikhail-Arkhangel'skii Cheremiskii monastery in 1868. Predictably, the Russian authorities aimed to use the monastery as part of its civilizing mission among the non-Russian population. The appointment of the Russian monk as abbot was surely a sign of this intention. The publication of *The Way of a Pilgrim*, which eventually gained huge readership and, probably, commercial success, was partly a result of Paisii's own background as a peasant in search of his spiritual ideal and that of the simple Mari people, who also became part of the ascetic model that the book promoted.

Like Bunyan's Pilgrim, the story about the Russian pilgrim enjoyed popular success. Between 1881 and 1894, there were four editions of the original text under various titles, to which different editors like Abbot Paisii and Bishop Feofan the Recluse contributed.[151] Amvrosii of Optina highly valued the book. Bishop Veneamin (Blagonravov) of Irkutsk believed that everyone, but especially monks, should read *The Way of a Pilgrim*.[152] In 1911 three additional "tales" of the wanderer were included in the new edition of the text published (and possibly authored) by Bishop Nikon (Rozhdestvenskii), the former superior of Trinity-Sergius Lavra.[153]

The text is a subtle but powerful critique of the Synodal theology of prayer, which was infused by scholasticism and a moralist stance.[154] The teaching of the *Dobrotoliubie* on the Jesus prayer was proposed as an antidote to the dominant spirituality of the Orthodox Church. In the end, the wanderer obtained grace not through catechism, sermons, and sacraments, but through personal asceticism, practicing mystical prayer, and reading of the Bible and the Philokalic Fathers. The only person the wanderer shared his spiritual experiences with was an anonymous "spiritual father," who could have been a simple monk or a parish priest. The message of the text was quite subversive: one could reach spiritual enlightenment outside of organized religion. In the past, this is exactly what the Synodal church had found disturbing and threatening in the practices of popular and even monastic eldership. Was it not a paradox that leading figures in the Church, such as bishops and leaders of monastic compounds, were involved in the making and publicizing of this provocative text?

The text could only have been published in the period following the Great Reforms that led to the relaxation of censorship laws. Its publication was also a response to the failure of the official church to carry out its social mission. The moderation of policies directed against religious dissenters also meant that the Church had to find methods other than the use of force to deal with Old Believers.[155] The fact that two persons involved in the creation of the text, Abbot Paisii and Archimandrite Mikhail, were involved in missionary work suggests that the text was aimed at raising the profile of mainstream Orthodox spirituality among new converts and dissenters. People learned the Jesus prayer from the book.[156] By rejecting the dominant forms of theological writing, such as polemical treatise or sermon, and placing a peasant mystic into the center of the narrative, *The Way of a Pilgrim* targeted a wider audience. The popularity of *Troitskie listki* (a cheap periodical published by Trinity-Sergius monastery aimed at a popular readership), for example, where the extended version of the tale was published in 1911, suggests that the story had a broad reach.[157]

HISTORIANS HAVE ARGUED that far from being the bulwark of conservatism, reaction, and resistance to social change, the Russian Orthodox Church actively engaged in various ways with social change and adapted to modernity. The forms of adaptation and social engagement included the emphasis on charity and social service.[158] Although the apophatic, mystical tradition of Orthodoxy, usually embodied in monastic spirituality, continues to be seen as reactionary and obscurantist, there are arguments that challenge this view.[159] Robert Nichols has interpreted the spiritual revival of the nineteenth century as a creative exchange between the Eastern and Western spiritual traditions, and has seen in elders a kind of spiritual intelligentsia that engaged in their own variant of social mission.[160] Laura Engelstein, on the other hand, has drawn attention to the resourceful reimagining of the Eastern hesychast tradition in the modern age that was neither a reaction to nor a defense of the timeless religious legacy in the face of modernity, but a kind of "cultural project" similar to those carried out by the religious elites in the West.[161]

In the second half of the nineteenth century, eldership transcended its earlier stage, when it had been mainly a localized, persecuted, and marginal phenomenon. Monasteries, in general, and elders, in particular, compensated for the shortcomings of pastoral care in rural areas. Pilgrimage, facilitated by the development of roads and transport, brought people closer to the centers of eldership at Mount Athos, Optina, Glinskaia, Trinity-Sergius Lavra, and to other less prominent monasteries. The popularization of elders through hagiographies and novels was another new development in post-Emancipation Russia. Social and economic changes also led to an increased social demand on elders; this breakdown of the institutions and rules that guided individuals' lives could account for the growth of elders' popularity.

But despite the elevation of eldership by religious and secular writers, the social impact of elders remained limited. Monks and nuns made up only a tiny proportion of the Orthodox population of the Empire (about 0.07 percent).[162] Elders were only present in a relatively small section of Russian monasticism, and could not provide guidance for all those who sought their help. The assimilation of eldership into the official church was problematic. Although in the post-Emancipation period the official church tended to hijack the popularity of elders for its own credit, the tensions between elders, on the one hand, and abbots and bishops, on the other, were not a thing of the past. The Synod confiscated the icons that were ordered by elders and admonished elders when they tried to use a portion of the income that they brought to the monastery for supporting weaker monastic communities. Moreover, in their eagerness to provide an official framework for eldership in cenobitic monasticism, the church authorities obliterated the elements of freedom, charisma, and mysticism that were characteristic of elders. If elders embodied the most buoyant spiritual segment of the Russian Orthodox Church in this period, their impact on the Church as a whole was ultimately limited.

CHAPTER FIVE

Appropriating the Elders

Elders and Political Crisis in Late Imperial Russia, 1890s–1917

Although the age of Modernism in Europe has been identified with secularization and dechristianization, religion continued to have a hold on people. It might have been true that politically, Western religion was "in full retreat" by the 1900s, partly as a consequence of urbanization,[1] yet it was too early to proclaim the "death of God," certainly from the point of view of many ordinary believers. The social, economic, political, and ideological transformations of the age had their impact upon the established church, such as the crisis in recruitment of men, anticlericalism, and the secularization of the church's privileges and estates, but such institutional depredations cannot be equated with a popular loss of faith. The increase in the number of pilgrimages and apparitions of the Virgin Mary, the emergence of new spiritual movements and teachings such as theosophical societies, and the expansion of nonestablished communities of faith suggested the vitality of the religious worldview.[2] The carnage of the First World War was accompanied by the revival of piety both at the front and in the rear.[3] Although church attendance might have plummeted during the war, religious images were a popular trope for those who were physically affected by the conflict, such as wounded soldiers, refugees, and widows and orphans. Many soldiers also claimed to have witnessed apparitions of Christ, Mary, and angels on the battlefields.[4]

Historians have conventionally used the word crisis to describe the position of the Russian Orthodox Church in fin-de-siècle Russia, recounting the internal divisions among the clergy, the growing criticism of the system of ecclesiastical administration implemented by Peter I, and cracks in the union between church and throne.[5] The upper echelons of the Church dissociated themselves from the crown as a response to the interference of the autocrat into ecclesiastical affairs. The bishops complained about the "unprecedented picture of decline and decomposition" in the tsar's court and corruption in the top levels of power during the last years of the ancién regime.[6] A section of the clergy believed that the only way to strengthen the institutional fabric and moral ground of Orthodoxy was through reform and liberation from what Minister Witte called the "policing church" model, cultivated by Pobedonostsev.[7] There were different visions of reform: while the majority of clerics advocated more autonomy for the clergy in matters of church administration, including the abolition of the hateful Synod, a minority of the liberal clergy campaigned for internal reform that would restructure ecclesiastical organization according to the principle of *sobornost'*, so that it allowed greater participation by the laity.[8] The liberal current within the church attracted the support of the intelligentsia, who initiated a dialogue with theologians through the "religious-philosophical meetings" that took place in St. Petersburg with the blessing of Metropolitan Antonii (Vadkovskii).[9] The religious searchings of the educated classes, who were "fascinated by color, sound, and mystical intuitions which had been lost on the previous generations," were not strictly bound to conventional Orthodoxy. [10] The religious-philosophical meetings—limited in scale and impact—revealed a huge gap between the ways of thinking of the clergy, on the one hand, and that of the artists and philosophers, on the other.

Despite the hectic, while not altogether unsuccessful, attempts by Orthodox clergymen to expand their social base by organizing brotherhoods, teetotalers' societies, public lectures, and charitable activities, the Church's position on the ground was growing weaker. Like elsewhere in Europe, the forces of anti-clericalism and secularism, coming from various political and cultural directions, gained support among educated society and a section of city workers.[11] The growth of sectarianism among the lower classes accelerated after the publication of the Manifesto on Religious Toleration in 1905, and the rise of esoteric doctrines and practices among the upper classes and intelligentsia meant that the Church had to deal not only with materialist and secularist tendencies, but also with the growing pluralism of spiritual experience and religious authority.[12] Prior to 1905, the main struggles of the Church were against rival religious confessions, religious dissent, and sectarianism, even to the neglect of the growing revolutionary tendencies among urban workers.[13]

One sign of the continued vitality of religion in society was the growth of monasteries and female communities between the 1880s and early 1900s: the total number of monks, nuns and novices was 58,283 in 1900 and 94,629 in 1914.[14] However, monasticism too experienced a crisis of identity: in the early 1900s monks, clergy, and the public actively debated the role of monasteries in Russian life. In 1901, Nicholas II ordered a full-scale investigation into disorders and crimes within monasteries.[15] The Synodal conclusion (drawing upon diocesan reports) was a pessimistic one: while noting the positive developments in monastic life, the Synod nevertheless complained about the decline of true monasticism; it criticized monks for idleness and a lack of interest in spiritual literature, and it bemoaned disorder in the economic sphere and the monasteries' lack of influence on the surrounding population.[16]

A dualistic attitude characterized public discourse about monasticism at the turn of the century. In their search for stability and roots, some members of educated society, including aristocrats, turned to the Orthodox Church and sought in the Russian *narod* the bearer of moral and spiritual values. For example, Sergei Bulgakov believed that monasteries traditionally represented the lighthouses where, through the centuries, people thronged in search of moral support and instruction.[17] Even so, in the opinion of the anticlerical intelligentsia, monasticism belonged to the corrupt establishment, while its holy men exhibited Pharisee-like pride.[18] The debates about the future of monasticism in the early 1900s revealed two polar positions: the reformist critics blamed the ascetics for their failure to engage with social service and for ignoring the commandment of Christ to "love thy neighbor"; the defenders of monasticism, most prominent among them the abbot of Trinity-Sergius Lavra and Bishop Nikon (Rozhdestvenskii), argued that without withdrawal from the world a monk would not be able to serve the world and contribute to its spiritual renewal. [19]

The situation of crisis and the challenge of modernization within the Russian Church highlighted the ambiguity of the elders' position in this period. On the one hand, in the eyes of the authorities, *startsy* served as the agents of monastic reform and the bulwark against the "external" attacks on the Church by "heretics" and revolutionaries. On the other hand, in the atmosphere of the pluralization of religious experience and the weakening of the church hierarchy, charismatic elders posed a danger and had to be disciplined and kept in check by the authorities. An important development of the period was the appropriation of the charisma of the Orthodox elders by the laity, including the aristocracy and illiterate peasants.

Monastic Elders
Changes and Continuity

In the late Imperial period, monastic *starchestvo* continued to progress from being a marginal and suspicious practice to a widely accepted and superior form of monastic profession (even more respectable than the position of the abbot). However, the disputes about monasticism in late Imperial Russia revealed that the status of elders in monasteries was subject to different, sometimes contradictory, interpretations. The debate primarily focused on the social roles of monasticism and its relevance to modern society. For the conservatives, monasticism was the bulwark against secularization, while for the liberal section of the Orthodox Church, monasticism had to be reinvented in order to respond to changing social demands.

While for some critics, elders were an integral part of Orthodox Christian monasticism, for others, they represented only a specific form of contemplative monasticism. The latter view was expressed in a polemical article about monasticism that appeared in the journal *The Monastery*, published in 1909. Author N. Faminskii advocated the professionalization of the Russian monasteries. He argued that in addition to "missionary monasteries"—brotherhoods of learned monks and female monastics that would provide society with nurses, teachers, and deaconesses—there should be ascetic monasteries where *starchestvo* was cultivated.[20]

The Monastic Council that first convened in 1909 demonstrated that eldership was perceived by many as the means to reform Russian monasticism. It was the first attempt to bring together monks, abbots, and bishops with the aim of creating a "brotherly union of mutual spiritual aid"—that is, a form of cooperation among the monasteries that provided an exchange of spiritual experience. The council was not inclusive and democratic: only senior monks, bishops, and abbots had the right to vote. Nuns and religious women, who numerically dominated Russian monasticism, were excluded from participation, although they were allowed to submit their proposals for consideration. The council believed that a primary function of eldership should be the education of monks, and imposed the task of cultivating eldership on the abbots, senior monks, and bishops.[21] The delegates lamented the scarcity of monks with adequate experience, an aura of piety, and sufficient spiritual gravitas to take up such role. As a whole, the members of the council interpreted eldership as a primarily monastic institution, placing it within the monastic hierarchy (the elder would be third in line after the abbot and a treasurer), although pointing out that an elder should be free from administrative responsibilities, acting only as an advisor to the abbot.[22] Thus, the council regarded elders as essentially spiritual leaders, pastors, and educators, who had no interest and involvement in the administration of the monastery. This view did not reflect the reality.

The Synod acted upon the recommendation of the council to introduce eldership into every Russian monastery. In 1910 it issued a circular that suggested that every monastery send selected monks, who were known for a strict ascetic life and good spiritual disposition, to Optina or Glinskaia pustyn' for practical training in the art of *starchestvo*. The Glinskaia elders were responsible for the dissemination of the practice of eldership in the monasteries of Kursk diocese. In 1910 and 1911, the Bishop of Kursk reported to the Synod that with the aid of Glinskaia monks, "the spiritual institution" of eldership has been introduced in other monasteries of the diocese, such as Korennaia, Belogorskaia and Sofronieva pustyn'.[23] During 1911 the abbots from Moscow, Kharkov, St. Petersburg, Kiev, Vladimir, and Mogilev dioceses (including such ancient monastic centers as the Kievo-Pecherskii monastery and Florishcheva pustyn') contacted the Optina monastery with a request to send their monks to observe the organization of *starchestvo*. The Optina monks were so overwhelmed with requests that they had to petition the Kaluga bishop to limit the visits to two monks at a time for a duration not exceeding one month. The legislation suggests, on the one hand, that the Synod had a very limited view of *starchestvo*, seeing it primarily as an instrument of monastic discipline; on the other hand, *starchestvo* ceased to be a marginal and disrespected phenomenon in the Russian monastic environment and received promotion from the church authorities. It is also clear that the attempt to introduce *starchestvo* "from above" could not achieve its goal, not only due to the limited definition of eldership, but also due to the lack of experienced monks who could fill that role. For example, in Kursk diocese *starchestvo* was "introduced" to three other monasteries apart from Glinskaia, all of which had already had historical roots of eldership. In the rest of the monasteries, however, it did not thrive.[24]

In those monasteries where eldership flourished, the social profile and outlook of elders was changing. There were more elders coming from the peasantry and lower urban orders who were, as a rule, more open to the world. They introduced new farming techniques, responded to popular demands, and became involved in local politics. An elder no longer had to be a celibate monk. The popular elder Aleksei (Solov'ev) of Zosimova pustyn' (1846–1928) was a widowed parish priest, who became a monk only at the age of 52. There were also other elders among parish priests, the most well-known being the Moscow preacher Valentin Amfiteatrov (1836–1908) and the priest Aleksei Mechev (1859–1924). The combination of ascetic theology and pastoral experience among parish priests at the turn of the century owes much to the phenomenon of Father John of Kronstadt, who according to Zinaida Gippius was linked with the holy men and elders of Russia by some invisible thread.[25] Liturgy and Eucharist were the main means through which John of Kronstadt provided believers with "spiritual nourishment" (*okormlenie*). Although Father John's relationship with nuns was very similar to the one that existed among elders and their female spiritual daughters, he cannot be regarded as a spiritual director in the style of Optina elders: surrounded by agitated crowds, he hardly had time for one-to-one confession and conversation.

Despite the insistence of the Synod and monastic authorities on the strict separation of the spiritual, administrative, and financial functions in the monastery, it was not unusual for elders to act as abbots and treasurers. German (Gomzin) of Zosimova pustyn', Agafangel (Amosov) of Aleksandr-Svirskii monastery, and Gavriil (Zyrianov) of Sedmiozernaia pustyn' in Kazan had to shoulder administrative burdens in addition to their duties as confessors and spiritual fathers. In fact, it was impossible to separate the spiritual from the material in the activities of the elders. The role of the elders as spiritual instructors of novices required the provision of conditions that would promote the ideal of contemplative life. Spiritual reformation could not be carried out without a reorganization of monastic life that involved the rearrangement of space (building of new churches, dormitories), provision of subsistence for cenobitic monks, and a reform of internal order. Abbot German actively safeguarded the brethren of Zosimova pustyn' from contacts with the outside world: he purchased the land around the monastery to prevent the building of dachas, diverted the road to the railway station in order to stop traffic in the vicinity of the monastery, and carried out extensive building activities that allowed every monk to have a separate room—a rare achievement in Russian monasteries.[26] Agafangel (Amosov), a disciple of the Valaam elders and a correspondent of Feofan the Recluse, enthusiastically fulfilled the task dispatched by the St. Petersburg consistory of reforming the dwindling Aleksandr-Svirskii monastery, the traditional citadel of Orthodoxy in dissent-ridden Olonets province. By 1891 the monastery had just 15 monks of poor reputation, who were compared by the Valaam monk Agapii to "rotten logs" that could not be used to build a decent house. Agafangel poured his energy into reforming liturgical life, which aimed to bring prayer back into the center of monastic routine. He changed the singing style of the monks from Italian Baroque to old Russian chant, he ensured that every member of the community was assigned to an elder, and he eventually introduced the cenobitic rule in the formerly idiorrythmic community. As a result, the monastery acquired a couple of new churches, hostels, a brick factory, and church schools, and became a magnet for novices, pilgrims, and donors.[27]

Elders and Monastic Life: Spirituality

In 1909 Ivan Kalinin, a novice in one of the Russian monasteries, contended that the biggest problem of the monastic life in Russia was the lack of spiritual guidance for novices.[28] The same concerns were expressed by a hieromonk of Solovetskii monastery, Paisii, during the monastic council in the same year. He argued that novices in Solovki had no access to *startsy* until they took monastic vows, which sometimes only happened after 10 to 20 years in the monastery; by that time it was too late to develop the bond between a *starets* and a monk.[29] The experience of elders in those few monasteries where eldership was established suggests that instruction of novices was the elders' primary responsibility. As a rule, every novice in Optina, Glinskaia, Zosimova, and Valaam monastery could count on advice from his elder in his preparation for monastic life. The nineteen-year-old Nikon (Nikolai Beliaev) was as eager to learn from the knowledge and experience of his elder Varsonofii (Plikhankov) as the latter was willing to share it. Nikon recorded daily his conversations with his *batiushka* ("little father") in his diary. Sometimes the novice spent days and nights in the cell of his elder, and he confessed his "thoughts" daily.[30] Elders passed to neophytes the art of the ascetic struggle with the passions and the Jesus prayer. Their aim was the cultivation of "inner monasticism" (*vnutrennee monashestvo*) with its focus on the development of the spirit. This was preceded by "outer monasticism," which consisted of judiciously recommended ascetic exercises (*podvig*), church attendance, and sobriety of the mind.[31] The methods of education varied: there was a regular "disclosure of thoughts" (also possible in written form), spiritual conversations, advice on reading, and personal example.[32] Although the goal of daily confession was to accelerate the progress of a novice, not all brethren were enthusiastic about this rule.[33]

Confession to elders was a practice distinct from sacramental confession; it required "charisma rather than authority."[34] Some elders replaced or complemented the auricular confession by public confession, an ancient practice made popular by Father John of Kronstadt. In the Iversko-Alekseevskaia community on the Black Sea, for example, the non-ordained spiritual elder Sofronii (Shevtsov) used to read a list of sins from his notebook, to which all those present could reply aloud "I have sinned." Then the penitents could perform their auricular confession individually, if they had anything else to add, followed by the prayer of absolution.[35] In the age of the decline of public penance, the attempt by popular spiritual leaders to revive what was believed to be a medieval penitential practice had an antimodernist propensity.[36] These practices carried out by elders, such as "disclosure of thoughts" and public penance, coexisted uneasily with the standard auricular confession and attracted the suspicion of church authorities.

The primary virtue of a novice was obedience (*poslushanie*), understood as an inner disposition to follow the will of an elder without questioning and criticism. Elder Nektarii criticized those novices who carried out the orders of their superiors but failed to develop the inner virtue of obedience, because of their anger and critical attitude.[37] Some elders were very strict, almost ruthless, in trying to root out self-will and pride in their spiritual children; others were gentle and careful to avoid rebellion.[38] In the monasteries and convents with a high prevalence of peasants, obedience to the elder monks or nuns was not dissimilar to the authority structures in patriarchal peasant families. The Synod and bishops demanded obedience from the black and white clergy and insisted that the clergy preach social conformity to their flock. Liberal and socialist critics challenged Church teaching on obedience and claimed that it was the ideology of slavery. Nevertheless, the spiritual virtue of obedience to the elder's will could neither be molded into the Synodal hierarchical and conservative ideal, nor adequately described by the intelligentsia critique. The spiritual ideology of elders that valorized obedience proved ultimately subversive to the established church.

Elders and the Laity
The Ways and Means of Moral Influence

Pilgrimage, a traditional form of interaction between the world of ascetic monasticism and lay piety, flourished in late Imperial Russia.[39] Even though statistical evidence cannot characterize adequately the extent of the elders' influence on the laity, it can at least give us an awareness of the massive number of pilgrims passing through the elders' reception rooms. In 1904,

5.1. Elders of Valaam.
Source: Rossiiskii gosudarstvennyi arkhiv kinofotodokumentov. Courtesy of the Russian Archives of Documentary Films and Photographs

monastery confessors in Solovki received 2,461 lay penitents.[40] This number did fall sharply the following year, but this is probably an effect of the Manifesto on Religious Toleration, which relaxed the rules on compulsory observance of the sacraments.[41] Even though confession was a duty, some men and women were attracted by the opportunity to confess to an experienced elder because they believed in the monk's spiritual insight. They were also attracted by the informal atmosphere of confession to the elders, which often took place outside of the public spaces of the church, in elders' private quarters, or specially designated reception rooms (called *khibarka* in Optina).[42] The widespread practice of confession outside the Church caused the Holy Synod to issue a warning in 1910 against this custom.[43]

Despite the Synodal regulations, the relationship between lay visitors and monks was relatively unconstrained. The pilgrims could stay in the monastery as long as they wished, or as long as they could afford. They were more or less free in their choice of a confessor, often visiting different monks before choosing the one they most liked. Contemporaries testified that elders had a gift of being able to draw people in by their personal warmth, knowledge of the human heart, and unfailing love to all those who sought their advice.[44] The elders made themselves available physically (keeping the doors of their cells open) and spiritually for anyone who needed them.[45] L. I. Veselitskaia (Mikulich), a popular writer at the turn of the century (and a friend of N. Leskov), came to Optina in the early twentieth century in search of an ideal confessor. She scrutinized her own motives, asking "Why do I want, like most women, to find the most worthy and faultless confessor so that he will hear all the impure things I have to tell him?"[46] Having come to Optina with a clearly defined purpose—to seek advice on how to settle a family conflict—she found Elder Anatolii very responsive to her needs. She tried to remember the elder's every word and felt an immediate relief of anxiety and distress about her family difficulties.[47]

In late Imperial Russia, institutionalized theology was no longer sharply separated from monastic spiritual life. Students of theological academies sought spiritual guidance from monastic confessors—simple monks who often lacked theological education (or any education for that matter). The learned professors and students at Kazan Theological Academy valued the spiritual authority of Gavriil (Zyrianov), a son of Siberian peasants, who had produced no theological treatises apart from a small collection of devotional homilies. The Moscow theology students, too, highly esteemed the authority of ordinary monks. Sergei Volkov, a student in the Moscow Theological Academy in the later prerevolutionary years, remembered Father Ippolit, who as a confessor successfully solved the moral problems that the young man shared with him: "Only then [after the confession] I realized that, apart from the approach of academic theology [to spiritual problems], there was another way—psychological (*dushevnyi*) and spiritual—incomparably higher than the former."[48]

Pilgrims who established personal links with monastic confessors could keep in touch with them through correspondence. The rise of literacy in late Imperial Russia allowed lower-class men and women to use letters as the means of maintaining spiritual unity with their guides. The massive correspondence of Optina elders provides a good illustration. The correspondents of Elder Nektarii—petty shopkeepers, servants, workers—had a poor mastery of grammar and style. Nektarii, who was known for his clairvoyance and *iurodstvo*, kept all letters addressed to him and prayed for their authors.

As in the earlier period, the laity also sought elders' advice for various needs in which spiritual concerns were not prevalent. The lay people asked monks to give advice on marriage, the choice of monastic life, whether or not to have surgery, and requested that they pray for health and success in business and exams. As in medieval times, people continued to believe that a blessing from a holy elder, who had renounced the world, would bring success to their worldly activities. One man asked an elder's blessing for his financial affairs, another wanted to construct turbine engines in his mill, while a married couple appealed for the elder's "fatherly advice" on how to build an extension to their house.[49] The majority of letters, especially by female correspondents, tell a story of material hardship. Many of Nektarii's spiritual daughters, either unmarried, widowed, or married to unreliable husbands, had to rely on their own efforts in life.[50] Perhaps they hoped to summon divine assistance through the intercession of the holy man. The First World War brought a new set of concerns: many lay men and women asked for elders' prayers to help them or their relatives avoid military conscription or death on the field of battle.[51]

Spiritual Families

Mariia Kisteneva, a teenage girl, began her letter to Father Nektarii of Optina in August of 1915 thus: "Dear *batiushka* [Little Father]. I am kissing your little hands and feet and asking for your prayers and your blessing." There was nothing unusual in this form of address. Many people developed strong emotional links with their spiritual directors. It was spiritual kinship that defined the relationship between the guide and the guided.[52]

Elders and their numerous spiritual children formed a new social structure, *communitas*—a social relationship emerging in the liminal or transitional situation of movement from structured and hierarchic relations to the antistructural center.[53] The relationship between the members of an elder's spiritual family was fluid and spontaneous, and marked by the spirit of fraternity and comradeship. The individuals in these groups related to each other independent of social status, rank, and distinction.

The relationships between the members of this fellowship were based upon an ethos of Christian love, equality, and mutual support. Elders could serve as mediators among their spiritual children, encouraging charity and brotherly love. Bishop Veneamin (Fedchenkov), during his time as a student of the Moscow Theological Academy, saved money to help his spiritual father Isidor of Gethsemane to go on pilgrimage to Sarov. He was surprised one day to receive a letter from an unknown invalid from Kursk begging for help. Elder Isidor, to whom the letter had been addressed, scribbled a quotation from Psalms on it. During Veneamin's next visit Isidor explained the puzzle: he proposed that the student use the money which he had put aside for pilgrimage to help the cripple from Kursk, who had lost his arm during a factory accident. This was the beginning of the relationship between the invalid and the theology student, who was often driven to despair because of his protégé's difficult character.[54] Although the relations between numerous spiritual siblings were not free from jealousy and rivalry, many of them built strong bonds, which in time of crisis allowed them to survive, both physically and spiritually. It should be noted that some letter writers were unable to visit their spiritual advisors. Therefore, their position in the spiritual family was defined more by the vertical links to their spiritual father, than by the horizontal ones that connected them to other members of the spiritual family.

The revival of spiritual families in late Imperial Russia, which in some sense replicated the medieval institution of the penitential family (*pokaial'naia sem'ia*), came about as the result of many factors. This revival could be seen as a response to the crisis of the institution of the parish in late Imperial Russia and the increased social mobility of the population.[55] Following the emancipation of the serfs and large-scale urbanization and industrialization in the 1880s–1890s, significant numbers of men and—to a lesser extent—women changed their places of residence.[56] Migrants found it difficult to integrate into the urban parishes, which were "so territorially amorphous, so socially heterogeneous, and so numerically overpopulated" that the personal bonds between a pastor and his flock that were enjoyed in the countryside were impossible to achieve.[57] Few letters exist that can be identified as originating from migrants: these are the letters from servants, workers, and clerks who expressed their sense of insecurity and hardship in the city.[58] Some spiritual children who were newcomers to the metropolis were not necessarily from the countryside, but from small towns in provincial Russia.

Thus *starchestvo* was not possible without a network of quasi-familial relationships that produced a flexible structure outside of any institutional framework. The community of spiritual fellowship that formed around an elder was representative of a relationship that provided emotional and social support for those who felt uprooted and confused, alienated and betrayed. These "spiritual families" were even more important during a period of social, economic, and political change, when traditional structures of the family, the rural community, and the parish were breaking down.

Tensions between the Elders and the Church Hierarchs

The recognition of the special place of elders in monasticism by the Synod and by the monastic council in 1909 did not put an end to the tensions between the institutional and charismatic authorities of the Russian Church. These tensions primarily took two forms: conflict over financial management and problems of spiritual discipline. In 1909, the monastic council made it clear that the role of an elder should be limited to spiritual affairs only. This view did not take into account the challenges that elders faced and the commitments they had to make. Spiritual elders who combined spiritual authority with administrative skills were able to turn mediocre and impoverished monasteries into prosperous monastic enterprises. However, the success of elders as administrators could also attract envy and malice. Favoritism, petty power struggles, bribery, denunciations, cavils, and vanity—typical features of provincial church life—poisoned the lives of elders and often brought them into conflict with the itinerant church hierarchs who sometimes sought to strengthen their own short-term leadership by weakening that of a successful monastic administrator.

The son of a Siberian peasant and a spiritual disciple of Amvrosii of Optina, Gavriil (Zyrianov), agreed to become the abbot of Sed'miozernaia pustyn' in Kazan diocese only after the persistent requests of Bishop Arsenii (Briantsev). He had to manage the community (which had 100 novices), the annual income of thirty-three thousand roubles, and substantial property. Despite his evident economic abilities, Gavriil suffered under the burden of administration and begged the bishop to release him from it. The bishop declined his request and rewarded Gavriil with an honorary mitre.[59] During his tenure as abbot, Gavriil built a new church, renovated monastic buildings, and organized an apiary, milk and butter production, a brick factory, and a grain dryer. Some of these innovations received much appreciation from the local gentry, who copied the model of Gavriil's grain dryer in their estates. Largely due to the efforts of the elder, the monastery was officially recognized as one of the best in the diocese. In 1908, Gavriil's competence as administrator was challenged by the merchant Polivanov from Kazan, who accused the elder of mismanagement and political unreliability. The new bishop, Nikanor (Kamenskii), acting on Polivanov's denunciation, hastily organized an inspection of the monastery and found some evidence of mismanagement, even though he failed to prove that Gavriil was a member of the Social-Democratic Party. The inspectors appointed by the bishop were faced with a difficult case. On the one hand, they praised the rationalization of the monastery's economy and the sophisticated agricultural machinery introduced by the abbot. On the other hand, they expressed persnickety criticism about a few faults: the paperwork was not up to scratch; the monastery had a debt of about 10,000 rubles; the monastic hostel was occupied by lodgers and not by pilgrims. In fact, some rooms in the hostel were occupied by *zemstvo* doctors, a midwife, and a nurse, thus helping to provide the local peasants with medical support.[60] The debt was not an extraordinary one. Every summer, the monastery collected donations during a procession with the wonderworking icon of Smolensk-Sed'miozernaia Mother of God in nearby villages. The collected sum was sufficient to cover all outstanding annual debts.[61]

The methods of inquiry and the manner with which the new abbot treated the well-respected elder, expelling the latter from his lodgings and expropriating his personal belongings, suggested that the inquest aimed at a change of leadership in the monastery. The spiritual consistory turned down Gavriil's request to retire to a farm three miles away from the monastery where his spiritual children, the Barkov family, would look after him. Instead, the authorities sent the elder to Pskov diocese, where he was banned for life from any involvement in economic matters.

Similar accusations of financial mismanagement affected other high-profile elders. In 1909, the council of the Trinity-Sergius monastery replaced the abbot of Zosimova hermitage, which was under its administrative jurisdiction.[62] The treasurer, Iona, complained to the council that Abbot German kept a secret account, sponsored some expensive building works, and incorrectly recorded monastic income. Following a brief investigation, the council replaced German with Iona, and appointed the former as abbot of the unpopular Stefano-Makhrishchskii monastery, which was, for all intents and purposes, tantamount to Siberian exile.[63] The Zosimova hermitage was prosperous and had a high reputation among Moscow intelligentsia, as well as enjoying the favors of Grand Duchess Elizabeth (who visited the monastery accompanied by the sisters of her Marfo-Mariinskii convent). This exceptional status was difficult to maintain as a satellite monastery of the Trinity-Sergius Lavra. In addition to the ambitions of the treasurer Iona, who temporarily replaced German, the Trinity-Sergius leadership was concerned about the excess of power concentrated in the hands of the Zosimova abbot and suspected that the financial affairs of the hermitage were not in their control.[64] Similarly, in 1912 the bishop of Kursk accused the abbot of Glinskaia pustyn' of financial incompetence and expelled him from the monastery.

In all these cases, it is striking that the authorities conducting the evaluation of the monastery focused entirely on the economic aspect. The achievements of monastic leaders were measured only in material terms: the number of cattle, amount of income, and the management of the agriculture and economy of the community. The Synod criticized abbots for their faults in management and gave them no credit for their spiritual and educational skills, which benefited a large number of clergy and laity. German's case was an exception: the inspectors admitted that he had the reputation of an experienced spiritual guide and therefore felt compelled to remove him without publicity.[65]

The attempts of the Synod and bishops to further centralize and control monastic life also affected informal spiritual leaders who guided female communities, which were integrated into the Synodal system through being granted the status of convents. In 1913, the vulnerability of spiritual elders and the signs of crisis in the late imperial church were further exposed by the affair of the Iveron-Alekseevskaia community in Ekaterinodar province. The community was founded in 1904 by a *meshchanka* (petty trader), Mavra Makarovskaia, and Elder Sofronii (Shevtsov). It received its official status in 1910, by which time it had 53 sisters, 8 to 10 novices, and assets estimated at 103,000 rubles. Makarovskaia was tonsured under the name of Mariam and became the abbess. The elder Sofronii, a spiritual father to the members of the community, lived in a small house (*pustyn'ka*) near the convent. Sofronii, a *meshchanin* from Ekaterinodar, was renowned for his asceticism and his experience in Optina pustyn' and Athos. Despite the number of years he spent in the monasteries, Sofronii did not take vows, and became the informal spiritual leader for a group of men and women in Tuapse in the early 1900s. Although Sofronii had no official role as a priest or confessor, he established the rules of the community based on those of other monasteries where *starchestvo* was practiced, such as the Optina and Glinskaia pustyn'. He also instructed the sisters and guided them in ascetic life.[66] Sofronii's spiritual authority was instrumental in raising funds from private donors in the Moscow and Ekaterinodar regions. For example, Sofronii's benefactors donated 5500 rubles towards the purchase of an estate in Tuapse, where the Iveron-Alekseevskaia community planned to build a compound (*podvor'e*).[67]

While the institutionalization of the Iveron-Alekseevskaia community by the Synod provided certain advantages in terms of status and recognition, it also brought new insecurities: the community's property was no longer under the total control of its founders, and with a change of leadership it would remain under the auspices of the new commune. This may explain the founders' unwillingness to provide transparency in their financial dealings: the Tuapse estate had been purchased in the name of Mother Mariam's brother, Fedor Makarovskii, while other donations were not properly recorded in the account books.

The involvement of male elders with female communities was another area of concern for ecclesiastical authorities. The frequent contact between religious women and elders raised the suspicions of the bishops. If in the 1830s the authorities were concerned with the spread of heresy among elders and their female disciples, in the late nineteenth century they were concerned with sexual morality. Elder Sofronii allegedly used to take baths in the presence of the sisters of Iveron-Alekseevskaia where they washed him while listening to his admonitions.[68] Incidentally, the fifty-five-year-old Sofronii did not deny that he spent long hours in the convent's bath, trying to relieve his rheumatic pains, but he rejected all accusations of sexual impropriety.[69] During the investigation insinuations were made regarding a possible sexual relationship between Mother Mariam and her adopted brother Fedor Makarovskii, both of whom were Sofronii's spiritual children.

Once the news of financial mismanagement reached the Synod, it launched a full-scale investigation that confirmed the concealment of large sums of private donations and the manipulative purchasing of estates in private names. As a result, Mother Mariam was replaced with a new abbess, called Ieronima, while Elder Sofronii and Fedor Makarovskii were banned from living near the convent. The new abbess, however, encountered stubborn opposition to her authority, with a large section of nuns remaining loyal to the previous abbess and Sofronii. The nuns expressed their dislike of the new abbess in a histrionic manner by fainting during the liturgy when her name was read in the prayers and during the prayers for her name day. Unrest and violence continued for several months: one sister was beaten up, another was threatened with an iron shovel.[70]

The Iveron-Alekseevskaia community affair demonstrated that the position of an elder could be appropriated for the wrong ends, and that the

Synod had only limited control. Despite the damaging evidence produced by the investigation, Elder Sofronii retained supporters among the nuns of the Iveron-Alekseevskaia community, the merchants of Tuapse and Krasnodar, and even among highly placed individuals like Grand Duchess Elizabeth and Count N. D. Zhevakhov. Moreover, despite the attempts of the investigators to try to bring the wrongdoers of Iveron-Alekseevskaia to justice, Makarovskii and Sofronii could not be tried by a church court because they were lay people. Hence, paradoxically, the elders who did not "professionally" belong to the organized church (i.e., were neither priests, monks, nor nuns) were relatively immune to interventions by the church authorities into the internal life of their communities.

Diversification and Appropriation of Charisma in Late Imperial Russia

Within the official Synodal discourse of late Imperial Russia there were several often contradictory interpretations of *starchestvo*. The charisma of an elder could be exercised by a variety of people that included abbots, monks, nuns, married parish priests, bishops, and even some members of the laity. If one applies a broader definition of *starchestvo*, as authority based on the gift of the Holy Spirit, then the diversification of *startsy* should not be surprising. However, this diversification has to be understood in the context of social and ecclesiastical changes in prerevolutionary Russia. By the late nineteenth century, the discourse on *starchestvo* had become mainstream, with a growing number of hagiographical publications in circulation, which were aimed at a broader audience. Popular pilgrimage had brought many lay people in contact with elders and resulted in the spread of monastic models outside their traditional context. It was not only the elites that appropriated popular models of holiness in order to strengthen or resanctify the domains of social and political power.[71] The lower classes, too, creatively engaged with forms of religious expression produced by the educated monks and church elites.

Even though the religious practice of eldership became part of popular spirituality, in its origins eldership was a monastic institution that aimed at the spiritual education of monks and guidance of the laity. The surfacing of the forms of eldership among groups that did not belong to the monastic clergy, therefore, can be characterized as cultural appropriation.[72] This appropriation provided multiple benefits to social groups and individuals: the lower classes made claims to spiritual and social power, while the elites tried to overcome the cultural distance between themselves and the people, and to bring about a greater integration of society. The differential access to power by social groups that practiced spiritual eldership and the consequences that derived from this inequality are of key importance for an understanding of the conflicts of the late imperial era.

Bishops and Elders

Although profoundly conservative in their outlook, by the late nineteenth century the most senior clerics in the Church (numbering 175 by the turn of the century) had become assertively critical of the Russian autocratic state's intervention into church affairs; they demanded the convocation of a church council that would redefine the Church's relationship to the state.[73] It is in the context of this new assertiveness and radicalism of the bishops that we should understand the appropriation of *starchestvo* as the means of invigorating church life. Embracing the authority of a charismatic elder, senior clergy could claim power in the Church, which they believed was corrupted by bureaucracy and secularism. Contrary to the voices that criticized the prevalence of the black clergy in the Church, a section of the Russian episcopate eagerly supported monasticism and monastic spirituality as the weapon to fight against liberalism, revolution, and secular thought.

Bishop Antonii (Khrapovitskii) (1863–1936), born into a gentry family, was an archenemy of Chief Procurator Pobedonostsev because of his openly expressed support for the restoration of the office of Russian patriarch. A rector of the St. Petersburg, Moscow, and Kazan theological academies, Antonii had enormous influence on young academy students, inspiring many of them to take monastic vows.[74] He believed that bright and educated young monks would form the avant-garde of the "militant church"—church understood as an active moral force for preserving and implementing God's commandments in society.[75] About sixty of the theology graduates who studied under Antonii became bishops.[76] Antonii made an emotional impact on his students. One of them wrote: "Very soon Antonii became my authority, almost like an idol. I was enchanted and fell in love with him."[77]

Although there were monastic elders in the vicinity of the Kazan academy, such as the respected Elder Gavriil, who was a spiritual father to many students, Bishop Antonii had certainly exercised the authority of a spiritual elder himself. The students of theology and young clergymen who gathered at his famous and exclusive tea-drinking parties imagined themselves as disciples and spiritual sons at the feet of the "Great *Abba*." Antonii's informal and paternalistic manner of address (he called his visitors by their familiar first names: "Serezha," "Misha," "Vania"), as well as his familiarity and humor, emphasized the "father-son" model on which the relationship between the bishop and his circle of friends was based—a relationship that typified the connection between elders and their spiritual children.[78]

Elders played an important role in Antonii's vision of the "militant church." In some of his writings, Antonii presented eldership as a pastoral model unique to Orthodoxy, contrasting it with the Roman Catholic ideal of priesthood. In a very biased work, "Two Methods of Pastorship, Latin and Orthodox," he argued that in contrast to Roman Catholic pastors, Orthodox spiritual elders never tried to adapt themselves to the tastes and interests of their congregation. Pilgrims had to overcome tremendous obstacles in order to reach some popular elder, many were often disappointed with their first impression and only with time did they discover the inner beauty and wisdom of the Orthodox elder.[79] Antonii believed that the central aspects of the elders' pastoral approach were spiritual healing and the "adoption" of a believer. Adoption (*usvoenie*) was understood as a gift of grace: an ability to love and accept every sinner (Matt 8:17).[80] The elder supposedly had the gift to "discover an inner man" in every person, even those who had transgressed.[81]

Antonii contributed to the development of Orthodox pastoral theology, which he conceived though the prism of his critical reading of Western theology and Schopenhauer. His aim was to promote the clerical profession as an attractive option to the graduates of theological institutions, many of whom were becoming disillusioned with the Synodal church and refusing to be ordained after graduation, claiming as justification an absence of priestly calling.[82] Antonii believed that the priesthood was a superior vocation, not just another profession in society, and he expressed indignation about the criticism of the Orthodox clergy by the educated public. He used Orthodox monastic elders as a model for the Orthodox clergy, thereby unwittingly promoting the idea of a celibate clergy despite his antipathy toward the Roman Catholic priesthood. The liberation of an educated clergyman from material, familial, and sexual concerns was the basis of spiritual freedom and selfless service to church and society. Antonii thus promoted a new model for the Orthodox pastorship, led by an avant-garde of educated celibate men, including bishops, who played the role of spiritual guides for the nation.

Yet Antonii's model had flaws. The bishop's interpretation of eldership was based on rationalism and psychological moralism rather than on the dogmatic and mystical aspects of Orthodox theology.[83] His ideas of the "militant church" provoked protest from the liberal clergy, who later tried to supplant the celibate church leadership with married bishops. Although Antonii praised the Optina style of spiritual eldership, he failed to apply it outside the context of monastic life. Antonii's influence on young theology students often led to tragic consequences: many young men who made the commitment to celibacy under Antonii's influence later regretted their premature decisions and renounced their vows.[84] And finally, the bishop's own brilliant and rapid career within the Church represented a sharp contrast to the humility and selflessness of the Russian spiritual elders.

Other bishops, too, borrowed the models of spiritual guidance from ascetic elders. Bishop Antonii (Florensov) (1847–1918), a spiritual father of Pavel Florenskii, was known as the "bishop-elder." Like Antonii Khrapovitskii, Antonii Florensov had experience in pedagogical activity, teaching and guiding students of theological seminaries in Samara, Volhynia, and Vologda. His success as a spiritual director was determined by his interest in human psychology, which—in his view—had much to do with the physical characteristics of a person, including their race, blood, pedigree, and temperament.[85]

Although the charisma of a spiritual elder was attractive to the Russian prelates who searched for new models of ecclesiastical leadership in times of crisis, the relationship between church hierarchs and monastic elders was riddled with tension. Local conflicts between charismatic holy men and senior clerics only sharpened in the prerevolutionary years, signifying the crisis of authority that preceded the Revolution of 1917.

Parish Priests as Elders

If for elders the main methods of spiritual influence were confession and conversation, parish priests used the Eucharist and sermons to the same effect. The mystical significance of the Eucharist was evident in the celebration of mass by Father John of Kronstadt. The clergy that co-celebrated with him in the cathedral of Kronstadt remembered that Father John treated *proskomide* (the preparation of the bread and wine for Eucharist before the beginning of the service) with great awe: he always prepared it himself, remembered the names of the people who asked him to pray for them, and often wept.[86] He treated the Eucharist with great respect and often refused to give Holy Communion to those who appeared to him as being unworthy. Father John's affectionate manner of celebration was imitated widely by the parish clergy but attracted the criticism of some hierarchs, such as Bishop Antonii Khrapovitskii, who dismissed it as *klikushestvo* (hysterics).[87] Father John's connection with the Russian elders was twofold: on the one hand, he was influenced by the ascetic and mystical theology that nourished the spiritual elders' teaching; on the other hand, his spiritual writings, which encapsulated his own religious experience, had a notable influence on the elders, especially those who were involved in the "Name of God" controversy in 1911–1914.

Yet despite the two-way exchange between charismatic parish priests like Father John and monastic elders, the appropriation of the charisma of elders by parish clergy was not a widespread phenomenon in fin-de-siècle Russia. Father Aleksei Mechev was one of the few urban parish priests who combined the gift of insightful confessor with that of a Eucharist celebrant. The son of the choirmaster of Chudov monastery in Moscow, Father Aleksei became a priest in 1893 at the small church of St. Nicholas in the unfashionable Moscow district of Maroseika. After the death of his wife in 1902, Aleksei dedicated his life to serving the people who came to him in search of advice or prayer. Father Aleksei's parishioners remembered the church's poor appearance and its very unremarkable, humble *batiushka* who moved casually about the church. During the first years of Father Aleksei's career as a priest he had a tiny congregation. However, between the years of 1905–1908 his reputation as a spiritual elder started to develop. He was compared to the Optina Elders: "Father Aleksei was an elder of Optina, only living in Moscow."[88] Father Pavel Florenskii too regarded Maroseika as an offshoot of Optina monastery. Father Aleksei indeed had a good relationship with the Optina monks Anatolii (Potapov) and Varsonofii (Plikhankov), but he did not imitate monastic elders. In the heady atmosphere of the 1905 revolution, Aleksei Mechev developed a new form of pastoral service that responded to the needs of educated Muscovites. Unlike monastic elders, he used methods typical of parish pastoral life, including sermons, spiritual talks, the Eucharist, and other sacraments and services. Unlike Antonii (Khrapovitskii), he did not see celibacy as the ultimate path to salvation: many of his spiritual children were married priests or lay people who had families. In the context of an urban parish, there was no need to practice the monastic "disclosure of thoughts." Only those very close to Aleksei Mechev revealed to him their inner thoughts and aspirations. However, his approach to confession, the essence of which was healing, not judgment, did have an affinity with the Optina elders.

Like the Optina elders, Father Aleksei appealed to people from various social ranks: professors, engineers, students, merchants, and civil servants. However, Father Aleksei's fame spread beyond the educated classes. Petty traders and illiterate peasants also were attracted by the reputation of the

Maroseika priest as a spiritual healer and clairvoyant. An educated Muscovite woman remembered that the first time she heard Father Aleksei's name was from a peasant on a train. This was in 1918, the year when all class distinctions in travel were abolished. People on the train were discussing the Bolshevik antireligious campaigns that targeted saints' relics. One passenger, a peasant who had moved from the Caucasus to Central Russia and established a small business, pointed out that never mind the dead saints, there were still some living saints around, such as Father Aleksei of Maroseika. The man told his fellow passengers about his first visit to the charismatic priest, during which Father Aleksei resolved his personal dilemma of whether or not to invest in a small tea shop. The advice proved very useful and the man continued to visit the priest from Maroseika.[89]

The negative impact that the social isolation of the parish clergy from their parishioners had on the tasks of the Church's urban mission in times of political and social crisis cannot be overestimated.[90] Yet the examples of Father John, his followers, and the circle of Priest Aleksei (Mechev) suggest that the urban parish clergy had resources for the development of a form of parish life that was characterized by several key features: an emphasis on the mystical essence of the Orthodox liturgy; more intensive forms of religious life (frequent communion and confession, regular church attendance); affectionate forms of worship, and the informal relationship between the pastor and his parishioners. The important characteristic of this form of pastoral mission was its intimate link with monastic spirituality, albeit in a form adapted for life in the world.

Village Spiritual Elders

The Russian village rarely had a shortage of indigenous holy men and women—wanderers, holy fools, hermits, clairvoyants—individuals who served as mediators between the ordinary villagers and God, who responded to the existential and social needs of the village folk. Village ascetics were usually the pious members of the community who sought a deeper religious commitment outside of the accepted church institutions. They practiced an ascetic way of life, withdrawing from the community to the back of the village or to a forest, or they behaved as holy fools. Undoubtedly, some of them were religious entrepreneurs who might have exploited the trust of the poor, but many others were men and women who at some point in their lives had experienced a spiritual conversion, and who attracted popular interest and imitation.

village elders

Biographical accounts of village spiritual elders often describe events that marked a transition from an "ordinary" to a new life, such as a meeting with a spiritual person, a pilgrimage, or an opportunity during army service to study with the army chaplains and access spiritual literature.[91] By embracing ascetic practices, which often took severe forms, these village elders drew a line between the sacred and profane, between a "normal" peasant way of life and a life of the spirit. Elder Vasilii Karpunin from the village of Ialtunovo in Riazan province (d. circa 1917) earned his reputation as a holy elder (*starets*) through his piety and extreme asceticism: he walked barefoot in winter and practiced severe fasting.[92] Elder Spiridon Sukhinin (1865–1929), from the village Ternovo in Voronezh province, was also very strict in his fasting: his followers claimed that as a baby he did not even nurse during the fasting days prescribed by the Church. The parents of the future elder Gavriil (Zyrianov), peasants from a village in the Urals, made a vow to God that they would never eat meat or have sexual intercourse. The son of lower-class urban dwellers, Sergei Shevtsov (known as Elder Sofronii), drafted into the army as a young man, chose to wear chains under his military uniform, which drew suspicions of sectarianism from his superiors.

The reputation of an ascetic was supported by tales of miracles. Vasilii Karpunin apparently healed people from incurable diseases, wrestled with demons, prophesied, and responded to locals who sought his prayers. Vasilii was a guide to several dozen young unmarried women who lived "in obedience" to their elder. Spiridon Sukhinin had a reputation for clairvoyance and healing.[93] From the peasant point of view, the way of life and spiritual power of these pious members of their community served as similar or superior religious credentials to those of officially recognized spiritual leaders, such as parish priests and monks.

While some holy men remained within their local setting, a few of them left the local orbit and "made a career" among the members of the upper class who were looking for genuine folk holiness, uncorrupted by culture and Synodal politics. Without a doubt, the most famous of all the village *startsy* in fin-de-siècle Russia was Grigorii Rasputin. Born to a peasant family in Tiumen' province, Siberia, Grigorii Rasputin was married and had three children. At the age of 28 this former horse thief and drunkard experienced a sudden conversion. According to one account, his behavior visibly changed after he had been violently beaten up by his fellow villagers. On his return to the village he became the leader of a small circle of men and women who practiced an ascetic way of life and gathered to listen to Grigorii's own commentary on the Gospel.

Village spiritual elders existed on the margins of institutional Orthodoxy, and their activities were often treated as "self-willed" religious behavior, a marginal form of religious offence that fell short of being defined as sectarianism or heresy.[94] In other cases, the extreme asceticism practiced by lay people brought accusations of sectarianism. Much depended on whether these local ascetics cooperated with the village priest rather than diverting people from the Church. If cooperation was evident, the representatives of the institutional church could delegate their spiritual power to the active and pious members of the parish.[95] In other cases, parish priests suspected heresy and tried to subvert the influence of local holy men.

Pilgrimages to monasteries and the tombs of the saints were a ritual journey that marked the separation of a regular member of the peasant community from its economic and social fabric and his transition to the new status of holy man, an outsider. It is likely that in their spiritual quest, peasant pilgrims would adopt some features of monastic spirituality. In particular, their meetings with elders gave them models for imitation and self-fashioning. The village elders, however, did not actively pursue a monastic vocation. These peasants, dissatisfied with the constraints of institutionalized religion, brought some of the forms of the virtuoso religion back to their native villages. The peasant elders, just like professional pilgrims (*stranniki*), were mediators between the world of monasticism and village spirituality. They adopted some features of the monastic way of life, including fasting, prayer, the reading of holy books, and the relationship of obedience between master and disciple. They also made use of sacred objects that they obtained on pilgrimages. For example, Vasilii Karpunin lived for a short while in Mount Athos, where—according to local legend—he took monastic vows. However, he decided to return to his village, where he healed villagers from a large bottle of boiled water to which he added holy oil taken from the Athonite monasteries.[96] Shevtsov describes the thirty-two-year-old illiterate layman Aleksandr Volkov, a peasant from the village Velikii Dvor, who built a hut decorated with icons; he began to wear a smock-like outfit that resembled a cassock and a *skuf'ia* (a monastic hat). He adopted five female followers who dressed in uniform fashion and resembled monastic novices. His choice of books also suggests that he adopted monastic spirituality and fashioned himself as an elder.[97]

The functions of the village elder were oriented to the community, not the individual. His roles were protective: shielding the community from enemies (including demonic forces) and the preservation of morality, health, and economic welfare (as in activities such as weather forecasting). A village elder also had a cultural function: he was the center of the village's spiritual gatherings or *sobesednichestva*, in which the members of the community sang hymns and listened to the elder's orations.[98] Popular folklore about certain elders, especially stories concerning punishment of the disobedient ones, ensured that individuals abided by the communal morality.

Apart from their influence on the village community, village spiritual elders exercised their authority on a close circle of followers, normally groups of single women—or occasionally married women—who dedicated their lives to God (*chernichki*).[99] They did not take part in agricultural work, and made their living from religious services to the villagers such as praying for the living and the dead or decorating icons with foil. In the village of Ialtunovo, Elder Grigorii Karpunin marked women who dedicated themselves to prayer by cutting their hair, a symbolic imitation of the Orthodox rite of taking monastic vows (*postrig*). It seems that some charismatic elders passed their gifts to religious women. Elder Grigorii gave "lessons" in holy foolishness to his favorite disciple, Anna Petrina. Although Anna was married and had children, she followed her spiritual father in everything. During spiritual gatherings in her house, she sat under the bench on the orders of her elder, acting irrationally and sometimes indecently: she was noticed wandering the streets wearing a bast shoe on one foot and a felt boot on the other, or praying in church while clutching two logs in her hands.[100]

The appropriation of models of spiritual guidance by the lower classes demonstrated that the power relations between the "producers" and "consumers" of the sacred became reversed. Even though in the past the Church had had difficulties controlling outbursts of popular piety that challenged the competence of official representatives of the Church, in the years preceding the revolution this became almost impossible. The practices of *starchestvo* could not be monopolized by the Church, and this partly explains the broad appeal of this form of spiritual organization to various groups of the laity. The use of charismatic power and the appropriation of the models of the "official" church by lower class individuals was also a result of growing literacy, improved communications, migration, and the further integration of the Russian village into the national community.[101]

The Upper Classes
The Appropriation of Popular Culture

Russian officialdom used charismatic popular elders as symbols of the unity between the tsar and the people, as epitomized in the canonization of Serafim of Sarov in 1903.[102] Serafim of Sarov's special significance for

Nicholas II's family was due to the efforts of the saint's energetic impresario, Archimandrite Serafim (Leonid Chichagov) (1856–1937).[103] For his participation in the Russo-Turkish war of 1878–1879, Leonid was decorated with the St. George's Cross. But the young officer experienced a profound religious conversion after meeting Father John of Kronstadt, under whose influence he decided to retire from the army and subsequently became a priest in 1891, despite the objections of his wife and relatives. In 1895, after the death of his wife, Leonid became a novice in the Trinity-Sergius monastery and in 1898 he took monastic orders, taking the name Serafim.

Chichagov's interest in Serafim of Sarov began around the time of his ordination as a priest, after his inspirational visit to the Diveevo community, which Serafim had founded. Chichagov conceived the idea of collecting testimonies about Serafim from those who remembered him. In 1896 he published the massive 800-page *Chronicles of Serafimo-Diveevo Convent*, a collection of written testimonies and documents from the archives of the monastery. The *Chronicles* portrayed Serafim as a visionary and prophet. Some of the most daring prophecies and sayings in the first edition were edited or deleted by the censor.[104] For example, Serafim's claim that he appointed twelve Diveevo sisters to represent twelve female disciples of the Virgin Mary was stricken from the *Chronicles*.

When Chichagov presented the *Chronicles* to Nicholas II, he must have been aware of the significance of the saint for the Romanov family.[105] While it is difficult to imagine that Nicholas II read the entire book, the emperor clearly was convinced that Serafim was a great saint whose canonization was impeded by the bureaucrats in the Holy Synod. Although the church authorities had established a formal commission for the canonization of Serafim in 1892, the official consideration of Serafim's candidacy for sainthood was unhurried, despite pressure from local ecclesiastical authorities and the court.[106] Chichagov, however, continued to promote Serafim's cult and alert the emperor to the deficiencies and red tape of the Synodal administration. In 1902, Chief Procurator Pobedonostev expressed his worries about the role of Chichagov in the "Serafim affair." In September of that year he warned the commandant of the royal palace, P. P. Gesse, about Archimandrite Serafim's planned visit to the emperor, calling Serafim "a man of sharp mind" who could ruin the reputations of many members of the clergy.[107]

The interest of the Romanovs in the Sarov wonder worker was connected with Serafim's prophecies concerning the ruling dynasty, as well as with the popular image of the monarchy. For example, Tsarina Alexandra consulted the writings of Nicholas Motovilov, an admirer of Serafim and donor of

5.2. Nicholas II carrying the casket with Serafim's relics. Sarov, 1903.
Source: Rossiiskii gosudarstvennyi arkhiv kinofotodokumentov. Courtesy of the Russian Archives of Documentary Films and Photographs

the Diveevo community, which were kept by the Personal Chancellery of Nicholas I, and contained a prediction concerning the successors of Nicholas I.[108] Apart from the personal piety of the royal couple and their hope for a male heir, there was a political calculation in the use of the image of a popular saint as the symbol of the unity between the tsar and his people. General Mosolov and a group of right-wing political ideologues believed that the tsar was trying to overcome *sredostenie*, or the cultural, political, and social separation between the ruling dynasty and the Russian people created by bureaucrats and the intelligentsia.[109] The tsar's participation in the celebrations in Sarov in 1903 was aimed at breaking this barrier and bringing the royal family into communion with ordinary people. It is debatable whether the royal family's involvement with the canonization was a wise political decision. The tsar's active intervention in the canonization process alienated the liberal intelligentsia as well as the church hierarchs.

At the same time, the controversy surrounding Serafim's relics damaged the image of the monarchy in the eyes of skeptical onlookers, among whom were many Old Believers. The fact that instead of an uncorrupted body, the Synodal commission found only a well-preserved skeleton of the saint, gave rise to rumours that Serafim's body was corrupted, and therefore, he was not a true saint. Despite the explanations given by Bishop Antonii (Vadkovskii) that posthumous preservation of the body did not necessarily indicate the person's saintliness, critics refered to the incident as "the Sarov affair" and to Serafim as "the corrupted [*istlevshii*] saint." [110]

The Tsarina Alexandra's religious temperament would have been a private matter if it had not had significance for Russia's political crisis. Father Georgii (Shavel'skii), a priest who served in the Russian army and navy, wrote that "Alexandra was fascinated with a specific kind of Orthodoxy that emerged in the last years before the revolution, the typical features of which were an insatiable thirst for omens, prophecies[,] and miracles coupled with a search for holy fools, wonder-workers[,] and saints who would be bearers of supernatural power. According to the Gospel, Christ himself warned his disciples against such religion (Matt 4:7)."[111] A convert to Orthodoxy from Lutheranism, Alexandra assimilated a version of Russian popular religion which was characterized by educated clerics and intellectuals as "superstitious." It is interesting that Father Georgii locates this type of religion in the last years preceding the upheaval of 1917. As a priest, he should have known that this type of religiosity had always existed among ordinary people. What he meant, perhaps, was that this form of Orthodoxy, traditionally associated with the ignorant and poor, was finding its way into the upper circles of society and was epitomized in the faith of the tsarina. Alexandra was not alone in her fascination with popular religion. Countess Orbeliani, who suffered from a paralysis of the legs, was eager to go to Sarov in the hope that she would be cured by being plunged into Serafim's holy spring. Countesses Militsa and Stana, wives of the Grand Dukes Paul and Nicholas Romanov, introduced Alexandra to Rasputin, while a number of women in the court shared Alexandra's views. Robert Nichols has argued that Nicholas and Alexandra's attraction to various holy men like holy fool Mitya Koliaba or *starets* Grigorii Rasputin derived not so much from traditional Orthodox sources as from popular Western mystical theories such as the notion of the "Friends of God."[112] This confirms the notion of cultural appropriation: the elites picked the forms and phenomena of local religion and interpreted them in light of the theories that were available to them. The heterogeneity of the sources of personal religiosity was a specific feature of late imperial religiosity.

The imperial couple's interest in popular holy men, including their "friend" Grigorii Rasputin, was inseparable from the ideology of simplicity preached by the Russian intelligentsia, most famously by Leo Tolstoy. Although the royal couple had a distrust of Russian intellectuals, they nevertheless shared the same ideology and confessed primitivism in their religious life. The relationships between Nicholas and Alexandra and the Romanov children, on the one hand, and soldiers or servants, on the other, were warm and affectionate, while the simple-hearted holy fools like Mitya Koliaba and the semiliterate "Elder" Grigorii embodied their faith in the "'natural'" Orthodoxy of the ordinary people who were uncontaminated by intellectualism.[113] Rasputin's preaching appealed to both parents and children in the royal family. In one of his telegrams to Great Duchess Anastasia he wrote, "God does not like pride. Simplicity will conquer the world. The one who has the reins of power should be humble like an angel … . A proud person will ruin everything and everyone."[114] Rasputin's egalitarianism was expressed in his use of the Russian "*ty*" (thou) with any individual regardless of age and status, his disregard for manners and subordination, and his hatred of aristocracy. These and other proclivities (even his sexual promiscuity) were accepted by the royal family as genuine expressions of Rasputin's affinity with the *narod*.

Rasputin's role epitomized the contradictions and discontinuities of the ancien régime. In the crisis of the revolutionary era, the autocracy tried to present itself as being above politics and as autonomous of rational bureaucracy, and it increasingly relied on rituals, symbols, and association with the traditional and mystical aspects of the Orthodox faith. The failures of the autocracy to reform in the manner of the European parliamentary monarchies, and to find a compromise with conservative liberals like Stolypin or Guchkov, led to the revival of a patrimonial style of politics, characteristic of the Muscovite state, that emphasized personal ties, kinship, friendship, dependency, and patronage.[115] Yet in the period of war and revolution, due to the breakdown of horizontal links between the members of traditional society, the monarchy began to rely disproportionately on various power brokers and mediators, of whom holy man Grigorii Rasputin was just one. Politicians, courtiers, bureaucrats, clergymen, and ordinary civil servants came to Rasputin asking for promotions, protection, and favors. The Jewish engineer A. V. Gerzon, for example, was advised to seek patronage in St. Petersburg in order to receive the post of military engineer in Lviv, which he allegedly could not obtain by other means because of his Jewish name. He was introduced to Rasputin in 1915 in St. Petersburg by a ballet dancer, and obtained from him a letter of recommendation, which he did not use because it was full of grammatical mistakes.[116] With the aid of Rasputin, the defrocked Athonite monks, accused of the "Name of God" heresy, were received by the tsar, to whom they expounded their grievances.[117] The Rasputin phenomenon was not an example of authentic peasant faith, unspoiled by the corrupt institutional church, as Rasputin's admirers in St. Petersburg circles wanted to believe. Quite the opposite, it was an expression of the growing cultural contact between the world of the Russian "noble savage" and educated society.[118]

The choice of religious models by the royal couple was not necessarily typical of all members of the court: some members of the aristocracy remained within the boundaries of mainstream religion and were guided by the authority of canonical tradition. Grand Duchess Elizabeth, Alexandra's sister, who was married to Grand Duke Sergei, was a Protestant convert to Orthodoxy who had great respect for the Orthodox spiritual elders. Despite her husband's skepticism, she enthusiastically dedicated herself to Orthodoxy, taking part in the management of the Imperial Palestine Society together with the Grand Duke, who was its official patron. After her husband's assassination by Kaliaev, a member of the Socialist-Revolutionary Party, during the Revolution of 1905, she founded and headed the Marfo-Mariinskii convent in Moscow. The community initially consisted of seventeen lay women who lived together and dedicated their lives to prayer and charity. Always very deliberate in her choice of attire, Elizabeth wore a special white habit designed for her and the sisters of the Marfo-Mariinskii convent by the famous Russian artist V. Vasnetsov. The architectural complex of the convent founded by Elizabeth in Bol'shaia Ordynka, not far from Christ the Savior Cathedral, was a masterpiece of style and elegance to which the best Moscow architects (Shchusev) and artists (Nesterov and Korin) had contributed.[119]

Elizabeth used her status and influence to promote a new vision of female monasticism and to restore the order of deaconesses, the female ministers who had had specific responsibilities (assisting the baptism of female adults, preserving order in church, visiting the sick, and helping the poor) in the ancient church.[120] Some clergy, like the Metropolitan Vladimir of Moscow, approved of these ideas, while others, like Bishop Germogen of Saratov, did not. The Synod reluctantly accepted the special status of the Marfo-Mariinskii convent, in which women between the ages of 21 and 40 enjoyed an uncharacteristic freedom of movement and autonomy from bishops. Elizabeth's support of eldership had much to do with her desire to enhance the role of women in the Church: personal connections with spiritual leaders, who were neither trained theologians nor church functionaries, appealed to women because of the non-hierarchical and egalitarian character of this relationship, based on the ideal of spiritual kinship.

Elizabeth traveled outside Moscow to visit elders in provincial Sed'miozernaia, Optina, and Zosimova pustyn'. Although the Marfo-Mariinskii convent had their own priest, Father Mitrofan (Srebrianskii), Elizabeth, with her fellow women religious, visited Gavriil (Zyrianov) of Sed'miozernaia and Aleksei (Solov'ev) of Zosimova for confession and spiritual advice.[121] For example, in 1909 the Grand Duchess visited Zosimova pustyn' (25 kilometers from Trinity-Sergius Lavra) nine times. During each visit she stayed in the monastery for an average of two days, spending the night in vigils. Some witnesses commented that the Grand Duchess's confession to Elder Aleksei lasted for four hours.[122] Elizabeth also befriended Gavriil (Zyrianov), visiting him annually in Kazan and helping him to resettle in Pskov after his expulsion from Sed'miozernaia pustyn'.[123]

Although contrary to the assertion of critics, Elizabeth's attempts to restore the order of deaconesses had little to do with her Protestantism, her inclination toward elders may have had roots in Protestant pneumatocentric ecclesiology, expressed in the writings of the German Pastor Mohler, who influenced Khomiakov. Perhaps, as a former Protestant, Elizabeth found it easier to assimilate the concept of eldership as charismatic authority, and the Church as the body of believers united in the Holy Spirit. Yet Elizabeth never put holy men and elders above the church hierarchy. In situations of conflict between the Synod and individual elders, she acted as a mediator between the two sides and avoided confrontation. As a supporter of eldership and the creator of an innovative community that embodied a novel religious aesthetic, she indeed pursued "subtly subversive goals" and opposed the "official" religion.[124]

During conflicts between charismatic elders and the established church hierarchy, the intervention of powerful lay persons was vital. Elizabeth used her influence to protect German, the abbot of the Zosimova monastery, who in 1909 was removed to another remote monastery following allegations of financial mismanagement. Elizabeth also acted as a patron of the Iversko-Alkseevskaia female community in Sukhumi diocese, which had an elder-in-residence, the nonordained monk Sofronii. The controversy that involved the community in 1912, however, demonstrated that even the Grand Duchess was not powerful enough to save the founders of the community from the wrath of the Holy Synod. Elizabeth believed that eldership was essential for the organization of spiritual life in monastic communities. She cited the examples of Optina, Glinskaia, and Sofronieva monasteries and pointed to benefits of close proximity between the elders of Optina and the nuns of Shamordino.

Although a great admirer of spiritual elders, Elizabeth was very critical of Rasputin. Elizabeth's attempts to speak to the tsar and tsarina about the "pseudo-*starets*" Grigorii, however, had no effect, resulting in a growing separation between the leader of the Marfo-Mariinskii convent and the court in St. Petersburg. Empress Alexandra sneered at the churchmen who came from Moscow and objected to the appointment of A. D. Samarin, who was close to the Novoselov circle, on the grounds that he came from the Muscovite "vicious and hypocritical clique of Ella" (Grand Duchess Elizabeth) and would present a threat to Rasputin.[125]

It is obvious that there was no unified model of eldership to which the upper circles adhered. Eldership was imagined by the elites as a spiritual union between the rulers and the common folk. The belief that, through their personal links with holy men, the elites could partake in the pure faith of the ordinary people functioned as a psychological defense mechanism against the increasing pressures and frustrations of traditional elites in the era of modern politics. At the same time, through a period of political and social crises, the role of religious entrepreneurs increased to the extent that it subverted the institutional logic of the bureaucratic state and had a corrosive effect on Russia's top echelons of power. Not all members of the aristocracy made such a sharp distinction between charisma and institution. In contrast to the royal family, other members of the court, such as Grand Duchess Elizabeth, showed more skill and tact in dealing with church administrators. Her assimilation of eldership as a legitimate form of spiritual organization unique to Orthodoxy expressed a better understanding of Orthodox theology than that of her sister and brother-in-law.

Spirituality and Protest (Imiaslavtsy)

The Reinforcement of Discipline in Monasteries

In late Imperial Russia the monastic population was made up predominantly of peasants, who accounted for well over half (between 60 and 90 percent) of the inhabitants of monasteries and convents.[126] The writer Vasilii Nemirovich-Danchenko used the term "the peasant kingdom" to describe the Valaam monastery, and this could well be applied to other communities, such as Solovki, Glinskaia, and the majority of convents. It has been argued that monasteries promised a better lifestyle to impoverished Russian peasants, but only an insignificantly small number of peasants would achieve the rank of a hieromonk or abbot.[127] The majority of peasant monks endured physical hardship, long hours of prayer, and lifelong celibacy. The father of a peasant monk from Glazov, Potapii Ladygin (b. 1866), visited his son in the St. Panteleimon monastery on Mount Athos. He was moved to tears when he saw the hardship and deprivations of monastic life and begged his son to come back home.[128]

Undoubtedly, rather than the promise of social and economic benefits, monasticism attracted peasants mainly because of its spiritual appeal. Monasteries were legitimate spaces where pious peasants could dedicate their lives to God, unhindered by family and economic pressures. In 1906, the repeal of legal restrictions that previously prevented peasants joining the monastic vocation allowed thousands of peasants to join monasteries and convents where they could practice and redefine ascetic ideals.[129] Changes in the social profile of monasteries created a different context for the interpretation of spiritual eldership and the religious experience it aimed to facilitate. Academic theologians and Synodal administrators found it difficult to control the interpretation of mystical experience by the uneducated members of the church. Once they realized their inability to win the conflict through theological argument, the church authorities felt compelled to employ force and coercion.

The *Imiaslavie* ("Name of God") affair of 1912–1914, which led to the forced expulsion of 833 Russian monks from Mount Athos by the military, was the expression of a major crisis in the Russian Church on the eve of the First World War. Although the conflict primarily concerned the Athonite monks, it affected monasticism in the heartland and provinces of Russia. The actions of the church authorities discredited even the most experienced Athonite monks, many of who were spiritual elders, for their adherence to *Imiaslavie*. Following their expulsion, many of these purged monks became spiritual leaders, especially after the end of the Synodal church in 1917.[130]

The *Imiaslavie* affair was linked to the controversial book *On the Mountains of the Caucasus*, a collection of meditations on the magnitude of God. The beauty of Caucasian nature inspired the narrator—a solitary monk living in the mountains—to contemplate the glory of the other world. The book was a treatise on the Jesus prayer presented in a poetic and non-didactic manner.

The author of the book, Monk Ilarion (b. 1845), the son of a priest and the graduate of a theological seminary, became a monk in the St. Panteleimon monastery on Mount Athos and then followed the Russian monks who had moved to the Caucasus from Athos to become hermits. The book was a semiautobiographical account describing the meeting of the author with Elder Disiderii, an Athonite monk in the Caucasus known for his spiritual experience. Disiderii was also a theological seminary student who left the seminary before finishing his course because he felt physically and spiritually corrupted by the low morals of the institution.[131]

The book began with the description of a passage by two monks through the high mountain terrain in search of some hermits. During their journey the monks met an old hermit, "tall and thin as a skeleton; [whose] long and white beard reached up to his waist," and who had led a solitary existence for 10 years following 20 years spent in a monastic community.[132] The eager visitors asked the hermit about the spiritual experience he acquired in solitary living—a traditional narrative device for a prolonged treatise on the practice of the Jesus prayer. The hermit related that he had reached a new level in his mastery of the prayer, the prayer of the heart, which led him to conclude that the name of God repeated in this prayer was inseparable from the mystical experience of unity with the divine. In sum, God was present in his name.

The book went through three editions in five years (1907–1912), and was avidly read in monastic and lay circles. Financial assistance for the publication was given by Abbot Varsonofii (Plikhankov) of Optina pustyn', Grand Duchess Elizabeth, and the Kievo-Pecherskaia Lavra. The publication was approved by the spiritual censors. Its popularity could be compared to *The Way of a Pilgrim*, as its genre was a contemplative work of prose, rather than a theological treatise. The nonelitist stance of the book appealed to lower-class monks and nuns: theological education was deemed redundant and the practice of the Jesus prayer would bring an ascetic into direct communion with God. The book conveyed the idea that Our Lady was the first practitioner of the Jesus prayer, which she learned while in the Temple and then taught to the apostles.[133] The legitimation of the spiritual practice by evoking the authority of Mary, by no means unusual for Orthodoxy, only contributed to the book's appeal for women.

Although by the turn of the century the Jesus prayer was a well-known spiritual practice popularized through the writings of Father John of Kronstadt, Feofan the Recluse, and Ignatii Brianchaninov, Ilarion made a theological statement when he claimed that God was present in His name. He asserted that the repetition of the name of Jesus Christ, recited rhythmically in the words of the prayer, could help the believer to achieve union with God. Although this statement was legitimated by the Old and New Testaments, by the writings of the hesychasts and of John of Kronstadt, the adoption of the teaching by the Athonite monks provoked a bitter controversy in the St. Panteleimon monastery. The book inadvertently became a manifesto for the militant defenders of *Imiaslavie*, and triggered a Synodal attack on what was interpreted as a heresy. In the

Optina monastery, Abbot Varsonofii (Plikhankov) expelled the critics of *Imiaslavie*, only to be purged as abbot a few years later. In St. Panteleimon, the book mobilized a number of active supporters, who replaced the abbot of the monastery unsympathetic to its teaching.

The Patriarch of Constantinople and the theologians of Chalcidice criticized the "Name of God Worshippers" and denounced their position as pantheism. Following the intervention of Bishop Antonii (Khrapovitskii), the Russian Holy Synod too declared the teaching on the Name of God a heresy. The Name Worshippers, who were in the majority, led by the monks David (Mukhranov) and Antonii (Bulatovich), refused to obey the orders of their superiors—accusing them of the heresy of *imiaborchestvo* (denying the name).[134] These monks replaced the abbot with an elected council of elders and put pressure upon those who did not subscribe to the new teaching. The complicated relationship between the Russian and Greek ecclesiastical authorities (who tried to clamp down on Russian influence on the Holy Mountain) required immediate intervention. On June 11, 1913, the steamers *Tsar*, *Kherson*, and *Chikhachev* brought 118 Russian soldiers under the command of five officers to Mount Athos. The soldiers helped the monastic authorities to pacify the disobedient Name Worshippers and, using hoses, forced the monks onto the steamers. In early July, 1913, 833 Athonite monks were deported to Russia. Upon their arrival, 40 were imprisoned, while the rest were defrocked and sent back to their places of origin.[135] Later, the Athonite exiles were allowed to join Russian monasteries where they often faced opposition from the local monks.[136]

The argument between the academic theologians who were representatives of the Synod, on the one hand, and the *Imiaslavtsy*, on the other, could be interpreted as a clash between two forms of knowledge, one traditional and the other institutionalized. The first was founded on spiritual experience, worship, and ascetic practices, while the second was a discourse of academic theology based upon the use of formal logic and appeal to reason. The theologians, who represented institutional expertise, dismissed the teaching on the name of God as primitive religion that worshipped creation and nature (including language), and as the dangerous heresy of *Khlystovshchina* (a derogatary definition of *Khristovshchina*, a popular religious movement characterized by ecstatic forms of worship and prophecy) that drew people away from the institutionalized church.[137]

The overwhelming majority of monks who were expelled from Athos (93 percent) had peasant origins.[138] They were not theologians, but in their view the Synod's attack on the idea that God was in his name was a form of iconoclasm. Yet their lack of theological education did not make them heretics. Educated theologians and philosophers like Pavel Florenskii and Aleksei Losev defended the theoretical basis of the Name Worshippers; in the opinion of Pavel Florenskii, *Imiaslavie* was a passionate protest against philosophical and theological subjectivism. The "Name of God" argument, according to Losev and Florenskii, had its basis in Neoplatonic thought and patristic theology.[139] Florenskii examined the shared philosophical perspective of Platonic idealism and the folkloric worldview. According to this theory, "Name" was a "materialization, the condensation of grace-bearing or occult forces, a mystical root by which man was connected with immaterial worlds."[140]

The *Imiaslavie* affair led to even further suspicion between the Synodal church and the Russian monasteries, which were policed on the subject of the new heresy: monks had to sign a circular condemning it, while abbots were required to report to the bishops on anyone who sympathized with the Name Worshippers.[141] Given the large circulation of Ilarion's book, it would have been impossible to confiscate every single copy of it. During the regular inspections of monastic cells, many nuns and monks hid the book from the inspectors.[142] In March 1914, the Optina elders Agapit and Anatolii were summoned by the Moscow consistory to participate in a "show trial" of the Name Worshippers from Athos. The Optina elders refused to go under the pretext of illness.

The Synod's victory over the *Imiaslavie* "heresy" was a nominal one: the schism continued to trouble the Russian Orthodox Church up until the end of the Synodal era in 1917. The Name Worshippers affair had a significant bearing on elders. The attack on *Imiaslavie* was associated by many with an attack on the Jesus prayer and contemplative monasticism. The Synod's employment of violence and coercion in dealing with religious issues led many lay men and women to lose their trust in the church hierarchy and simultaneously raised the profile of nonordained monastic elders. Even if the *Imiaslavtsy* were in the wrong, their experience as victims and martyrs gave greater credibility to their movement. Many of the monks expelled from Athos became spiritual fathers, forming small communities in various parts of Russia. Because of the war and revolution, it became very difficult to locate the historical traces of the eight hundred monks expelled from Athos in 1911, but fragmentary evidence suggests that some of the monks were reintegrated into Russian monasteries and became informal spiritual leaders.[143] Ilarion himself earned the status of a spiritual elder in the Caucasus, guiding a small number of men and women with his spiritual advice.[144] Several unofficial communities of Name Worshippers continued to exist until the late 1920s in the Caucusus.[145] It would be wrong, however, to describe Name Worshippers as *startsy*-oriented and "Name Deniers" as anti-*startsy*. Broadly speaking, there were two ecclesiological positions taken by the interpreters of the Athonite "heresy" that affected the Russian Church in the following epoch. Neither of these positions was alien to the concept of eldership. According to one, voiced by Father Sergii Bulgakov, *Imiaslavie* was an obvious example of the lack of discipline in the Orthodox Church, which put the Church in danger of self-destruction at times of extreme theological debate and internal strife.[146] Bulgakov thought that questioning the right of the Holy Synod, supported by the Patriarch of Constantinople, to condemn heresy entailed a great danger of fragmentation and schism. Neither Bishop Antonii (Khrapovitskii) nor Nikon (Rozhdestvenskii), opponents of the Name Worshippers, had any theological objections to monasticism and eldership.

The ecclesiastical authorities used the language of the time to condemn the nonconformist behavior of monks. The most frequent term employed to describe these conflicts was *bunt* (mutiny), while the disobedient were known as "mutineers" and firebrands (*smut'iany*). To punish the heresy the authorities sent in official missionaries, threatened nonconformists with excommunication, and used other administrative punishments.[147] The missionary Mikhail Vinogradov reported to Bishop Agafodor that the promotion of the Jesus prayer by Ilarion and his disciples aimed at the "annihilation of church rituals [*obriadnost'*]," subverted the order and discipline of monastic life, and encouraged passivity (*nichegonedelanie*).[148] Thus despite their apparent quietism, these contemplatives were perceived as subversive and dangerous by the Synod.

Thus monasteries did not remain immune to the broader processes of social conflict and challenge to authority that Russian society experienced in the period between 1905 and 1917. Faced by attempts to democratize monastic life, the Synod and monastic hierarchy tried to appeal to elders as figures of traditional authority to ensure discipline and order. Here eldership was used only as a mechanism of discipline while obedience was emphasized as a central virtue. In order to strengthen the opposition to *Imiaslavie* the Synod invited Optina Elders Anatolii and Iosif to participate in the trial of *Imiaslavtsy* in 1913; the indisposed *startsy* discharged themselves on the grounds of illness.[149]

IN THE LATE IMPERIAL ERA, elders' charisma appealed to various groups within the Russian Orthodox Church. Bishops and theologians fashioned themselves as spiritual fathers, while parish priests combined traditional pastoral methods with a more intensive approach to confession and the guidance of their parishioners' souls. Among the laity the forms of ascetic life became widely practiced due to growing literacy, mobility, and the development of transport that allowed better access to faraway monasteries. The elites imagined spiritual elders as alternative leaders who could replace the corrupt church hierarchy and provide leadership in times of crisis and disorientation. Thus, spiritual elders unintentionally came to play a predominantly symbolic role in the discourse of the late imperial era, illustrating Wilson's belief that in the modern era charisma was a romantic idea, an attempt to re-enchant and animate the "sclerotic" system of the church, which was based on impersonality and routine procedures.[150]

The question of the strength or weakness of the Russian Orthodox Church in the revolutionary period cannot be answered adequately without taking into account the Orthodox elders. Due to their mediatory position in the Church, elders could be seen as part of both the institutional framework of the Church and of popular culture. The haziness of the definition of eldership and the general openness of the concept to interpretation provided an additional element of appeal in respect to the elders' charisma. Although elders did not take part in urban social missions or preach the Gospel to masses of discontented migrants and urban workers, they did provide relief and pastoral support to those afflicted individuals who sought a deeper engagement with the divine.

While perhaps this "social mission" was not statistically significant, it was certainly a sign of the array of moral and spiritual resources in the Russian Orthodox Church that could be mobilized in times of revolutionary turmoil. There were two primary reasons for the failure to mobilize these resources. The first reason was the growing cultural and epistemological gap between two groups in the Orthodox Church, the bishops and the monastic elders. The influx of peasants into the monastic profession coupled with the proliferation of elders outside monastic walls brought about a significant change in the social profile of elders; this caused tensions between the church hierarchy and charismatic spiritual leaders. The gap between the educated church elite and the elders who had little or no formal education grew even wider than it had been during most of the nineteenth century, when elders often had a seminary or home education. The second reason was the problem of discipline. The church hierarchs—who were already concerned about the weakening of their power—overreacted to the involvement of elders in actions that they perceived as disobedience and heresy. They resorted to the use of traditional methods of control, such as the use of the police force, violence, and inflexibility in discussions about the theological issues at stake. The *Imiaslavie* affair discredited the church hierarchy even further in the eyes of ordinary believers and gave credit to the nonconventional ecclesiological views of the Russian God-seeking intelligentsia. The ecclesiological crisis of the 1920s was a logical continuation of the tensions and scandals of the late imperial era.

CHAPTER SIX

The Legacy of the Elders after the Revolution, 1917–2000

The overthrow of the monarchy in February 1917 marked a new era in the history of the Russian Orthodox Church and affected the fortunes of Russian eldership. In the immediate postrevolutionary period a more democratic model of authority took the upper hand within Russian Orthodoxy. The initial democratization and liberalization of society could not but affect the Church and was expressed in the condemnation of the *Rasputinshchina*, the downfall of the bishops and the clergy that had connections with "Elder" Grigorii, and the dismissal of such conservative prelates as Antonii Khrapovitskii, Tikhon Nikanorov, and Ioakim Levitskii, who were strongly associated with the defeated regime. Clergy and parishioners called for diocesan councils (often without the permission of the ruling bishop), which were characterized by the active participation of the laity and frequent radicalism of proceedings and decisions.[1] The liberal forces within the Church advocated for the abolition of celibacy for bishops and for an electoral principle in church administration.[2] While overall the Church supported the Provisional Government, it protested against the legislation of the summer of 1917 that lowered the age of "religious self-determination" to 14 years and transferred the parish schools to the Ministry of Education. The summoning of the Church Council in August 1917 took place in an atmosphere of social radicalization and political crisis. The election of the new leader of the Church, Patriarch Tikhon (Belavin), following more than two hundred years of Synodal administration, signified that the Church "had affirmed its status as an organizing principle for society alternative to any that might be proposed by the state."[3] The Church Council also reinstated the principles of celibacy for bishops, respect for monasticism, and spiritual eldership. Respect for eldership was expressed in the method of choosing the new patriarch: Elder Aleksei (Solov'ev) of Zosimova pustyn' drew lots and produced Tikhon's name from a list of three candidates. The council continued the prerevolutionary policy of monastic reform and recommended cenobitic rule and elections of the abbot or abbess by the entire community. The introduction of elders well versed in holy scripture and patristic writings was also advocated.[4]

The Bolshevik Revolution and the Civil War threw the ecclesiastical structure of Russian Orthodoxy into disarray and threatened the natural environment for eldership—monasticism. The decree separating the church from the state in 1918 and the Red Terror led to huge material and human losses within an institution that previously had enjoyed a privileged and protected existence. As a result of the Brest-Litovsk peace with Germany and the Civil War, a large number of Russian Orthodox parishes, monasteries, clergy, and believers found themselves outside the borders of Russia. Within the remaining Orthodox clergy, a schism developed between the pro-Soviet Living Church and the church led by Patriarch Tikhon. This rupture was aggravated by the Cheka (the Extraordinary Commission for the Battle with Counterrevolution, Sabotage, and Speculation). The Living Church, or Renovationists (*obnovlentsy*), who in 1922 controlled more than 70 percent of parishes, were based on the premise of the prerevolutionary "group of 32 priests," and liberal clergy led by Antonin Granovskii. They objected to the requirement of celibacy for bishops and, more generally, regarded monasticism as irrelevant for modern life. The Church Council of 1923 ruled that all monasteries should be closed on the grounds that these institutions deviated from their original ideals of nonpossession. Despite the belated attempts by some members of the Renovationist clergy to reverse the radical condemnation of monasticism, the majority of monks moved into the camp of Patriarch Tikhon.[5]

Starchestvo indeed experienced several changes in the atheist state. Firstly, it became more significant for monastic life, which was set adrift from its formal foundations. Secondly, it even further transcended the boundaries of monastic practice, and began to be employed by parish priests. Thirdly, due to the arrest and displacement of monks, *starchestvo* spread beyond the traditional centers of eldership in Russia. Finally, the number of women who possessed the charismatic authority of *staritsy* grew.

These developments had a direct impact on spiritual eldership. Now spiritually experienced monks and nuns were in much closer contact with the laity of both genders, while the church authorities had little control over the content and form of such contact. Towards the end of the NEP period (1921–1928), ideological arguments for the abolition of monasticism, even in the form of agricultural communes, gained the upper hand.[6] The presence of the religious in the landscape of socialist agriculture was perceived as dangerous; it created competition and demonstrated better agricultural practices than those promoted by the state; in addition, monasteries continued to attract the laity for pilgrimage and prayer.[7] By the end of the 1930s, the remaining monastic communes had been closed, leaving their members homeless. Some elderly monks and nuns were taken in by local parish priests and dedicated parishioners.[8] In other cases, the monks from provincial monasteries found refuge in the cities, forming new informal communes in parish churches. For example, six monks from Zosimova pustyn', which was closed down by the authorities in 1923, moved to Moscow Vysoko-Petrovskii monastery, where under the leadership of Bishop Varfolomei (Remov) they continued their monastic life and offered spiritual guidance to the laity.[9] This close-knit group of monks attracted men and women from various districts of Moscow who sought a deeper engagement with monastic spirituality.[10]

After the forced closure of monasteries, monastic life became decentralized and informal. Monks and nuns had to remove their habits, as they lived and worked among ordinary people in the countryside and the city. Unable to attend church services, they gathered to pray in private houses. When priests were not available, nuns conducted parts of the monastic services. Several nuns of the Novo-Tikhvinskii and Kasli convents in the Urals continued to live as a community even after the closure of their convents in the 1920s. After the closure of three convents in Verkhotur'e, Nizhnii Tagil, and Krasnoe Selo, their nuns moved to Turinskii okrug, to be near their spiritual father, the monk Damian (Lisitsyn), who lived in the taiga together with 20 hermits. The hermits survived by fishing and honey-making until 1924, when the secret police arrested four of them, forcing the others to flee.[11]

Indeed, in the late 1920s and the 1930s, the importance of informal spiritual leaders recruited out of monastic clergy within the oppositionist church movements grew. The declaration of loyalty to Soviet power in 1927 by Metropolitan Sergii (Stragorodskii),who replaced Tikhon in 1927, weakened Renovationism but gave rise to new schisms.[12] The conservative clergy that opposed Sergii, numbering about 3500, and led by Bishops Iosif (Petrovykh), Bishop Aleksei (Bui), Victor (Ostrovidov), and Niktarii (Trezvinskii), embraced in total about 11.5 percent of all parishes.[13] During the period 1929–1933 the Soviet authorities arrested 4,000 men and women as part of their assault on the church opposition in Moscow, Leningrad, Voronezh, Ukraine, and Belorussia.[14] Although the composition of the opposition movement was quite heterogeneous, it was united by a common distrust of the established church hierarchy, which had damaged its reputation by its support of the Soviet state. Some prominent spiritual elders belonged to the anti-Sergii opposition, such as Father Sergii (the son of Moscow elder Aleksei Mechev), who was arrested and executed in 1941. A large number of ordinary nuns and monks joined the opposition, supporting the bishops and serving as channels between the laity and the clergy. According to secret police records, the blind schema-monk Maksim (Pelevtsev) from Samara, who had a reputation for clairvoyance, was visited by peasants from nearby villages and preached that collective farms embodied the darkness of the Antichrist.[15] In Bashkiria after the arrest of anti-Sergian bishop Veneamin (Troitskii), Abbess Evdokiia Panferova from Sterlitamak became the leader of the opposition. Orthodox believers regarded her as a prophetess and clairvoyant, calling her "holy Avdot'ia."[16] It is unlikely that these leaders were instrumental in the anti-kolkhoz movement: the local holy men and women who categorized collective farms as the work of the Antichrist were simply articulating a sentiment that was already widespread among the peasantry.[17]

The popular opposition to Soviet authority and the compromised position of the Russian Orthodox Church also incorporated the prerevolutionary religious movements that emerged around the cult of some charismatic personality, which made these movements typologically similar to *starchestvo*. These included the *Ioannites*, who believed that Father John of Kronstadt was the incarnation of the Holy Trinity; *Imiaslavtsy* expelled from Athos and their supporters in Russia; *Innokentievtsy*, the followers of the Moldavian monk Innokentii accused of heresy in 1913; *Fedorovtsy*; and *Stefanovtsy*, the followers of Elder Stefan (Podgornyi), a monk from Suzdal' Spaso-Evfim'evskii monastery who around 1912 preached temparence to peasants. After the revolution, the movement of *Stefanovtsy* was led by Stefan's grandson, Vasilii Podgornyi, and the Suzdal' monk Isaia (Kushnarev). Most of these movements were inspired by the eschatological prophecies that proliferated in the early Soviet countryside. The *Fedorovtsy*, the followers of peasant Fedor Rybalkin, who was a prisoner of war from 1914–1917, believed that their leader Fedor was the incarnation of Christ, who came to the world to judge the unrighteous in 1922.[18] The followers of charismatic leaders refused to join collective farms, refused to take part in elections, practiced strict asceticism including celibacy, and believed that their leaders were embodiments of divinity. Although we can draw similarities between Orthodox elders and these charismatic leaders of popular eschatological movements, the latter differed from the former in the deification (or self-deification) of the charismatic leader and the localized and sectarian character of the eschatological movements. The popularity of elders within these movements attracted the attention of the Bolsheviks, who commented that eldership was widespread in Soviet Russia and that this was a new phenomenon, directly linked with opposition to the regime.[19]

Monasticism began to play a more significant role among the laity because the hierarchical structure of the Church was weakened. During the 1920s–1930s, many more monks could be ordained as priests and bishops promptly and without the complex procedures of the Synodal period. The links between ordinary believers and the monastic clergy became more intense: the clergy depended on the laity for food, accommodation, and moral support. In addition, the ascetic practices of monasticism found their way into the lives of the laity.

The post-revolutionary change in Russian society was understood by many Christians as both a return to apostolic times when Christians were persecuted, and the beginning of the new era prophesied by the saints in the past. One of the leaders of the opposition, priest Valentin Sventsitskii, expounded the idea of "monasticism in the world." In the *Dialogues*, written during his exile, he argued that during the first centuries of Christianity monasticism did not exist, because the ideals of monasticism (except celibacy) were practiced by all Christians. Following an influx of heathens into the Church, the demarcation between the "world" and the Church eroded, which stimulated some Christians to leave the world for the desert where they could live according to the Gospel. Sventsitskii referred to prophecies of Antony the Great, which foretold that in the future monks would live not in the desert but in the midst of cities and their task would be more difficult than that of traditional monasticism, as they would have to resist the values of the material world.[20] Under the new regime, all Christians had to become monks and nuns in the sense that in order to live in the new Soviet society they had to build invisible walls around themselves, which would protect them from contamination by the secular, anti-Christian culture and ideology of Bolshevik Russia. This new model of ascetic life in the world was practiced by lay men and women who gathered around popular spiritual leaders like hieromonk Varsonofii (Iurchenko) in Ukraine, Father Sergei Mechev, and others. These groups of laity practiced an intense liturgical and spiritual life, celebrating all church services according to the *Typicon*, keeping all Orthodox fasts, and practicing more frequent and concentrated confessions.[21]

These new forms of spiritual life required a deeper relationship between a Christian and his or her spiritual director. Paradoxically, the revolution had actually released the constraints that existed on individualism in the search for the sacred, and allowed for a proliferation of unorthodox interpretations of religious texts. The growth of Baptist choirs and prayer groups, Old Believer conferences and pilgrimages, and the activity of the Christian Student Movement in the 1920s and early 1930s signified that the disappearance of the old regime did not suppress, but rather stimulated religious activities.[22] The members of the Christian Student Movement, inspired by the evangelicals, were sympathetic to Orthodox elders, who—they believed—opposed the rigidity of the church hierarchy and lived by evangelical ideals.[23] Thus, the search for spiritual guidance was an expression of the individual striving to find religious fulfillment. As the experience and knowledge of monastic ascetic practices became more accessible to the laity, a greater popular interest in the development of a more intense form of religious life arose. "When people came to the elder they found not a judge or persecutor but their ideal self, with all their thoughts about eternity and God and with their striving to heaven," wrote a member of an informal religious community in Moscow that had formed around the elder Ignatii (Lebedev).[24] The search for moral support and certainty during difficult times also motivated religious involvement. The urban intelligentsia and educated classes, who lost their social and economic privileges and civil rights during the Civil War and the NEP, and had become social pariahs (the so-called "*lishentsy*"), looked for some form of recognition and encouragement in the Church. One-to-one communication with an experienced and caring pastor, who concentrated on inward spiritual problems, helped people to cope with daily hardship and social exclusion. Finally, the search for a spiritual guide was a form of protest and resistance to the regime. Following the advice of their spiritual fathers, some Christians felt empowered to challenge the authorities by participating in underground religious activities, spreading leaflets, and preaching among peasants about the Antichrist.

The contacts between spiritual children and their elders were often interrupted by arrests and exile. Prisons and labor camps became spaces that Orthodox priests could use as new arenas for pastoral work and the

6.1. Father Sergii Mechev among his spiritual children. Moscow, 1930s. Courtesy of Vladimir I. Petrov

spreading of the evangelical message. Father Maksim (Zhizhilenko), who had a medical degree, worked as a doctor in the hospital of Solovki labor camp in 1929–1930. It was said that he was able to give correct diagnoses to his patients without using any instruments or analyses.[25] Despite hardship and deprivation, prisons and camps became locations where monks could learn more about life. Bishop Veneamin (Milov), arrested as a monk in Danilov monastery in 1929, wrote about the camp: "Before my arrest I was cut off from daily life and could not see what people live by, what they are interested in, what is the spirit of contemporary society."[26] The camps, which held about 20 percent of Russia's population of clergy and believers, could become a ground for protest against the regime. For example, the nuns of Shamordino convent who came to Solovki in the 1930s refused to perform any common work, justifying their actions through their moral opposition to the Antichrist. Despite the advice of the prison doctors who happened to be Orthodox priests, they declined any compromise that could help them to survive in the camp.[27]

The disintegration of the institutional structure of Orthodoxy in the early Soviet era had several effects on spiritual eldership. It opened the door to informal spritual leaders, removing the constraints that existed in the Synodal church. Due to the closure of monasteries and convents, monasticism became more intimately connected with the life in the world, while ascetic values often became guiding principles for the laity. In the heated ideological climate of the 1920s, against the background of several antireligious campaigns and unpopular collectivization policies, spiritual elders often expressed anti-Bolshevik attitudes and encouraged their spiritual children to resist. Yet the most prudent of them tried to ensure the Church's survival and advised their followers to focus on spiritual life.[28] *Starchestvo* in postrevolutionary Russia functioned as a form of religious collective memory in the sense that it served as a link with the Orthodox community's past, as well as a practice that brought the believer into closer contact with the divine.[29] Followers of the *startsy* commemorated their spiritual guides and thus maintained the continuity of ascetic and hesychast tradition, which would be revived during the post-war period.

Monasticism and Elders in Soviet Society after the War

The return of the Russian Orthodox Church into the orbit of Soviet public life and the ceasing of repressions against its clergy during the Second World War had a revitalizing effect on monasticism. Immediately before the war there were no monasteries and convents left in the Soviet Union, whereas in 1945 there were 75, of which 46 were located in the territories of Ukraine, Belorussia, and Moldova (annexed in 1939). Twenty-nine of these had reopened during the German occupation.[30] Compared to the prerevolutionary period, monasteries and convents had fewer monks and nuns: there were 3,125 nuns in 42 convents and 855 monks and novices in 33 monasteries. About two-thirds of the inhabitants of monastic communities were above 60 years old.[31] The monasteries and convents that reemerged in the occupied territories often recruited their previous inhabitants who, following the closure of a monastery by the Soviet authorities, had remained nearby.[32] Some monks served in parish churches as priests.[33] When the war ended, the government did not return to earlier policies directed at the eradication of organized religion. Recognizing the Russian Orthodox Church's contribution to the war effort, Stalin turned a blind eye to the seeming incompatibility of the coexistence of organized monasticism and the Soviet way of life, and tried to incorporate religious institutions into the Soviet economic system. According to a decree of the Council of Ministers in 1945, monasteries and convents functioned as auxiliary (*podsobnye*) state agricultural enterprises and as cooperative institutions that had to supply the country with milk and meat in accordance with fixed quotas established from above.[34] The authorities' attitude towards monasticism, and the Church in general, was guided by considerations of loyalty to the Soviet motherland. During the war the Soviet military administration did not hesitate to use monasteries as bases for intelligence on the occupied territories: for example, several Soviet NKVD officers were housed in the Pskovo-Pecherskii monastery, disguised as novices.[35]

Although the reemergence of Orthodox monasticism in Soviet Russia had, on the whole, a revitalizing effect on popular religion, internal life in monasteries and convents lacked discipline and spiritual direction. In 1955, the abbots and abbesses in Moldova gathered to discuss the problems that arose in their institutions: they commented on instances of alcoholism, fights between monks, and laziness. Bishop Nektarii of Kishinev suggested that the older and more experienced monks and nuns should use their authority to instruct the younger monks and novices, to whom the latter could recount their actions and thoughts daily. The bishop certainly had in mind the ascetic practice of eldership, which by that time seemed to have lost its significance in the Moldavian monasteries. Other bishops also tried to use experienced monks to revive spiritual life in monasteries where it was lacking. For example, Bishop Grigorii of Leningrad was concerned that the Pskovo-Pecherskii monastery, which had about 60 monks and novices, lacked experienced administrators and elders. In 1947, he wrote to the New Valaam monastery in Finland, which had emerged as a result of the evacuation of Russian monks from the island during the Winter War, with a request for the dispatch of some monks to Pechery, in order to help it revive its spiritual life.[36]

In postwar Soviet society the monastic spiritual elders symbolized continuity with the religious life of prerevolutionary Russia. Old age was generally a typical feature of the Orthodox clergy in the 1950s; this demographic generational imbalance may also have been responsible for the conservatism of the spiritual leaders.[37] The core of revived monasticism was embodied in the monks and nuns who took the veil either before or just after the Revolution of 1917. For example, between 1953 and 1957, more than one third of the monks in Glinskaia pustyn', which was restored during the war, were those who took their vows before 1922.[38] These monks—many of whom had suffered in the prisons and camps—paid particular attention to the preservation of tradition as they had learned it during their novitiate. In Glinskaia, the conservatism of elders (many of whom had little or no formal education) entailed not only abiding by the ancient Rule of Mount Athos (including the practice of spiritual guidance of novices by the elders and the emphasis on correct ritual performance), but also criticism of modernist tendencies, such as frequent communion, introduced by some members of the clergy.[39] After the closure of Glisnkaia pustyn' under Khrushchev, many elders left for the Caucasus, where they could continue contemplative life.

In the wake of the disappearance of the Renovationist movement in 1946–1948, the attitude toward monasticism among the church leadership was generally quite positive: the hierarchy supported monasteries and encouraged the restoration of the institution of spiritual guidance. Bishops relied on elders and they expressed their appreciation by awarding distinguished monks with the title of archimandrite and giving them symbolic awards.[40] The use of elders for the purposes of discipline and education echoed the prerevolutionary Synodal policy. In a reflection of the past, members of the clergy who transgressed had to serve public penance in one of the monasteries under the supervision of an experienced senior monk, normally known as "an elder." For example, Patriarch Aleksii I ordered two monks of the Pskovo-Pecherskii monastery to be transferred to Glinskaia pustyn' in 1957 for "spiritual growth under the guidance of experienced elders."[41] Yet despite this policy, tensions between the elders and members of the church hierarchy continued during the Soviet period, and reflected a traditional confrontation between the institution and charismatic leaders. It was not unusual for some popular elders to suffer misunderstanding and persecution from the church authorities. Elder Sampson (Sivers), a descendant of the noble family of Count Sivers, was especially prone to creating confrontations at the various monasteries in which he lived. In his memoirs he claimed that his troubles with church administrators could be accounted for by political discrimination and slander. In Astrakhan and Stalingrad, where he served as a priest after the war, his preaching and the practice of public confession attracted thousands of people. This extraordinary popularity, he implied, put the clergy of these cities in an uncomfortable position vis-à-vis the party authorities. The bishop of Astrakhan, Sergii (Larin), prohibited Sampson from celebrating the liturgy and sent the defrocked priest under escort to the Pskovo-Pecherskii monastery, where Sampson, predictably, fell out with the abbot of the monastery. In the 1950s a mentally unstable female pilgrim called Lidia charged Elder Sampson with rape. The affair, accompanied by the attention of the media, led to the expulsion of Sampson from the community.[42] Despite these clashes with the hierarchy and monastic administrators, Sampson enjoyed the reputation of a spiritual guide and faith healer among his lay supporters, who started to press the church hierarchy for the canonization of their venerable elder in the post-Soviet period.

Elders, Their Influence on the Laity, and Popular Religion

In 1956 believers throughout Russia retold the tale of a young female worker, Zoia from Kuibyshev, who fell into catalepsy during a youth party while dancing with an icon of St. Nicholas. According to this tale, during a New Year celebration in her flat, Zoia, who was offended by her fiancé Nikolai's failure to turn up at the party, declared cockily that she would dance instead with the icon of St. Nicholas that hung in the house. As soon as she declared her intention and laid hands upon the icon, she was struck by some invisible force and could no longer move her limbs. Despite the efforts of doctors to bring her out of her stupor, she remained standing on the same spot with the icon in her hands for four months until Easter of 1956.[43] Rumors about how the girl had turned to stone as a punishment for her sacrilegious behavior circulated across various Russian regions and led to an upsurge in church attendance.[44] The local party authorities, who denied that such an incident had taken place, discussed the popular rumor about Zoia throughout 1956 in connection with the failure of antireligious propaganda.[45] According to one version of this legend, a popular elder from Belgorod, the monk Serafim (Tiapochkin) (1894–1982), managed to sneak into Zoia's house (which was guarded by militia), and remove the icon of St. Nicholas from the "stone girl's" hands.[46]

During this time religion was denigrated within Soviet discourse and was categorized pejoratively as "superstition," "mysticism," "paganism," and "fanaticism." The party was especially worried about the revival of unsanctioned mass pilgrimages to holy springs, during which unauthorized persons carried out religious services, preached, and practiced faith healing. The shrieks and convulsions of those who were believed to be demonically possessed provided a shocking yet fascinating spectacle for the pilgrims.[47] In many ways, elders represented an alternative form of religious authority somewhere on the borderline between the sanctioned and unsanctioned that could channel expressions of popular piety into a legitimate outlet, i.e. parish or monastic life. The popularity of elders grew in proportion to the miracles they supposedly performed: faith-healing, exorcisms, and prophecies. A large number of people sought help from elders in relation to their health problems. It is striking that although more people had access to medical care than during the prewar era, believers continued to rely on divine intervention in matters of health. Many people approached elders with requests for their approval of surgery or some other medical treatment, and—in addition to medical treatment—believers resorted to faith healing (prayer, anointment with oil, or with soil taken from the grave of a popular elder).[48] More often than not, elders discouraged a believer from following through on forthcoming surgery or treatment, thus implying that the power of God was stronger than the advance of modern medicine.

The social base of elders probably included all social groups within Soviet society, even the Soviet elite. The spiritual children of Serafim (Murav'ev) of Vyritsa, for example, included prominent members of the Leningrad intelligentsia, professionals, bishops, and patriarchs. Elder Sampson too boasted that among his spiritual children were the academician I. P. Pavlov and the Politburo member N.A. Tikhonov.[49] Glinskaia monastery and its elders, on the other hand, were popular among the rural population of Sumy oblast. The scale of popular interest in monasticism and elders can be deduced from the number of pilgrims and the growing income of the few remaining monasteries in the Soviet Union. Official Soviet data suggests that in the late 1940s and 1950s the number of pilgrims traveling to monasteries during religious feasts could reach 60,000 people. According to the same source, Kievo-Pecherskii monastery attracted more than 500,000 pilgrims each year.[50] Glinskaia pustyn' had more modest and, perhaps, more reliable data that suggested that in the first half of 1954, 720 pilgrims stayed in the monastery hostels.[51] At Piukhtitsa convent between two and three thousand pilgrims usually gathered for the feast of the Dormition of Mother of God in August.[52] Donations accounted for about 66 percent of Glinskaia's total income; in addition, lay supporters of the elders provided them with food, clothes, and, if necessary, with lodging.

The surge of lay interest in elders in Soviet society had parallels with the prerevolutionary era. People came to elders in search of the meaning of life and looking for psychological help during personal crises. In addition, nonbelievers or nonpracticing Christians, who had experienced a renewal of their faith, were seeking the support and guidance of experienced spiritual leaders. Antonina, an accountant from Pechery, told the story of her conversion. In 1954 she suffered a personal crisis, which led her to attempt suicide by gas poisoning. She failed in this endeavor but remembered saying a last prayer before she was temporarily overcome by the fumes. She woke up feeling like a different person. At work she asked a colleague who regularly visited the Pskovo-Pecherskii monastery to take her to the monastery and she managed to fund the trip through a providential lottery win. At the monastery she went to confession with Elder Simeon (Zhelnin), who met her as if he had known her before and had expected her. He managed to win the repentant woman's trust and helped her to overcome her crisis, and the two developed a long-term spiritual bond.[53] Although Antonina did not make an explicit connection between her attempt on her own life (a grave sin in the Orthodox Church) and the meeting with Elder Simeon, her story suggests that she managed to escape from her depressive state through the intervention of the divine, which eventually brought her into contact with Simeon. The decision to change her life radically, which even led to her repudiation of her unbelieving husband, was linked with the more radical form of spirituality represented by monasticism and the practice of spiritual guidance.

The elders' means of influence upon the laity varied, from direct contact during confession and conversation, to indirect forms of communication via letters and tape recordings. The followers of Elder Sampson transmitted his sermons and spiritual talks on audiotapes to groups of believers across Russia, thus using the same means that were employed to broadcast the songs of Russian semiunderground popular artists like Vladimir Vysotskii or Bulat Okudzhava.[54] Despite the activities of the Moscow Patriarchate's publishing house, hesychast and ascetic literature were in short supply. Elders encouraged people to read the works of the Byzantine and Russian hesychast writers, such as the *Dobrotoliubie* or the writings of Ignatii Brianchaninov, which had been copied by hand or borrowed from private or monastic libraries.[55]

The antireligious campaigns of the late 1950s closed the majority of monasteries (only 18 remained by 1964), with the aid of police and the KGB, the expulsion of monks and nuns, raising the age of novitiate to 30 years, and the raising of taxes on the Church. Local authorities also targeted popular spiritual leaders by either removing them from their monasteries or incarcerating them in mental hospitals. For example, in 1963, the militia of Pochaev in the Ukrainian Republic detained a popular *starets* from the Pochaev Lavra monastery, monk Iosif (Golovatiuk), who had been instrumental in organizing resistance to the plan of closing the monastery. He was forced to undergo "treatment" in a local mental hospital, and was subsequently transferred to the care of his relatives.

The forced closure of monasteries and the attacks on believers in the Khrushchev period had several consequences for spiritual eldership.[56] On the one hand, the closure of a monastery could lead to the spread of elders' influence outside their cloisters, which, in some ways, was a replication of the situation of the 1920s–1930s. The expelled monks (more than 1,500) found new accommodation either among the laity or in areas that were less troubled by the antireligious campaigns. For example, following the closure of their monastery in 1961, the monks of Glinskaia moved to the Caucasus, where some of them lived as hermits and others served as priests in Sukhumi cathedral.[57] Since the remaining monasteries in the Soviet Union served as showcases for foreign visitors and the activity of monks and nuns was under the strict control of the local administraiton and the party, the centers of spiritual guidance once again transferred to the parishes. On the other hand, the style and methods of Khrushchev's antireligious campaign alienated some sections of believers and the clergy from the Soviet project, and created a fertile breeding ground for more radical forms of religious expression that drew a sharp division between the sacred world of religious belief and practice and the profane world of Soviet society. This may explain why some believers were attracted to charismatic religious leaders who were in opposition to the Soviet regime.

The new political investment in the antireligious campaigns and the destructive policies that were used against the institutions and personnel of the Russian Orthodox Church led to a growth of conformism on the part of the church hierarchy and the emergence of dissent among the lower ranks of the clergy and intelligentsia. Some vociferous priests like G. Iakunin, N. Eshliman, and the deacon A. Krasnov-Levitin accused the hierarchy of cowardice and complicity and criticized their neglect of the reformist spirit of the Church Council of 1917–1918.[58] In 1972, Alexander Solzhenitsyn adopted a similar position in his open "Great Lent Letter," addressed to Patriarch Pimen. He lamented the devastation of religious life in Russia and blamed the hierarchy for their silence, passivity, and submissiveness to the destroyers of the Church.[59]

Apart from the forced closure of monasteries and ecclesiastical seminaries, in the 1960s–1970s there were signs of the declining influence of the Church in social life. This was expressed in the falling number of parishes and shrinking number of the clergy. For example, between 1961 and 1967 the number of priests fell by 1,500.[60] The reasons for such a decline were social as well as political. An outflow of population from rural areas was accompanied by the decline of village parishes, while in the cities almost no new parishes were created despite the religious needs of a growing urban population. There was a scarcity of churches in many of the new cities within the Soviet Union, and often only cemetery churches remained active.[61] Although the years of antireligious campaigns, strict prohibitions on religious activities among children and youth, and the surveillance of the clergy and active believers were certainly instrumental in a decline in religious belief and the alienation of believers from their churches, in many ways the Soviet Union also experienced the general weakening of Christian religion that occurred in the Western European countries. Decline of religious belief and activity, driven by a combination of factors, including urbanization, mass culture, and education, led to the emergence of a generation that, if not atheistic, was at least indifferent to religion.[62]

Yet precisely within this "indifferent generation" there was a religious revival, although limited in scale, among the city intelligentsia who came to faith in the late 1950s and 1960s. According to Jane Ellis, there were two major reasons for this religious revival: first, the moral and intellectual revival provoked by de-Stalinization and, secondly, the breaking of the long silence that followed the years of terror.[63] In big cities, educated youth began to explore religious philosophy. Many baby boomers were converted to Christianity through reading Solov'ev, Berdiaev, or Dostoevsky, practicing yoga and meditation, or watching Western films, such as *The Gospel according to St. Matthew* by Pasolini (1964).[64] The questioning members of the intelligentsia formed small discussion groups and circles, including religious-philosophical seminars that were organized by artists and intellectuals in the 1970s. They tended to lean towards clergy that had a similar background and intellectual outlook, including Orthodox priests such as Sergei Zheludkov, Alexander Men', Dmitrii Dudko, Vsevolod Shpiller, Valerii Povedskii, and Vladimir Zalipskii, as well as the Latvian monk Tavrion (Batozskii). All these priests carried out missionary work among the intelligentsia, catechizing and baptizing adults, and drawing on world literature, the arts, and music to convey the Gospel to Soviet-educated circles.[65] Disregarding the ideological differences between the "democrats" and "nationalists," the missionary clergy used pastoral methods of the Russian Orthodox Church that were traditional, as well as innovative. They employed the traditional teachings of the Church Fathers, combining them with universalist and ecumenical currents.[66] The personal relationship between the pastor and the neophyte, based on the model of spiritual fatherhood, was especially valuable in the development of personal ties between the members of these dissident or semidissident circles around the parishes of Alexander Men''s church in Novaia Derevnia near Moscow, Vsevolod Shpiller's Nikolaevskaia church in Kuznetsy (Moscow), or Dmitrii Dudko's commune in Grebnevo, 40 kilometers outside Moscow. Father Alexander Men', whose spiritual directors had belonged to Aleksei and Sergei Mechev's circles in Moscow, valued the relationship of spiritual paternity between the pastor and the believer; he believed that no important life decisions should be made by a believer without a blessing and advice from his spiritual director, who was to instruct the believer in the matters of fasting, prayer, communion, and charity. Yet he considered the monastic concept of obedience inapplicable to the life in the world, because lay people, unlike monks, did not make vows of obedience. He compared his role as a pastor with that of a midwife, saying that he only wanted to help the person to find his or her own way to God: "what is born from within is more valuable than what is brought from without."[67]

Elders, Monasticism, and Russia Abroad

The story of Russian spiritual elders would be incomplete without a brief overview of Russian emigration and the Russian émigrés' religious quests and concerns about tradition. The presence of a large Russian diaspora was the result of two world wars, the Civil War, border changes, and the pressure of political regimes. There were significant social, ideological, and cultural differences between these Russians. Some of them suddenly and involuntarily found themselves to be citizens of a different state as a result of First World War border arrangements, which led to the creation of border or limitrophe states. Others came to Europe alongside the retreating White armies in 1920. According to some estimates, the number of Russians in Europe following the end of the Civil War was between 668,000 and 772,000.[68]

The Second World War significantly increased the size of the Slavic population in Europe: thousands of displaced Russians, Ukrainians, and Belorussians chose not return to their homeland and settled in the West. In addition to this massive population shift between 1914 and 1945, in the post-Stalin era there was a further migration of individuals motivated by political, ideological, or religious reasons. In reference to the first two waves of migration, Mark Raeff observed that many exiles experienced "a renewal of faith [that] proved to be a consolation and a source of the inner strength needed to confront the ordeal of exile."[69] The overwhelming number of Russian Orthodox Christians among the migrants, and the fact that many clergy retreated with the White Armies, guaranteed the emergence of a lively and energetic religious life in exile. However, competing loyalties split the émigré community into camps, some of which remained faithful to the Moscow Patriarch, while others joined the newly formed Russian Church in Exile or came under the jurisdiction of the Patriarch of Constantinople. Despite these split loyalties, the Russians—many of whom experienced a profound religious conversion in exile—believed that through the Orthodox Church they would be able to maintain a mystical inner connection with Russia and its fate.[70]

Mark Raeff, in his thoughtful and elegantly written *Russia Abroad*, points out that monasticism "played little part in the cultural life and everyday consciousness of the emigration."[71] This statement needs to be qualified. Monasticism continued to influence Russian émigré writers such as Boris Zaitsev and Ivan Shmelev, whose writings were inspired by monastic spirituality and the saints.[72] Boris Zaitsev developed the religious theme in his prose only after his emigration in 1922, when he discovered "Holy Russia," which he would never have noticed without the suffering inflicted by the revolution.[73] Russians, including émigré writers, who lived either in the border states, the Balkans, or Western Europe, made regular pilgrimages to such centers of monastic life as Valaam, the Pskovo-Pecherskii monastery, Mount Athos, and the Piukhtitsa convent. As a result of postwar border treaties these religious hubs remained outside Soviet Russia.[74] The literary pilgrims often made a connection with the prerevolutionary tradition of writing about monasteries, wherein these religious institutions were a topos of Russian culture associated with history, spirituality, tradition, eternity, and otherworldliness.[75] Thus, monasteries and convents retained their significance for the Russian diaspora's consciousness as visible sites of tradition and religious commitment. Monasteries served as venues for the popular conferences of the Russian Student Christian Movement, they published liturgical and devotional literature, and they continued—albeit on a limited scale—their charitable activities.[76] Yet the chief aims of Russian monks and nuns in exile were preservation and management of the Russian Orthodox monastic tradition in an alien environment, often in countries such as Great Britain, Finland, or the United States, where the tradition of monasticism was either absent or weak.

The émigrés continued to venerate Russian holy men, focusing on those figures that were known as spiritual guides and intercessors for the people: Sergius of Radonezh, Serafim of Sarov, and Father John of Kronstadt. The cult of St. Serafim of Sarov among émigrés was developed not only because of its association with the royal family, but because it represented an embodiment of Russian holiness.[77] In the ecumenically inclined periodicals, such as *Vestnik RKhD*, St. Serafim was compared to the popular French confessor Cure D'Ars, and he was treated as an exceptionally holy figure, an icon of Orthodoxy.[78] Boris Zaitsev bemoaned the behavior of the Russian intelligentsia who had treated the canonization of the Sarov monk with skepticism in the years around 1903, and came to Sarov only for picnics and not for worship.[79] Ivan Shmelev revealed to his readers that St. Serafim supernaturally entered his life, helping to cure an illness and avoid surgery.[80] Serafim's apparent intervention also signified a spiritual reunion of the writer with his native land: "I am not alone here, there are likeminded souls including Him, who is of our kin, the very Russian, from Sarov . . . here, in this Europe alien to everything I believe in."[81]

Another icon of Orthodoxy for the Russian émigrés was Father John of Kronstadt: recollections of encounters with the "Kronstadt little father" and accounts of miracles performed by the popular pastor were published widely in the émigré press, and his portrait decorated people's homes. Eventually his canonization was carried out by the Russian Church in Exile.[82] However, despite the deprivations suffered by the exiles and the renewal of religious enthusiasm among many of their number, educated Russian émigrés did not search for a living charismatic spiritual figure of similar status to Serafim or Father John of Kronstadt, and had no parallel to the spiritual movements that took place in Soviet Russia.

While not necessarily in search of a charismatic authority and often wary of monastic spirituality, the church in exile was nevertheless a fertile ground for the cultivation of spiritual fatherhood. Many church hierarchs and ordinary parish priests gained the reputation of a *pater spirituelle* and were able to build intimate links with their parishioners and serve their needs in a truly evangelical way. Although known better for their public roles or theological writings, religious figures of the Russian emigration such as the priests Sergii Bulgakov, Aleksandr Elchaninov, Aleksei Neliubov, and Vasilii Zenkovskii, Archimadrite Kiprian (Kern), and bishops Ioann (Shakhovskoi) and Antonii (Khrapovitskii) were also known as skilful confessors and much-loved pastors.[83]

While recognizing the historical role of monasticism, some segments of the Russian emigration, especially the circles around the Paris Institute of Theology and the groups of intellectuals associated with the religious-philosophical journal *The Way* (*Put'*), questioned the relevance of ascetic withdrawal from the world in modern society. These intellectuals were not a homogeneous grouping and counted among their number the poet and Socialist-Revolutionary-turned-Orthodox-nun Mother Mariia Skobtsova, and Bishop Ioann (Shakhovskoi) of San Francisco, who was also a poet. Together, diverse characters such as these contributed to a radical change of thinking about monasticism. Mother Mariia (neè Pilenko) experienced a profound religious conversion that helped her turn away from the grief associated with tragic losses (her husband and two of her children died of hunger) to evangelical service for poor and destitute Russians in France. She organized kitchens to feed poor workingmen in Paris and organized shelter for the homeless. Her attempts to hide Jews during the Vichy regime resulted in her imprisonment in a Nazi concentration camp where—according to witnesses—she died saving the life of another woman.[84]

According to Mother Mariia, it was not sufficient to love one's neighbor by praying for him and giving him Christian consolation. She believed one had to feed him if he was hungry and give him shelter if he was homeless. Embracing the monastic habit and taking monastic vows of poverty and celibacy, she rejected traditional Orthodox cloistering for nuns and could be observed shopping in the markets for her kitchen or sitting in Parisian cafes with her intellectual friend Nicholas Berdiaev. She was an outspoken critic of traditional monasticism. During her visit to Piukhtitsa convent in Estonia she described the attitude of the nuns as concern about personal piety and a comfortable retreat from social evil. She authored articles in which she criticized monastic spiritual guidance, or *starchestvo*, as outdated practice and bad religion. According to her interpretation, the absolute remittance of one's own will into the hands of the elder implied that a monk carried no personal responsibility for his actions. She certainly exaggerated the case by suggesting that a monk could have no opinion, values, or choice. The extreme case, she suggested, would be a disciple who followed a heretical elder. She argued that under the circumstances in which the Church found itself in exile, eldership had no connection to its roots and could not be restored because there were no monks capable of being *startsy*.[85] Mother Mariia aimed at creating a new form of monasticism in the world, which would be "semimonastery, semifellowship."[86] In the communities she founded in Paris, several lonely poor women lived together, providing food for those in need and carrying out numerous social and religious activities. While she alienated her collaborators, the nun Evdokiia (Meshcheriakova) and Hieromonk Kiprian (Kern), who defended traditional ascetic monasticism, she found support and understanding in the person of the Frenchman Father Lev (Gillet), a Benedictine monk who had converted to Orthodoxy.[87]

Monastic Eldership in Russia Abroad

Monastic life in Soviet Russia faced challenges in its struggle for survival in a state that attempted to eliminate organized religion. Yet the position of the Russian monasteries beyond the borders of the USSR was only slightly better. As a result of the emergence of the border states and independent Finland, about 50 Orthodox Russian monasteries found themselves in the new countries of Poland, Estonia, Latvia, Finland, and Romania. The new border treaties signed in 1920 between Russia and limitrophe states changed the fortunes of several major Russian monasteries and convents.

The famous Valaam monastery on Ladoga Lake, known as the "Northern Athos," became part of Finnish Karelia following the successful offensive by General Mannerheim in 1919–1920. Together with its satellite monasteries (the Konevets and the St. Trifon monasteries), the Lintula convent, and numerous hermitages situated on the islands, it represented an important center for the cultivation of monastic life and became a magnet for pilgrims. The tradition of spiritual guidance as it had been shaped in the Synodal era persisted even during the turbulent era of wars and revolutions. However, the monastery that had boasted more than 1,000 monks, novices, and voluntary laborers before 1914, lost much of its fortune and many of its younger men during the First World War. In 1917–1918 the monastery was cut off from its compounds (*podvor'e*) in Moscow and St. Petersburg and from the Russian pilgrims that used to come to the monastery in large numbers.[88] By the mid-1920s only 450 monks and novices lived in Valaam.[89] The Finnish authorities put pressure upon the monks to apply for Finnish citizenship and—when the Finnish Church declared its autonomy from Moscow—to switch from the Old Style (the Julian calendar) to the New Style (the Gregorian calendar). The calendar question proved to be very controversial: several monks in Valaam actively resisted the arbitrary change of dates pertaining to the celebration of Easter and other feasts and accused the church authorities of the violation of church canons. The monks continued to celebrate according to the Old Style: for example, during the visit of the Greek bishop Germanos in 1922, several hieromonks refused to co-celebrate, while deacons refused to take communion. The church authorities continued to put pressure on the monks and in 1925 the ecclesiastical court reprimanded several senior monks (including the respected Elder Mikhail) for their disobedience to the sanctioned authority and their role in igniting a schism among the brethren.[90]

Valaam's reputation for the cultivation of spiritual elders was well-known: every new novice was assigned to an experienced monk-elder in the monastery or its sketes, while some Valaam monks became very popular as confessors and spiritual guides of the laity. Schemamonk Efrem (Khrobostov) (1871–1947), for example, had been confessor of Grand Duke Nicholas and his family. He was believed to continue the legacy of the Valaam hermit-elders, Aleksei and Antipa. Afanasii (Nechaev) (1886–1944), a novice in Valaam during 1925–1926, felt that his understanding of Christianity had changed after meeting the Valaam elders, Mikhail and Efrem. Afanasii was a lay missionary who in 1923 had escaped from Russia across the Finnish border and visited Valaam as a tourist. After his meeting with Elder Mikhail, whom he described as a "True Man," he decided to become a monk. Afanasii's intention to save the world through missionary efforts was replaced by a belief that it was more important to save one's own soul.[91] He saw in the Valaam eldership the Socratic ideal of self-knowledge, and he believed that this knowledge of one's own self could be achieved through interaction with an elder. According to Afanasii, it was the ability of the elder to embrace the entire self of the person in question that promoted a wonderful sense of freedom from everything that caused suffering.

However, the practice of providing spiritual guidance for novices and the laity had fallen into disuse after 1917, when the number of novices had shrunk and the pilgrims from Russia stopped coming. After the evacuation of the monastery in 1940 to a Finnish area near Hüvaskula, there was almost no new blood in the community. The majority of monks, including novices, were born in the 1870s, so that by the end of the Second World War they were in their 70s and 80s.[92] In the 1940s–1950s some elders officially carried out the duties of confessors (Elders Efrem and Ioann), while others withdrew from monastic affairs because of their refusal to accept the New Style (Elder Mikhail).

Elder Ioann (Alekseev) (1873–1958) was one of many peasant youths who, after the emancipation of the serfs in 1861, decided to choose a monastic vocation. His education was limited to lessons from a village tailor and at a parish school, but during his life in Valaam from the age of 28 he learned the Bible, sacred history, and catechism. The letters he wrote to his spiritual children show an excellent knowledge of scripture and of the writings of the Fathers of the Church. Although deeply attached to Valaam, Ioann realized the deficiencies of monastic spiritual life. He criticized monks for their blind attachment to outward piety and institutional rules and their neglect of the essence of monastic life: inner prayer.[93] He understood spiritual guidance as a form of transmission of one's own experience: "the mentor should point in the direction which he himself followed. If he only guides on the basis of books, he will make mistakes . . . a [true] guide should be free from passions and have the gift of judgment."[94] Elder Ioann's correspondents included men and women of Russian or Karelian descent who lived in Finland, as well as some former Lutherans who had converted to Orthodoxy. Because there were fewer pilgrims and novices, the elder could develop deep bonds with his spiritual children and respond to their letters with particular thoroughness.

Elder Mikhail (1871–1959), from the *meshchane* (petty traders) of Kronstadt, came to Valaam as an eighteen-year-old youth, and by 1921, at the age of just 40, he was elected as the confessor of the community. After taking an active part in the opposition against the new calendar, he lost his position of confessor and all other honors. After the war, when relations with the Russian Church had been restored, several monks expressed a wish to return to the old Valaam. Yet negotiations between the Moscow patriarch and the Soviet authorities regarding the restoration of the former "Northern Athos" did not succeed. Bishop Grigorii of Leningrad came up with the offer to send several experienced monks to Pskov-Pechery monastery, where there was a dearth of skillful administrators and spiritual leaders.[95] Responding to this call, seven monks, including Elder Mikhail, returned to the Soviet Union in 1957 and settled in the Pskov-Pechery monastery. Due to the old age of the repatriates, four of them died in 1959.

By the late 1950s there were just 53 monks in Valaam monastery, and by the 1970s this number had dwindled to only 10. The monastic tradition of Valaam vanished for several reasons. It was partly due to the deaths of the monks born in Tsarist Russia, who were the heirs of the traditions developed under Abbots Nazarii and Damaskin. Also, the Finnish church authorities, concerned with remolding Valaam as a Finnish or, at least, Karelian monastery, tried to protect the young Finnish monks against the "corrupting Russian spirit."[96] The Russian monks in Valaam made little effort to adapt to the needs of Finnish society, extending their work with the laity only to Russian emigrants. As a result, the Finnish successors of the Russian monks had very little contact with the tradition of spiritual guidance.[97] The generational transition was very rapid: by the 1970s there were no older monks who could act as the spiritual fathers of the newcomers. Both Valaam in Hüvaskula and the female convent in Lintulla were successfully indigenized by the Orthodox Finns: the concept of Valaam as the "spiritual mother " of the Finnish Orthodox Church excluded the element of Russianness from its legacy, only minor traces of which are visible in the outlook and tradition of both communities.[98]

Decline of the "Russian Athos"

While avid anti-Russian feelings had been evident among the Greek monks of Mount Athos since the second half of the nineteenth century, the Balkan wars in 1912–1913 led to a consistent policy of Hellenization on Athos. The *Imiaslavie* affair, the First World War, and more profoundly, the revolution in Russia, weakened the once powerful Russian religious presence on the Holy Mountain. After the withdrawal of the "Name of God Worshippers" from Athos and the military conscription of 90 monks during the war, 1,914 Russian monks remained on Athos, the majority of whom lived in the St. Panteleimon monastery and in the sketes of St. Andrew and St. Elijah, while 186 monks lived autonomously in separate cells (*kellioty*) and 263 lived as hermits.[99] The monastery continued to attract Russian men of émigré background, especially from the evacuated White Army forces in Gallipoli, despite the restricted access of foreign nationals to Athos.[100] The interruption of links with Russia brought with it a sharp fall in income, which had previously consisted of donations collected both in Russia and from pilgrims, as well as from sales of books and icons. To survive, St. Panteleimon monks had to sell the monastic fleet and some of the precious manuscripts in their possession. The monks were grateful to their correspondents in European countries who supported them from time to time.[101] They could hardly have afforded postage stamps and writing paper without the charity of their spiritual children in the world.

Despite demographic and economic decline, spiritual life in Athos continued to thrive. The monks followed strict ascetic rules and celebrated church services that lasted many hours; the novices lived in obedience to their elders. The monk Savva (b. 1881), who was tonsured in Athos in 1912, recalled that despite his previous monastic experience, he only managed to find a true spiritual father in Mount Athos. According to Savva, every elder had about 30 disciples (sometimes fewer), who supported one another with advice and conversation.[102] The old St. Panteleimon monastery, known as "Old Russik," was a laboratory of spiritual discipline and mental prayer. It had a special regime that was stricter than that of the main monastery, and the monks engaged each other with discourses on ascetic life.

While many Russian monks in Mount Athos led exemplary ascetic lives, few of them became known far beyond Athos and the Russian milieu. In the mid-twentieth century, the traditions of ascetic life and spiritual guidance of the Russian Athonites received international recognition when the book *Elder Siluan* was published in Paris in 1948, and subsequently translated into several European languages. Siluan (Semen Antonov) (1866–1938), a peasant from Tambov province, came to Athos because of its exceptionally good reputation, which was promoted by cheap booklets available to a mass readership. Having attended a local parish school for two winters, Semen worked as a carpenter and served in the sapper battalion of the Life Guards in St. Petersburg. Semen's piety, his interest in Athos, and his reverence before Father John of Kronstadt were not unusual for a peasant in post-Emancipation rural Russia, and did not necessarily predetermine his choice of monastic vocation. Siluan had wavered between a life in the world and monasticism: in his youth he drank vodka, played harmonica, took part in village brawls, and courted girls.[103] Spending a few years in St. Petersburg during his army service strengthened the young man's desire to join the Athonite community, because in the capital Siluan might have been able to visit the compound of St. Panteleimon monastery and access literature about Athos. After joining the monastery in 1892, Siluan worked in the mill and served as a manager and foreman at St. Panteleimon. After several years of struggle with demonic visions, Siluan experienced a vision of Christ during a vigil service. This vision stimulated the monk to write down his thoughts and meditations about the soul's relationship of love with God, the loss of grace, and the search for the peace and sweetness of God's love. His notes are pervaded by deep compassion for all living creatures, including poor workers on Mount Athos, fellow monks, animals, and insects (the monk grieved over a fly which he had killed and over a snake chopped into pieces that he had found on a mountain path). Siluan's notes include a passionate call to pray for one's enemies. This message was, perhaps, his response to the violent clashes between St. Panteleimon monks during the "Name of God" affair in 1913; it was also a response to the political events in Russia that divided the Russian émigré community into hostile camps. Siluan's notes, edited and published by his disciple, strike the reader as artless and profound at the same time. The language is influenced by the Psalms and Orthodox prayers; yet the intonation is very personal and emotional. It is difficult to think of a similar example of spiritual prose in Russia, and it could, perhaps, be compared to the writings of medieval mystics.[104]

Siluan was never ordained as a priest, thus he could not serve as a confessor. Nevertheless, he had several disciples and correspondents outside Athos. Monks and lay people asked for Siluan's advice and blessings in situations where they had to make crucial decisions. Nadiezhda Soboleva, a Russian émigré in Paris, struggled to turn her husband away from atheism, but had to care for him when he fell ill. She turned to Siluan for advice and intercession.[105] Both Bishop Veneamin (Fedchenkov) and his aide, the nun Anna (a noble émigré, Olga Obukhova) corresponded with Siluan. Nun Anna followed Bishop Veneamin to America, but due to her clashes with the bishop's secretary, wanted to leave her service and return to Europe. Siluan advised her to stay with the bishop, a suggestion to which she adhered.[106]

In the 1930s Siluan found himself at the center of a small circle of intellectuals-turned-monks who discovered in this peasant-monk an endless source of renewal for their faith and deemed him to be an essential guide in their mystical search for God. Among them were two former students of the theological seminary in Paris, Sergei Sakharov and Vasilii Krivosheine, and the English middle-class Catholic David Balfour.[107] Sofronii (Sergei Sakharov) (1896–1993), was a talented artist who was tormented by metaphysical questions. When he came to Athos in 1925, he found in Siluan a person who was—despite the huge cultural and social distance between the two men—able to engage with his philosophical and spiritual search; the two were very close until Siluan's death in 1938. In order to find a publisher for Siluan's writings, Sofronii left Athos in 1947.[108]

Father Sofronii's book *Starets Siluan* consisted of two sections: the edited writings of the Athonite monk and a larger section that contained a theological interpretation of Siluan's teaching. In contrast to the Russian intelligentsia's romantic idelaization of the *narod*, Sofronii's book is a fair tribute to Siluan's way of thinking and style: Sofronii neither tries to imitate

6.2. St. Siluan the Athonite. Contemporary Icon.
Courtesy of Nikita V. Andrejev

his teacher's manner of writing, nor patronizes the semiliterate peasant by rationalizing and dissecting his thoughts. The book is a dialogue between the master and his disciple, the loving account of a unique life that had an important message for modern times.

Returning from Athos to Paris in 1947, Sofronii found his experience and ideas unwelcome within a Russian émigré milieu that looked down on monasticism as an irrelevant institution in the modern world. He found a retreat in a quiet suburb of Paris, Sainte-Geneviève-des-Bois, where a small community of like-minded people had gathered. Failing to receive permission to return to Russia, where he had hoped to join Trinity-Sergius monastery, Sofronii moved to England, where his supporters helped to purchase a derelict house in Essex, which became a new monastic community. There was nothing conventional about this project: the community consisted of men and women of different nationalities (Swiss, Swedish, German, French, joined later by Greeks and Russians) who were all theologically educated; the services included an unusual monotonous recitation of the Jesus prayer while the lights were off, and each member of the community contributed to each reading. The community had no written code of monastic rules to regulate the daily routine of the monastery: every member of the community had the freedom to develop his full potential, and to find God in an atmosphere of communion and serving one's brother. In this, the Russian and Athonite traditions of spiritual guidance had merged and found a new meaning in Western society.

The Impact of Eldership on the Russian Emigration and Beyond

The practice and theory of spiritual eldership was inseparable from monasticism as a form of organized asceticism. In the philosophical and social thought of the religiously minded Russian émigré intelligentsia, intellectually rooted in the Russian Silver Age, asceticism had very little currency. Firstly, an influential current of Orthodox thought in the West, associated with the brilliant constellation of Russian intellectuals in Paris, questioned the traditional centrality of ascetic spirituality and monasticism in Orthodoxy.[109] They believed that there were alternative, more appropriate forms of Orthodox witness to the world, including charitable activities, theological education, parish life, and the gatherings of the Christian Student Movement. This current fell short of producing a new ecclesiology that would remove organized asceticism from Orthodox life, however. Father Sergii Bulgakov, for example, recognized the contradiction between the prophetic role of monasticism, which "bears the character of creative daring, often accompanied by struggle, by the breaking of fleshly and spiritual ties," on the one hand, and the tendency toward institutionalization and the spirit of "legalism," which is the opposite of "creative daring," on the other. Legalism in spiritual life meant "slavery to grand and little inquisitors, with their pretensions to infallibility and assertion of spiritual despotism under the pretext of monastic spiritual guidance."[110] He believed that channeling inspiration into preestablished patterns such as the *Philokalia* was opposite to the spirit of creativity in the Church.[111]

Furthermore, the Russian émigrés suggested that the older forms of cloistering and rigid separation of monks from the rest of the Christian community had to be replaced by new ways of fully living the ideals of Christian life without tonsure, celibacy, and the wilderness, such as "white monasticism" (*beloe inochestvo*, an oxymoron because the term "white" is reserved for life in the world, as in "white priesthood") and monasticism in the world.The Bishop of San Francisco, Ioann (Shakhovskoi), dreamed that all pious Christians would live intense spiritual lives like nuns and monks: bishops would be treated as abbots of these idiorrythmic "white" monasteries, while parish priests would be elders (*startsy*).[112]

Yet the traditional view of ascetic endeavor as inseparable from monastic vows continued to draw a small but influential following among émigrés and converts to Orthodoxy in the West. Examples include the aforementioned circle around the monk Siluan, and later the monastic community led by Father Sofronii. There were men and women who practiced asceticism and a life of prayer despite the displacement and destitution brought by emigration. Despite Father Sergii Bulgakov's caution against the legalism of the *Philokalia*, it was precisely hesychast spirituality and the experience of eldership that produced many creative forms of Orthodox life. Many of those who gained charismatic gifts became magnets for others who were searching for eternal life. The influence of the Russian spiritual fathers in emigration extended beyond the Russian émigré milieu: they attracted converts to Orthodoxy who were seeking more intense and deeper engagement with the divine. The Russian bearers of the tradition of *starchestvo* also had an influence on religious movements within Orthodox countries. For example, a monk from Optina monastery, Ioan Kuligin, became a spiritual authority for many members of the Romanian revivalist group "The Burning Bush." This group, hosted by Antim monastery in Bucharest before and after the Second World War, was a cultural and theological movement that attempted to revive hesychast theology in Romania. It involved lay people and clergymen, all inspired by the presence of Father Ioan Kuligin, known as John the Stranger, who instructed his followers in the Jesus prayer. A member of this group, theologian André Scrima, wrote a book that provided an interpretation of the function and meaning of the spiritual fatherhood of the Eastern Orthodox Church.[113]

Orthodox Elders under Gorbachev and in Post-Soviet Russia

The Gorbachev era (1985–1992) opened up a new opportunity for the Orthodox Church to restore its national prestige and reclaim the privileges and property that were lost during the previous decades. The Church sponsored a full-scale revival of monasticism and by 1988, 22 monasteries had been returned to ecclesiastical use, including the legendary Optina pustyn'. The political liberalization of the Perestroika era stimulated a growth of interest in such traditional sources of spirituality as pilgrimage, holy springs, wonder-working icons, holy graves, and of course, spiritual elders.

Travel companies organized bus excursions to monasteries that had popular elders in residence, and these tours were often operated on a commercial basis: belonging to Orthodoxy was not a requirement for potential pilgrims. During these visits the tourists venerated icons, placed requests for prayers, and bought candles and souvenirs. Some of them managed to pass a note to an elder with a request to pray for a specific person or a specific cause. There were specialized tours designed with the sole purpose of visiting an elder. Yet apart from the "occasional" pilgrims and more or less catechized Orthodox believers, Gorbachev's Russia also developed a number of lay "professional worshippers" or "church people" (*tserkovnye liudi*), who were the bearers of esoteric knowledge about Russia's messianic role in the world, and who defined themselves solely by their place in the symbolic universe of Russian Orthodoxy.[114] Spiritual elders were central figures in the life and activities of "church people," who formed eremetic and self-sufficient social communities—spiritual families, by means of which they separated themselves from larger religious institutions (parish, monastery) and secular life.[115]

The revival of popular interest in religion was accompanied by the growth of new parishes that often were understaffed and overcrowded. To address the lack of clergy, the Church ordained new priests in haste, turning a blind eye to the lack of theological education or moral unsuitability of some candidates. In monasteries too, there was a noticeable shortage of experienced monks and nuns. Despite the empowerment of the Russian Orthodox Church after Perestroika, the church hierarchy found it more difficult to control the emergence of the numerous little centers that formed around individual monks, parish priests, and charismatic lay men or women.

As a result of this diversity of popular belief, and due to the disruptions in recent religious and political history, spiritual eldership in post-Soviet Russia was a heterogeneous phenomenon. On the one hand, there were a handful of spiritual leaders (all born before or shortly after the revolution) who were greatly respected by the church hierarchy and had the reputation of "national elders." Among those were Ioann (Krest'iankin) from Pskov-Pechery monastery, Nikolai (Gur'ianov) from Pskov oblast, Archimandrite Kiril (Pavlov) and Archimandrite Naum (Baiborodin) from Trinity-Sergius Lavra. There were also a few less high-profile spiritual leaders in the monasteries and parishes, who exercised the various forms of spiritual discipline that were traditionally associated with *starchestvo*.

The reputations of Father Nikolai Gur'ianov (1909–2004) and Hieromonk Ioann Krest'iankin (1910–2006) as clairvoyant elders began to form as early as the 1970s and 1980s. Both were well-educated and pious young men, both suffered arrests for "anti-Soviet agitation," and both spent time incarcerated in prisons and camps. Both had little interest in making a career in the church. Father Nikolai was a parish priest in Latvia and Lithuania after the war and, from 1958, he served as a parish priest on the small island of Zalit in Pskov oblast. Ioann Krest'iankin served as a parish priest in Pskov and Riazan dioceses before he took monastic vows in 1966, and spent forty years as a monk in the Pskov-Pechery monastery, where he acted as a confessor to monks and the laity. His series of talks about the construction of a proper confession, given during the 1960s, has become the basis for the manual for confession used in all Russian parishes in the post-Soviet era.

The religious temperaments of these two elders could not be more different. Nikolai was known for his simpleheartedness and poetic inclinations: he liked to sing spiritual verses, some of which he composed himself, and he surprised his visitors with unpredictable and comic aphorisms. The meaning of these irrational utterances would only be revealed in the future. There is a story about a group of mafia men who came to Elder Nikolai to receive a blessing. During the visit, the elder anointed one of them with oil: not just the forehead, as tradition recommended, but the man's entire naked back. It turned out that the man happened to be involved in a shoot-out between two rival Mafia groups, and despite sustaining several wounds was the only one of the entire group to survive.

During the 1990s the popularity of Father Nikolai as a living saint grew disproportionately. Testimony from Igor Stoliarov, a sailor on the atomic submarine *Komsomolets*, who survived the dramatic fire and sinking of the

6.3. Elder Nikolai Gur'ianov, Zalit.
Courtesy of Maksim A. Antipov

craft in 1989, was much publicized by the Russian media. He claimed that during his escape from the fire into the icy waters of the Atlantic he saw an apparition of a white-bearded elder who introduced himself as Nikolai and told the man "You must swim, I am praying for you, you will be saved." Several years later Stoliarov, who was one of 25 people rescued, visited the island of Zalit and recognized Elder Nikolai as his miraculous rescuer.[116] As a result of Nikolai's reputation, some people gave up their careers and urban lifestyle and came to live in the remote island community so that they could be closer to the elder. In the last years of Elder Nikolai's life, the aging *starets* became an emblem of the fundamentalists' camp (those in favor of canonization of Rasputin), which included two of his female cellmates. Conflicts between the various groups of Elder Nikolai's admirers, and between the fundamentalists and Bishop of Pskov Evsevii, suggest that *starchestvo* remained a highly contentious phenomenon in post-Soviet Russia.

In contrast, Father Ioann's style was characterized by a sober, even rational approach. Ioann's letters could be compared to those of Amvrosii of Optina: he did not hesitate to challenge his correspondents and always reminded them of the Gospel's commandments and Christ's cross as the main conditions of salvation.[117] In the words of one of his spiritual children, Moscow priest Vladimir Volgin, Elder Ioann from the very first "burned him with his love," the kind of love that had none of the possessiveness of human love, but which left the person in question with a sense of unlimited freedom.[118] It was Ioann who received the dubious honor of blessing President Putin in 2000 when the acting president (who had yet to win the vote of the Russian people) came to visit the elder in the Pskov-Pechery monastery, accompanied by his ally Archimandrite Tikhon Shevkunov.

Elders like Fathers Nikolai and Ioann were treated with respect by the ecclesiastical and secular establishment because of their popularity, authority, and general compliance with the church hierarchy. During the campaign against INN (the individual tax code) in 2000–2001, which was perceived as the mark of the Antichrist by conservative believers and the clergy, both elders were specifically targeted by the church establishment and were asked to express their opinion about INN. Tikhon Shevkunov interviewed three of the most respectable elders (including Kiril Pavlov), who generally opposed the campaign against INN, and extensively publicized his findings.[119]

The "national elders," because of their prestige, were hard to reach for ordinary churchgoers in search of a spiritual guide. In response to popular demand, spiritual elders and faith healers mushroomed in contemporary Russia, often to the consternation of the church hierarchy.[120] Several charismatic elders were instrumental in the movement against INN and influenced the campaign for the canonization of Grigorii Rasputin and Tsar Ivan the Terrible.[121] The forms of religious life that developed around some of these charismatic leaders, many of whom were ordained or tonsured in the Orthodox Church, attracted criticism for their distorted concept of obedience. These self-appointed "elders" (also known as "young" or immature elders, *mladostartsy*) exercised unprecedented power over their spiritual children in such a way that many lay people were traumatized and bitterly disappointed. For example, there were an inordinate number of cases in which *mladostartsy* interfered in the marriages, raising of children, fertility choices, and personal finances of those who trusted them.[122] Patriarch Aleksii II condemned those spiritual fathers who arranged marriages between their spiritual children and discouraged them from voting, studying, or serving in the army.[123] The official campaign against "young elders" revealed an ongoing tension between the two poles within the Church: the church hierarchy and charismatic elders. Yet no specific actions were taken against the pastors in question, many of whom continued their activities.[124]

Perceptions of elders by contemporaries in post-Soviet Russia varied from outright rejection to uncritical idolization. The hierarchy and many theologians deferred to the elders who complied with the Church's internal discipline and who did not interfere with the civil and social duties of their spiritual children, but at the same time criticized the *mladostartsy*, describing them as leaders of "totalitarian sects."[125] Agnostic intellectuals perceived contemporary *starchestvo* as an informal network that existed parallel to the church hierarchy and performed economic and social functions under the façade of spiritual life.[126] The artistic elite found in elders a source of inspiration and spiritual comfort.[127] The film "The Island" (*Ostrov*, 2006) by Pavel Lungin, for example, popularized the image of a clairvoyant monastic elder, played in the film by Petr Mamonov, a former punk turned pious Orthodox.

There remains a dearth of studies that focus on contemporary Russian eldership and, therefore, all interpretations of this phenomenon can only be seen as tentative. According to the critical Orthodox clergy, there are several reasons for the distorted forms of spiritual guidance of the *mladostartsy*, all of which are related to the communist legacy. On the one hand, communism suppressed individualism and personal responsibility; the psychological need to find someone who took the responsibility for decision-making led many people to search for new authorities and guidelines. The presence of Soviet influence was expressed in the spiritual and social passivity of *Homo Soveticus Christianus*, according to Andrei Desnitskii, who believed that for many Soviet citizens who came to church during the 1990s, Christianity was a substitute for the Soviet ideology and way of thinking.[128] On the other hand, some authors have suggested that the years of militant atheism destroyed the Christian worldview and led to the revival of pagan, archaic forms of religion that had nothing to do with Christianity.[129] The Church too was partly to blame: the lack of clergy in the 1990s led to many hasty ordinations of candidates who lacked moral rectitude.[130] Furthermore, Nikolai Mitrokhin has pointed out that people had more trust in elders than in the priests and bishops, who had compromised themselves by their compliance with the communist authorities.[131] He has also emphasized the paradoxically modern character of *starchestvo*, because it has allowed believers a choice of their spiritual lifestyle and certain independence from the administrative structure of the church.[132]

While the popularity of elders and distorted forms of spiritual guidance predated the Soviet regime, the relative freedom with which elders operated in post-Soviet Russia was novel. This freedom suggests the lack of ecclesiastical means of control. Popular interest in the elders surged in the 1990s, a time when the introduction of Western institutions, particularly the capitalist marketplace and democracy, brought risk, challenge, and unpredictability into people's lives to an unprecedented degree. According to Galina Lindquist, in contrast to Western society, in postcommunist Russia the role of legal mechanisms that controlled risk was minimal, which left people with only two methods of dealing with breach of contract between individuals and institutions: the help of "muscle men," and magic.[133] Studies of evangelical Protestantism have also demonstrated that people living in an increasingly insecure world are more likely to be attracted to the ideas of formulaic prayers, guidebooks, and the concepts of spiritual and moral discipline.[134] The appeal of Orthodox elders, especially those who provided much stricter sets of rules and guidance, was that believers could renounce responsibility for their own decisions and trust in the preternatural powers of the holy men, thus minimizing (in their view) the potential risks they might encounter in an unpredictable social world. Trust in the charismatic leader provided individuals with a psychological sense of security in situations over which they had little control.

THE WEAKENING OF INSTITUTIONAL Orthodoxy in the years that followed the Revolution of 1917 had several consequences for *starchestvo*. The disintegration of the imperial church, with its network of organized monasticism and Synodal administration, led to a further diffusion to the grassroots level of the specific form of ascetic spirituality associated with elders. Although traditionally the elders' spirituality was focused on withdrawal from the world, inner prayer, and struggle against passions, in the Soviet era it took the form of resistance to the regime, which was associated with the domain of the Antichrist. The enclosed and conservative outlook within the Church, that of the so-called *tserkovnye liudi*, could be traced back to the late imperial era and the specific Orthodox discourse produced by the right-wing writers like Nilus. A number of nonconformist groups within the Church, more or less suppressed by the Stalinist police in the 1930s–1950s, were inclined to charismatic spiritual leadership.

Another novel development in the Soviet era was that the differences between "black" (monastic) and "white" (parish priesthood) forms of spiritual guidance faded away. Homeless monks and nuns, withdrawn from their monasteries, often replaced missing priests in rural areas. The communities of Aleksei and Sergei Mechev and the Orthodox brotherhoods conducted their pastoral work in parish churches and among the laity, using the experience of the Optina elders.

Popular religion, described as superstition by the Soviet authorities, did not disappear despite Soviet education programs and atheist propaganda. People sought advice and sanctification from reputable elders, whether they were monks or parish priests, and sometimes lay men or women. Although the Church was pressed by the Soviet authorities to put an end to popular pilgrimage and other expressions of religious enthusiasm, there were considerable limits on the Church's ability to achieve this.

In the face of attacks by the Soviet state, the Church developed an even more conservative position than during 1917–1918. *Startsy* signified an affinity with the past, and asceticism and hesychast theology represented an ideology that asserted the traditional values of Orthodoxy. Yet at the same time, the involvement of the urban intelligentsia in Christian networks, the attempts to look beyond the traditional models of Orthodoxy, and the influences from the West (both of non-Orthodox Christianity and Orthodoxy abroad) led to the emergence of new forms of spiritual guidance in which the traditional model of spiritual fatherhood was reinvented in the context of an egalitarian Eucharistic community.

While the Russian Orthodox outside Russia lived under political regimes that were less antagonistic to religion than those of their counterparts in Russia, they too had to assert their faith and construct their own version of Holy Russia, in which real and fictional elders, including Dostoevsky's Zosima, played an important role. Despite the intellectual émigrés' questioning of the vitality of the old forms of ascetic life, a section of the Russian diaspora recreated the tradition of eldership, creatively engaging with tradition and finding a place for it in a new cultural environment.

Contemporary Russia

The revival of eldership in contemporary Russia is a subject that merits a separate study. Provisionally, it can be interpreted as an expression of the persistence of religious memory as well as a response to specific social and cultural factors brought about by the political reforms of the 1980s–1990s. The critical position of the church hierarchy towards abuses of pastoral authority by some self-proclaimed elders is reminiscent of the attempts of the imperial Synod to deal with the charismatic *startsy*. Yet even the replication of this controversy in the modern period signifies the durability of this fascinating religious phenomenon within Russian culture.

Conclusion

The role of the spiritual elder (*startsy*) was not immutable. A variety of behaviors, lifestyles, and experiences has been described as constituting "eldership" (*starchestvo*). Indeed, opposite types such as the holy fools of Diveevo, renowned for their bizarre conduct, and the theologically literate elders of Optina or Zosimova pustyn' all enjoyed the reputation of *startsy*. Although the theological definition of *starchevstvo* is rather narrow, it is clear that as it was defined within popular culture, *starchestvo* was in fact quite complex. In the eyes of ordinary believers, a *starets* was a living saint, a mediator between heaven and earth, who—by virtue of his or her special relationship with divine powers—could perform miracles, heal the sick, and predict the future, and who often possessed a rare insight into human nature.[1] *Startsy* did not necessarily have to be priests or monks, but many of them did have a preference for the ascetic life. Although these popular *startsy* sometimes had a precarious relationship with the institutional church, undoubtedly they saw themselves as part of the Eastern Christian tradition.

The tradition of spiritual guidance in the narrow theological sense originated among ascetics of the Byzantine Empire. These theologians developed and began to pass on a specific method of achieving spiritual perfection associated firstly with hesychastic prayer, and secondly with an ascetic struggle against the destructive impulses of flesh and mind. These techniques of spiritual guidance fell into obscurity within the Orthodox world between the fifteenth and eighteenth centuries. Similar practices of spiritual guidance revived in the Balkans during the Enlightenment, which were linked to the hesychastic theology that was also revived in this period. The situation in Russia was somewhat complicated due to the religious schism of the seventeenth century and the antimonastic reforms of the eighteenth. During this period, official theological discourse marginalized practices related to *starchestvo*, equating them with religious dissent and superstition. The revival of spiritual guidance in Russia, either within Paisii Velichkovskii's tradition or independent of it, had to face—with some exceptions—much resistance and misconception on the part of the church administrators and the clergy. This was partly due to the clergy's worldview, which was under the sway of scholastic theology and the Enlightenment, and partly due to their social and economic dependence and political submissiveness.[2]

Guiding persons in their spiritual development was a distinct skill which was not necessarily related to personal holiness. While an experienced ascetic could also be a charismatic leader, not every charismatic person who had a reputation for the holy life could be a good teacher. That is why the Russian Church had no shortage of elders who were accepted as reputable ascetics, yet monasteries suffered from a paucity of spiritual guidance, especially among novices, and from the lack of conditions necessary for the development of such guidance (for example, good libraries, cooperation between administrators and *startsy*, and acceptance of the "disclosure of thoughts" as a legitimate practice). The belated attempt to extend the experience of *starchestvo* within Optina and Glinskaia pustyn' to other Russian monastic institutions was not fully implemented due to practical difficulties and the disruption caused by the Revolution of 1917.

The different forms of ascetic life and traditions of *starchestvo* did not always coexist peacefully. The elders who positioned themselves as descendants of Paisii Velichkovskii's lineage looked askance at possessors of popular charisma, such as holy fools and various prophets. In the twentieth century, the notorious reputation of Grigorii Rasputin had an altogether discouraging effect on many Orthodox believers in regard to *starchestvo*. However, these various forms of popular spirituality did not exist in isolation: spiritually ambitious peasants also adopted monastic forms of life, read monastic literature, and practiced severe forms of asceticism. There was obviously a great lack of experienced leaders; even the anonymous pilgrim from *The*

Way of the Pilgrim scarcely received any instruction from his spiritual father, but educated himself by reading the Gospel and the *Dobrotoliubie*.

In addition, the overlap between the pastoral authority of a priest and that of a *starets* was a significant problem. The fact that many monastic elders were ordained as priests (including most of the elders in Optina pustyn', and the majority of the twentieth-century elders) confused even further the distinction between the authority of ordination and the authority of the elders' charisma. In the eighteenth and nineteenth centuries, many monastic elders chose to be ordained as priests simply as a strategic means of evading Synodal criticism while practicing spiritual guidance. (Needless to say, this option did not exist for nuns). During this period there was, as a rule, little sympathy between parish priests and monastic elders.[3] This was due to the parish priesthood's miserable and isolated social position, combined with their seminary education, which rarely focused on ascetic theology. Not until the turn of the twentieth century did some Orthodox parish priests start taking up the methods and approaches of elders in order to try to improve the spiritual life of their parishioners. It was no coincidence that around this time the public image of priests began to improve.[4] The emergence of a succession of elders who were also married priests had an impact on parish life both in Soviet Russia and in the diaspora.

The Russian *startsy* were differentiated by their social and religious functions (i.e., guidance of neophytes or primarily charismatic roles), but they also differed by taking quite contradictory approaches to Christian life, thus producing a dichotomy, described by Margaret Ziolkowsky, between the "kenotic" versus "rigorous hero."[5] The "rigorous hero," typified by the figures of Priest Avvakum and Monk Ferapont from *Brothers Karamazov*, exhibited the Josephite type of sainthood that was characterized by ascetic severity and an external demonstration of piety. The Russian Church had no shortage of "rigorous" *startsy* like Fedor Ushakov, Fedor Polzikov (Elder Leonid's teacher), and Abbot Varlaam of Valaam monastery. In addition, there were the numerous self-appointed elders in post-Soviet Russia who demanded absolute obedience from their spiritual children and insisted on the strict observance of church regulations. Kenotic spirituality, which was "more inwardly directed, and grounded in a keen sense of humility" was typical for elders such as Nazarii of Valaam, the elders of Optina, Serafim of Sarov, Father Aleksei Mechev, Serafim of Vyritsa and, of course, the fictional Elder Zosima. The presence of these opposite approaches demonstrates the fallacy of taking Optina pustyn' as the typical model of Russian eldership. Despite Optina's prominence as a symbol of the ideological construction of Holy Russia, its elders employed just one of the several existing styles of spiritual eldership.[6]

That is why it would be wrong to conclude that eldership was an alternative to the dominant religious culture of the Russian Church, because, in many ways, it mirrored the existing cultural trends within the Church.

There was also an exchange between religious dissent and Orthodox eldership: some elders came from Old Believer communities, others benefited from visiting Old Believer monastic foundations and borrowing their books (even if this was done under the pretext of missionary activities). There are traces of Old Believer influence on the key texts of Russian spiritual prose, such as *The Way of a Pilgrim*. In prerevolutionary Russia, the authorities often encouraged (or at least tolerated) hesychastic practices and spiritual guidance within monasteries, as long as they could be presented as remedies against religious dissent. Some church hierarchs believed that the reputation of elders could bring dissenting peasants and middle-class members back to the Orthodox fold.[7] The links and exchanges between Old Belief and Orthodox elders, however, do not imply parallels between popular mystical movements such as the Skoptsy and the world of the elders. Even though the Jesus prayer had an impact on Skoptsy practices, the spirituality of this sect was communal in character, with folkloric imitation of the liturgy and the practice of *radeniie* (a collective ecstatic prayer). The elders' practices were instead centered on one-to-one communication between a *starets* and an adherent, while the Jesus prayer was practiced individually, not collectively. Moreover, the ideology of self-sacralization, characteristic of the leaders of Russian mystical sects, was not typical for the Orthodox *startsy*.[8] In the twentieth century, the exchanges between Old Believers and the Orthodox Church lost their relevance, and the role of eldership faded due to the antagonism between organized religion and the atheist state. However, elders did survive despite the arrests of the clergy, the consistent policy of bringing the Church to submission to the political regime, and the destruction of monasticism. While in its formal appearance the Church minimized its social service and missionary zeal, focusing instead on liturgical life and the performance of sacraments, spiritual guidance continued to be practiced informally by some parish priests and monks. Despite the decline of popular trust in the clergy (one could not be sure whether a confessing priest was an informer of the KGB or not), a number of reputable members of the clergy gained the reputations of elders to whom people came with their questions and personal grievances. In the post-Soviet era, the revival of popular interest in eldership coincided with bitter debates among the clergy over the meaning of *starchestvo* and the limits of the elders' power. The proliferation of heterogeneous practices of *starchestvo* and the absence of a theological consensus about the place of *startsy* within the ecclesiastical structure supports the observation that the contemporary Russian Church is not a monolith but divided along ideological and political lines.[9]

The spiritual elders highlighted in equal measure the weaknesses and strengths of Russian Orthodoxy's response to the challenges of modernity. In the eighteenth and nineteenth centuries the attempts of *startsy*-supporting groups within the Orthodox Church to promote ascetic and hesychast teaching as the basis for the revival of Orthodoxy met misunderstanding and resistance. It was not until the late nineteenth century that hesychast theology became accepted within theological institutions. The churchmen's inability to define the Orthodox confessional position, as Dixon suggests, certainly weakened the Church's resilience to the challenges from its religious rivals as well as from unbelief, while their "reliance on Western scholarship and pastoral methods made their attempts to differentiate Orthodoxy both complex and controversial."[10] Shevzov, too, has remarked on the lack of consensus within the Church on such important aspects of ecclesial life as hierarchy and community, religious authority, and parish and patriarch.[11] In spite of the popularity of *starchestvo*, there was little agreement among church administrators and theologians about what precisely were the ecclesiological roles, status, functions, and limits to the power of *startsy*.

While some *startsy* owed their success to the support of such prominent prelates as Gavriil Petrov, Platon Levshin, and Filaret Drozdov, in an average Russian monastery *starchestvo* was unlikely to flourish because of numerous constraints imposed by the Synodal system. The intervention of the ecclesiastical authorities into the elders' activities antagonized elders' supporters and further added to the popular distrust of bishops and the Synod. At the same time, in some sectors the Russian Church showed a capacity for employing resources to carry out reform and improvement. Even though the reasons for the revival of monasticism in the late eighteenth and nineteenth centuries were not limited to *starchestvo*, elders were both contributors to and beneficiaries of the internal reform of monasticism, which in many aspects was spontaneous and independent of official initiative.[12] The renewed monastic institutions were more socially oriented, open to missionary ideals, and focused on the cultivation of an intense spiritual life.

The persistence of a decentralizing tendency within the Russian Church was a feature that it shared with the Byzantine Church, in which "little centers of power competed with the vested hierarchy of church and state."[13] This was both a weakness and a strength. The decentralizing tendency, which led to a growth of informal relationships such as those between elders and their spiritual children and those between members of spiritual families, signified that for many believers in Russia, neither the parish church nor the church hierarchy with a bishop as a spiritual authority were necessarily the central elements of their religious identity. People came to elders to seek spiritual renewal, solace in hardship, and counsel in minor and major predicaments. It is not surprising that many of these supplicants had very vague ideas about church tradition, the history of the church, and theological matters. It was not the tradition that mattered to them, but relevance to their present experience. This is why, for some elders' adepts, their personal relationship with an elder was more important than a life in church that included following the commandments and taking part in sacraments. Despite this particular tendency among elders' admirers, spiritual elders should not be divorced from the context of the Russian Orthodox Church, and neither should they be regarded as sectarians or primarily as faith healers.[14] Spiritual elders represented a specific form of ministry within the Orthodox Church, carrying out the roles of teacher, spiritual director, counselor, and prophet. The study of the Russian elders from a historical perspective enriches our understanding of Orthodoxy and contributes to further discussion of the problems of spiritual authority, popular belief, the impact of religious identity on national identity, and the interactions between church and society in the modern world.

Notes

Introduction

1. As cited in Bishop Kallistos (Ware), "The Spiritual Guide in Orthodox Christianity," in *The Inner Kingdom*, vol. 1, *The Collected Works* (Crestwood, NY: St. Vladimir Seminary Press, 2001), 128.

2. "Vospominaniia arkhimandrita Afanasiia Nechaeva," *Sever* 9 (1991): 82.

3. Isidor (Bogoiavlenskii), "Slovo na sobor Sergiia i Germana, Valaamskikh churdotvortsev [July 11, 1948]," *Mir pravoslaviia*, no. 6 (39), (June 2001): 1.

4. An attempt to collate the accounts of locally and centrally venerated holy men and women of the eighteenth and nineteenth centuries was made by Archimandrite Nikodim Kononov in his nineteen-volume collection. Nikodim (Kononov), *Zhizneopisaniia otechestvennykh podvizhnikov blagochestiia vosemnadtsatogo i deviatnadtsatogo vv.* 19 vols. (Athos: Sviato-Pantelemonovskii monastyr', 1906–1910).

5. Gregory Freeze, "Subversive Piety: Religion and Political Crisis in Late Imperial Russia," *Journal of Modern History* 68, no. 2 (1996): 324.

6. A. L. Beglov, "Starchestvo v trudakh russkikh tserkovnykh uchenykh i pisatelei," in *Put' k sovershennoi zhizni: o russkom starchestve* (Moscow: Pravoslavnyi Sviato-Tikhonovskii Gumanitarnyi Universitet, 2006), 5. Various authors point out the significance of elders for the religious identity of the Russian people. See, M. M. Gromyko and A. V. Buganov, *O vozzreniiakh russkogo naroda* (Moscow: Palomnik, 2000).

7. M. Pye, "Religious Tradition and the Student of Religion," in *Religion, Tradition, and Renewal*, ed. A. W. Geertz and J. S. Jensen (Aarhus: Aarhus University Press, 1991), 29.

8. Eric Hobsbawm and Terence Ranger, eds., *The Invention of Tradition* (Cambridge: Cambridge University Press, 1983), 1–14.

9. Jan Assmann, *Religion and Cultural Memory: Ten Studies*, trans. Rodney Livingstone (Stanford: Stanford University Press, 2006), 31.

10. Peter Berger, *The Heretical Imperative: Contemporary Possibilities of Religious Affirmation* (Garden City, NY: Anchor Press), 46–54.

11. Maurice Halbwachs, *On Collective Memory* (Chicago: University of Chicago Press, 1992), 84–119.

12. Ibid., 102–5.

13. On asceticism, see V. L. Wimbush, ed., *Ascetic Behaviour in Greco-Roman Antiquity: A Sourcebook* (Minneapolis: Fortress Press, 1990); Vincent. L. Wimbush and Richard Valantasis, eds., *Asceticism* (New York: Oxford University Press, 2002).

14. Gavin Flood, *The Ascetic Self: Subjectivity, Memory, and Tradition* (Cambridge: Cambridge University Press, 2004), 8, passim.

15. For example, Maurists (the Benedictine monks of the Congregation of St. Maur) produced critical editions of the Latin and Greek Fathers in the seventeenth century.

16. For example, the Oxford movement. See Geoffrey Rowell, ed., *Tradition Renewed: The Oxford Movement Conference Papers* (Allison Park, PA: Pickwick Publications, 1986); Owen Chadwick, *The Spirit of the Oxford Movement: Tractarian Essays* (Cambridge: Cambridge University Press, 1990). See also Laura Engelstein, "Holy Russia in Modern Times: an Essay on Orthodoxy and Cultural Change," *Past and Present* 173 (2001): 129–56.

17. P. Syrku, *K istorii ispravleniia knig v Bolgarii v XIV veke* (St. Petersburg: Tip. Imperatorskoi akademii nauk, 1890); A. I. Iatsmirskii, "Vizantiiskii religioznyi mistitsizm XIV veka pered perekhodom ego k slavianam," *Strannik* 10 (1908): 55–140, 167–219; I. Popov, "Ideiia obozheniia v drevne-vostochnoi tserkvi," *Voprosy filosofii i psikhologii* 2, no. 97 (1909): 165–213; A. N. Iatsmirskii, *Vozrozhdenie vizantiisko-bolgarskogo religioznogo mistitsizma i slavianskoi asketicheskoi literatury v XVIII veke* (Khar'kov, 1905), 185–203; idem, *Slavianskie i russkie rukopisi rumynskikh bibliotek* (St. Petersburg: Izd. Imperatorskoi akademii nauk, 1905). Although two dissertations were published (by Kazankli and P. Regentskii) on Paisii Velichkovskii in the Kazan' and St. Petersburg Spiritual Academies, Iatsmirskii's work represent the first published scholarly attempt to deal with Paisii's legacy.

18. See Faith C. M. Kitch, *The Literary Style of Epifanii Premudryi "Pletenije Sloves"* (Munich: Verlag Otto Sagner, 1976), 26–29; G. M. Prokhorov, *"Tak vossiiaiut pravedniki . . ." Vizantiiskaia literatura XIV veka v Drevnei Rusi* (St. Petersburg: Izd. Olega Abyshko, 2009).

19. Georges Florovsky, *Puti russkogo bogosloviia* (1937; repr., Vilnius, 1991), 123.

20. Weber, *Wirtschaft und Gesellschaft*, in Jack T. Sanders, *Charisma, Converts, Competitors: Societal and Sociological Factors in the Success of Early Christianity* (London: SCM Press, 2000), 22.

21. Ware, "The Spiritual Guide in Orthodox Christianity," 129; Metropolitan Trifon (Turkestanov), *Drevnekhristianskie i Optinskie startsy* (Moscow: Martis, 1997); Sergii Chetverikov, *Moldavskii starets Paisii Velichkovskii: ego zhizn', uchenie, i vliianie na pravoslavnoe monashestvo* (Paris: YMCA Press, 1988); P. I. Smirnov, *Dukhovnyi otets v drevnei Vostochnoi tserkvi* (1906; repr., Moscow: Pravoslavnyi Sviato-Tikhonskii Bogoslovskii Institut, 2003); I. M. Kontsevich, *Stiazhanie sviatogo dukha v putiakh Drevnei Rusi* (1952; repr., Moscow: Lepta, 2002).

22. Charles Lindholm, *Charisma* (Cambridge: Blackwell, 1990), 26.

23. Sanders, *Charisma, Converts, Competitors*, 22–23.

24. Max Weber, *Economy and Society: An Outline of Interpretive Sociology*, vol. 3 (New York: Bedminster Press, 1968), 1121–24.

25. Ibid., 1148–49.

26. Sanders, *Charisma, Converts, Competitors*, 26. Bryan Wilson, *Magic and Millennium: A Sociological Study of Religious Movements of Protest among Tribal and Third-World Peoples* (St. Albans: Paladin, 1975); idem, *The Noble Savages: the Primitive Origins of Charisma and Its Contemporary Survival* (Berkeley: University of California Press, 1975); Roy Wallis, ed., *Millennialism and Charisma* (Belfast: Queen's University, 1982); Thomas Csordas, *Language, Charisma, and Creativity: The Ritual Life of a Religious Movement* (Berkeley: University of California Press, 1997); Lindholm, *Charisma*.

27. Wilson, *The Noble Savages*, 7.

28. Csordas, *Language, Charisma*; Galina Lindquist, *Conjuring Hope: Magic and Healing in Contemporary Russia* (New York: Berghahn Books, 2005), 114–16.

29. John Milbank, *Theology and Social Theory: Beyond Secular Reason* (London: Blackwell, 1993), 91.

30. Peter Brown, "The Rise and Function of the Holy Man in Late Antiquity,"

The Journal of Roman Studies 61 (1971): 80–101; see also the discussion of Brown's contribution in James Howard-Johnston and Paul Antony Hayward, eds., *The Cult of Saints in Late Antiquity: Essays on the Contribution of Peter Brown* (Oxford: Oxford University Press, 1999).

31. For the summary and critique of this position see Gregory Freeze, "Handmaiden of the State? The Church in Imperial Russia Reconsidered," *Journal of Ecclesiastical History* 36, no. 1 (1985): 82–102; despite Freeze's compelling revisionism, Russian historians continue to speak of the subservient status and weak position of the Russian Church vis-à-vis the Russian state. See, for example, V. A. Fedorov, *Russkaia pravoslavnaia tserkov' i gosudarstvo: Sinodal'nyi period, 1700–1917* (Moscow: Russkaia Panorama, 2003).

32. The elements of such interpretation are present in some evaluations of elders' conflicts with bishops and monastic administrators; see Freeze, "Subversive Piety," 308–50; N. Mitrokhin, *Russkaia pravoslavnaia tserkov': sovremennoe sostoianie i aktual'nye problemy* (Moscow: Novoe literaturnoe obozrenie, 2004).

33. Bishop Kallistos (Ware), "The Spiritual Guide," 129, 150.

34. Scott Kenworthy, "The Revival of Monasticism in Modern Russia: the Trinity-Sergius Lavra, 1825–1921" (PhD diss., Brandeis University, 2002).

35. Brown, "The Rise and Function of the Holy Man," 95.

36. P. Florenskii, *Perepiska s M. A. Novoselovym* (Tomsk: Vodolei, 1998), 31.

37. Vera Shevzov, *Russian Orthodoxy on the Eve of Revolution* (Oxford: Oxford University Press, 2004), 28.

38. Ibid., 29.

39. The summary of Khomiakov's views are presented in Georges Florovsky, *Puti russkogo bogosloviia*, 277.

40. Augustine of Hippo as quoted in Sergii Mansurov, *Ocherki iz istorii tserkvi* (Klin: Khristianskaia zhizn', 2002), 23.

41. The members of this circle were primarily members of the Moscow lay intelligentsia and white priests, including F. D. Samarin, V. A. Kozhevnikov, N. N. Mamonov, P. B. Mansurov, Princes E. N. and G. N. Trubetskoi, Father Iosif Fudel', Pavel Florenskii, S. Bulgakov, V. F. Ern, L. A. Tikhomirov, Father Evgenii Sinadskii, and V. P. Sventsitskii. Philosophers Nicholas Berdiaev and Vasilii Rozanov were occasionally present.

42. Florenskii, *Perepiska s M. A. Novoselovym*, 19–20.

43. Pavel Florenskii, *Stolp i utverzhdenie istiny: Opyt pravoslavnoi feoditsei v dvenadtsaty pis'makh* (Moscow, 1914), 7–8, 125. For the English translation see P. Florensky, *The Pillar and Ground of the Truth*, trans. Boris Jakim (Princeton: Princeton University Press, 1997).

44. Mansurov, *Ocherki iz istorii tserkvi*, 4.

45. Sergei Firsov, *Russkaia tserkov' nakanune peremen (konets 1890-kh–1918 gg)* (Moscow: Kruglyi stol po religioznomu obrazovaniiu i diakonii, 2002), 23–53.

46. Carlo Ginzburg, *The Cheese and the Worms: The Cosmos of a Sixteenth-Century Miller*, trans. John and Anne Tedeschi (Baltimore: Johns Hopkins University Press, 1980); Aron Gurevich, *Categories of Medieval Culture*, trans. G. L. Campbell (London: Routledge, Keegan, & Paul, 1985); idem, *Medieval Popular Culture: Problems of Belief and Perception*, Cambridge Studies in Oral and Literate Culture 14 (Cambridge: Cambridge University Press, 1988). The influence of medieval and early modern historians is evident in the work of Ruth Harris, *Lourdes: Body and Spirit in the Secular Age* (New York: Viking, 1999), which is dedicated to popular religion in postrevolutionary France.

47. Bob Scribner, "Is a History of Popular Culture Possible?" *History of European*

Ideas 10, no. 2 (1989): 175. For discussion of recent trends in the literature on Russian popular religion, see Simon Dixon, "How Holy was Holy Russia? Rediscovering Russian Religion," in *Reinterpreting Russia*, ed. Geoffrey A. Hosking and Robert Service (London: Arnold, 1999), 21–39. See also Eve Levin, "Dvoeverie and Popular Religion," in *Seeking God: the Recovery of Religious Identity in Orthodox Russia, Ukraine, and Georgia*, ed. Stephen K. Batalden (DeKalb: Northern Illinois University Press, 1993), 31–52; Chris Chulos, "Myths of the Pious or Pagan Peasants in Post-Emancipation Central Russia (Voronezh province)," in *Russian History* 22, no. 2 (1995): 181–216; Vera Shevzov, "Letting the People into Church," 61–62; Stella Rock, *Popular Religion in Russia: "Double Belief" and the Making of an Academic Myth* (London: Routledge, 2007).

48. See Peter Burke and Bob Scribner, "Is a History of Popular Culture Possible?" *History of European Ideas* 10, no. 2 (1989): 177.

49. Laura Engelstein, "Old and New, High and Low: Straw Horsemen of Russian Orthodoxy," in *Orthodox Russia: Belief and Practice Under the Tsars*, 29; Robert Nichols, "The Orthodox Elders of Imperial Russia" *Modern Greek Studies Yearbook* 1 (1985): 4.

50. Peter Burke, *Popular Culture in Early Modern Europe* (Burlington: Ashgate, 2009), 65–87.

51. Ibid., 28, 68–77.

52. Nichols, "The Orthodox Elders," 10.

53. Old Believers (*starovery* or *staroobriadtsy*) were religious dissidents who split from the Russian Orthodox Church in protest against the church reforms carried in the 1660s under the leadership of Patriarch Nikon. The main division was between the priestly (*popovtsy*) and priestless (*bespopovtsy*) Old Believers. *Popovtsy* differed from the mainstream Orthodox Church only on the issue of ritual, while *bespopovtsy* justified lay ministry and had fewer sacraments than the Orthodox Church (notably, the Eucharist was absent). With the exception of the period of enlightened toleration between 1763 and 1814, the imperial government did not recognize the legal rights of Old Believers and tried to assimilate them into the Orthodox population. It was only in 1905 that Old Believers received rights equal to those of Orthodox believers. A great deal of Russian scholarly literature on Old Belief presents it as an autonomous traditional culture, ignoring exchanges with society at large. For a critique of this position, see Douglas Rogers, *Old Faith and the Russian Land: A Historical Ethnography of Ethics in the Urals* (Ithaca: Cornell University Press, 2009), 169–72.

54. Engelstein, "Old and New, High and Low," 31.

55. Christ-Faith (*Khristovshchina*) and Skoptsy originated in the seventeenth century as a result of eschatological expectations among the Russian peasants. Both groups were characterized by ecstatic rituals and prophecy, while some members practiced self-mutilation. The state authorities and the church persecuted Skoptsy and Khrysty as "pernicious sects."

56. A. A. Panchenko, *Khristovshchina i skopchestvo: fol'klor i traditsionnaia kul'tura russkikh misticheskikh sekt* (Moscow: Ob"edinennoe gumanitarnoe izdatel'stvo, 2002); and Eugene Clay, "The Theological Origins of the Christ-Faith (*Khristovshchina*)," *Russian History/Histoire Russe* 15, no. 1 (1988): 21–41.

57. See Nichols on the elders' crossover between "high" and "low." Nichols, "The Orthodox Elders," 1–30.

58. G. P. Fedotov, *A Treasury of Russian Spirituality* (London: Sheed & Ward, 1952), 242.

59. In medieval hagiography, the authenticity of a saint was determined not by his or her individual characteristics, but by conformity with a specific hagiographic canon.

See Iu. E. Arnautova, "Zhitie kak dukhovnaia biografiia: k voprosu o "tipicheskom" i "individual'nom" v latinskoi agiografii," in *Istoriia cherez lichnost': Istoricheskaia biografiia segodnia*, ed. Lorina P. Repina (Moscow: Krug, 2005), 126.

60. K. N. Leont'ev, "Otets Kliment (Zendergol'm) ieromonakh Optinoi pustyni," in *Pravoslavnyi nemets: ieromonakh Klement (Zendergol'm)* (Kozel'sk: Izd. Vvedenskoi Optini Pustyni, 2002), 99–101.

1—Spiritual Guidance, *Pneumatikos Patir*, and the Mystical Prayer *Lost and Found*

1. Antoine Guillaumont, "L'enseignement spirituel des moines d' Egypte," in *Maitre et disciples dans les traditions religieuses*, ed. Michel Meslin (Paris: Editions du Cerf, 1990), 143–54; Irénée Hausherr, *Spiritual Direction in the Early Christian East*, trans. Anthony P. Gythiel (Kalamazoo, MI: Cistercian Publications, 1990).

2. The earliest surviving document (discovered in 1977) containing the word monk (*monakhos*) derives from 324 CE (24 years earlier than Athnasius's *Life of Antony*). This papyrus suggests that by 324 the monk was an accepted figure and monasticism was a public institution. William Harmless, *Desert Christians: An Introduction to the Literature of Early Monasticism* (New York: Oxford University Press, 2004), 420.

3. Traditionally attributed to St. John Climacus.

4. Cenobitic (Gk. *koinobios*, "living in a community") is the accepted term for communal monasticism. See Edwin A. Judge, "The Earliest Use of *Monachos* for 'Monk,' and the origins of monasticism," *Jährbuch für Antike und Christentum* 20 (1977): 72–89.

5. *The Sayings of the Desert Fathers*, trans. Benedicta Ward (London: Mowbray 1975), xviii-xix.

6. It should not be forgotten that Basil was greatly influenced by his sister Makrina, the founder of female ascetic communities in Cappadocia.

7. In the early monastic texts *abbas* were not ordained. Neither Pachomius nor his successors were priests.

8. P. Smirnov, *Dukhovnyi otets*, 15. Asceticism (Greek: exercise) originated from the system of exercises, including both physical training and sexual abstinence, practiced by Olympic athletes. The sporting connotations are particularly evident in the Life of St. Anthony and in Cassian's writings. Harmless, *Desert Christians*, 61, 385. Monks were compared to the Olympic athletes who trained and subjected their bodies to fierce discipline.

9. Philip Rousseau, "Ascetics as Mediators and as Teachers," in *The Cult of Saints in Late Antiquity and the Middle Ages*, 55.

10. Isaac Newman, "Talmudic discipleship," in *Le Maître spirituel dans les grandes traditions d'Occident et d'Orient*, Hermes: recherches sur l'expérience spirituelle 4 (Paris: Tournai, 1967), 49–55; Gabriel Germain, "Les maîtres spirituels dans l'antiquité classique," in *Le Maître spirituel*, 36–48.

11. Hausherr, *Spiritual Direction*, 84.

12. Ibid., 77.

13. Smirnov, *Dukhovnyi otets*, 20–22.

14. *The Sayings of the Desert Fathers*, xxii. There were also female ascetics who were regarded as spiritual mothers (*ammas*) in early Christian society. The frequent use of the

term "spiritual father" in this book and references to *his* disciples are not intended to diminish the importance of spiritual mothers.

15. As cited in Hausherr, *Spiritual Direction*, 26.

16. V. I. Ekzempliarskii, "Starchestvo," in *Put' k sovershennoi zhizni: O russkom starchestve* (Moscow: Pravoslavnyi Sviato-Tikhonovskii Gumanitarnyi Universitet, 2006), 165; Nicholas Sakharov, *I Love, Therefore I Am: The Theological Legacy of Archimandrite Sophrony* (New York: St. Vladimir Seminary Press, 2002); Smirnov, *Dukhovnyi otets*.

17. *Sayings of the Desert Fathers*, 85–86; Sakharov, *I Love, Therefore I Am*, 270–71.

18. Sakharov, *I Love, Therefore I Am*, 270–71.

19. Smirnov, *Dukhovnyi otets*, 61.

20. I. V. Popov, *Misticheskoe opravdanie asketizma v tvoreniiakh prep. Makariia Egipetskogo* (Kozel'sk, 1905).

21. Vladimir Lossky, *The Vision of God* (New York, 1983), 55, as cited in A. Sidorov, "Evagrii Pontiiskii: zhizn', literaturnaia deiatel'nost', i mesto v istorii," in *Tvoreniia Avvy Evagriia: asketicheskie i bogoslovskie traktaty* (Moscow: Martis, 1994), 30.

22. Gabriel Bunge, *Akedia: die geistliche Lehre des Evagrios Pontikos vom Uberdruss* (Koln: Luthe, 1989), 12, as cited in Sidorov, "Evagrii," 52.

23. John Meyendorff, *Zhizn' i trudy sviatitelia Grigoriia Palamy*, trans. G. Nachinkin (St. Petersburg: Vizantinorossika, 1997), 188–89.

24. Hausherr, *Spiritual Direction*, 106–7.

25. Julia Konstantinovsky, *Evagrius Ponticus: The Making of a Gnostic* (Farnham and Burlington: Ashgate, 2008), 38.

26. Letter of Leonid (Lev Nagolkin) to the nuns of Belev convent. *Zhitie optinskogo startsa ieromonakha Leonida, v skhime L'va* (Kozel'sk: Izd. Vvedenskoi Optinoi pustyni, 1994), 298–99.

27. Hausherr, *Spiritual Direction*, 181–86.

28. Smirnov, *Dukhovnyi otets*, 54. Christian theology defines charisma as "a gratuitous gift from God, supernatural, transitory, given to the individual for the good of others, for the benefit of the church." *The New Catholic Encyclopedia*, 2nd ed. (Washington, DC: Thomson Gale, 2003), 3:389–90, s.v. "charisma."

29. Brown, "The Rise and Function of the Holy Man," 87.

30. Smirnov, *Dukhovnyi otets*, 67.

31. Smirnov, *Dukhovnyi otets*, 89; Sakharov, *I Love, Therefore I Am*.

32. I. M. Kontsevich, *Stiazhanie sviatogo dukha v putiakh Drevnei Rusi* (1952; repr., Moscow: Lepta, 2002), 35.

33. John Meyendorff, "O bozhestvennom dostoinstve sviatogo dukha," in *Svidetel' istiny: pamiati protopresvitera Ioanna Meiendorfa*, ed. A. V. Levitskii (Ekaterinburg: Ekaterinburgskaia eparkhiia, 2003), 110–11.

34. Giles Constable, *Monks, Hermits, and Crusaders in Medieval Europe* (London, Variorum Reprints, 1988).

35. Constable, *Monks, Hermits*, 191–93; Jean Leclercq, "Spiritual Direction in the Benedictine Tradition," in *Traditions of Spiritual Guidance*, ed. Lavinia Byrne (London: Geoffrey Chapman, 1990), 17.

36. Constable, *Monks, Hermits*, 193.

37. Ibid.; Leclercq mentions the correspondence between Ida, Countess of Boulogne, and St. Anselm of Canterbury (d. 1109) who regarded himself as her spiritual father. Yet the correspondence suggests very little spiritual guidance and contains mainly general advice. See Leclercq, "Spiritual Direction," 22.

38. Leclercq, "Spiritual Direction," 23.

39. Constable, *Monks, Hermits*, 203.

40. Smirnov, *Dukhovnyi otets*, 103; John Philip Thomas, *Private Religious Foundations in the Byzantine Empire* (Washington, DC: Dumbarton Oaks Research Library and Collection, 1987).

41. Joan Mervyn Hussey, *The Orthodox Church in the Byzantine Empire* (Oxford: Clarendon Press, 1986), 25.

42. Hausherr, *Spiritual Direction*, 102. This point needs to be qualified by the fact that under Leo V (813–820) some monasteries actually defected to the iconoclasts. Hussey, *The Orthodox Church*, 50.

43. Hilarion Alfeyev, *St. Symeon the New Theologian and Orthodox Tradition* (Oxford: Oxford University Press, 2000), 200–1.

44. Michael Angold, *Church and Society in Byzantium under the Comneni, 1081–1261* (Cambridge: Cambridge University Press, 1995), 269.

45. John A. McGuckin, "Symeon the New Theologian (d. 1022) and Byzantine Monasticism," in *Mount Athos and Byzantine Monasticism: Papers from the Twenty-eighth Spring Symposium of Byzantine Studies, Birmingham March 1994*, ed. Anthony Bryer and Mary Cunningham. Society for the Promotion of Byzantine Studies Publications 4 (Aldershot: Variorum, 1996), 19.

46. Simeon Novyi Bogoslov, "Poslaniie o ispovedi," in Simeon Novyi Bogolov and Nikita Stifat, *Asketicheskie proizvedeniia*, ed. and trans. Ilarion (Alfeev) (Klin: Khristianskaia zhizn', 2001), 79–94.

47. Nikita Stifat, "Zhizn' i podvizhnichestvo izhe vo sviatykh ottsa nashego Simeona Novogo Bogoslova," in *Asketicheskie proizvedeniia*, 97–222.

48. McGuckin, "Symeon the New Theologian," 32.

49. According to the Typicon of Ioann Tsimiskhii (c. 972) the abbots of communal monasteries as well as leaders of anchorites were represented at the annual Athonite councils. *Pravoslavnaia Entsiklopediia* (Moscow: Pravoslavnaia entsiklopediia, 2000), 110–14, s.v. "Afon."

50. Ibid., 112.

51. Kallistos Ware, "St. Anastasios the Athonite: Traditionalist or Innovator," in *Mount Athos and Byzantine Monasticism*, 10–13.

52. Ibid., 11.

53. On Palamas, see John Meyendorff, *Zhizn' i trudy*.

54. Jaroslav Pelikan, *The Spirit of Eastern Christendom (600–1700)* (Chicago: The University of Chicago Press, 1974), 203.

55. Kitch, *Literary Style*, 37–38.

56. A. Pozov, *Logos-meditatsiia drevnei tserkvi: umnoe delanie* (Munich: Tovarishchestvo zarubezhnykh pisatelei, 1964), 106.

57. The *Alphabet Jerusalem Paterikon* was translated during or before the eleventh century, and the *Sinai Paterikon* is known from an Old Russian copy of eleventh to twelfth centuries. There were references to the Lives of St. Sabbas and John of Climacus in the Vita of Feodosii of the Kievo-Pecherskii monastery.

58. *Kievo-Pecherskii Paterik: Polnoe sobraniie zhitii sviatykh v Kievo-Pecherskoi Lavre podvizavshikhsia*, trans. E. Poselianin, 3rd ed. (Moscow: Stupin, 1911), 133.

59. G. P. Fedotov, *Sviatye Drevnei Rusi (X-XVII st.)* (Paris: YMCA Press, 1985), 35.

60. G. M. Prokhorov, "O vizantiiskoi bogoslovsko-filosofskoi literature v kul'ture Rusi XIV-XVI vv.," in *Svidetel' istiny*, 430–31.

61. Kitch, *Literary Style*, 43–44.

62. George A. Maloney, *Russian Hesychasm: The Spirituality of Nil Sorskii* (The Hague: Mouton, 1973), 146.

63. N. V. Sinitsyna, "Tipy monastyrei i russkii asketicheskii ideal (XV-XVI vv.)," in *Monashestvo i monastyri v Rossii XI-XX vv.* (Moscow: Nauka, 2002), 135.

64. B. M. Kloss, "Monashestvo v epokhu obrazovaniia tsentralizovannogo gosudarstva," in *Monashestvo i monastyri v Rossii*, 63–64.

65. Amvrosii (Ornatskii), *Drevnerusskie inocheskie ustavy: ustavy rossiiskikh monastyrenachal'nikov* (Moscow: Severnyi palomnik, 2001), 37. Under Hegumen Trifon (1435–1448), the Kirillo-Belozerskii monastery became cenobitic and the ties between individual elders and novices became less prominent. See Robert Romanchuk, *Byzantine Hermeneutics and Pedagogy in the Russian North: Monks and Masters at the Kirillo-Belozerskii Monastery, 1397–1501* (Toronto: University of Toronto Press, 2007), 128–74.

66. Amvrosii (Ornatskii), *Drevnerusskie inocheskie ustavy*, 45.

67. Ibid., 122.

68. Ibid., 123.

69. E. V. Krushel'nitskaia, *Martirii Zelenetskii i osnovannyi im Troitskii monastyr'* (St. Petersburg: Aleteiia, 1998).

70. Kontsevich examined the lives of about 80 saints, most of whom were included in his "succession" of *starchestvo*. Their function as spiritual instructors is often assumed from the references in hagiographical literature to the popularity of these saints among the laity. No attention was paid to the narrative strategies of his material and to the frequent *topoi* of the ascetic vitae. Kontsevich, *Stiazhanie sviatogo dukha*, 111–202.

71. Ibid., 196.

72. Eve Levin, "Monks and their Devotees in Muscovite Russia" (Paper presented to the Convention of American Association for the Advancement of Slavic Studies, 2005).

73. Smirnov, *Dukhovnyi otets*, 23, 449.

74. Ibid., 223.

75. P. S. Stefanovich, *Prikhod i prikhodskoe dukhovenstvo v Rossii v XVI-XVII vekakh* (Moscow: Indrik, 2002), 295.

76. Ibid., 296.

77. Paul Bushkovitch, *Religion and Society in Russia: The Sixteenth and Seventeenth Centuries* (New York: Oxford University Press, 1992), 10.

78. Stefanovich, *Prikhod i prikhodskoe dukhovenstvo*, 297.

79. If, as Smirnov suggests, the model of the Russian penitential family can be reconstructed from Priest Avvakum (Petrov)'s relationship with his numerous spiritual children, then, at least in relation to their spiritual father, obedience and humility were the main virtues cultivated in his circle.

80. On the decline of the popularity of Desert Fathers and Hesychast texts among monks from the end of the sixteenth century, see G. M. Prokhorov, "Keleinaia isikhastskaia literatura v biblioteke Kirillo-Belozerskogo monastyria s XIV po XVII v.," in *Monastyrskaia kul'tura: Vostok i Zapad*, ed. E. Vodolazkin (St. Petersburg: Pushkinskii Dom, 1999), 44–58.

81. Kh. Iannaras, *Orthodoxia kai Dysi sti Neoteri Ellada* (Athens, 1966), 188, as cited in S. Govorun, "Epokha grecheskogo prosveshcheniia: istoriia i polemika," <http://www.krotov.info>.

82. D. Tsakonas, *Istoria tis neoellinikis logotechnias* (Athens, 1981), as cited in Govorun, "Epokha grecheskogo prosveshcheniia."

83. Afanasii Parios, *Apologia Christianiki* (Constantinople, 1798), as cited in Govorun, "Epokha grecheskogo prosveshcheniia."

84. S. N. Govorun, "Dvizhenie kolivadov," *Tserkov' i vremia* 16, no. 3 (2001): 90–96.

85. Ibid., 98.

86. S. N. Govorun, "Iz istorii dobrotoliubiia," *Tserkov' i vremia* 14, no. 1 (2001): 291.

87. According to Molinos (1628–1696), the prayer of quietude required total submission to the will of God and the guidance of an expert spiritual director. *The Oxford Dictionary of the Christian Church*, ed. F. L. Cross and E. A. Livingstone (Oxford: Oxford University Press, 1997): 1100–1. s.v. "Molinos." It is possible that Molinos was familiar with the patristic sources on prayer. Nevertheless, as with other works, the Orthodox authors of the eighteenth century recognized familiar ideas in the writings of the representatives of competing faiths.

88. C. Papoulidis, "Portée oecuménique du renouveau monastique au XVIII siécle dans l'église Orthodoxe," *Balkan Studies* 10, no. 1 (1969): 111–12.

89. Both Iannaras and Govorun locate the *Kollyvades* within the anti-Enlightenment camp.

90. S. J. Barnett, *The Enlightenment and Religion: The Myths of Modernity* (Manchester: Manchester University Press, 2003), 136.

91. Govorun, "Iz istorii dobrotoliubiia," 289–94.

92. During the Cossack uprising in 1648 large numbers of Jews were killed and thousands fled. It is possible to surmise that many families, like the ancestors of Paisii's mother, elected to convert to Christianity and—by the eighteenth century—had assimilated into Ukrainian Orthodox society. See M. Nadav, "The Jewish Community of Nemyriv in 1648: Their Massacre and Loyalty Oath to the Cossacks," *Harvard Ukrainian Studies* 8, nos. 1–2 (1984): 376–77.

93. On the methods of teaching in the Kiev Academy, see James Cracraft, "Theology at the Kiev Academy during its Golden Age," *Harvard Ukrainian Studies* 8, nos. 1–2 (1984): 75.

94. Sergii Chetverikov, *Starets Paisii Velichkovskii: ego zhizn', uchenie, i vliianie na pravoslavnoe monashestvo* (Paris: YMCA Press, 1988), 10–64.

95. Porfirii Uspenskii, *Vostok Khristianskii: Istoriia Afona* (St. Petersburg: Izd. Imperatorskoi akademii nauk, 1892) as cited in Iatsmirskii, *Slavianskie i russkie rukopisi*, 539.

96. Steven Runciman, *The Great Church in Captivity: A Study of the Patriarchate of Constantinople from the Eve of the Turkish Conquest to the Greek War of Independence* (London: Cambridge University Press, 1968), 365, 374.

97. The Habsburgs came into possession of Transylvania, home to many Orthodox monasteries, in 1711, and actively promoted the Uniate faith in this region, provoking an uprising of Orthodox Romanians in 1760. Nigel Aston, *Christianity and Revolutionary Europe, 1750–1830* (Cambridge: Cambridge University Press, 2002), 19.

98. Valentina Pelin, "The Correspondence of Abbot Paisie from Neamts," *Revue des Études Sud-Est Européennes* 22, nos. 1–2 (1994): 75–80.

99. "Zhitie i podvigi ottsa nashego startsa Paisiia," in *Zhitie i pisaniia moldavskogo startsa Paisiia Velichkovskogo* (1847; repr., Kozel'sk: Sviato-Vvedenskaia Optina Pustyn', 2001), 23–25; Mitrofan, "Zhitie i podvigi blazhennogo otsa nashego Paisiia," in *Prep. Paisii Velichkovskii: Avtobiografiia, zhizneopisanie, i izbrannye tvoreniia po rukopisnym istochnikam XVIII-XIX vv.*, ed. D. A. Pospelova, O. A. Rodionova, P. B. and M. A. Zhgun (Moscow: Russkii na Afone Sviato-Panteleimonov Monastyr', 2004), 134–37.

100. Pelin, "The Correspondence of Abbot Paisie," 80. Paisii wrote about his supervision of the two monasteries in Sekul and Neamt, which contained both Romanian and Slavic speakers: ". . . two days before my departure . . . the brothers gather in the refectory: one day those speaking the Slav language, the other day—those speaking the Moldavian language. And I instruct them: one day in Slav, and on the other in Moldavian." Ibid., 80. It seems that Paisii was using Church Slavonic as a *lingua franca* for monks of Slavic origin.

101. The signs of ethnic tension had already been present in the 1780s before the war. The Rule of Sofronieva hermitage, for example, stipulated the acceptance of Wallachian monks in the monastery. "Sofronieva i Glinskaia pustyni," *Strannik* 12 (1862): 529–68.

102. "Povest' o sviatem sobore," in *Prep. Paisii Velichkovskii*, 32.

103. "Pis'ma startsa Paisiia," in *Zhitie i pisaniia moldavskogo startsa*, 215. Later in this letter Paisii mentions that ancient manuscripts could be found in other monasteries in Athos, but one should make a generous donation to the impoverished Greek monasteries in order to get access to their libraries. Ibid., 228–29.

104. N. N. Lisovoi, "Dve epokhi, dva dobrotoliubiia (prepodobnyi Paisii Velichkovskii i sviatitel' Feofan Zatvornik)," in *Tserkov' v istorii Rossii*, ed. Iaroslav Shchapov and Pavel Zyrianov (Moscow: Institut Rossiiskoi istorii Rossiiskoi Akademii nauk, 1998), 2:137–38.

105. Cracraft, "Theology at the Kiev Academy," 75.

106. "Pis'ma startsa Paisiia," 226.

107. Florovsky, *Puti russkogo bogosloviia*, 126–27.

108. Lisovoi, "Dve epokhi," 122. The inaccurate view that Paisii was merely a translator of the Greek edition is suggested in Govorun's article and repeated elsewhere. Govorun, "Iz istorii Dobrotoiubiia," 262–95. Ilarion (Alfeev), *Sviashchennaia taina tserkvi: vvedenie v istoriiu i problematiku imiaslavskikh sporov* (St. Petersburg: Aleteiia, 2002), 1:222.

109. Lisovoi, "Dve epokhi," 125–27.

110. Leonid (Poliakov), "Literaturnoe nasledstvo Paisiia Velichkovskogo," *Zhurnal Moskovskoi Patriarkhii* 4 (1957): 60.

111. Chetverikov, *Starets Paisii*, 144.

112. Ibid., 145.

113. "Povest' o sviatem sobore," 61.

114. Ibid., 85.

115. Ibid., 111–12.

116. Ibid., 105. Paisii regarded himself as unworthy of priesthood.

117. Paisii, "Avraamskikh del podrazhateliu," in *Zhitie i pisaniia moldavskogo startsa*, 250.

118. "Zhitie i podvigi ottsa nashego startsa Paisiia," in ibid., 23–25.

119. Ibid., 30–31.

120. Ibid., 45–46.

121. Paisii, "Prechestnoi gospozhe Marii," in ibid., 265.

122. Ibid., 266.

123. "Avraamskikh del podrazhateliu," 253.

124. Il'ia Chitterio, "Uchenie prep. Paisiia Velichkovskogo," in *Prep. Paisii Velichkovskii*, 308.

125. Poliakov, "Literaturnoe nasledstvo," 59.

126. S. Govorun, "Iz istorii Dobrotoiubiia," 293.

127. Florovskii, *Puti russkogo bogosloviia*, 126.

128. F. J. Thomson, *The Reception of Byzantine Culture in Medieval Russia* (Aldershot: Ashgate Variorum, 1999), 117–18.

2—Monasticism and Elders between Reform and Revival, 1721–1801

1. For more on the Russian spiritual renaissance that began in the late eighteenth century see I. Smolitsch, *Russisches Mönchtum: Entstehung, Entwicklung, und Wesen, 988–1917* (Würzburg: Augustins-Verlag, 1953) and G. Florovskii, *Puti russkogo bogosloviia*, as well as the contemporary Russian study of monasticism by P. I. Zyrianov, *Russkie monastyri i monashestvo v XIX i nachale XX v.* (Moscow: Russkoe Slovo, 1999). For a thorough and archivally based treatment of the subject of institutional reorganization see William Wagner, "The Transformation of Female Orthodox Monasticism in Nizhnii Novgorod Diocese, 1764–1929, in Comparative Perspective," *Journal of Modern History* 78, no. 12 (2006): 793–845.

2. On superstition and its use in Petrine Russia see E. Smilianskaia, "Pravoslavnyi pastyr' i ego suevernaia pastva," in *Chelovek mezhdu tsarstvom i imperiei: sbornik materialov mezdunarodnoi konferentsii*, ed. M. S. Kiseleva (Moscow: Institut cheloveka RAN, 2003), 407–15.

3. Ivanovskii regarded Peter's reforms, first, as an attempt to purify monasticism of abuses, and second, as driven by an intention to guard the rights and interests of society at large. V. Ivanovskii, "Russkoe zakonodatel'stvo 18 i 19 st. v svoikh postanovleniiakh otnositel'no monashestvuiushchikh lits i monastyrei," *Vera i razum* 1, no. 3 (1904): 149.

4. James Billington, *The Icon and the Axe: An Interpretive History of Russian Culture* (New York: Vintage Books, 1996), 181.

5. On the Solovetskii uprising see Georg Michels, "The Violent Old Belief: An Examination of Religious Dissent on the Karelian Frontier," *Russian History* 19 (1992): 203–29; O. V. Chumicheva, *Solovetskoe vosstanie, 1667–1676 gg.* (Novosibirsk: Izd-vo SO RAN, 1998).

6. For example, in 1733 monks of Sarov and Berliukov monasteries copied and circulated the treatise by Rodyshevskii "On Monasticism," advocating the restoration of the patriarch. I. Chistovich, *Feofan Prokopovich i ego vremia* (St. Petersburg: Izd. Imperatorskoi Akademii nauk, 1868), 4:524–25.

7. Ivanovskii, "Russkoe zakonodatel'stvo," *Vera i razum* 1, no. 8 (1904): 429.

8. Chistovich, *Feofan Prokopovich*, 515.

9. RGADA, f. 248, op. 14, d. 81, kn. 781, l. 1320–1320 ob.

10. Ibid., ll. 1377–78.

11. Quotas (*shtaty*) were introduced in some monasteries by Peter I in 1724. Ivanovskii, "Russkoe zakonodatel'stvo," *Vera i razum* 1, no. 3 (1904): 270–71.

12. Ibid., 171–72.

13. Lavrov, *Koldovstvo i religiia v Rossii, 1700–1740* (Moscow: Drevlekhranilishche, 2000), 345.

14. A. I. Komissarenko, *Russkii absolutism i dukhoventsvo v XVIII veke: ocherki istorii sekulariazatsionnoi reformy 1764 g.* (Moscow: Izd-vo Vses. zaochnogo politekhnicheskogo instituta, 1990), 121; V. A. Fedorov, *Russkaia pravoslavnaia tserkov'*, 59.

15. Wagner, "The Transformation of Female Orthodox Monasticism," 801.

16. Memo of Prince Potemkin to Catherine, "On Monasteries" (October 1786) as

quoted in N. Lisovoi, "Vosemnadtsatyi vek v istorii russkogo monashestva," in *Monashestvo i monastyri v Rossii XI-XX veka: Istoricheskie ocherki*, ed. N. V. Sinitsyna (Moscow: Nauka, 2002), 200.

17. P. V. Kalitin, ed., *Vysokopreosviashchennyi Gavriil (Petrov), Mitropolit Novgorodskii i Sanktpeterburgskii: Vopreki veku prosveshcheniia; zhizn', tvorchestvo, konchina* (Moscow: Palomnik, 2000), 167.

18. Ibid.

19. Ibid.

20. Ibid., 169.

21. Ibid.

22. Wagner, "The Transformation of Female Orthodox Monasticism," 804–5.

23. M. S. Popov, *Arsenii Matsieevich i ego delo* (St. Petersburg: Tip. M. Frolovoi, 1912), 128.

24. Ibid., 157.

25. Ibid.

26. Kalitin, *Vysokopreosviashchennyi Gavriil*, 194–95.

27. E. Smilianskaia, *Volshebniki, bogokhul'niki, eretiki: narodnaia religioznost' i "dukhovnye prestupleniia" v Rossii XVIII v.* (Moscow: Indrik, 2003), 39.

28. Brenda Meehan-Waters, "Popular Piety, Local Initiative, and the Founding of Women's Religious Communities in Russia, 1764–1904," *St. Vladimir's Theological Quarterly* 30 (1986): 117–42.

29. Serge Zenkovsky, *Russkoe staroobriadchestvo: dukhovnye dvizheniia semnadtsatogo veka* (Munich: Wilhelm Fink Verlag 1970), 126, 447, passim.

30. Eugene Clay, "The Theological Origins of the Christ-Faith," 21–42; Panchenko, *Khristovshchina i skopchestvo*, 141–43.

31. Old Believers copied many ascetic writings by hand (the so-called "Starchestvo" collections), and printed the most popular ones, such as the "Alphabetic Paterikon," a collection of the lives of the desert saints. *Paterik Azbuchnyi* (Suprasl', 1791); D. D. Smirnov, "Stat'i 'Ot starchestva' v rukopisnykh sbornikakh XVII-XIX vv.," in *Russkaia kniga v dorevoliutsionnoi Sibiri: rukopisnaia i pechatnaia kniga na Vostoke strany*, ed. N. N. Pokrovskii (Novosibirsk: RAN Sibirskoe otd-nie, 1992), 156–74.

32. E. M. Iukhimenko, *Vygovskaia staroobriadcheskaia pustyn': Dukhovnaia zhizn' i literatura*, vols. 1-2 (Moscow: Iazyki slavianskoi kul'tury, 2002); P.S. Smirnov, *Spory i razdeleniia v russkom raskole v pervoi chetverti XVIII veka* (St. Petersburg, 1909).

33. N. N. Pokrovskii, *Antifeodal'nyi protest uralo-sibirskikh krest'ian-staroobriadtsev v XVIII veke* (Novosibirsk: Nauka, 1974); RGADA, f. 248, op. 14, d. 21, kn. 783, l. 1403.

34. [Porfirii], *Zhitie i podvigi skhimonakha Ioanna, osnovatelia i pervonachal'nika Sarovskoi pustyni* (Murom, 1892), 53–54; TsGA RM, f. 1, op. 1, d. 73, ll. 10–37.

35. GABO, f. 7, op. 1, d. 5, ll. 5–7.

36. Feofan (Sokolov), "Zapiski o. Feofana, arkhimandrita Kirillo-Novoezerskogo monastyria," *Strannik* 1, no. 2 (1862): 39.

37. For example, Old Believer monks who wished to come back to Orthodoxy were held under supervision, but eventually were allowed to join the monastery.

38. Monk Neofit compiled a list of questions for a priestless group of Old Believers, the Vyg Pomorians, who wrote a treatise by the way of answers to these questions known as *Pomorskie otvety*. *Pomorskie otvety: Otvety pustynnozhitelei na voprosy ieromonakha*

Neofita. (Ural'sk: Staroobriad. Tip. Simakova, 1911).

39. M. Iu. Nechaeva, *Monastyri i vlasti: upravlenie obiteliami Vostochnogo Urala v XVIII v.* (Ekaterinburg: UrO RAN, 1998), 162–63.

40. *Prepodobnogo ottsa avvy Ioanna, igumena Sinaiskoi gory: Lestvitsa v russkom perevode* (St. Petersburg: Tipografiia No. 6, 1995), 22, 26. See also Paisii Velichkovskii, "Poslanie Avraamovskikh del podrazhateliu . . .," in *Zhitie i pisaniia moldavskogo startsa* (1847), 238–56.

41. *Nila Sorskogo predanie i ustav* (Moscow: Tip. M. A. Aleksandrova, 1912), 3–9.

42. As quoted in Ivanovskii, "Russkoe zakonodatel'stvo," *Vera i razum* 1, no. 19 (1904): 433.

43. G. V. Piasetskii, *Istoriia Orlovskoi eparkhii* (Orel, 1899), 188–89.

44. OR RGB, f. 214, d. 214, ll. 28–30.

45. Ibid., ll. 37–38.

46. TsGA RM, f. 1, op. 1, d. 243, l. 92.

47. OR RGB, f. 214, d. 214, l. 31.

48. It is possible that the plant used by St. Serafim was the so-called *boiarskaia snit'* (*Bupleurum aureum*) also known as "rabbit cabbage." *Snit'* was traditionally used by peasants for making soups (*snitnye shchi, botvin'e*). Vladimir I. Dal', *Tol'kovyi slovar' zhivogo velikorusskogo iazyka*, <http://vidahl.agava.ru/>, s. v. "snit'."

49. RGIA, f. 796, op. 205, d. 536, l. 4.

50. OR RGB, f. 214, d. 283, ll. 22–23 ob.

51. Piasetskii, *Istoriia*, 184–85; [Kavelin], "Poslednie russkie pravoslavnye pustynnozhiteli," *Domashniaia beseda* 21 (1862): 487–89.

52. Piasetskii, *Istoriia Orlovskoi eparkhii*, 186.

53. OR RGB, f. 214, d. 214, ll. 38 ob.–42 ob.

54. GAOO, f. 220, op. 1, d. 55, l. 2.

55. Ignatii Brianchaninov, "Zhizn' skhimonakha Feodora," in *Polnoe sobranie tvorenii sviatitelia Ignatiia Brianchaninova* (Moscow: Palomnik, 2002), 4:430–45.

56. Among them were, for example, Schemamonk Gerasim (Georgii) (b. 1740) who lived as a hermit in the Briansk forests, Leonid Nagolkin, Maksim (Sokol'nikov), and Ioannikii (Bocharov), a monk in the Aleksander-Nevskaia Lavra and Optina Pustyn'. OR RGB, f. 214, d. 283, l. 31.

57. SPb FIRI RAN, f. 3, op. 3, d. 21, l. 85, as cited in Nestor (Kumysh), "Prepodobnyi Feodor Svirskii," *Sankt-Peterburgskii tserkovnyi vestnik*, no. 12 (2003), <http://mitropolia-spb.ru> >, under *Voda zhivaia*.

58. Brianchaninov, "Zhizn' skhimonakha Feodora," 435.

59. A. Zorin, *Kormia dvuglavogo orla . . . Literatura i gosudarstvennaia ideologiia v Rossii v poslednie treti XVIII-pervoi treti XIX veka* (Moscow: Novoe literaturnoe obozrenie, 2001), 31–64.

60. Tikhon of Zadonsk, *Tvoreniia izhe vo sviatykh ottsa nashego Tikhona Zadonskogo* (Moscow: Sinodal'naia Tip., 1889), 2:323–24.

61. Charles François Philibert Masson, *Sekretnye zapiski o Rossii vremeni tsarstvovaniia Ekateriny II i Pavla I* (Moscow: Novoe literaturnoe obozrenie, 1996), 40.

62. Both parish priests and monks were involved in cases of blasphemy, the use of magic, and irreverence. Smilianskaia, *Volshebniki*, 224.

63. P. Znamenskii, *Prikhodskoe dukhovenstvo v Rossii so vremeni reformy Petra*

(Kazan, 1873), 632–33. In 1825 Alexander I ordered Bishop Evgenii (Bolkhovitinov) to compile a set of general rules "on the restraint of the clergy from improper behavior."

64. Gregory Freeze, *The Russian Levites: Parish Clergy in the Eighteenth Century* (Cambridge: Harvard University Press, 1977), 218.

65. Ibid., 221.

66. St. John Chrysostom as quoted in A. P. Lebedev, *Iz istorii nravstvennogo sostoianiia dukhovenstva ot II po VIII vek* (Sergiev Posad, 1903), 31–32.

67. Sergei Bakhmustov, *Monastyri Mordovii* (Saransk: Mordovskoe knizhnoe izdatel'stvo, 2000), 737.

68. B. V. Titlinov, *Gavriil Petrov, Mitropolit Novgorodskii i Sankt-Peterburgskii: Ego zhizn' i deiatel'nost' v sviazi s tserkovnymi delami togo vremeni* (Petrograd: Tip. M. Melkusheva, 1916), 751.

69. Ibid., 752.

70. Ibid.

71. Lisovoi, "Vosemnadtsatyi vek v istorii russkogo monashestva," 208.

72. V. M. Zhivov, *Iazyk i kul'tura v Rossii XVIII v.* (Moscow: Iazyki russkoi kul'tury, 1996), 425.

73. Ibid., 371.

74. Titlinov, *Gavriil Petrov*, 742–43. Since Valaam monastery was outside the official "*shtaty*," Nazarii was appointed as *stroitel'*, which was the equivalent of the title of abbot.

75. Ibid., 750.

76. *Valaamskii monastyr'* (St Petersburg, 1864); *Starcheskie nastavleniia o. Nazariia s kratkim ukazaniem o ego zhizni i podvigakh* (Moscow, 1853). The new Rule of Valaam monastery was approved by Gavriil.

77. Titlinov, *Gavriil Petrov*, 749.

78. Makarii, "Skazanie," as cited in Kalitin, *Vysokopreosviashchennyi Gavriil*, 210.

79. Feofan himself was one of the central figures in the promotion of "new monasticism." He advised the bishops of St. Petersburg and Novgorod dioceses on matters of monastic reform; he also was responsible for the appointment and replacement of abbots, many of whom had links with the spiritual elders. In 1799, Gavriil promoted Feofan to supervisor of five monasteries, including the female Goritskii convent.

80. OR RGB, f. 214, d. 214, ll. 42–51.

81. Tikhon, *Tvoreniia*, 39–40.

82. Lisovoi, "Dve epokhi," 125.

83. Titlinov, *Gavriil Petrov*, 745.

84. *Vysokopreosviashchennyi Gavriil*, 204–5.

85. GABO, f. 7, op. 1, d. 30, ll. 13–15.

86. Erast (Vytropskii), *Istoricheskoe opisanie Kozel'skoi Optinoi pustyni i Predtecheva skita* (Kozel'sk: Izd. Sviato-Vvedenskoi Optinoi Pustyni, 2000), 45–48.

87. Ibid., 53–54.

88. R. V. Kaurkin, "Obraz ideal'nogo pravitelia v religioznoi i obshchestvennoi mysli Rossii XVIII v.," paper presented at the conference "State, Church, Society: Historical Experience and Contemporary Problems," Institute of World History RAN, Moscow, April 12, 2005.

89. Erast, *Istoricheskoe opisanie*, 46.

90. "Zapiski Feofana Novoezerskogo," in *Starcheskie sovety Feofana Novoezerskogo: Valaamskikh i Solovetskikh podvizhnikov XVIII i XIX vv.* (Moscow: Preobrazhenie, 2000), 40; Israil', "Startsy Brianskoi Beloberezhskoi pustyni," *Orlovskie eparkhial'nye*

vedomosti 4 (1909): 1043.

91. "Zapiski Feofana Novoezerskogo," 198–99.

92. "Sofronieva i Glinskaia pustyni," 564–65.

93. The fifteenth-century controversy between the Nonpossessors and Josephites developed under very different circumstances and cannot be directly applied to the elders. While Paisii Velichkovskii and the like-minded monks in Russia read the writings of Nil Sorskii, they did not necessarily take his Rule as the optimal form of monastic organization.

94. Zhivov, *Iazyk i kul'tura*, 376.

95. Ivanovskii, "Russkoe zakonodatel'stvo," *Vera i razum* 1, no. 3 (1904): 162; Lavrov, *Koldovstvo i religiia*, 295.

96. This sample is from Beloberezhskaia Pustyn' in 1805, and includes monks and novices. GABO, f. 7, op. 1, d. 34, ll. 46–48. This is compared to the sample provided by P. Zyrianov on the basis of 35 monasteries in Moscow diocese. Zyrianov, *Russkie monastyri i monashestvo*, 25.

97. Lavrov, *Koldovstvo i religiia*, 275–93.

98. Ibid., 297.

99. *Zhizn' ottsa Feodora byvshego nastoiatelia Sanaksarskia obiteli prestavl'shagosia v 1791 g.* (Moscow: Universitetskaia tipografiia, 1847), 6.

100. OR RGB, f. 214, d. 214, l. 11 ob.

101. E. Gorchakova, *Obitel' startsa Zosimy Verkhovskogo* (Moscow: Izd-vo im. sviatitelia Ignatii Stavropol'skogo, 1998), 3.

102. Twelve members of the Court Guards received the Empress' personal permission to join Fedor's community. Feofan (Sokolov), "Zapiski o. Feofana," 35.

103. OR RGB, f. 214, d. 284, ll. 21–21 ob.

104. Z. P. Kovalenko, "Lev Nagolkin i Beloberezhskaia pustyn'," in *Stranitsy istorii Karacheva*, ed. V. V. Krasheninnikov (Briansk: Brian. obl. Nauch. b-ka, 1996), 18–19. Kovalenko revised the date of birth of Elder Lev (Leonid), claiming that he was born in 1768. She believes that the official monastic documents made Lev older to circumvent the legislation that stipulated the minimum age for monastic profession at 30. Thus Lev became a monk at 25 in 1797.

105. David L. Ransel, "An Eighteenth-Century Russian Merchant Family in Prosperity and Decline," in *Imperial Russia: New Histories for the Empire*, ed. Jane Burbank and David L. Ransel, Indiana-Michigan Series in East-European Studies (Bloomington: Indiana University Press, 1998), 265.

106. Ransel demonstrates that Russian merchants spent most of the year on the road, gaining experience of life and invaluable insights into different local cultures. Ransel, "An Eighteenth-Century Russian Merchant," 263.

107. A. Kovalevskii, "Vospominaniia o dukhovnike Kievo-Pecherskoi Lavry, ieroskhimonakhe Antonii," *Dushepoleznoe chtenie* (1881), 350.

108. *Zapiski o zhizni i podvigakh Petra Alekseevicha Michurina, pustynnozhitelia Vasiliska, i nekotorye cherty iz zhizni iurodivogo monakha Iony* (Moscow, 1849), 49.

109. Ibid., 22.

110. Zosima Verkhovskii, *Tvoreniia* (Sergiev Posad: Sviato-Troitskaia Sergieva Lavra, 2006), 112.

111. Laura Engelstein, *Castration and the Heavenly Kingdom: A Russian Folktale* (Ithaca: Cornell University Press, 1999).

112. OR RGB, f. 214, d. 409; ibid., d. 450.

113. A. Pentkovskii, "Ot 'Iskatelia neprestannoi molitvy' do 'Otkrovennykh rasskazov strannika' (k voprosu ob istorii teksta)," *Simvol* 27 (1992): 151–52.

114. With the exception of widowed priests who were forced to join monasteries rather than marry again.

115. OR RGB, f. 213, op. 58, d. 26, l. 28.

116. The calculation is made on the basis of Synodal records of canonized and non-canonized Russian saints. RGIA, f. 796, op. 182, d. 2497, l. 57 ob.

117. This was typical for Nizhnii Novgorod diocese, but also was a pattern in other regions of Russia. See Wagner, "The Transformation of Female Orthodox Monasticism," 807.

118. Ibid., 801. Wagner accounts for different figures produced by various scholars.

119. Ibid., 797.

120. Meehan-Waters, "Popular Piety," 117–42.

121. [Serafim (Chichagov)], *Letopis' Serafimo-Diveevskogo monastyria* (Moscow: Palomnik, 2002), 1–3; *Afonskii Paterik, ili Zhizneopisanie sviatykh na Sviatoi Afonskoi Gore prosiiavshikh* (Moscow: Blagovest, 2001), 520.

122. *Letopis' Serafimo-Diveevskogo*, 5. On the attitude of spiritual authorities in other cultural contexts to visionaries, see William Christian, *Apparitions in Late Medieval and Renaissance Spain* (Princeton: Princeton University Press, 1981).

123. On property and noble women see Michelle Lamarche Marrese, *A Woman's Kingdom: Noblewomen and the Control of Property in Russia, 1700–1861* (Ithaca: Cornell University Press, 2002).

124. Caroline Bynum Walker, *Jesus as Mother: Studies in the Spirituality of the High Middle Ages* (Berkeley: University of California Press, 1982), 259–65.

125. E. Poselianin, *Russkaia tserkov' i russkie podvizhniki XVIII veka* (St. Petersburg: Izd. I. L. Tuzova, 1905), 276–78.

126. Paisii Velichkovskii, "Prechestnoi Gospozhe Marii s bogosobrannymi sestrami," in *Zhitie i pisaniia moldavskogo startsa* (1847), 262.

127. Ibid., 263.

128. Ibid., 264–67.

129. Ibid., 267.

130. Poselianin, *Russkaia tserkov'*, 279.

131. Theodor of Sanaxar, *Saint Theodore of Sanaxar*, vol. 5, *Little Russian Philokalia* (Platina, CA: St. Herman of Alaska Brotherhood, 2000), 178.

132. Ibid., 182.

133. *Zhitie i pisaniia moldavskogo startsa* (1892), 253–55.

134. Ibid., 254.

135. TsANO, f. 570, op. 558, d. 236, ll. 11–43.

136. Florovskii, *Puti russkogo bogosloviia*, 122.

3—The Institutionalization of Spiritual Guidance, 1810–1860
Achievements and Tensions

1. For more on "mystical universalism," see A. Zorin, *Kormia dvuglavogo orla*, 297–336. For a critical evaluation of this concept see the forum in *Ab Imperio* 1 (2002), 470–554.

2. *Polnoe sobranie zakonov Rossiiskoi Imperii, poveleniem Gosudaria Imperatora*

Nikolaia Pavlovicha sostavlennoe, sobranie pervoe s 1649 po 12 Dekabria 1825 goda, 1-aia seriia (St. Petersburg: Tipografiia II Otdeleniia Sobstvennoi Ego Imperatorskogo Velichestva Kantseliarii, 1830), vol. 26, no. 19.7876, 588 (manifesto of March 15, 1801). Subsequent citations will be identified as *PSZ*, 1, followed by volume, number, and page.

3. RGIA, f. 1374, op. 4, d. 221, ll. 1–5.

4. RGIA, f. 796, op. 101, d. 890, ll. 2–5 ob.

5. *Zhizneopisanie Optinskogo startsa ieromonakha Leonida*, 12.

6. RGIA, f. 796, op. 2, d. 5355, ll. 1–30 ob.

7. The members of the society included A. S. Shishkov, M. Speranskii, M. Magnitskii, S. Uvarov, and N. M. Karamzin. They published a literary journal and had regular gatherings in the salon of Derzhavin.

8. Iu. Kondakov, *Dukhovno-religioznaia politika Aleksandra I i russkaia pravoslavnaia oppozitsiia, 1801–1825* (St. Petersburg: Nestor, 1998), 98–99.

9. A. F. Labzin wrote: "There is now a young Russian priest who preaches every Sunday and attracts many listeners, especially from merchants and ordinary people, so that many have stopped going to the Alexandro-Nevskaia Lavra to listen to Bishop Mikhail and have started to patronize this new preacher." Kondakov believes that this young Russian priest was Fotii. Kondakov, *Dukhovno-religioznaia politika*, 110.

10. G. Florovskii, *Puti russkogo bogosloviia*, 159.

11. Prior his appointment to Iur'ev monastery, Fotii was briefly an abbot in the Derevianitskii and Skovorodskii monasteries.

12. The Holy Union was formed at the Congress of Vienna (1814–1815). Its participants maintained conservative religious values in opposition to liberal and revolutionary movements.

13. Weber, *Economy and Society*, 122.

14. The calculation is made from the data presented in *Pravoslavnaia entsiklopediia*, s.v. "Monastyri i monashestvo."

15. During Paul I' s reign, every monastery received 30 desiatins (about 81 acres) of land. Under Alexander I (on June 8, 1905), a decree allowed monasteries to receive donations from private donors, which should have only consisted of uninhabited land. According to the decree of May 24, 1810, monasteries could purchase land independently. During Nicholas I's reign, property owned by monasteries increased even more. In 1838, every monastery received some parcels of woodland. New monasteries had the right to claim 100 desiatins of land or a compensatory equivalent in cash. Ibid.

16. Zyrianov, *Russkie monastyri i monashestvo*, 15.

17. S. Chetverikov, "Iz istorii russkogo starchestva," *Put'* 1 (1912): 3, 7, 38.

18. Hereafter Optina Pustyn' and Ioanno-Predtechenskii skete are used interchangeably.

19. Erast, *Istoricheskoe opisanie*, 65–72.

20. Ibid., 87–88. The Rule of Optina Skete was based on the officially approved Rule of Konevets monastery that promoted cenobitic principles of monastic life.

21. D. Sokolov, "Zasluga Optinoi pustyni v dele izdaniia sviatootecheskikh tvorenii," *Pribavleniia k tserkovnym vedomostiam*, no. 30 (July 27, 1902): 1001. See also OR RGB, f. 23, op. 39, d. 5, l. 1.

22. Sokolov, "Zasluga Optinoi," 1005.

23. Leonard J. Stanton, *The Optina Pustyn Monastery in the Russian Literary Imagination: Iconic Vision in Works by Dostoevsky, Gogol, Tolstoy, and Others*, Middlebury

Studies in Russian Language and Literature 3 (New York: Peter Lang, 1995).

24. *Zhitie i pisaniia moldavskogo startsa* (1847), i-xvi; N. Kauchtschischwili, A. N. Tachiaos and V. Pelin, eds., *Paisij, lo starec* (Comunita di Bose, Magnano: Edizioni Qiqajon, 1997), 11 and passim.

25. For example, Optina published the biography and writings of Zosima (Verkhovskii) and Elder Vasilisk. The Optina library had handwritten copies of the life of Elder Adrian (Blinskii) and memoirs of the Roslavl' hermits.

26. Vsevolod Roshko, *Prepodobnyi Serafim: Sarov i Diveevo; Issledovaniia i materialy* (Moscow: Sam & Sam, 1997), 48.

27. V. Stepashkin, *Prepodobnyi Serafim Sarovskii: predaniia i fakty* (Sarov, 2002), 38–39.

28. TsGA RM, f. 1, op. 1, d. 243, ll. 94–94 ob.

29. Zosima Verkhovskii, *Tvoreniia* (Sviato-Troitskaia Sergieva Lavra, 2006), 443–47.

30. Constable, *Monks, Hermits*, 202–3.

31. The monks of the Sofronieva and Glinskaia Pustyn' were granted a special right to elect their superiors. "Sofronieva and Glinskaia pustyni," *Strannik* 12 (1862): 529–68.

32. V. Ivanovskii, "Russkoe zakonodatel'stvo 18 i 19 st.," *Vera i razum*, no. 10 (1894): 537.

33. OR RGB, f. 213, op. 86, d. 14, l. 57–57 ob.

34. In one of his letters he remarked that he was happy with Moisei and, especially, with his brother Antonii. *Pis'ma Optinskogo startsa L'va k monakhu Ioannikiiu (Bocharovu)* (Kozel'sk: Sviato-Vvedenskaia Optina Pustyn', 2002), 71.

35. *Zhizneopisanie optinskogo startsa ieromonakha Leonida*, 9–10.

36. Onufrii (Makhanov), *Prichal molitv uedinennykh: Valaamskii monastyr' i ego nebesnye pokroviteli prepodobnye Sergii i German* (St. Petersburg: Tsarskoe delo, 2005), 83.

37. *Zhizneopisanie optinskogo startsa ieromonakha Leonida*, 11–12.

38. Onufrii (Makhanov), *Prichal molitv uedinennykh*, 137.

39. Ioann (Maslov), *Glinskaia Pustyn': Istoriia obiteli i ee dukhovno-prosvetitel'skaia deiatel'nost' v XVI–XX vekakh* (Moscow: Izdatel'skii otdel Moskovskogo patriarkhata, 1994), 122.

40. Ibid., 128–30.

41. Ibid., 133.

42. Leonid Nagolkin headed Belobrezhskaia pustyn' between 1804 and 1808. It has been suggested that his election as abbot took place without his awareness.

43. Wagner, "The Transformation of Female Orthodox Monasticism," 793–845.

44. In 1891 Bishop Vitalii of Kaluga tried to prevent the close involvement of Optina monks with Shamordino women's community. Erast, *Istoricheskoe opisaniie*, 199; Elder Sofronii (Shevtsov)'s association with the women's community in Tuapse was also found inappropriate in 1911. RGIA, f. 796, op. 205, d. 277, l. 6 ob.

45. Also compare with the concept of the "inner man" that was influential in Russian literature. E. G. Etkind, "*Vnutrennii chelovek" i vneshniaia rech': Ocherki psikhopoetiki russkoi literatury XVIII-XIX vv.* (Moscow: Iazyki ruskoi kul'tury, 1998); Zorin, *Kormia dvuglavogo orla*, 306.

46. Ignatii (Brianchaninov), "Pis'mo k igumenu Damaskinu" [September 25, 1853] in *Polnoe zhizneopisaniie sviatitelia Ignatiia Kavkazskogo* (Moscow: Izdatel'stvo im. svt. Ignatiia Stavropol'skogo, 2002), 196.

47. V. Kotel'nikov, *Pravoslavnaia asketika i russkaia literatura: na puti k Optinoi* (St. Petersburg: Prizma-15, 1994), 59.

48. In the eighteenth and nineteenth centuries, popular biographies of holy men and women used the generic term *podvizhniki* (ascetics) to describe these unofficially venerated saints. Poselianin, *Russkaia tserkov'*; idem, *Prepodobnyi Serafim Sarovskii, chudotvorets i russkie podvizhniki XIX veka* (Moscow: Aksios, 2003).

49. Kozel'sk merchant Briuzgin made comments in the presence of Leonid that ancient ascetics were slender. OR RGB, f. 213, op. 49, d. 5, l. 11.

50. OR RGB, f. 213, op. 49, d. 5, l. 5–6.

51. Kotel'nikov, *Pravoslavnaia asketika*, 59.

52. A private rule (*pravilo*) was usually a daily selection of prayers and psalms (accompanied by bows and prostrations) read by a Christian in private, in addition to all necessary church services that one was expected to attend.

53. OR RGB, f. 213, op. 75, d. 4, ll. 5–6 ob.

54. Ibid.

55. The epistles of the apostles contained a theological message and dealt with problems in early Christian communities.

56. Joseph Power and Wendy Wright, eds. *Francis de Sales, Jane de Chantal: Letters of Spiritual Direction* (New York: Paulist Press, 1988). The published works contain 2,000 letters which are estimated to be one tenth of the actual number he wrote. *New Catholic Encyclopedia*, s.v. "Francis de Sales;" Ruth Manning, "A Confessor and his Spiritual Child: François de Sales, Jeanne de Chantal, and the Foundation of the Order of the Visitation," in *The Art of Survival: Gender and History in Europe, 1450–2000*, Past and Present Supplements 1, ed. Lyndal Roper and Ruth Harris (Oxford: Oxford Journals, 2006), 101–17.

57. The Optina Pustyn' monks collected, edited, and published the letters of elders Leonid, Makarii (Ivanov), Amvrosii (Grenkov), and Anatolii (Zertsalov).

58. W. F. Ryan, *The Bathhouse at Midnight: An Historical Survey of Magic and Divination in Russia* (University Park: Pennsylvania State University Press, 1999), 311.

59. Ignatiia (Puzik), *Starchestvo na Rusi* (Moscow: Izd-vo Moskovskogo Podvor'ia Sviato-Troitskoi Sergievoi Lavry, 1999), 112.

60. Georgii (Mashurin), *Pis'ma v Boze pochivaiushego zatvornika Zadonskogo Bogoroditskogo monastyria Georgiia*, 6th ed. (St. Petersburg, 1894).

61. T. R. Rudi, "Rannie zhitiia Serafima Sarovskogo: voprosy literaturnoi istorii," *Trudy otdela drevnerusskoi literatury* 51 (1999): 429.

62. There were several copies of the treatise in the libraries of the Optina, Simonov, and Trinity-Sergius monasteries, and in the library of Hegumen Parfenii (Ageev), the former Old Believer and founder of Spaso-Preobrazhenskii monastery in Guslitsy.

63. "Povestvovanie o deistviiakh serdechnoi molitvy startsa pustynnozhitelia Vasiliska, spisannogo ego uchenikom Zosimoi Verkhovskim," as cited in Pentkovskii, "Ot iskatelia neprestannoi molitvy," 152.

64. Leonid (Nagolkin), "Undated letter (c. 1830s) to a nun named 'O.,'" in *Pis'ma velikikh optinskikh startsev: XIX vek* (Moscow: Sretenskogo monastyria, 2001), 56.

65. Ibid., 57.

66. OR RGB, f. 213, op. 75, d. 48, l. 4; *Zhizneopisanie Optinskogo startsa ieromonakha Leonida*, 80.

67. Leonid, "Letter to Mother N.," [May 15, 1817] in *Pis'ma velikhikh*, 32.

68. Pentkovskii, "Ot iskatelia neprestannoi molitvy," 152.

69. Ignatii (Brianchaninov), "O molitve Iisusovoi," in *Polnoe sobranie tvorenii*, 1:212–239. On Brianchaninov, see Irina Paert, "'An Unmercenary Bishop': Ignatii Brianchaninov

(1807–1867) and the Making of Modern Russian Orthodoxy," *Slavonica* 9, no. 2 (2003): 99–112.

70. As quoted in Hausherr, *Spiritual Direction*, 7.

71. OR RGB, f. 213, op. 80, d. 1, l. 154.

72. OR RGB, f. 213, op. 75, d. 1, l. 32 (Letter from Leonid to Akilina Cherkassova, March 21, 1827).

73. RGIA, f. 797, op. 28, d. 217, 1 otd., 2 st., l. 54 ob.

74. Paert, *Old Believers*, 37–38.

75. Ignatii (Brianchaninov), "O molitve Iisusovoi," in *Polnoe sobranie tvorenii*, 1:212–14.

76. Georges Florovsky, "The Byzantine Ascetic and Spiritual Fathers," in *The Collected Works of Georges Florovsky*, ed. Richard S. Haugh (Vaduz: Büchervertriebanstalt, 1987), 10:134. Florovsky described a clash of two religious types in the fourth century: "[T]he anthropomorphites were visionaries: their religious experience turned on graphic, perceptible visions. On the other hand, the "Origenists" strove to overcome perceptible contemplation and for a nonimagery intellectual vision." See also Konstantinovsky, *Evagrius Ponticus*, 27–45.

77. Brianchaninov, "O molitve Iisusovoi," 220.

78. Ibid., 221.

79. Hausherr, *Spiritual Direction*, 157.

80. *Zhizneopisanie optinskogo startsa ieromonakha Leonida*, 59.

81. *PSZ*, 1, vol. 6, no. 4042, 710 (Supplement to the Ecclesiastical Regulation, 1721).

82. TsGIA SPb, f. 19, op. 29, d. 27, l. 109 ob.

83. Ibid.

84. On the development of the confessional discipline see A. Almazov, *Tainaia ispoved' v Pravoslavnoi Vostochnoi Tserkvi*, vols. 1–3 (Odessa, 1894); on a variety of confessional practices see Nadieszda Kizenko, "Written Confessions and the Construction of Sacred Narrative," in *Sacred Stories: Religion and Spirituality in Modern Russia*, ed. Mark D. Steinberg and Heather J. Coleman (Bloomington, IN: Indiana University Press, 2007): 93–118.

85. OR RGB, f. 425, op. 3, d. 49, l. 17 ob.

86. OR RGB, f. 213, op. 75, d. 1, 1. 54.

87. OR RGB, f. 425, op. 3, d. 49, l. 17 ob.

88. Father Alexei Malov, a member of the Academy of Science and a Freemason, is also known for his celebration of the memorial service (*panikhida*) at Alexander Pushkin's funeral in 1837. "Zhizneopisanie episkopa Ignatiia Brianchaninova," in *Polnoe sobranie tvorenii*, 1:17.

89. Zorin, *Kormia dvuglavogo orla*, 339–74.

90. Richard Wortman, *Scenarios of Power: Myth and Ceremony in Russian Monarchy* (Princeton: Princeton University Press, 1995), 1:402, as cited in Michelle Viise, "Filaret Drozdov and the Language of Official Proclamations in Nineteenth-Century Russia," *The Slavic and East European Journal* 44, no. 4 (2000): 565.

91. Metropolitan Makarii, I. K. Smolitsch, and Vladislav Tsypin, *Istoriia russkoi tserkvi*, vol. 8, part 1, I. K. Smolitsch (Moscow: Izdatel'stvo Spaso-Preobrazhenskogo Valaamskogo monastryia, 1996), 266–67.

92. For the argument that institutional expansion of the church was driven by the ambition to surmount religious dissent and, generally, extend its sphere of influence, see Simon Dixon, "Church, State and Society in Late Imperial Russia: the Diocese of St. Petersburg, 1880–1914" (PhD diss., University College London, 1993), 38–40.

93. OR RGB, f. 213, op. 49, d. 5, l. 4.

94. *Zhizneopisanie optinskogo startsa ieromonakha Leonida*, 97–98.

95. On the controversial image of Filaret, see O. E. Maiorova, "Mitropolit Moskovskii Filaret v obshchestvennom soznanii kontsa XIX v.," *Lotmanovskii sbornik* 2 (1997): 626–27 and passim.

96. Brenda Meehan-Waters, "Metropolitan Filaret (Drozdov) and the Reform of Russian Women's Monastic Communities," *The Russian Review* 50 (1991): 310–23.

97. For more on the relationship between the male clergy and the female religious communities see Wagner, "The Transformation of Female Orthodox Monasticism," 807.

98. This was also typical for bishops of Kaluga who supervised Optina Pustyn'. For example, see GAKO, f. 903, op.1, d. 61, ll. 65, 69, 70, 71 ob., 76–76 ob., 135 ob.

99. RGADA, f. 1183, op. 2, d. 40, l. 2–2 ob.

100. *Polnoe sobranie tvorenii*, 3:410. See also TsGIA SPb, f. 19, op. 29, d. 27, l. 194.

101. RGIA, f. 797, op. 28, d. 217, 1 otd., 2 st., ll. 1–56.

102. The importance of such incidents in creating the cults of saints was typical for premodern Russia, where believers often worshipped unidentified corpses found by chance. Eve Levin, "From Corpse to Cult in Early Modern Russia," in *Orthodox Russia: Belief and Practice under the Tsars*, ed. Valerie. A. Kivelson and Robert H. Green (University Park: Pennsylvania State University Press, 2003), 81–103.

103. RGIA, f. 797, op. 28, d. 217, 1 otd., 2 st., ll. 55–56.

104. Levin, "From Corpse to Cult," 103.

105. GAKO, f. 903, op. 1, d. 61, l. 65–65 ob.

106. Following the reunification of the Uniates with the Orthodox Church, hundreds of Uniate monks were relocated to various Russian monasteries, where they had to confirm themselves in the Orthodox faith under the supervision of abbots and elders. Makarii et al., *Istoriia russkoi tserkvi*, 2:342.

107. OR RGB, f. 213, op. 63, d. 1, ll. 18–19 ob.

108. OR RGB, f. 213, op. 10, d. 9, l. 243.

109. David Goldfrank, "Recentering Nil Sorskii: The Evidence from the Sources," *The Russian Review* 66 (July 2007): 367.

110. OR RGB, f. 213, op. 49, d. 5, l. 29 ob.

111. OR RGB, f. 213, op. 10, d. 9, l. 11.

112. This is the argument of Ekzempliarskii, *Taina stradanii*, 166.

113. Marcel Mauss, *The Gift: the Form and Reason for Exchange in Archaic Societies* (London: Routledge Classics, 2002); Ilana F. Silber, *Virtuosity, Charisma, and Social Order: A Comparative Sociological Study of Monasticism in Theravada Buddhism and Medieval Catholicism*, Cambridge Cultural and Social Studies (Cambridge: Cambridge University Press, 1995), 33.

114. Silber, *Virtuosity, Charisma, and Social Order*, 33.

115. Monasteries that received meager subsidies from the state could not survive and required extra income from private donors or from the profitable use of their property.

116. For example, Motovilov bequeathed 157 desiatins of land to the Diveevo communities. Olga Bukova, *Zhenskie obiteli prepodobnogo Serafima Sarovskogo: Istoriia desiati nizhegorodskikh zhenskikh monastyrei* (Nizhnii Novgorod: Knigi, 2003), 207.

117. RGIA, f. 796, op. 142, d. 809, ll.1–14; Erast, *Istoricheskoe opisanie*, 187.

118. Daniel Kaiser, "Testamentary Charity in Early Modern Russia: Trends and Motivations," *Journal of Modern History* 76, no. 3 (2004): 23.

119. For example, Trinity-Sergius pustyn' near St. Petersburg contained the burial vaults of the Kochubei and Kushelev families, who contributed to the construction of churches in the monastery. The building of St. John the Baptist Church in the pustyn' over the vault of General Kushelev in 1857 cost 75,000 rubles. In 1843 Prince M. V. Kochubei began to build the church of the Protection of the Mother of God, investing about 250,000 rubles. The lower part of this church contained the tomb of Princess Kochubei (née Bariatynskaia). RNB, f. 1000, op. 2, d. 53, l. 112 ob.

120. Marrese, *A Woman's Kingdom*, 167.

121. Zyrianov, *Russkie monastyri i monashestvo*, 80.

122. Donors often specifically indicated that their gifts were intended for the provision of Predtechev skete, not Optina Pustyn' monstery as a whole. Therefore, often unwillingly Predtechev skete became an agent of property relations. Erast, *Istoricheskoe opisanie*, 134–35; RGIA, f. 796, op. 142, d. 809.

123. OR RGB, f. 213, op. 40, d. 10, l. 2.

124. When Moisei became the abbot of Optina in 1826, the monastery had debts of 12,000 rubles, which had not been paid in full by the end of his office. Leonid (Kavelin), *Istoricheskoe opisanie Kozel'skoi Vvedenskoi Optinoi Pustyni* (Moscow Tip. Got'e, 1876), 97.

125. Erast, *Istoricheskoe opisanie*, 134–35.

126. Bukova, *Zhenskie obiteli*, 64.

127. Ibid., 212–13.

128. OR RGB, f. 213, op. 63, d. 1, l. 5 ob.

129. Elder Makarii of Optina and Adrian Iugskii complained that replying to letters took up all their time. Erast, *Istoricheskoe opisanie*, 116.

130. OR RGB, f. 213, op. 75, d. 48, ll. 1–2 (April 11 and June 30, 1841).

131. Ibid., l. 1.

132. I. V. Kireevskii, *Razum na puti k istine: Filosofskie stat'i, publitsistika, pis'ma; Perespiska s prep. Makariem (Ivanovym). Dnevnik* (Moscow: Pravilo very, 2002), 400.

133. Ibid.

134. Ibid., 393.

135. Ibid., 404, 407.

136. Makarii, "Letter of February 20, 1859," in *Pis'ma velikikh Optinskikh startsev*, 138.

137. *Zhizneopisaniie Optinskogo startsa ieromonakha Leonida*, 74.

138. Ibid., 80.

139. Ibid.

140. Peter Brown, *The Cult of the Saints: Its Rise and Function in Latin Christianity* (Chicago: University of Chicago Press, 1981), 76.

141. *Zhizneopisanie Optinskogo startsa ieromonakha Leonida*, 83.

142. TsGA RM f. 1, op. 1, d. 510, l. 40 ob.

143. TsGA RM f. 1, op. 1, d. 388, l. 84 ob.

144. RGIA, f. 797, op. 5, d. 17979, ll. 1–6.

145. Ibid, l. 73.

146. TSGA RM f. 1, op. 1, d. 90, l. 71.

147. Brown, *Cult of the Saints*, 78–79.

148. "K proslavleniiu sviatoi pamiati Serafima Sarovskogo," *Russkii arkhiv* 3, no. 9 (1902): 142.

149. Brown, *The Cult of Saints*, 49.

150. *Dukhovnye nastavleniia ottsa Serafima Sarovskoi pustyni ieromonakha, pustynnika i zatvornika* (Moscow, 1847).

151. This passage is influenced by Brown's discussion of the role of the impresarios of cults in late antiquity. Brown, *The Cult of the Saints*, 49.

152. RGIA, f. 807, op. 2, d. 1221, ll. 22 ob.–25.

153. A. Grigor'ev, "Oppozitsiia zastoia: Ocherki iz istorii mrakobesiia," <http://smalt.karelia.ru/~filolog/vremja/1861/MAY/oppozast.htm>.

154. Stanton, *The Optina Pustyn Monastery*, 101.

155. I. Kireevskii, *Razum na puti k istine*, 567, 569.

156. Ibid., lxii, 151–213, and passim.

157. Bukova, *Zhenskie obiteli*, 281.

158. Ibid., 285–86.

159. Zorin, *Kormia dvuglavogo orla*, 374.

4—Elders, Society, and the Russian People in Post-Emancipation Russia, 1860–1890

1. Freeze, "Handmaiden of the State?" 100–1.

2. Florovskii, *Puti russkogo bogosloviia*, 339–41.

3. A. Iu. Polunov, *Pod vlast'iu ober-prokurora: Gosudarstvo i tserkov' v epokhu Alexandra III* (Moscow: AIRO XX, 1996), 72–73.

4. Ibid., 74.

5. Ibid., 75.

6. Gerhard Simon, *Konstantin Petrovic Pobedonoscev und die Kirchenpolitik des Heiligen Sinod, 1880–1905* (Göttingen: Vandenhoeck u. Ruprecht, 1969), <http://www.krotov.info/history/19/1880/1885simo.html>.

7. Igumen Modest, *Sviatyi Grigorii Palama, mitropolit Solunskii: Pobornik pravoslavnogo ucheniia o favorskom svete i o deistviiakh bozhiikh* (Kiev: V Tip. Antona Gammershmida, 1860); F. I. Uspenskii, "Filosofskoe i bogoslovskoe dvizheniie v XIV veke (Varlaam, Palama, i priverzhentsy ikh)," *Zhurnal Ministerstva Narodnogo Prosveshcheniia* 279, no. 1 (1892): 1–64; ibid., no. 2: 348–427; the opinion that Palamas was a heretic is present in S. V. Bulgakov, *Nastol'naia kniga dlia sviashchenno-tserkovno-sluzhitelei: sbornik svedenii, kasaiushchikhsia preimushchestvenno prakticheskoi deiatel'nosti otechestvennago dukhovenstva* (Kiev: Tip. Kievo-Pecherskoi Uspenskoi Lavry, 1913).

8. I. S. Belliustin, *Description of the Clergy in Rural Russia: The Memoir of a Nineteenth-Century Parish Priest*, trans., with an interpretive essay by Gregory L. Freeze (Ithaca: Cornell University Press, 1985). Although Belliustin was not a mystic, he had a great respect for Russian holy men, notably Serafim of Sarov.

9. NART, f. 4, op. 1, d. 5845, l. 1 (Synodal Decree of March 20, 1862).

10. The members of idiorrythmic monasteries had a bad reputation because of loose discipline. V. S. Markov, ed., *Polnoe sobranie rezoliutsii Filareta, Mitropolita Moskovskogo* (Moscow: Izd. redaktsii "Dushepoleznago chteniia" vo Universitetskoi tip-ii, 1906), 3:27–29, 37.

11. Filaret (Drozdov), *Mneniia, otzyvy, i pis'ma Filareta, Mitropolita Moskovskogo i Kolomenskogo po raznym voprosam za 1821–1867 gg.* (1905; repr., Westmead: Gregg International, 1971), 74.

12. Meehan-Waters, "Metropolitan Filaret (Drozdov)," 316.

13. *Pravoslavnaia entsiklopediia*, s.v. "Monastyri i monashestvo;" NART, f. 4, op. 1, d. 5845, ll. 1–1 ob., 16.

14. Ibid., l. 1.

15. RGIA, f. 796, op. 142, d. 1011.

16. The official circular addressed to bishops pointed out that the reform of monasteries was necessary because of the growing criticism of monasticism in society. S. Firsov, *Russkaia tserkov' nakanune peremen (konets 1890-kh–1918 gg.)* (Moscow: Kruglyi stol po religioznomu obrazovaniiu i diakonii, 2002), 84.

17. GIANO, f. 513, op. 1, d. 1368, ll. 3, 6 ob.

18. Freeze, introduction to *Description of the Clergy*, 52–53.

19. Joseph (Sanin) (1439/40–1515) was the abbot of Volokolamsk monastery and was the founder of a large community based on a strict rule that emphasised obedience, work, and lengthy liturgical services. Unlike his opponent, Nil Sorskii, the promoter of a contemplative ideal, Joseph welcomed large donations of money and land to monasteries, and was in favor of learned monks pursuing careers in church administration.

20. For example, the Belev nuns and Leonid Nagolkin affair in 1839–1841. See Chapter 3.

21. Ioann (Maslov), *Glinskaia pustyn'*, 233.

22. GAKO, f. 903, op. 1, d. 212, ll. 27–28.

23. S. V. Rimskii, *Rossiiskaia tserkov' v epokhu velikikh reform: tserkovnye reformy v Rossii 1860–1870-kh godov* (Moscow: Krutitskoe patriarsh'e podvor'e, Obshchestvo liubitelei tserkovnoi istorii, 1999), 68–71.

24. Ioann (Maslov), *Glinskaia Pustyn'*, 211, 313.

25. In 1855 Valaam monastery had 189 monks and novices, whose number increased to 500 by 1881. Onufrii (Makhanov), *Prichal molitv uedinennykh*, 169, 258. Optina pustyn' also saw the increase of its community.

26. Zyrianov, *Russkie monastyri i monashestvo*, 172. Zyrianov located the process of "peasantization" to the 1900s, but data suggest that it had taken place already in the 1860s–1880s. See a critical review of Zyrianov in Kenworthy, "Monasticism in Russian History," *Kritika* 10, no. 2 (2009): 323.

27. Ioann (Maslov), *Glinskaia pustyn'*, 313.

28. G. M. Zapal'skii, *Optina Pustyn' i ee vospitanniki v 1825–1917 godakh* (Moscow: Rukopisnye pamiatniki drevnei Rusi, 2009), 103.

29. William Wagner, "Paradoxes of Piety: The Nizhegorod Convent of the Exaltation of the Cross, 1807–1935," in *Orthodox Russia: Belief and Practice Under the Tsars*, ed. Valerie Kivelson and Robert Green (University Park: Pennsylvania State University Press, 2004), 211–38; Wagner, "The Transformation of Female Orthodox Monasticism," 818.

30. GAKO, f. 903, op. 1, d. 62, ll. 24–30, 32–34.

31. "Pamiatnye zapiski igumenii Evgenii (Ozerovoi)," in *Zhenskaia Optina: materialy k letopisi Boriso-Glebskogo zhenskogo monastyria*, ed. Sergei Fomin and Tamara Fomina (Moscow: Palomnik, 2005), 162. The twelve-year-old daughter of a merchant was brought by her father to Metropolitan Filaret, who personally gave his blessing for her admission to Anosin Boriso-Glebskii convent in 1860.

32. Ioann (Maslov), *Glinskaia pustyn'*, 313..

33. Ibid., 255, 313, passim.

34. Andronnik (Trubachev), *Prepodobnyi Amvrosii Optinskii* (Kiev: Izdatel'stvo imeni

sviatitelia L'va papy Rimskogo, 2003), 32–57; *Zhizneopisanie v boze pochivshego startsa-uteshitelia ottsa Varnavy* ([Vyksa]: Iverskaia obitel', 1907); Ioann (Maslov), *Glinskaia pustyn'*, 236.

35. Zyrianov, *Russkie monastyri i monashestvo*, 77–93.

36. Wagner, "The Transformation of Female Orthodox Monasticism," 824; Ioann (Maslov), *Glinskaia pustyn'*, 327, passim.

37. *Zhenskaia Optina*, 161 and elsewhere.

38. Erast, *Istoricheskoe opisanie*, 185.

39. Fedor Dostoevskii, *Brat'ia Karamazovy*, in *Polnoe sobranie sochinenii*, 14:49.

40. Erast, *Istoricheskoe opisanie*, 185–91.

41. *Zhizneopisanie v boze pochivshego startsa-uteshitelia ottsa Varnavy*, 25–26, 88, passim.

42. Rimskii, *Rossiiskaia tserkov'*, 90–91.

43. Weber, *Economy and Society*, 1113.

44. Onufrii (Makhanov), *Prichal molitv uedinennykh*, 185.

45. S. Chetverikov, *Pravda khristianstva* (Moscow: Krutitskoe patriarsh'e podvor'e, 1998), 379.

46. The links between medieval and early Modern Russian monasticism and Athos were quite lively until the seventeenth century. Kievo-Pecherskii monastery, the community of Nil Sorskii, and many others were linked with Athos.

47. *Pravoslavnaia entsiklopediia*, s.v. "Afon."

48. Uspenskii, *Vostok Khristianskii*, 557.

49. Ioakim (Sabel'nikov), *Velikaia strazha: zhizn' i trudy blazhennoi pamiati afonskikh startsev ieroskhimonakha Ieronima i skharkhimandrita Makariia* (Moscow: Izdatel'stvo Moskovskoi Patriarkhii, 2001), 1:577.

50. "Ustav pustynnoi mestnosti imenuemoi Fivaida," in Ioakim (Sabel'nikov), *Velikaia strazha*, 515.

51. Ioakim (Sabel'nikov), *Velikaia strazha*, 498–99.

52. The ban on theater performances during Great Lent was abandoned in 1876 but reintroduced after the assassination of Alexander II in 1881 and cancelled again in 1890. Polunov, *Pod vlast'iu ober-prokurora*, 82.

53. The proposal was sent to Count Ignat'ev, but nothing is known about its impact on Synodal policy. Ioakim (Sabel'nikov), *Velikaia strazha*, 501–2.

54. Ibid., 503–4.

55. Nicholas Fennell, *The Russians on Athos* (New York: Peter Lang, 2001), 70–71.

56. GATO, f. 1409, d. 1404, l. 160 ob.

57. Although many of Brianchaninov's works were composed in the 1830s–1840s, they appeared in print only after the Emancipation.

58. As cited in N. Lisovoi, "Dve epokhi," 108–78.

59. This was a proposal by P. Velikanov of Moscow Spiritual Academy at the conference dedicated to the tenth anniversary of the Russian internet in 2004.

60. *Tvoreniia izhe vo sviatykh ottsa nashego Feofana Zatvornika* (Moscow: Pravilo very, 2000), 2:53.

61. Ibid., 2:13.

62. Arkhiv SPb FIRI RAN, f. 3, op. 3, d. 186a, ll. 28–29 ob. (Letter to Agafangel (Amosov) of August 30, 1892).

63. Ibid., l. 121 (Letter to Bishop Arkadii of Olonets of April 17, 1856).

64. *Tvoreniia izhe vo sviatykh ottsa nashego Feofana Zatvornika*, 2:195.

65. Arkhiv SPb FIRI RAN, f. 3, op. 3, d. 186a, l. 28 ob.

66. *Tvoreniia izhe vo sviatykh ottsa nashego Feofana Zatvornika*, 2:195, 221.

67. Ibid., 195.

68. Ibid., 191.

69. Sven Linnér, *Starets Zosima in The Brothers Karamazov: A Study in the Mimesis of Virtue* (Stockholm: Almqvist & Wiksell, 1975), 20–26.

70. Shamordino nuns published memoirs and collections of letters from Elder Amvrosii. For example, *Venok ot Shamordina na mogilu optinskogo startsa ieroskhimonakha Amvrosiia* (Shamordino, 1916). Mother Taisiia of Leushino published hagiographical accounts of the female elders and holy women of local monasteries. Igumenia Taisiia (Solopova), *Zhizneopisanie iurodivoi staritsy Evdokii Rodionovoi, zhivshei pri nachale osnovaniia Ioanno-Predtechenskogo Leushinskogo pervoklassnogo zhenskogo monastyria Cherepovetskogo uezda Novgorodskoi gubernii* (St. Petersburg: Izd. Leushinskogo podvor'ia, 2003); idem, *Staritsa Sergiia—pervonachal'nitsa Leushinskoi obshchiny* (St. Petersburg: Izd. Leushinskogo podvor'ia, 2002).

71. William Wagner, "'Orthodox Domesticity': Creating a Social Role for Women in Late Imperial Russia," in *Sacred Stories: Religion and Spirituality in Modern Russia*, ed. Mark D. Steinberg and Heather J. Coleman, Indiana-Michigan Series in Russian and East European Studies (Bloomington: Indiana University Press, 2007), 134.

72. *Igumenia Arseniia, Nastoiatel'nitsa Ust'-Medveditskogo monastyria oblasti voiska Donskogo* (Pskovo-Pecherskii monastyr', 1994), 29–34, 65.

73. Ibid., 143.

74. For more information on holy fools and Russian culture see Ewa Thompson, *Understanding Russia: The Holy Fool in Russian Culture* (Lanham, MD: University Press of America, 1987); Boris Uspenskii, *Izbrannye trudy*, 2 vols. (Moscow: Gnozis, 1994).

75. Aleksandr Strizhev, *Serafimo-diveevskie predaniia: zhitie, vospominaniia, pis'ma, tserkovnye torzhestva* (Moscow: Palomnik, 2001), 301.

76. Ibid., 311–28.

77. Ibid., 311–13.

78. S. A. Ivanov, *Blazhennye pokhaby: Kul'turnaia istoriia iurodstva* (Moscow: Iazyki slavianskikh kul'tur, 2005), 167–85.

79. Ibid., 45–46; Derek Krueger, *Symeon the Holy Fool: Leontius's Life and the Late Antique City* (Berkeley: University of California Press, 1996), 71.

80. *Letopis' Serafimo-Diveevskogo*, 228–29.

81. Ivanov, *Blazhennye pokhaby*, 51–53; Krueger, *Symeon the Holy Fool.*

82. Ioann Kovalevskii, *Iurodstvo o Khriste i Khrista radi Iurodivye Vostochnoi i Russkoi tserkvi: istoricheskii ocherk i zhitiia sikh podvizhnikov* (Moscow: Pech. A. I. Snegirovoi, 1895).

83. *Serafimo-diveevskie predaniia*, 276–78.

84. Ibid.

85. Ibid., 99.

86. *Zhizneopisanie v boze pochivshego startsa-uteshitelia ottsa Varnavy*, 62.

87. Ibid., 59–61.

88. Zyrianov, *Russkoe monashestvo i monastyri*, 121.

89. Faith Wigzell, *Reading Russian Fortunes: Print Culture, Gender, and Divination in Russia from 1765* (Cambridge: Cambridge University Press, 1998).

90. Ibid., 49.

91. *Serafimo-diveevskie predaniia*, 311.

92. Ibid., 311.

93. *Zhizneopisanie v boze pochivshego startsa-uteshitelia ottsa Varnavy*, 65–66.

94. *Serafimo-diveevskie predaniia*, 319.

95. Zyrianov, *Russkie monastyri*, 120–21.

96. Brown, "The Rise and Function of the Holy Man," 99.

97. Ekzempliarskii, *Taina stradanii*, 168; S. S. Khoruzhii, "Fenomen russkogo starchestva v ego dukhovnykh i antropologicheskikh osnovaniiakh," *Tserkov' i vremia*, no. 21 (2002): 208; Andronik (Trubachev), *Prepodobnyi Amvrosii Optinskii: Zhizn' i tvoreniia* (Kiev: Obshchestvo liubitelei pravoslavnoi literatury, 2003), 17.

98. Archimandrite Agapit, *Zhizneopisanie v boze pochivshego optinskogo startsa ieroskhimonakha Amvrosiia* (Zagorsk: Izd. Sviato-Troitskoi Sergievoi Lavry, 1900), 25–26.

99. Ibid., 27–29.

100. Ibid., 37.

101. Andronik (Trubachev), *Prepodobnyi*, 60.

102. References to Amvrosii as a national elder appear after his death in the hagiographical and biographical texts. See Andronik (Trubachev), *Prepodobnyi*, 257–58, 264.

103. OR RGB, f. 213, op. 49, d. 11, l. 32. For examples, see Andronik (Trubachev), *Prepodobnyi*, 161–256.

104. OR RGB, f. 213, op. 49, d. 11, ll. 32 ob.–33.

105. Amvrosii (Grenkov), *Sbornik pisem i statei Optinskogo startsa ieroskhimonakha ottsa Amvrosiia* (Moscow 1894), 1:37–38.

106. Ibid., 1:95–96.

107. Andronik (Trubachev), *Prepodobnyi Amvrosii*, 113.

108. Ibid., 84.

109. OR RGB, f. 213, op. 51, d. 11, l. 2 ob.

110. Andrei Maylunas and Sergei Mironenko, eds., *A Lifelong Passion: Nicholas and Alexandra, Their Own Story* (New York: Doubleday, 1997), 222, passim.

111. OR RGB, f. 213, op. 51, d. 11, ll. 9 ob.–10, 16 ob., 19 ob., 40.

112. Ibid., l. 19 ob.

113. OR RGB, f. 213, op. 49, d. 11, ll. 69, 86. On the phenomenon of possession, see Christine Worobec, *Possessed: Women, Witches, and Demons in Imperial Russia* (DeKalb: Northern Illinois University Press, 2001).

114. OR RGB, f. 213, op. 51, d. 11, l. 35.

115. For example, he duly paid 150 rubles to the peasants of Rudnevo who wanted to charge the monastery for the use of their road between Shamordino and Optina. Witnesses insisted that it was an unreasonable request, since the road had long been in public use, but the elder tried to avoid conflicts between monastic communities and the local population.

116. Erast, *Istoricheskoe opisanie*, 209.

117. RGIA, f. 777, op. 4, d. 6, l. 66 (1896); Vera Shevzov, *Russian Orthodoxy on the Eve of Revolution* (New York: Oxford University Press, 2004), 210.

118. Andronik (Trubachev), *Prepodobnyi Amvrosii*, 141.

119. Weber, *Economy and Society*, 1122.

120. For the most recent reverberation of this myth, see Orlando Figes, *Natasha's Dance: A Cultural History of Russia* (New York: Metropolitan Books, 2002), 292.

121. Anna Akhmatova, "Predystoriia," 1940–1943. <http://www.akhmatova.org>.

122. Andronik (Trubachev), *Prepodobnyi Amvrosii*, 126–27.

123. K. V. Mochul'skii, "Dostoevsky: Zhizn' i tvorchestvo," in *Russkie emigranty o Dostoevskom*, ed. Sergei V. Belov (St Petersburg: Andreev i synov'ia, 1994), 278–80.

124. Stanton, *The Optina Pustyn' Monastery*, 151–78. Linnér unearths the European influences on Zosima in *Starets Zosima in The Brothers Karamazov*, 129–32.

125. On representation of the clergy in the Russian literature of the 1860s–1890s, see Makarii et al., *Istoriia Russkoi Tserkvi*, vol. 8, part 1, 375–76.

126. Vasilii Nemirovich-Danchenko, a writer exploring the "monastic theme," described real monastic characters in his travelogues. V. I. Nemirovich-Danchenko, "Iz knig palomnichestv i puteshestvii," in *Sobranie sochinenii v 3 tomakh* (Moscow: Terra, 1996), 3:367–542.

127. Vladimir Golstein, "Accidental Families and Surrogate Fathers: Rochard, Grigory, and Smerdiakov," in *A New Word on The Brothers Karamazov*, ed. Robert Louis Jackson, with an introductory essay by Robin Feuer Miller (Evanston: Northwestern University Press, 2004), 90–91.

128. Saltykov-Shchedrin, "Otstavnoi Soldat Pimenov" (c. 1857), in *Sobranie sochinenii v 20 tomakh* (Moscow: Khudozhestvennaia literatura, 1965), 2:124–32; Lev Tolstoi, "Tri startsa" (1886), in *Sobranie sochinenii v 20 tomakh* (Moscow: Khudozhestvennaia literatura, 1982), 10:342–47; Leskov, "Chas voli Bozhiei (skazka)" (1890), in *Sobranie sochinenii v 11 tomakh* (Moscow: Gos. Izd-vo khudozhestvennoi literatury, 1956), 9:5–31.

129. M. E. Saltykov-Shchedrin, *Sobranie sochinenii v desiati tomakh* (Moscow: Pravda, 1988), 1:405.

130. Tolstoi, *Sobranie sochinenii*, 10:342–47.

131. For example, the hermit Vassian from Saltykov-Shchedrin's story "Otstavnoi Soldat Pimenov" is not harmed by a hungry wolf in winter.

132. Erast, *Istoricheskoe opisanie*, 173–74.

133. S. L. Frank, *Russkoe mirovozzrenie* (St. Petersburg: Nauka, 1996), 414.

134. *Pravoslavnyi nemets*, 74–75.

135. Ibid., 79–80.

136. Ibid., 82.

137. Ibid., 83.

138. V. Rozanov, "Religiia kak svet i radost," in *Okolo tserkovnykh sten*, ed. Aleksandr Nikolinkin and V. V. Rozanov (Moscow: Respublika, 1995), 12.

139. Danilevskii, as quoted in Stanton, *The Optina Pustyn' Monastery*, 105.

140. Ibid., 101–5.

141. Ibid.

142. Billington, *The Icon and the Axe*, 384.

143. M. Gromyko, *Pravoslavie i russkaia narodnaia kul'tura* (Moscow: Instituta etnologii i antropologii RAN, 1993); Steven Graham, *With the Russian Pilgrims to Jerusalem* (London: Macmillan and Co., 1913).

144. B. P. Vysheslavtsev, *Otkrovennye rasskazy strannika dukhovnomu svoemu ottsu* (Paris: YMCA Press, 1930), 1.

145. Ibid., 2.

146. Anat Vernitski, "The Way of a Pilgrim: Literary Reading of a Religious Text," *Slavonica* 4, no. 12 (2003): 113–22; S. A. Ipatova, "Otkrovennye rasskazy strannika dukhovnomu svoemu ottsu: paradigmy siuzheta," in *Khristianstvo i russkaia literatura*, ed. V. A. Kotel'nikov (St Petersburg: Nauka, 2002), 4:300–35.

147. Ipatova, "Otkrovennye rasskazy strannika," 300–35.

148. It has also been suggested that *The Way of a Pilgrim* was a compilation of the writings of Father Mikhail and Hieromonk Arsenii Troepol'skii (1801–1870), a prolific but unpublished monastic author. Zapal'skii, *Optina Pustyn'*, 182–200. The contribution of monk Arsenii, who studied at Moscow University, to the production of the popular text explains the literary closeness of *The Way of a Pilgrim* to Bunyan's tale.

149. NART, f. 10, op. 5, d. 515, l. 81.

150. Ibid., ll. 6–7 ob.

151. I. Basin, "Avtorstvo 'Otkrovennykh rasskazov strannika,'" *Simvol* no. 27 (1992): 175.

152. Ibid., 168.

153. A. Pentkovskii, "Ot iskatelia neprestannoi molitvy," 156.

154. Mikhail (Kozlov), "Rasskaz strannika, iskatelia molitvy," *Simvol* no. 27 (1992): 7–13.

155. Makarii et al., *Istoriia russkoi tserkvi*, vol. 8, part 2, 161–65.

156. For example, Feofan's correspondent wrote about a novice who learned the Jesus prayer by reading *The Way of a Pilgrim*. *Tvoreniia izhe vo sviatykh ottsa nashego Feofana Zatvornika*, 2:210.

157. *Troitskie listki* were initiated by Nikon (Rozhdestvenskii) in 1879; they were cheap ten-page brochures that cost 1 kopeck and immediately sold out to pilgrims of Trinity-Sergius Lavra.

158. Wagner argues that monasticism was far more adaptive and responsive to social change than previously had been believed. Wagner, "The Transformation of Female Orthodox Monasticism"; Freeze, "Handmaiden of the State?"

159. On the reactionary role of monastic apophatic spirituality as embodied in the views of Pobedonostsev and Khrapovitskii, see Simon Dixon, "Church, State, and Society in Late Imperial Russia: the Diocese of St. Petersburg, 1880–1914" (PhD diss., University of London, 1993).

160. Nichols, "The Orthodox Elders (Startsy) of Imperial Russia," 1–30.

161. Engelstein, "Old and New, High and Low," 28–31.

162. In 1900 there were 58,283 monks, nuns, and novices among the Orthodox population of 87,384,480 (1897 census). Zyrianov, "Russkie monastyri i monashestvo v XIX–nachale XX veka," in *Monashestvo i monastyri v Rossii*, ed. N. V. Sinitsyna, 305.

5—Appropriating the Elders: Elders and Political Crisis in Late Imperial Russia, 1890s–1917

1. Eric J. Hobsbawm, *The Age of Empire, 1875–1914* (London: A Cardinal Book, 1991), 266.

2. David Blackbourn, *Marpingen: Apparitions of the Virgin Mary in Bismarckian Germany* (Oxford: Clarendon Press, 1993); Maria Carlson, *"No Religion Higher than Truth": A History of the Theosophical Movement in Russia, 1875–1922* (Princeton: Princeton University Press, 1993); Joy Dixon, *Divine Feminine: Theosophy and Feminism in England* (Baltimore: Johns Hopkins University Press, 2001); Ruth Harris, *Lourdes: Body and Spirit in the Secular Age* (New York: Viking, 1999). For studies that focus on secularization in Europe see Hugh McLeod, *Secularization in Western Europe, 1848–1914* (Basingstoke: Macmillan, 2000); Callum Brown, *The Death of Christian Britain: Understanding Secularization, 1800–2000* (London: Routledge, 2001).

3. Michael Snape, *God and the British Soldier: Religion and the British Army in the*

First and Second World Wars (London: Routledge, 2005).

4. Ibid., 38–42; Peter Gatrell, *A Whole Empire Walking: Refugees in Russia during World War I* (Bloomington: Indiana University Press, 1999), illustration 1.

5. P. N. Zyrianov, *Pravoslavnaia tserkov' v bor'be s revoliutsiei 1905–1907 gg.* (Moscow: Nauka, 1984); Gregory Freeze, "Church and Politics in Late Imperial Russia: Crisis and Radicalization of the Clergy," in *Russia under the Last Tsar: Opposition and Subversion, 1897–1917*, ed. Anna Geifman (Malden, MA: Blackwell, 1999), 269–97; Firsov, *Russkaia tserkov' nakanune peremen*. The most recent scholar to use the concept "crisis" in referring to Russian Orthodoxy before the revolution is Vera Shevzov, *Russian Orthodoxy*. See also Gregory Freeze, "'Pious Folk?' Religious Observance in Vladimir Diocese, 1900–1914," *Jahrbücher für Geschichte Osteuropas* 52 (2004): 323–40.

6. Freeze, "Church and Politics," 269, 278.

7. S. Iu. Vitte, *Vospominaniia* (Tallinn: Skif-Aleks, 1994), 2:344.

8. The so-called "Group of 32 Priests" from St. Petersburg, supported by Bishop Antonii Vadkovskii, submitted their proposals to the Synod in March 1905. Zyrianov, *Pravoslavnaia tserkov'*, 68–69. On disenchantment with the state see Freeze, *Parish Clergy*; idem, "Going to the Intelligentsia": The Church and its Urban Mission in Post-Reform Russia," *Between Tsar and People: Educated Society and the Quest for Public Identity in Late Imperial Russia*, ed. Edith W. Clowes, Samuel D. Kassow, and James L. West (Princeton: Princeton University Press, 1991), 224.

9. Nicholas Zernov, *The Russian Religious Renaissance of the Twentieth Century* (London: Dartmon, Longman, & Todd, 1963).

10. Ibid., 89.

11. The degree to which secularization took hold among the working classes should not be overestimated. See Reginald Zelnik, "'To the Unaccustomed Eye': Religion and Irreligion in the Experience of St. Petersburg Workers in the 1870s," *Russian History* 16, nos. 2–4 (1989): 214–36; Page Herrlinger, *Working Souls: Russian Orthodoxy and Factory Labor in St. Petersburg, 1881–1917*, Allan K. Wildman Group Historical Series 2 (Bloomington: Slavica, 2007).

12. A. I. Klibanov, *Istoriia religioznogo sektanstva v Rossii: 60-e gody XIX v.–1917 g.* (Moscow: Nauka, 1965); Charles J. Ryan, *H. P. Blavatsky and the Theosophical Movement: A Brief Historical Sketch* (Pasadena, CA: Theosophical University Press, 1975); Edmund Heier, *Religious Schism in the Russian Aristocracy, 1860–1900: Radstockism and Pashkovism* (The Hague: Nijhoff, 1970).

13. Zyrianov, *Pravoslavnaia tserkov'*, 58–59.

14. Zyrianov, "Russkie monastyri i monashestvo," 305.

15. Freeze, "Church and Politics," 272, 287.

16. Kenworthy, "The Revival of Monasticism," chapter 7.

17. Ibid.

18. For example, Tolstoy's story "Father Sergii," in Tolstoi, *Sobranie sochinenii v 20 tomakh* (Moscow: Khudozhestvennaia literatura, 1982), 12:342–84.

19. The polemic on the future of monasticism was published in the journals *Khristianskoe chtenie* and *Bogoslovskii vestnik*. The critics of Bishop Nikon's position, professors S. Smirnov and N. Kapterev of the Moscow Theological Academy, drew examples from history, showing the immense role of monasteries in service to society. Kenworthy, "The Revival of Monasticism," chapter 7.

20. N. Faminskii, "O monashestve," *Monastyr'* 4 (1909): 262–65.

21. RGADA, f. 1204, op. 1, d. 17518, l. 5.

22. Ibid., l. 47.

23. RGIA, f. 796, op. 442, d. 2395, l. 14; ibid., d. 2461, l. 9.

24. RGIA, f. 796, op. 442, d. 2461, l. 9.

25. S. Firsov, *Sviatoi Ioann Kronshtadtskii v vospominaniiakh sovremennikov* (St. Petersburg: Izdatel'skii Dom Neva 2003), 19.

26. Arsenii (Zhadanovskii), *Vospominaniia* (Moscow: Pravoslavnyi Sviato Tikhonovskii Bogoslovskii Institut, 1995), 77–79.

27. Nikodim (Kononov), *Nastoiatel' Aleksandro-Svirskogo monastyria arkhimandrit Agafangel. Krat. biogr. ocherk* (Petrozavodsk: Olonets. gub. tip., 1910); Ieromonakh Nestor (Kumysh), "Svirskii nastoiatel' arkhimandrit Agafangel (Amosov) (1841–1909)," in *Sankt-Peterburgskii tserkovnyi vestnik*, <http://www.mitropoliia-spb.ru >.

28. Ivan Kalinin, "O Poslushnichestve," *Monastyr'* 6 (1909): 437–38.

29. RGADA, f. 1204, op. 1, d. 17518, ll. 90–90 ob.

30. Nikon (Beliaev), *Dnevnik poslednego dukhovnika Optinoi pustyni* (Minsk: Luchi Sofii, 2002), 147, 163.

31. The teaching on inner monasticism is based on the works of Ignatii Brianchaninov and Feofan the Recluse. See also the formulation by Varsonofii (Plikhankov) in Nikon, *Dnevnik*, 135.

32. Arkhiv SPb FIRI RAN, f. 3, op. 3, d. 429, l. 15 ob. (Krasnovskii's memoir about Hegumen Agafangel (Amosov)); Ioann (Maslov), *Glinskaia pustyn'*, 398–401.

33. Georgii (Tertyshnikov), "Zhitie ieromonakha Varnavy (Merkulova), startsa Gefsimanskogo skita pri Sviato Troitse-Sergievoi Lavre," *Zhurnal Moskovskoi Patriarkhii*, no. 9/10 (1994): 45.

34. Richard Price, "Informal Penance in Early Medieval Christendom," in *Retribution, Repentance, and Reconciliation: Papers Read at the 2002 Summer Meeting and the 2003 Winter Meeting of the Ecclesiastical History Society*, ed. Kate Cooper and Jeremy Gregory (Woodbridge, Suffolk: Boydell Press, 2004), 34. On sacramental confession, see Kizenko, "The Mystery of Confession in Imperial Russia," *Modern Greek Studies Yearbook* 20/21 (2004/2005): 1–15.

35. RGIA, f. 796, op. 205, d. 275, l. 73.

36. On public penance see Freeze, "The Wages of Sin: The Decline of Public Penance in Imperial Russia," in *Seeking God*, 53–82.

37. OR RGB, f. 213, op. 96, d. 18, l. 4.

38. Elder Iulian of Glinskaia emphasised obedience and demanded total submission to his authority. Ioann (Maslov), *Glinskaia pustyn'*, 402. The elders of Optina, on the contrary, were quite liberal; their authority was purely spiritual and based on voluntary agreement.

39. On pilgrimage, see Roy R. Robson, "Transforming Solovki: Pilgrim Narratives, Modernization, and Late Imperial Monastic Life," in *Sacred Stories*, 44–60.

40. On general numbers of pilgrims see Robson, "Transforming Solovki," 49.

41. Arkhiv SPb FIRI RAN, f. 3, op. 7, d. 32a, ll. 1–103.

42. Most elders had a special reception room attached to their cells, where they slept and prayed. I. Chetverukhin and E. Chetverukhina, *Prepodobnyi Aleksei, starets-zatvornik Smolenskoi Zosimovoi pustyni* (Zagorsk: Sviato-Troitskaia Sergieva Lavra, 2003), 74.

43. RGADA, f. 1183, op. 1, d. 67, l. 2 ob.

44. Ibid., l. 58; see also Arkhiv SPb FIRI RAN, f. 3, op. 3, d. 429, l. 15 ob.; RGADA, f.

1204, op. 1, d. 17480, ll. 72–72 ob.; Ioann, *Glinskaia pustyn'*, 398–401.

45. Ioann (Maslov), *Glinskaia pustyn'*, 399.

46. RGALI, f. 101, op. 1, d. 18, l. 45 ob.

47. Ibid., l. 58.

48. Sergei Volkov, *Vozle monastyrskikh sten: Memuary, Dnevniki, Pis'ma* (Moscow: Izdatel'stvo gumanitarnoi literatury, 2000), 105–6.

49. OR RGB, f. 213, op. 97, d. 15, l. 44; ibid., op. 96, d. 26, ll. 56, 91.

50. OR RGB, f. 213, op. 97, d. 15, ll. 45, 65, 72; ibid., op. 96, d. 26, ll. 39, 55, 56.

51. OR RGB, f. 213, op. 97, d. 15, ll. 45; ibid., op. 96, d. 18, l. 13; ibid., d. 26, ll. 34, 47, 103.

52. OR RGB, f. 213, op. 96, d. 26, ll. 17–36.

53. Victor Turner, *The Ritual Process: Structure and Anti-Structure* (Chicago: Aldine de Gruyter, 1969).

54. Mitropolit Veneamin (Fedchenkov), *Bozh'i liudi: moi dukhovnye vstrechi* (Moscow: Otchii dom, 2004), 38–44.

55. On the penitential family, see S. Smirnov, *Drevne-russkii dukhovnik: issledovanie po istorii tserkovnogo byta* (Moscow: Sinodal'naia Tipografiia, 1913), 31. The clergy and the laity complained about the crisis in parish life, and there were calls for reform of the parish structure set by Peter I and for the return of the elected priesthood. Firsov, *Russkaia tserkov'*, 136, 149.

56. On migrant labor, see Barbara Engel, *Between the Fields and the City: Women, Work, and Family in Russia, 1861–1914* (Cambridge: Cambridge University Press, 1996).

57. Freeze, "Going to the Intelligentsia," 230.

58. OR RGB, f. 213, op. 97, d. 15, ll. 5, 6, 10–11, 71.

59. NART, f. 4, op. 1, d. 122924, l. 129.

60. Ibid., l. 46.

61. Ibid., l. 70.

62. In the nineteenth century the Trinity-Sergius monastery had five small monasteries (hermitages and sketes) under its jurisdiction, which were established as places for contemplative monasticism. Kenworthy, "The Revival of Monasticism," 62. The Council included the prior, treasurer, the sacristan, the steward, and the supervisor (*blagochinnyi*), as well as senior monks.

63. Ibid., 66.

64. RGADA, f. 1204, op. 1, d. 17479, ll. 2–8 ob.

65. Ibid, l. 4.

66. RGIA, f. 796, op. 205, d. 274, l. 13. The Optina pustyn', for example, used the Rule of the Konevets monastery, which distinguished between the roles of confessor (responsible for the sacrament of confession) and *starets* (responsible for guidance and advice). See Erast, *Istoricheskoe opisanie*, 87. Allegedly, Sofronii participated in the compilation of the Rule for the hermitage of Glinskaia pustyn'.

67. RGIA, f. 796, op. 205, d. 274, l. 142.

68. Ibid.

69. N. D. Zhevakhov, *Vospominaniia tovarishcha ober-prokurora Sv. Sinoda kniazia N. D. Zhevakhova* (Moscow: Rodnik, 1993).

70. RGIA, f. 796, op. 198, 1 otd., 5 st., d. 338, ll. 5–6.

71. Freeze, "Subversive Piety," 308–50.

72. For a discussion of the concept of cultural appropriation, see Bruce Ziff and Pratima V. Rao, eds., *Borrowed Power: Essays on Cultural Appropriation* (New Brunswick: Rutgers University Press, 1997).

73. Freeze, "Church and Politics," 268–78.

74. Kiprian (Kern), *Vospominaniia o mitropolite Antonii (Khrapovitskom) i episkope Gavriile (Chepure)* (Moscow: Pravoslavnyi Sviato-Tikhonovskii Institut, 2002), 9–10.

75. A. Khrapovitskii, "Nravstvennaia ideia dogmata tserkvi," <www.rodzianko.org>.

76. Antonii (Khrapovitskii), *Polnoe sobranie sochinenii* (Kazan: Tip-lit. Imperatorskogo Universiteta, 1900), 1:647.

77. Kiprian (Kern), *Vospominaniia*, 13.

78. Ibid., 16–17.

79. Antonii (Khrapovitskii), "Dva puti pastorstva, latinskii i pravoslavnyi," in idem, *Polnoe sobranie sochinenii*, 2:269.

80. Ibid., 272.

81. Ibid., 273.

82. Ibid., 188–96.

83. *Pravoslavnaia entsiklopediia*, s.v. "Antonii (Khrapovitskii);" Kiprian (Kern), *Vospominaniia*, 45.

84. Kiprian (Kern), *Vospominaniia*, 27.

85. A. El'chaninov, "Episkop-starets," *Put'* 4 (June-July 1926): 157–65.

86. In the Eastern Church, *proskomide* is the second part of the offertory moved back to the beginning of the service. Firsov, *Sviatoi Ioann Kronshtadtskii*, 71. See also Nadiezda Kizenko, *A Prodigal Saint: Father John of Kronstadt and the Russian People* (University Park: Pennsylvania State University Press, 2000).

87. Kiprian (Kern), *Vospominaniia*, 34–35.

88. Sergei Formin, ed.,*"Pastyr' dobryi": Zhizn' i trudy pravednogo startsa Aleksiia Moskovskogo* (Moscow: Palomnik, 2004), 153.

89. Ibid., 237–38.

90. Simon Dixon, "The Orthodox Church and the Workers of St. Petersburg 1880–1914," in *European Religion in the Age of the Great Cities*, ed. Hugh Mc Leod (London: Routledge, 1995): 129–31; Freeze, "Going to the Intelligentsia," 215–32.

91. O. V. Kirichenko, "Znachenie pravednika-startsa dlia sela," *Nauchnyi pravoslavnyi zhurnal: Traditsii i sovremennost* 1, no. 1 (2002): 62. Sergei Shevtsov began practicing ascetic life in the army: RGIA, f. 796, op. 205, d. 274, l. 205. Chris Chulos, *Converging Worlds: Religion and Community in Peasant Russia, 1861–1917* (DeKalb: Northern Illinois University Press, 2003), 19.

92. *Sestry: ocherk zhizni sester Anisii, Matrony, i Agafii, podvizhavshikhsia i pochivshikh v sele Ialtunovo, Shatskogo raiona, Riazanskoi eparkhii* (Moscow: Novospasskii monastyr', 2004), 14–24.

93. Kirichenko, "Znachenie pravednika-startsa," 61–76.

94. On self-willed religious behavior, see Vera Shevzov, "Popular Orthodoxy in Imperial Rural Russia" (PhD diss., Yale University, 1994), 620–712.

95. *Sestry*, 152.

96. *Sestry*, 14–24.

97. Shevzov, "Popular Orthodoxy in Imperial Rural Russia," 680–94.

98. Kirichenko, "Znachenie pravednika-startsa," 61–76.

99. M. Gromyko, "O edinstve pravoslaviia v tserkvi i v narodnoi zhizni," *Nauchnyi*

pravoslavnyi zhurnal: Traditsii i sovremennost' 1, no. 1 (2002): 21.

100. *Sestry*, 33–34.

101. Compare with the argument made by Chulos, *Converging Worlds*, 67.

102. Freeze, "Subversive Piety," 308–50.

103. Peter Brown writes about "impresarios" of the saint, or individuals who establish personal links with their invisible friends and protectors. Brown, *The Cult of the Saints*, 38.

104. OR RGB, f. Chichagova, op. 79/iii, d. 27, ll. 209, 228, 252, 276, 278, 433, 435, passim.

105. "K proslavleniiu sviatoi pamiati Serafima Sarovskogo," *Russkii arkhiv* 3, no. 9 (1902): 141–43.

106. Freeze, "Subversive Piety," 317–19.

107. Metropolitan Serafim (Chichagov), *Da budet volia tvoia* (Moscow: Palomnik, 1993), 2:79.

108. GARF, f. 109, 1 eksp., op. 29, d. 93, 1. 109; A. A. Mosolov, *Pri dvore poslednego imperatora: zapiski nachal'nika kantseliarii ministra dvora* (St Petersburg: Nauka, 1992), 173–74.

110. Freeze, "Religion and Political Crisis," 320; I. Basin, "Mif moshchei prepodobnogo Serafima Sarovskogo," *Stranitsy: Bogoslovie, Kul'tura, Obrazovanie* 2, no. 3 (1997): 385–97; ibid., no. 4 (1997): 538–49.

111 Georgii Shavel'skii, *Vospominaniia poslednego protopresvitera russkoi armii i flota* (Moscow, 1996), 2:296.

112. Robert Nichols, "The Friends of God: Nicholas II and Alexandra at the Canonization of Serafim of Sarov, July 1903," in *Religious and Secular Forces in Late Tsarist Russia: Essays in Honor of Donald Treadgold*, ed. Charles E. Timberlake (Seattle: University of Washington Press, 1992): 206–29.

113. Aleksandr Etkind, "Diskurs i revolutsiia: Grigorii Rasputin," *Revue Études Slaves* 69, nos .1–2 (1997): 230–31; Dominic Lieven, "Nicholas II," in *Critical Companion to the Russian Revolution, 1914–1921*, ed. Edward Acton, Vladimir Cherniaev, and William Rosenberg (Bloomington: Indiana University Press, 1997), 177.

114. GARF, f. 612, op. 1, d. 5, l. 1.

115. Nancy Shields Kollmann, *Kinship and Politics: The Making of the Muscovite Political System, 1345–1547* (Stanford: Stanford University Press, 1987).

116. GARF, f. 612, op. 1, d. 4, ll. 1–3.

117. Aleksandr Etkind, *Khlyst: Sekty, literatura, i revoliutsiia* (Moscow: Novoe literaturnoe obozrenie, 1998).

118. Etkind suggested that the "Rasputin phenomenon" could be explained by the assimilation of the ideas of the Enlightenment among the lower classes. My argument differs from his by indicating the contact and exchange between the official church (which to some extent was also influenced by the Enlightenment) and peasant religion. See Etkind, "Diskurs and revolutsiia," 233.

119. A. Shchusev's career as an architect continued in the Soviet era, resulting in the design of two conspicuous objects, Lenin's Mausoleum and Hotel "Moscow" in the center of Moscow. See also Elina Kahla, "Art as Glorious Deed: Creating the Community of Martha and Mary in Moscow," *Russian Review* 66 (January 2007): 73–94.

120. Ibid.

121. Father Mitrofan, a married priest, also gained the reputation of an elder. N. N. Sokolova, *Pod krovom Vsevyshnego* (Novosibirsk: Pravoslavnaia gimnaziia, 1998), 89–102.

122. Chetverukhin and Chetverukhina, *Prepodobnyi Aleksei*, 89.

123. Liubov' Miller, *Grand Duchess Elizabeth of Russia: New Martyr of the Communist Yoke* (Redding, CA: Nikodemos Orthodox Publication Society, 1991), 159.

124. Kahla, "Art as Glorious Deed," 94.

125. M. N. Pokrovskii, *Perepiska Nikolaia i Aleksandry Romanovykh, 1914–1915* (Moscow: Gos. Izd-vo, 1925), 3:217, 219, as cited in I. V. Nikitina and S. M. Polovinkin, "Moskovskii avva," in Florenskii, *Perepiska s M. A. Novoselovym*, 28.

126. Zyrianov, *Russkie monastyri i monashestvo*, 172–74.

127. Ibid.

128. "Kratkoe opisanie biografii menia nedostoinogo episkopa Petra Ladygina," in *Zabytye stranitsy russkogo imiaslaviia*, ed. A. M. Khitrov and O. L. Solomina (Moscow: Palomnik, 2001), 423.

129. Zyrianov, *Russkie monastyri*, 165–74; Kenworthy, "The Revival of Monasticism in Modern Russia", Chapter 5

130. For example, Schemamonk Kuksha "the New," who was accepted into the Kievo-Pecherskaia Lavra after the expulsion in 1913–14, became an authoritative spiritual guide. (He was canonized as a saint in the 1990s.) Ilarion (Alfeev), *Sviashchennaia taina*, 1:600–3.

131. Ibid., 293.

132. Schemamonk Ilarion, *Na gorakh Kavkaza: Beseda dvukh startsev pustynnikov o vrutrennem edinenii s Gospodom nashikh serdets* (1907, repr., St. Petersburg: Voskresenie, Lestvitsa, Dioptra, 2002), 116–17.

133. Ibid.

134. The dashing cavalry officer Bulatovich, who had headed the mission of the Russian Red Cross in Abyssinia, became a monk in Athos under the influence of Father John of Kronstadt. His ambition was to establish an Orthodox mission among Abyssinians, but instead he became an energetic proponent of the teaching on the name of God.

135. "Posleslovie," in Ilarion, *Na gorakh Kavkaza*, 912.

136. Ilarion (Alfeev), *Sviashchennaia taina*, 1:600.

137. Ibid., 484–547.

138. The calculations are based on the lists of 415 monks deported from Athos on the boat "Kherson" on July 3, 1913. Khitrov and Solomina, *Zabytye stranitsy russkogo imiaslaviia*, 68–97.

139. Florenskii, "Imeslavie kak filosofskaia predposylka," *Sochineniia v dvukh tomakh*, vol. 2, *U vodorazdelov mysli* (Moscow: Pravda, 1990).

140. Pavel Florenskii, *Opravdanie kosmosa* (St Petersburg: Russkii khristianskii gumanitarnyi institut, 1994), 52–53.

141. OR RGB, f. 213, op. 3, d. 25, ll. 1–26.

142. For example, Valaam library had four copies of the dangerous book, according to the catalog of the Valamo library at Helsinki University.

143. Father David from Athos was the spiritual guide of the philosopher Losev and his wife.

144. Ilarion (Alfeev), *Sviashchennaia taina*, 2:422–424; "Pis'mo iz Stavropol'skoi dukhovnoi konsistorii nachal'niku Kubanskoi oblasti ot 17.11.1914," in Ilarion (Alfeev), *Sviashchennaia taina*, 2:404–5.

145. Sergiia (Klimenko), *Minuvshee razvertyvaet svitok* (Samara: Samarskii dom pechati, 2008), 6–12.

146. Nikitina and Polovinkin, "Moskovskii avva," 31.

147. Ilarion (Alfeev), *Sviashchennaia taina*, 2:425.
148. Ibid., 423–25.
149. OR RGB, f. 214, op. 3, d. 25, l. 14.
150. Wilson, *The Noble Savages*, x.

6—The Legacy of the Elders after the Revolution, 1917–2000

1. Makarii et al., *Istoriia russkoi tserkvi*, 9:12; P. V. P., "Svet i teni tserkovnoi zhizni," *Rizhskie eparkhial'nye vedomosti*, nos. 7–8 (July-August 1917): 180–84.

2. "Chrezvychainyi s'ezd klira i mirian rizhskoi eparkhii v g. Iur'eve, Estliandskoi gubernii, 25–26 maia 1917 g.," *Rizhskie eparkhial'nye vedomosti*, nos. 5–6 (May-June 1917): 154.

3. Catherine Evtuhov, "The Church in the Russian Revolution: Arguments for and against Restoring the Patriarchate at the Church Council of 1917–1918," *Slavic Review* 50, no. 3 (Fall 1991): 511.

4. Makarii et al., *Istoriia russkoi tserkvi*, 9:46.

5. A. I. Kuznetsov, "Obnovlencheskii raskol v Russkoi tserkvi," in *"Obnovlencheskii" raskol: materially dlia tserkovno-istoricheskoi i kanonicheskoi kharakteristiki*, ed. I. V. Solov'ev (Moscow: Obshchestvo liubitelei tserkovnoi istorii, 2002), 439–40.

6. Edward E. Roslof, *Red Priests: Renovationism, Russian Orthodoxy, and Revolution, 1905–1946* (Bloomington: Indiana University Press, 2002), 124.

7. On agricultural communes organized by nuns see Jennifer Wynot, *Keeping the Faith: Russian Orthodox Monasticism in the Soviet Union, 1917–1939* (College Station, TX: Texas A&M University Press, 2004), 62.

8. ChTKhD, f. 2, op. 6, d. 6, l. 101.

9. Ibid., l. 62. The authorities of Cherepovets ordered priests from local parish churches to take care of the aged nuns from Goritskii convent in Vologda.

10. Aleksei Beglov, *V poiskakh "bezgreshnykh katakomb": Tserkovnoe podpol'e v SSSR* (Moscow: Izdatel'skii sovet russkoi pravoslavnoi tserkvi, Arefa, 2008), 46–47.

11. Protoierei Valerii Lavrinov, *Ekaterinburgskaia eparkhiia: Sobytiia, Liudi, Khramy* (Ekaterinburg: Izdatel'stvo Ural'skogo universiteta. 2001), 45.

12. M. V. Shkarovskii, *Russkaia pravoslavnaia tserkov' pri Staline i Khrushcheve* (Moscow: Krutitskoe patriarsh'e podvor'e, 1999), 217–19.

13. M. V. Shkarovskii, *Iosiflianstvo: techenie v Russkoi Pravoslavnoi Tserkvi* (St. Petersburg: Memorial, 1999), 34.

14. Ibid., 171–72.

15. Ibid., 149.

16. Ibid., 145.

17. Lynne Viola, "The Peasant Nightmare: Visions of Apocalypse in the Soviet Countryside," *Journal of Modern History* 62 (December 1990): 747–70.

18. S. Navaginskii, *Tserkovnoe podpol'e (o sekte fedorovtsev)* (Voronezh, 1929); Aleksandr Dem'ianov, *Istinno-proavoslavnoe khristianstvo: Kritika, ideologii, i deiatel'nosti* (Voronezh: Izdatel'stvo Voronezhskogo universiteta, 1977).

19. A. G. Eristov, *Ural'skii Sever: Antireligioznye ocherki Tobol'skogo kraia* (Sverdlovsk-Moscow: UOGIZ, 1933), 86–87.

20. V. P. Sventsitskii, *Dialogi* (Saratov: Izdatel'stvo Mosk. Podvor'ia Sviato-Troitskoi

Sergievoi Lavry, 1999).

21. M. Polskii, comp., *Novye mucheniki rossiiskie* (Jordanville, NY: Holy Trinity Monastery, 1949–1957), 161.

22. Heather Coleman, *Russian Baptists and Spiritual Revolution, 1905–1929* (Bloomington: Indiana University Press, 2005); V. F. Martsinkovskii, *Zapiski veruiushchego* (Novosibirsk: Posokh, 1994).

23. Martsinkovskii, *Zapiski veruiushchego*, 27–33.

24. Ignatiia, *Starchestvo v gody gonenii*, 92.

25. Pol'skii, *Novye mucheniki rossiiskie*, 27.

26. Veneamin (Milov), *Dnevnik inoka: pis'ma iz ssylki* (Zagorsk: Sviato-Troitskaia Sergieva Lavra, 1999), 139.

27. Pol'skii, *Novye mucheniki rossiiskie*, 260–61.

28. Ignatiia, *Starchestvo v gody gonenii*, 194–97.

29. Halbwachs, *On Collective Memory*, 45–103.

30. O. Iu. Vasil'eva, *Russkaia pravoslavnaia tserkov' v politike sovetskogo gosudarstva v 1943–1948 gg.* (Moscow: Institut rossiisskoi istorii RAN, 1999), 66.

31. GARF, f. 6991, op. 2, d. 18, l. 3. The calculations are based on data of 1945.

32. Ibid., d. 664, l. 66.

33. M. V. Shkarovskii, *Tserkov' zovet k zashchite rodiny: religioznaia zhizn' Leningrada i Severo-Zapada v gody Velikoi Otechestvennoi voiny* (St. Petersburg: Satis, 2005), 363.

34. Decree of September 25, 1945. Vasil'eva, *Russkaia pravoslavnaia tserkov'*, 66–67. For example, in 1945 Glinskaia pustyn' paid 53,000 rubles in state taxes. Ioann (Maslov), *Glinskaia pustyn'*, 449. The monastery regularly helped the local collective farm with the harvest.

35. Shkarovskii, *Tserkov' zovet*, 376–77.

36. VLA, f. Ea 160, d. 10.

37. N. V. Shabalin, *Russkaia pravoslavnaia tserkov' i sovetskoe gosudarstvo v seredine 40–50-e gg. XX v.: na materialakh Kirovskoi oblasti* (Kirov, 2004), 103–5.

38. Ioann (Maslov), *Glinskaia pustyn'*, 477.

39. For example, the Glinskaia monks protested against the new abbot Tavrion (Batozskii)'s attempts to introduce a different version of church chant, perceived as pro-Western, and his emphasis on frequent communion. Ibid., 513.

40. Ibid., 465, 476.

41. Ibid., 495–96.

42. *Zhivyi i po smerti: Ieroskhimonakh Sampson, graf Sivers* (Moscow: Derzhava, 2004), 25, 29–30.

43. Shabalin, *Russkaia pravoslavnaia tserkov'*, 100. Film director Aleksandr Proshkin has turned the story of Zoia into a film, "Miracle" (*Chudo*, 2009).

44. For example, Kirov believers told the story of Zoia as if it happened in the suburb of Kirov, not in Kuibyshev. Shabalin, *Russkaia pravoslavnaia tserkov'*, 99–100.

45. Ibid., 100.

46. Sofronii (Makritskii), *Belgorodskii starets arkhimandrit Serafim (Tiapochkin): zhizneopisanie, vospominaniia dukhovnykh chad, propovedi*, 6th ed. (Moscow: Khram Sofii Premudrosti Bozhiei, 2004), 33–47.

47. "Dobit'sia zakrytiia tak nazyvaemykh sviatykh mest [1958]," *Istochnik*, nos. 4–5 (1997): 120–29.

48. Arkhimandrite Tavrion (Batozskii), *Vsia zhizn' – Paskha Khristova:*

Zhizneopisaniie, vospominaniia dukhovnykh chad, propovedi (Moscow: Otchii dom, 2001), 106; *Zhivyi i po smerti*, 161, 184, 195–96, passim.

49. *Zhivyi i po smerti*, 28.

50. Report of the Council of Religious Affairs in 1970, reproduced in Gerd Stricker, ed., *Russkaia pravoslavnaia tserkov' v Sovetskoe vremia: materialy i dokumenty po istorii otnoshenii mezhdu gosudarstvom i tserkov'iu* (Moscow: Propilei, 1995), 2:83–84.

51. Ioann (Maslov), *Glinskaia pustyn'*, 567.

52. ERA, f. 1, op. 163, d. 12, l. 7.

53. *Starets Simeon Pskovo-Pecherskii*, 2nd ed. (Moscow: Sretenskii monastyr', 2004), 37–44.

54. *Zhivyi i po smerti*, 144, passim.

55. Ioann (Maslov), *Glinskaia pustyn'*, 503, 506, 534; *Zhivyi i po smerti*, 140; Natal'ia Zalipskaia, interview by Irina Paert, September 1, 2006. Zalipskaia's husband, Father Vladimir Zalipskii, copied patristic works by hand in the 1950s–1960s.

56. In 1959 the authorities closed 14 monasteries and 5 sketes, in 1960 11 monasteries. T. A. Chumachenko, *Gosudarstvo, pravoslavnaia tserkov', veruiushchie, 1941–1961*, Pervaia monografiia, ed. G. A. Bordiugov (Moscow: AIRO-XX, 1999), 205.

57. Ioann (Maslov), *Glinskaia pustyn'*, 468, 474, 503. Rafail (Karelin), *Taina spaseniia: besedy o dukhovnoi zhizni* (Moscow: Izd. Podvoria Sviato-Troitskoi Sergievoi Lavry, 2001), 82–83.

58. Makarii et al., *Istoriia russkoi tserkvi*, 9:411–12.

59. Ibid., 436–37.

60. Between 1961 and 1967 the number of Orthodox priests fell from 8,252 to 6,694, and deacons from 809 to 653. Ibid., 417.

61. Ibid., 416–17, 445.

62. Sociological surveys in the 1960s–1970s consistently demonstrated the decline of religiosity, primarily due to the lack of believers of the younger generation A. A. Lebedev, *Konkretnye issledovaniia v ateisticheskoi rabote* (Moscow: Politizdat, 1976).

63. Jane Ellis, *Russkaia pravoslavnaia tserkov': Soglasie i inakomyslie*, trans. G. Sidorenko (London: Overseas Publications Interchange, 1990), 6–7.

64. Yves Hamant, *Alexandre Men, un témoin pour la Russie de ce temps* (Paris: Mame, 1993). Translated by N. V. Garskaia as Iv Aman, *Aleksander Men'—svidetel' svoego vremeni* (Moscow: Rudomino, 1994), <http://krotov.info/library/01_a/ama/n_08.htm>

65. Makarii et al., *Istoriia Russkoi tserkvi*, 9:448–49.

66. Philip Boobbyer, *Conscience, Dissent, and Reform in Soviet Russia* (London: Routledge, 2005), 104–7.

67. Iv Aman, *Aleksander Men'*, <http://krotov.info/library>; Vladimir Levi "Ia ved' tol'ko instrument", <http://krotov.info/library>. Father Alexander was probably referring to the "maeutic" method, a device of intellectual or spiritual midwifery applied by Socrates. It is mentioned by Plato in *Theaetetus*.

68. Mark Raeff, *Russia Abroad: A Cultural History of the Russian Emigration, 1919–1939* (New York: Oxford University Press, 1990), 202–3.

69. Ibid., 119.

70. N. Arsen'ev, "Emigratsiia—na fone Rossii," *Vozrozhdenie* 191 (November 1967): 78.

71. Raeff, *Russia Abroad*, 125.

72. Boris Zaitsev, *Prepodobnyi Sergii Radonezhskii* (Paris: YMCA Press, 1925); idem, *Afon* (Paris: YMCA Press, 1928).

73. A. M. Liubomudrov, *Dukhovnyi realizm v literature russkogo zarubezh'ia: B. K.*

Zaitsev, I. S. Shmelev (St. Petersburg: Dmitrii Bulanin, 2003), 49.

74. Mikhail Ianson, *Valaamskie startsy* (Berlin: Izd-vo "Za tserkov'", 1938); I. Bogoiavlenskii, "Valaamskie vpechatleniia," *Pravoslavnyi sobesednik*, no. 8 (1939): 3–5; I. Kaigorodova, "Valaamskii monastyr'," *Nov': Pervyi sbornik molodezhi ko "Dniu russkoi kul'tury"* 1 (1928): 3; K. E. Arenskii, "Valaam," *Vozrozhdenie*, no. 225 (1970): 113–21; V. Davidenkova, "Palomnichestvo v Piukhtitskii zhenskii monastyr'," *Pravoslavnaia zhizn'*, no. 1 (1968): 15–18; E-v, "Troitsa v Pecherakh," *Vozrozhdenie*, no. 1880 (1930): 1.

75. For example, A. A. Osipov, *Putevaia tetrad' (Na Valaam!)* (Tallinn, 1940).

76. Raeff, *Russia Abroad*, 125, 130.

77. V. N. Il'in, *Prepodobnyi Serafim Sarovskii* (Paris: YMCA Press, 1925).

78. V. A. Zander, "Dve Pamiati," *Vestnik RKhD* 53 (1959): 25–36; P. N. Evdokimov, "Prepodobnyi Serafim kak ikona pravoslaviia," *Vestnik RKhD* 70–71 (1963): 43–54.

79. Boris Zaitsev, "Okolo Sv. Serafima (k stoletiiu ego konchiny)," in *Sobranie sochinenii v piati tomakh* (Moscow: Russkaia kniga, 2000), 7:364–69; Liubomudrov, *Dukhovnyi realizm*, 82.

80. Shmelev, "Milost' prepodobnogo Serafima," in *Sobranie sochinenii* (Moscow: Russkaia kniga, 2001), 2:343.

81. As quoted in Liubomudrov, *Dukhovnyi realizm*, 140.

82. A. V. Tyrkova-Williams, "Vstrecha s o. Ioannom Kronshtadtskim," *Vozrozhdenie*, no. 1630 (1929): 2–3; F. V. Segadaev, "Predskazanie Ioanna Kronshtadtskogo," *Russkaia mysl'*, no. 2960 (1973): 11; I. I. Sakhnovskii, "Chudesnaia pomoshch po molitvam o. Ioanna Kronshtadtskogo," *Pravoslavnaia zhizn'* no.11 (1955): 14–17; D. A. Ozerov, "Otets Ioann Kronshtadtskii," *Pravoslavnaia zhizn'* no. 11 (1964): 14–21; ibid., no. 12: 8–14; Aleksandr [Semenov-Tian-Shan'skii], *Otets Ioan Kronshtadtskii* (New York: Izdatel'stvo im. Chekhova, 1955).

83. M. Gizetti, "Pamiati moemu dukhovnomu ottsu [Vasilii Zenkovskii]," *Vestnik RKhD*, nos. 66–67 (1962): 35–36; Kiprian (Kern), *Pravoslavnoe pastyrskoe sluzhenie: iz kursa lektsii po pastyrskomu bogosloviiu* (Paris: Zhurnal Vechnoe, 1957), 141.

84. According to some evidence this woman was Mother Elisabeth Reve from a Catholic convent in Lyon, but it has also been suggested that Mother Mariia (Skobtsova) was dispatched to the gas chamber as one of the mortally exhausted prisoners.

85. Mariia (Skobtsova), *Vospominaniia, stat'i, ocherki* (Paris: YMCA Press, 1992), 156–57.

86. K. Mochul'skii, "Monakhinia Mariia (Skobtsova)," as cited in *"Peterburg menia pobedil . . .": Dokumental'noe povestvovanie o zhizni E. Iu. Kuz'minoi-Karavaevoi, materi Marii*, ed L. Ageeva (St. Petersburg: Zhurnal Neva, 2003), 310.

87. Father Lev Gillet was born in 1893 in the south of France, and he learned about Russia through reading Tolstoy and Dostoevsky. In 1920 he joined a Benedictine order in England and in 1924 lived in Lviv, where he took vows and was ordained as a priest. In 1928, while living in a mission at Cote d' Azure among Russian émigrés, he converted to Orthodoxy.

88. VLA, Ea. 135, file 19, l. 3 ob.

89. "Vospominaniia arkhimandrita Afanasiia (Nechaeva)," *Sever* 9 (1991): 77.

90. VLA, Ba. 81–83, ll. 23–24.

91. "Vospominaniia arkhimandrita Afanasiia," 78–79.

92. VLA, Ea 158 (lists of monks in 1945).

93. Ioann (Alekseev), *Zagliani v svoe serdtse: zhizneopisanie, pis'ma* (St Petersburg: Severnoe siianie, 2002), 16, 138, 199.

94. Ibid., 68.

95. VLA, Ea 160, file 10.

96. Hannu Kilpeläinen, *Valamo—karjalaisten luostari? Luostarin ja yhteistkunnan interaktio maailmansotien välisenä aikana* (Helsinki: Suomalaisen kirjallisuuden seura, 2000), 464.

97. Abbot Sergii of New Valaam monastery, interview by Irina Paert, November 22, 2006.

98. For example, the Lintulla convent is using Russian-style chant and some previous traditions passed on by the Russian nuns. In Valaam, the Greek forms of the liturgical service, music, and icon painting prevail. The rich archives of Valaam and the unique library are hardly used by the community, and mainly serve the interests of visiting scholars.

99. I. Smolitsch, "Sviataia Gora Afonskaia," *Vestnik RKhD*, 70–71 (1963): 40.

100. In 1924 the new rules of governing Mount Athos were adopted, according to which all monks regardless of their nationality had to become Greek subjects. *Pravoslavnaia entsiklopediia*, s.v. "Afon."

101. Siluan's letter to Nadiezhda Soboleva included thanks for one dollar she enclosed with her letter. Viktor (Mamontov), "Pis'ma startsa Siluana k dukhovnoi docheri," *Khristianos* 1 (1991): 71–76.

102. Skhimonakh Savva, "Shest'desiat let monasheskoi zhizni," *Pravoslavnaia Rus'* 14 (1959): 6.

103. Sofronii (Sakharov), *Starets Siluan* (Maldon, Essex: Monastery of St. John the Baptist), 8–10.

104. Siluan's writings have received appreciation among critics, theologians, and ordinary readers. One reviewer of Father Sofronii's book wrote that no anthology of Russian literature would be possible without "Adam's Lament," Siluan's meditation on the soul's loss of God's grace. Arhimandrit Sofronii, *Pis'ma v Rossiiu* (Essex-Moscow: Sviato-Ioannovskii Predtechenskii monastyr', 1997), 67. The patriarch of Constantinople canonized Siluan in 1987.

105. Viktor (Mamontov), "Pis'ma startsa Siluana," 71–76.

106. Veneamin (Fedchenkov), *Pis'ma o monashestve* (Moscow: Prensa, 2003), 82, 187.

107. Balfour studied in Rome and in 1922 joined the Benedictine monastery in Farnborough near London. In 1926 he transferred to Amay-sur-Meuse, a Catholic community in Belgium that used Eastern rites, where he took vows and was ordained as a priest. See Sofronii (Sakharov), *Podvig bogopoznaniia: Pis'ma s Afona (k D. Balfuru)* (Moscow: Palomnik, 2001).

108. Sakharov, *I Love, Therefore I Am*, 23–33.

109. "Diskussiia o monashestve: iz perepiski o. Vasiliia Zen'kovskogo s s. Ioannoi Reitlinger," *Vestnik RKhD* 1, no. 185 (2003): 53–64.

110. Sergei Bulgakov, *Uteshitel'*, vol. 2, *O bogochelovechestve* ([Tallinn]: YMCA Press, 1936), 345–56, as cited in Paul Valliere, *Modern Russian Theology: Bukharev, Solov'ev, Bulgakov: Orthodox Theology in a New Key* (Grand Rapids: Eerdmans, 2000), 365.

111. Ibid, 366.

112. Ioann (Shakhovskoi), "Beloe inochestvo," <http://azbyka.ru/tserkov/monashestvo/shahovskoy_beloe_inochestvo.shtml>.

113. André Scrima, *Il padre spirituale*, trans. Adalberto Mainardi (Bose: Edizioni Quiqajon/Comunità di Bose, 200).

114. A. V. Tarabukina, "Fol'klor i kul'tura protserkovnogo kruga" (Kand. diss., St.

Petersburg University, 2000), <http://www.ruthenia.ru/folktee/CYBERSTOL/books/Tarabukina/arina_tarabukina.html>

115. Ibid.

116. V. Emel'ianenko, "Privatizatsiia startsa," *Izvestiia*, February 2, 2001.

117. *Pis'ma arkhimandrita Ioanna (Krest'iankina)* (Pskov: Sviato-Uspenskii Pskovo-Pecherskii monastyr', 2006).

118. Vladimir Volgin, interview by Irina Paert, July 9, 2006, Moscow.

119. Tikhon (Shevkunov), interview with the Radio Radonezh, January 29, 2001, <http://www.pravoslavie.ru/jurnal/society/arhimtihon_radonezh.htm>.

120. Vladimir Sokolov, *Mladostarchestvo i pravoslavnaia traditsiia* (Moscow: Palomnik, 2005), 10.

121. Thanks to the efforts of Father Nikolai (Gur'ianov)'s cellmates, the authority of the *starets* was used to sanction these dubious campaigns. Jeanne Kormina, "Contesting the Sacred: Debates about Faith at the Grave of a *Starets*," paper presented at the conference "Reform Movements in Eastern Christian Culture: Renewal, Heresy, and Compromise" organized by the Association for the Study of Eastern Christian History and Culture, Columbus, Ohio, October 1–3, 2009.

122. "Opredelenie Sviashchennogo Sinoda Russkoi pravoslavnoi tserkvi," in *O dukhovnichestve* (Klin: Fond "Khristianskaia zhizn'," 2000), 25–33.

123. Ibid.

124. Mitrokhin, *Russkaia pravoslavnaia tserkov'*, 93–94.

125. Sokolov, *Mladostarchestvo*, 57.

126. Mitrokhin, *Russkaia pravoslavnaia tserkov'*, 96–102.

127. Popular figures like pop stars Andrei Makarevich and Valentina Tolkunova, actress Tatiana Vasil'eva, and dancer Maris Liepa all appealed to elders at some point of their lives.

128. Andrei Desnitskii, "Homo Soveticus Christianus," <http://reshma.nov.ru/alm/pr_sov/homo_sov.htm>.

129. Sokolov, *Mladostarchestvo*, 25–27.

130. Ibid., 27.

131. Mitrokhin, *Russkaia Pravoslavnaia tserkov'*, 96.

132. Ibid., 92–93.

133. Galina Lindquist, *Conjuring Hope*, 230–31.

134. Robert Wuthnow, *After Heaven: Spirituality in America since the 1950s* (Berkeley: University of California Press, 1998), 89–92.

Conclusion

1. Brown, "The Rise and Function of the Holy Man," 80–101.

2. Freeze, *The Russian Levites*; Florovsky, *Puti russkogo bogosloviia*, 56, passim.

3. On the position of parish priesthood see Freeze, *The Russian Levites*; idem, *Parish Clergy*.

4. T. A. Bernshtam, *Prikhodskaia zhizn' russkoi derevni: ocherki po tserkovnoi etnografii* (St. Petersburg: Peterburgskoe vostokovedenie, 2005), 128.

5. Margaret Ziolkowski, *Hagiography and Modern Russian Literature* (Princeton University Press, 1988), 131, 190.

6. Stanton, *The Optina Pustyn Monastery*, 79, 92, passim.

7. Arkhiv SPb FIRI RAN, f. 3, op. 3, d. 186a, l. 121 (Letter to Bishop Arkadii of Olonets of April 17, 1856).

8. A. A. Panchenko, *Khristovshchina i skopchestvo: fol'klor i traditsionnaia kul'tura russkikh misticheskikh sekt* (Moscow: Ob"edinennoe gumanitarnoe izdatel'stvo, 2002), 113–15, 141–43.

9. Zoe Knox, *Russian Society and the Orthodox Church: Religion in Russia after Communism* (London: RoutledgeCurzon, 2005); Mitrokhin, *Russkaia pravoslavnaia tserkov'*, 92–95.

10. Simon Dixon, "The Russian Orthodox Church in Imperial Russia, 1721–1917," in *The Cambridge History of Christianity*, vol. 5, *Eastern Christianity*, ed. Michael Angold (Cambridge: Cambridge University Press, 2008), 347.

11. Shevzov, *Russian Orthodoxy*, 258.

12. William Wagner, "The Transformation of Female Orthodox Monasticism," 793–845; Meehan-Waters, "Popular Piety, Local Initiative," 117–41.

13. Brown, "The Rise and Function of the Holy Man," 95. On the decentralizing tendency, see Shevzov, *Russian Orthodoxy*, 262.

14. On the latter view of elders see Knox, *Russian Society and the Orthodox Church*, 89.

Select Bibliography

Primary Sources

Archives

Arkhiv SPb FIRI RAN	Arkhiv Sankt-Peterburgskogo filiala Instituta rossiiskoi istorii RAN
ChTKhD	Cherepovetskii tsentr khraneniia dokumentatsii
GARF	Gosudarstvennyi arkhiv Rossiiskoi Federatsii
GABO	Gosudarstvennyi arkhiv Brianskoi oblasti
GAKO	Gosudarstvennyi arkhiv Kaluzhskoi oblasti
GAOO	Gosudarstvennyi arkhiv Orlovskoi oblasti
GATO	Gosudarstvennyi arkhiv Tverskoi oblasti
GIANO	Gosudarstvennyi istoricheskii arkhiv Novgorodskoi oblasti
ERA	Eesti Riigiarhiiv
NART	Natsional'nyi arkhiv respubliki Tatarstan
OR RGB	Otdel rukopisei Rossiiskoi gosudarstvennoi biblioteki
RGADA	Rossiiskii gosudarstvennyi arkhiv drevnikh aktov
RGALI	Rossiiskii gosudarstvennyi arkhiv literatury i iskusstva
RGIA	Rossiiskii gosudarstvennyi istoricheskii arkhiv
TsGA RM	Tsentral'nyi gosudarstvennyi arkhiv respubliki Mordoviia
TsANO	Tsentral'nyi arkhiv Nizhegorodskoi oblasti
VLA	Valamon Luostari Arkisto

Published Works

Afonskii paterik, ili Zhizneopisanie sviatykh na Sviatoi Afonskoi Gore prosiiavshikh. Moscow: Blagovest, 2001.

Agapit, Archimandrite. *Zhizneopisanie v boze pochivshego optinskogo startsa ieroskhimonakha Amvrosiia.* Zagorsk: Izd. Sviato-Troitskoi Sergievoi Lavry, 1900.

(Alekseev), Ioann. *Zagliani v svoe serdtse: zhizneopisanie, pis'ma.* St. Petersburg: Severnoe Siianie, 2002.

(Beliaev), Nikon. *Dnevnik poslednego dukhovnika Optinoi pustyni.* Minsk: Luchi Sofii, 2002.

Belov, Sergei V., ed. *Russkie emigranty o Dostoevskom.* St. Petersburg: Andreev i synov'ia, 1994.

Bulgakov, S. V. *Nastol'naia kniga dlia sviashchenno-tserkovno-sluzhitelei: sbornik svedenii, kasaiushchikhsia preimushchestvenno prakticheskoi deiatel'nosti otechestvennago dukhovenstva*. Kiev: Tip. Kievo-Pecherskoi Uspenskoi Lavry, 1913.

Chaila, Du. "Vospominaniia o S. A. Niluse i 'Sionskikh Protokolakh' (1909–1920)." *Evreiskaia tribuna* 72 (May 1921), 1–7.

Chetverukhin, I., and E. Chetverukhina. *Prepodobnyi Aleksei, starets-zatvornik Smolenskoi Zosimovoi pustyni*. Zagorsk: Sviato-Troitskaia Sergieva Lavra, 2003.

[(Chichagov), Serafim], ed. *Letopis' Serafimo-Diveevskogo monastyria*. Moscow: Palomnik, 2002.

"Diskussiia o monashestve: iz perepiski o. Vasiliia Zen'kovskogo s s. Ioannoi Reitlinger." *Vestnik RKhD* 1, no. 185 (2003): 53–64.

"Dobit'sia zakrytiia tak nazyvaemykh sviatykh mest [1958]," *Istochnik*, nos. 4–5 (1997): 120–29.

Dostoevskii, Fedor. *Brat'ia Karamazovy* [The Brothers Karamazov], in *Polnoe sobranie sochinenii v tridsati tomakh*. Vol. 14. Leningrad: Nauka, 1976.

(Drozdov), Filaret. *Mneniia, otzyvy, i pis'ma Filareta, Mitropolita Moskovskogo i Kolomenskogo po raznym voprosam za 1821–1867 gg*. Moscow: Sinodal'naia tipografiia, 1905. Reprint, Westmead: Gregg International, 1971.

Dukhovnye nastavleniia ottsa Serafima Sarovskoi pustyni ieromonakha, pustynnika i zatvornika. Moscow, 1847.

Emel'ianenko, V. "Privatizatsiia startsa." *Izvestiia*. February 2, 2001.

Faminskii, N. "O monashestve." *Monastyr'* 4 (1909): 262–65.

(Fedchenkov) Veneamin. *Pis'ma o monashestve*. Moscow: Prensa, 2003.

Firsov, S. *Sviatoi Ioann Kronshtadtskii v vospominaniiakh sovremennikov*. St. Petersburg: Izdatel'skii Dom Neva, 2003.

Florenskii, Pavel. *Opravdanie kosmosa*. St. Petersburg: Russkii khristianskii gumanitarnyi institut, 1994.

———. *Perepiska s M. A. Novoselovym*. Tomsk: Vodolei, 1998.

———. *Stolp i utverzhdenie istiny: Opyt pravoslavnoi feoditsei v dvenadtsaty pis'makh*. Moscow, 1914.

Fomin, Sergei, ed. "*Pastyr' dobryi": Zhizn' i trudy Moskovskogo startsa protoiereia Alekseia Mechova*. Moscow: Palomnik, 2004.

(Georgievskii) Evlogii. *Put' moei zhizni: vospominaniia Mitropolita Evlogiia*. Paris: YMCA Press, 1947.

Gorchakova, E. *Obitel' startsa Zosimy Verkhovskogo*. Moscow: Izd-vo im. Sviatitelia Ignatiia Stavropol'skogo, 1998.

(Govorov), Feofan. *Tvoreniia izhe vo sviatykh ottsa nashego Feofana Zatvornika*. 3 vols. Moscow: Pravilo very, 2000–2001.

Graham, Steven. *With the Russian Pilgrims to Jerusalem*. London: Macmillan and Co., 1913.

(Grenkov) Amvrosii. *Sbornik pisem i statei Optinskogo startsa ieroskhimonakha ottsa Amvrosiia*. Vol. 1. Moscow, 1894.

Ianson, Mikhail. *Valaamskie startsy*. Berlin: Izd-vo "Za tserkov'", 1938.

I. S. [Hieromonk Sergii]. *Skazanie o zhizni i podvigakh blazhennyia pamiati startsa Sarovskoi pustyni ieromonakha Serafima*. Moscow: Izd. D. I. Priesnova, 1880.

Ilarion, Schemamonk. *Na gorakh Kavkaza: Beseda dvukh startsev pustynnikov o vrutrennem edinenii s Gospodom nashikh serdets*. Moscow, 1907. Reprint, St. Petersburg: Voskresenie, Lestvitsa, Dioptra, 2002.

Ivanovskii, V. "Russkoe zakonodatel'stvo 18 i 19 st. v svoikh postanovleniiakh otnositel'no monashestvuiushchikh lits i monastyrei." *Vera i razum* 1, no. 3 (1904): 145–73; no. 4: 261–74; no. 8: 426–40 ; no. 10: 527–94; no. 19: 432–46; no. 21: 493–510.

(Karelin) Rafail. *Taina spaseniia: besedy o dukhovnoi zhizni*. Moscow: Izd. Podvoria Sviato-Troitskoi Sergievoi Lavry, 2001.

(Kavelin), Leonid. *Istoricheskoe opisanie Kozel'skoi Vvedenskoi Optinoi Pustyni*. Moscow: Tip. Got'e, 1876.

(Kern) Kiprian. *Vospominaniia o mitropolite Antonii (Khrapovitskom) i episcope Gavriile (Chepure)*. Moscow: Pravoslavnyi Sviato-Tikhonovskii Institut, 2002.

Khitrov, A. M., and O. L. Solomina, eds. *Zabytye stranitsy russkogo imiaslaviia*. Moscow: Palomnik, 2001.

(Khrapovitskii), Antonii. *Polnoe sobranie sochinenii*. 3 vols. Kazan: Tip-lit. Imperatorskogo Universiteta, 1900.

Kievo-Pecherskii Paterik: Polnoe sobraniie zhitii sviatykh v Kievo-Pecherskoi Lavre podvizavshikhsia. 3rd ed. Moscow: Stupin, 1911.

Kireevskii, I. V. *Razum na puti k istine: Filosofskie stat'i, publitsistika, pis'ma; Perespiska s prep. Makariem (Ivanovym). Dnevnik*. Moscow: Pravilo very, 2002.

(Kononov), Nikodim. *Zhizneopisaniia otechestvennykh podvizhnikov blagochestiia vosemnadtsatogo i deviatnadtsatogo vv*. 19 vols. Athos: Sviato-Pantelemonovskii monastyr', 1906–1910. Reprint, Kozel'sk: Sviato-Vvedenskaia Optina Pustyn', 1994–1999.

Kovalevskii, A. "Vospominaniia o dukhovnike Kievo-Pecherskoi Lavry, ieroskhimonakhe Antonii." *Dushepoleznoe chtenie* (1881): 337–68, 444–69.

(Kozlov) Mikhail. "Rasskaz strannika, iskatelia molitvy." *Simvol*, no. 27 (July 1992): 7–76.

"K proslavleniiu sviatoi pamiati Serafima Sarovskogo." *Russkii arkhiv* 3, no. 9 (1902): 141–43.

Leskov, N. S. *Sobranie sochinenii v 11 tomakh*. Moscow: Gos. Izd-vo khudozhestvennoi literatury, 1956–1958.

(Makritskii), Sofronii. *Belgorodskii starets arkhimandrit Serafim (Tiapochkin): zhizneopisanie, vospominaniia dukhovnykh chad propovedi*. 6th ed. Moscow: Khram Sofii Premudrosti Bozhiei, 2004.

(Mamontov), Viktor. "Pis'ma startsa Siluana k dukhovnoi docheri." *Khristianos* 1 (1991): 71–76.

Markov, V. S., ed. *Polnoe sobranie rezoliutsii Filareta Mitropolita Moskovskogo*. 5 vols. Moscow: Izd. Redaktsii Dushepoleznago chteniia vo Universitetskoi tip-ii, 1904–1916.

Martsinkovskii, V. F. *Zapiski veruiushchego*. Novosibirsk: Posokh, 1994.

[Mashurin, Georgii]. *Tvoreniia Georgiia, zatvornika Zadonskogo*. St. Petersburg, 1894. 6th ed. Reprint, Moscow: Palomnik, 1994.

Masson, Charles François Philibert. *Sekretnye zapiski o Rossii vremeni tsarstvovaniia Ekateriny II i Pavla I*. Moscow: Novoe literaturnoe obozrenie, 1996.

(Milov), Veneamin. *Dnevnik inoka: pis'ma iz ssylki*. Zagorsk: Sviato-Troitskaia Sergieva Lavra, 1999.

Mosolov, A. A. *Pri dvore poslednego imperatora: zapiski nachal'nika kantseliarii ministra dvora*. St. Petersburg: Nauka, 1992.

Nila Sorskogo predanie i ustav. Moscow: Tip. M. A. Aleksandova, 1912.

"Opredelenie Sviashchennogo Sinoda Russkoi pravoslavnoi tserkvi (28.12.1998)." In *O dukhovnichestve*, 25–33. Klin: Fond "Khristianskaia zhizn'," 2000.

(Ornatskii), Amvrosii. *Drevnerusskie inocheskie ustavy: ustavy rossiiskikh monastyrenachal'nikov*. Moscow: Severnyi palomnik, 2001.

Osipov, A. A. *Putevaia tetrad' (Na Valaam!)*. Tallinn, 1940.

Otkrovennye rasskazy strannika dukhovnomu svoemu ottsu. Paris: YMCA Press, 1930.

"Pamiatnye zapiski igumenii Evgenii (Ozerovoi)." In *Zhenskaia Optina: materialy k letopisi Boriso-Glebskogo zhenskogo monastyria*, ed. Sergei Fomin and Tamara Fomina. Moscow: Palomnik, 2005.

Pelin, Valentina. "The Correspondence of Abbot Paisie from Neamts." *Revue des Études Sud-Est Européennes* 22, nos. 1–2 (1994): 75–80.

Piasetskii, G. V. *Istoriia Orlovskoi eparkhii*. Orel, 1899.

Pis'ma arkhimandrita Ioanna (Krest'iankina). Pskov: Sviato-Uspenskii Pskovo-Pecherskii monastyr', 2006.

Pis'ma Optinskogo startsa L'va k monakhu Ioannikiiu (Bocharovu). Kozel'sk: Sviato-Vvedenskaia Optina Pustyn', 2002.

Pitirim. *Pis'ma velikikh optinskikh startsev: XIX vek*. Moscow: Izd. Sretenskogo monastyria, 2001.

Pokrovskii, M. N., ed. *Perepiska Nikolaia i Aleksandry Romanovykh: 1914–1915*. Vol. 3. Moscow: Gos. Izd-vo, 1925.

Polnoe sobranie tvorenii sviatitelia Ignatiia Brianchaninova. 5 vols. Moscow: Palomnik, 2001–2002.

Polnoe zhizneopisanie sviatitelia Ignatiia Kavkazskogo. Moscow: Izdatel'stvo im. svt. Ignatiia Stavropol'skogo, 2002.

Polskii, Mikhail, comp. *Novye mucheniki rossiiskie*. Jordanville, NY: Holy Trinity Monastery, 1949–1957.

[Porfirii]. *Zhitie i podvigi skhimonakha Ioanna, osnovatelia i pervonachal'nika Sarovskoi pustyni*. Murom, 1892.

Pospelova, D. A., O. A. Rodionova, and P. B. and M. A. Zhgun, eds. *Prep. Paisii Velichkovskii: Avtobiografiia, zhizneopisaniia, i izbrannye tvoreniia po rukopisnym istochnikam XVIII-XIX vv*. Moscow: Russkii na Afone Sviato-Panteleimonov monastyr', 2004.

Pravoslavnyi nemets: ieromonakh Kliment (Zendergol'm). Kozel'sk: Izd. Vvedenskoi Optini Pustyni, 2002.

Prepodobnogo ottsa avvy Ioanna, igumena Sinaiskoi gory: Lestvitsa v russkom perevode. St. Petersburg: Tipografiia No. 6, 1995.

Rasputin, Grigorii. *Vospominaniia opytnogo strannika*. N.p., [1907].

(Sabel'nikov), Ioakim. *Velikaia strazha: zhizn' i trudy blazhennoi pamiati afonskikh startsev ieroskhimonakha Ieronima i skhiarkhimandrita Makariia*. Vol. 1. Moscow: Izdatel'stvo Moskovskoi Patriarkhii, 2001.

(Sakharov), Sofronii. *Podvig bogopoznaniia: Pis'ma s Afona (k D. Balfuru)*. Moscow: Palomnik, 2001.

———. *Starets Siluan*. Maldon, Essex: Monastery of St. John the Baptist, 1990.

Sakhnovskii, I. I. "Chudesnaia pomoshch po molitvam o. Ioanna Kronshtadtskogo." *Pravoslavnaia zhizn'*, no. 11 (1955): 14–17.

Saltykov-Shchedrin, M. E. *Sobranie sochinenii*. 20 vols. Moscow: Khudozhestvennaia literatura, 1965.

Savva, Skhimonakh. "Shest'desiat let monasheskoi zhizni." *Pravoslavnaia Rus'* 14 (1959): 6–7.

Scrima, André. *Il padre spirituale*. Translated by Adalberto Mainardi. Bose: Edizioni Quiqajon/Comunità di Bose, 2000.

[Sebriakova], Arseniiia. *Zhizneopisanie*. Moscow: Sviato-Troitskaia Lavra, 1998.

Segadaev, F. V. "Predskazanie Ioanna Kronshtadtskogo." *Russkaia mysl'*, no. 2960 (1973): 11.

Sestry: ocherk zhizni sester Anisii, Matrony, i Agafii, podvizhavshikhsia i pochivshikh v sele Ialtunovo, Shatskogo raiona, Riazanskoi eparkhii. Moscow: Novospasskii monastyr', 2004.

(Sokolov), Feofan. "Zapiski o. Feofana, arkhimandrita Kirillo-Novoezerskogo monastyria." *Strannik* 1, no. 2 (1862): 33–53.

Solov'ev, I. V., ed."Obnovlencheskii" raskol: materialy dlia tserkovno-istoricheskoi i kanonicheskoi kharakteristiki. Moscow: Obshchestvo liubitelei tserkovnoi istorii, 2002.

Stricker, Gerd, ed. *Russkaia pravoslavnaia tserkov' v Sovetskoe vremia: materialy i dokumenty po istorii otnoshenii mezhdu gosudarstvom i tserkov'iu.* Vol. 2. Moscow: Propilei, 1995.

Shmelev, Ivan. "Milost' prepodobnogo Serafima." In *Sobranie sochinenii.* Vol. 2. Moscow: Russkaia kniga, 2001.

Sidorov, A. I., ed. *Tvoreniia Avvy Evagriia: asketicheskie i bogoslovskie traktaty.* Moscow: Martis, 1994.

(Skobtsova), Mariia. *Vospominaniia, stat'i, ocherki.* Paris: YMCA Press, 1992.

"Sofronieva i Glinskaia pustyni." *Strannik* 12 (1862): 529–68.

(Sokolov), Tikhon. *Tvoreniia izhe vo sviatykh ottsa nashego Tikhona Zadonskogo.* 2 vols. Moscow: Sinodal'naia Tip., 1889.

Sokolova, N. N. *Pod krovom Vsevyshnego.* Novosibirsk: Pravoslavnaia gimnaziia, 1998.

Starcheskie nastavleniia o. Nazariia s kratkim ukazaniem o ego zhizni i podvigakh. Moscow, 1853.

Starets Simeon Pskovo-Pecherskii. 2nd ed. Moscow: Sretenskii monastyr', 2004.

Strizhev, A., ed. *Po sledam Nilusa: razdum'ia, vstrechi, razyskaniia.* Moscow: Palomnik, 1999.

———. *Serafimo-diveevskie predaniia: zhitie, vospominaniia, pis'ma, tserkovnye torzhestva.* Moscow: Palomnik, 2001.

Sventsitskii, V. P. *Dialogi.* Saratov: Izdatel'stvo Mosk. Podvor'ia Sviato-Troitskoi Sergievoi Lavry, 1999.

Taisiia, Monakhinia. *Russkoe pravoslavnoe zhenskoe monashestvo XVIII-XX vv.* Moscow: Sviato-Troitskaia Sergieva Lavra, 1992.

Tolstoi, Lev. *Sobranie sochinenii v 20 t.* Moscow: Khudozhestvennaia literatura, 1978–1985.

Vitte, S. Iu. *Vospominaniia.* 2 vols. Tallinn: Skif-Aleks, 1994.

Volkov, Sergei. *Vozle monastyrskikh sten: Memuary, Dnevniki, Pis'ma.* Moscow: Izdatel'stvo gumanitarnoi literatury, 2000.

"Vospominaniia arkhimandrita Afanasiia (Nechaeva)," *Sever* 9 (1991): 74–88.

(Vytropskii), Erast. *Istoricheskoe opisanie Kozel'skoi Optinoi Pustyni i Predtecheva skita.* Kozel'sk: Izd. Sviato-Vvedenskoi Optinoi Pustyni, 2000.

Zaitsev, Boris. *Afon.* Paris: YMCA Press, 1928.

———. "Okolo Sv. Serafima (k stoletiiu ego konchiny)." In *Sobranie sochinenii.* Vol. 7. Moscow: Russkaia kniga, 2000.

———. *Prepodobnyi Sergii Radonezhskii.* Paris: YMCA Press, 1925.

Zander, V. A. "Dve Pamiati." *Vestnik RKhD* 53 (1959): 25–36.

"Zapiski o. Feofana, arkhimandrita Kirillo-Novoezerskogo monastyria." *Strannik* 1, no. 2 (1862): 33–58.

Zapiski o zhizni i podvigakh Petra Alekseevicha Michurina, pustynnozhitelia Vasiliska, i nekotorye cherty iz zhizni iurodivogo monakha Iony. Moscow, 1849.

(Zhadanovskii), Arsenii. *Vospominaniia*. Moscow: Pravoslavnyi Sviato-Tikhonovskii Bogoslovskii Institut, 1995.

Zhevakhov, N. D. *Vospominaniia tovarishcha ober-prokurora Sv. Sinoda kniazia N. D. Zhevakhova*. Moscow: Rodnik, 1993.

Zhitie i pisaniia moldavskogo startsa Paisiia Velichkovskogo. 3rd ed. Moscow, 1892.

Zhitie i pisaniia moldavskogo startsa Paisiia Velichkovskogo. Moscow, 1847. Reprint, Kozel'sk: Sviato-Vvedenskaia Optina Pustyn', 2001.

Zhitie optinskogo startsa ieromonakha Leonida, v skhime L'va. Kozel'sk: Izd. Vvedenskoi Optinoi pustyni, 1994.

Zhivyi i po smerti: Ieroskhimonakh Sampson, graf Sivers. Moscow: Derzhava, 2004.

Zhizneopisanie Optinskogo startsa Leonida. Zagorsk: Sviato-Troitskaia Sergieva Lavra, 1991.

Zhizneopisanie Troekurovskogo zatvornika startsa Ilariona. Moscow: Moskovskoe podvor'e Sviato-Troitskoi Sergievoi Lavry, 1998.

Zhizneopisanie v boze pochivshego startsa-uteshitelia ottsa Varnavy osnovatelia i stroitelia Iverskogo Vyksunskogo zhenskogo monastyria. Iverskaia obitel', 1907.

Zhizn' ottsa Feodora byvshego nastoiatelia Sanaksarskia obiteli prestavl'shagosia v 1791 g. Moscow: Universitetskaia tipografiia, 1847.

Secondary Sources

Ageeva, L., ed. "*Peterburg menia pobedil . . .*": *Dokumental'noe povestvovanie o zhizni E. Iu. Kuz'minoi-Karavaevoi, materi Marii*. St. Petersburg: Zhurnal Neva, 2003.

(Alfeev), Ilarion. *Sviashchennaia taina tserkvi: vvedenie v istoriiu i problematiku imiaslavskikh sporov*. Vol. 1. St. Petersburg: Aleteiia, 2002.

Almazov, A. I. *Tainaia ispoved' v Pravoslavnoi Vostochnoi Tserkvi: Opyt vneshnei istorii*. 3 vols. Odessa: Tip. Shtaba odesskago voennago okruga, 1894.

Aman, Iv. *Aleksander Men'—svidetel' svoego vremeni*. Translated by N. V. Garskaia. Moscow: Rudomino, 1994.

Angold, Michael. *Church and Society in Byzantium under the Comneni, 1081–1261*. Cambridge: Cambridge University Press, 1995.

Arnautova, Iu. E. "Zhitie kak dukhovnaia biografiia: k voprosu o 'tipicheskom' i 'individual'nom' v latinskoi agiografii." In *Istoriia cherez lichnost': Istoricheskaia biografiia segodnia*, edited by Lorina P. Repina, 112–38. Moscow: Krug, 2005.

Assmann, Jan. *Religion and Cultural Memory: Ten Studies*. Translated by Rodney Livingstone. Stanford: Stanford University Press, 2006.

Aston, Nigel. *Christianity and Revolutionary Europe, 1750–1830*. Cambridge: Cambridge University Press, 2002.

Bakhmustov, Sergei. *Monastyri Mordovii*. Saransk: Mordovskoe knizhnoe izdatel'stvo, 2000.

Barnett, S. J. *The Enlightenment and Religion: The Myths of Modernity*. Manchester: Manchester University Press, 2003.

Basin, I. "Avtorstvo 'Otkrovennykh rasskazov strannika.'" *Simvol*, no. 27 (1992): 167–87.

Basin, I. "Mif moshchei prepodobnogo Serafima Sarovskogo." *Stranitsy: Bogoslovie, Kul'tura, Obrazovanie* 2, no. 3 (1997): 385–97; no. 4 (1997): 538–49.

Beglov, Aleksei. "Starchestvo v trudakh russkikh tserkovnykh uchenykh i pisatelei." In *Put' k sovershennoi zhizni: o russkom starchestve*, edited by A. L. Beglov, 5–29. Moscow: Pravoslavnyi Sviato-Tikhonovskii Gumanitarnyi Universitet, 2006.

———. *V poiskakh "bezgreshnykh katakomb": Tserkovnoe podpol'e v SSSR*. Moscow: Izdatel'skii sovet russkoi pravoslavnoi tserkvi Arefa, 2008.

Belliustin, I. S. *Description of the Clergy in Rural Russia: The Memoir of a Nineteenth-Century Parish Priest*. Translated with an interpretive essay by Gregory L. Freeze. Ithaca: Cornell University Press, 1985.

Berger, Peter. *The Heretical Imperative: Contemporary Possibilities of Religious Affirmation*. Garden City, NY: Anchor Press, 1979.

Bernshtam, T. A. *Prikhodskaia zhizn' russkoi derevni: ocherki po tserkovnoi etnografii*. St. Petersburg: Peterburgskoe vostokovedenie, 2005.

Billington, James H. *The Icon and the Axe: An Interpretative History of Russian Culture*. New York: Vintage Books, 1996.

Boobbyer, Philip. *Conscience, Dissent, and Reform in Soviet Russia*. London: Routledge, 2005.

Brown, Peter. *The Cult of the Saints: Its Rise and Function in Latin Christianity*. Chicago: University of Chicago Press, 1981.

———. "The Rise and Function of the Holy Man in Late Antiquity." *The Journal of Roman Studies* 61 (1971): 80–101.

Bukova, Olga. *Zhenskie obiteli prepodobnogo Serafima Sarovskogo: Istoriia desiati nizhegorodskikh zhenskikh monastyrei*. Nizhnii Novgorod: Knigi, 2003.

Burke, Peter. *Popular Culture in Early Modern Europe*. Burlington: Ashgate, 2009.

Burke, Peter, and Bob Scribner, "Is a History of Popular Culture Possible?" *History of European Ideas* 10, no. 2 (1989): 175–91.

Bushkovitch, Paul. *Religion and Society in Russia: The Sixteenth and Seventeenth Centuries*. New York: Oxford University Press, 1992.

Byrne, Lavinia, ed. *Traditions of Spiritual Guidance*. London: Geoffrey Chapman, 1990.

Chetverikov, Sergii. "Iz istorii russkogo starchestva." *Put'* 1 (1912): 3, 7, 38.

———. *Moldavskii Starets Paisii Velichkovskii: ego zhizn, uchenie, i vliianie na pravoslavnoe monashestvo*. Paris: YMCA Press, 1988.

Chistov, K. V. *Russkie narodnye sotsial'no-utopicheskie legendy XVII-XIX vv*. Moscow: Nauka, 1967.

Chistovich, Ilarion. *Feofan Prokopovich i ego vremia*. Vol. 4. St. Petersburg: Izd. Imperatorskoi Akademii nauk, 1868.

Christian, William. *Apparitions in Late Medieval and Renaissance Spain*. Princeton: Princeton University Press, 1981.

Chulos, Chris J. *Converging Worlds: Religion and Community in Peasant Russia, 1861–1917*. DeKalb: Northern Illinois University Press, 2003.

———. "Myths of the Pious or Pagan Peasants in Post-Emancipation Central Russia (Voronezh Province)," *Russian History* 22, no. 2 (1995): 181–216.

Chumachenko, T. A. *Gosudarstvo, pravoslavnaia tserkov', veruiushchie, 1941–1961*. Pervaia monografiia. Edited by G. A. Bordiugov. Moscow: AIRO-XX, 1999.

Clay, Eugene. "The Theological Origins of the Christ-Faith (*Khristovshchina*)." *Russian History/Histoire Russe* 15, no. 1 (1988): 21–41.

Coleman, Heather. *Russian Baptists and Spiritual Revolution, 1905–1929*. Bloomington: Indiana University Press, 2005.

Constable, Giles. *Monks, Hermits, and Crusaders in Medieval Europe*. London: Variorium Reprints, 1988.

Csordas, Thomas. *Language, Charisma, and Creativity: The Ritual Life of a Religious Movement*. Berkeley: University of California Press, 1997.

Dem'ianov, Aleksandr. *Istinno-pravoslavnoe khristianstvo: Kritika ideologii i deiatel'nosti*. Voronezh: Izdatel'stvo Voronezhskogo universiteta, 1977.

Dixon, Joy. *Divine Feminine: Theosophy and Feminism in England*. Baltimore: John Hopkins University Press, 2001.

Dixon, Simon. "Church, State and Society in Late Imperial Russia: the Diocese of St. Petersburg, 1880–1914." PhD diss., University of London, 1993.

———. "Orthodox Church and Workers of St. Petersburg, 1880–1914." In *European Religion in the Age of the Great Cities, 1830–1930*, edited by Hugh Mc Leod, 119–45. London: Routledge, 1995.

———. "The Russian Orthodox Church in Imperial Russia, 1721–1917," In *The Cambridge History of Christianity*. Vol. 5, *Eastern Christianity*, edited by Michael Angold, 325–47. Cambridge: Cambridge University Press, 2008.

Dvorkin, A. L. "Religiia v postsovetskoi Rossii: sindrom 'svobodnogo rynka,'" *Vestnik RKhD* 169, nos. 1–2 (1994): 275–85.

Ekzempliarskii, Vasilii. *Taina stradanii i khristianstvo*. St. Petersburg: Satis, 1996.

El'chaninov, A. "Episkop-starets." *Put'* 4 (June–July 1926): 157–65.

Ellis, Jane. *Russkaia pravoslavnaia tserkov': Soglasie i inakomyslie*. Translated by G. Sidorenko. London: Overseas Publications Interchange, 1990.

Engelstein, Laura. *Castration and the Heavenly Kingdom: A Russian Folktale*. Ithaca: Cornell University Press, 1999.

———. "Holy Russia in Modern Times: an Essay on Orthodoxy and Cultural Change." *Past and Present* 173 (2001): 129–56.

———. "Old and New, High and Low: Straw Horsemen of Russian Orthodoxy." In *Orthodox Russia: Belief and Practice Under the Tsars*, edited by Valerie Kivelson and Robert Greene, 23–33. University Park: Pennsylvania State University Press, 2003.

Etkind, Aleksandr. "Bremia britogo cheloveka ili vnutrenniaia kolonizatsiia Rossii." *Ab Imperio* 1 (2002): 265–98.

———. "Diskurs i revolutsiia: Grigorii Rasputin." *Revue Études Slaves* 69, no. 1–2 (1997): 233–48.

———. *Khlyst: Sekty, literatura, i revoliutsiia*. Moscow: Novoe literaturnoe obozrenie, 1998.

Evdokimov, P. N. "Prepodobnyi Serafim kak ikona pravoslaviia." *Vestnik RKhD*, no. 70/71 (1963): 43–54.

Evtuhov, Catherine. "The Church in the Russian Revolution: Arguments for and against Restoring the Patriarchate at the Church Council of 1917–1918." *Slavic Review* 50, no. 3 (Fall 1991): 497–511.

Fedorov, V. A. *Russkaia pravoslavnaia tserkov' i gosudarstvo: Sinodal'nyi period, 1700–1917*. Moscow: Russkaia Panorama, 2003.

Fedotov, G. P. *Sviatye Drevnei Rusi (X-XVII st.)*. Paris: YMCA Press, 1985.

Fennell, Nicholas. *The Russians on Athos*. New York: Peter Lang, 2001.

Firsov, Sergei. *Russkaia tserkov' nakanune peremen (konets 1890-kh–1918 gg.)*. Moscow: Kruglyi stol po religioznomu obrazovaniiu i diakonii, 2002.

Flood, Gavin. *The Ascetic Self: Subjectivity, Memory, and Tradition*. Cambridge: Cambridge University Press, 2004.

Florenskii, Pavel. *Stolp i utverzhdenie istiny: Opyt pravoslavnoi feoditsei v dvenadtsaty pis'makh*. Moscow, 1914.

Florovsky, Georges. *Puti russkogo bogosloviia*. Paris: YMCA Press, 1937. Reprint, Vilnius, 1991.

Freeze, Gregory. "Church and Politics in Late Imperial Russia: Crisis and Radicalization of the Clergy." In *Russia under the Last Tsar: Opposition and Subversion, 1897–1917*, edited by Anna Geifman, 269–97. Malden, MA: Blackwell, 1999.

———. "'Going to the Intelligentsia': The Church and its Urban Mission in Post-Reform Russia." In *Between Tsar and People: Educated Society and the Quest for Public Identity in Late Imperial Russia*, edited by Edith W. Clowes, Samuel D. Kassow, and James L. West, 215–32. Princeton: Princeton University Press, 1991.

———."Handmaiden of the State? The Church in Imperial Russia Reconsidered." *Journal of Ecclesiastical History* 36, no. 1 (1985): 82–102.

———. *The Parish Clergy in Nineteenth-Century Russia: Crisis, Reform, Counter-Reform*. Princeton: Princeton University Press, 1983.

———."'Pious Folk?' Religious Observance in Vladimir Diocese, 1900–1914." *Jahrbücher für Geschichte Osteuropas* 52 (2004): 323–40.

———. *The Russian Levites: Parish Clergy in the Eighteenth Century*. Cambridge: Harvard University Press, 1977.

———."Subversive Piety: Religion and Political Crisis in Late Imperial Russia." *Journal of Modern History* 68, no. 2 (1996): 308–50.

Geertz, A. W and J. S. Jensen, eds. *Religion, Tradition, and Renewal*. Aarhus: Aarhus University Press, 1991.

Greyerz, Kaspar V. *Religion and Society in Early Modern Europe, 1500–1800*. London: George Allen and Unwin, 1984.

Ginzburg, Carlo. *The Cheese and the Worms: The Cosmos of a Sixteenth-Century Miller*. Translated by John and Anne Tedeschi. Baltimore: Johns Hopkins University Press, 1980.

Golubinskii, E. *Istoriia kanonizatsii sviatykh v russkoi tserkvi*. Moscow: Universitetskaia tip., 1903.

Govorun, S. "Dvizhenie kolivadov." *Tserkov' i vremia* 16, no. 3 (2001): 86–106.

Govorun, S. "Iz istorii Dobrotoliubiia." *Tserkov' i vremia* 14, no. 1 (2001): 262–95.

Gromyko, M. M. "O edinstve pravoslaviia v tserkvi i v narodnoi zhizni." *Nauchnyi pravoslavnyi zhurnal: Traditsii i sovremennost'* 1, no. 1 (2002).

———, ed. *Pravoslavie i russkaia narodnaia kul'tura*. Moscow: Instituta etnologii i antropologii RAN, 1993.

Gromyko, M. M., and A. V. Buganov, *O vozzreniiakh russkogo naroda*. Moscow: Palomnik, 2000.

Guillaumont, Antoine. "L'enseignement spirituel des moines d' Egypte." In *Maitre et disciples dans les traditions religieuses*, edited by Michel Meslin, 143–54. Paris: Editions du Cerf, 1990.

Gurevich, Aron J. *Categories of Medieval Culture*. Translated by G. L. Campbell. London: Routledge, Keegan, & Paul, 1985.

———.*Medieval Popular Culture: Problems of Belief and Perception*. Cambridge Studies in Oral and Literate Culture 14. Cambridge: Cambridge University Press, 1988.

Hagemeister, Michael. "Sergej Nilus und die 'Protokolle der Weisen von Zion': Überlegungen zur Forschungslage." *Jahrbuch für Antisemitismusforschung* 5 (1996): 127–47.

Halbwachs, Maurice. *On Collective Memory*. Chicago: University of Chicago Press, 1992.

Harmless, William. *Desert Christians: An Introduction to the Literature of Early Monasticism*. New York: Oxford University Press, 2004.

Harris, Ruth. *Lourdes: Body and Spirit in the Secular Age*. New York: Viking, 1999.

Hausherr, Irénée. *Spiritual Direction in the Early Christian East.* Translated by Anthony P. Gythiel. Kalamazoo, MI: Cistercian Publications, 1990.

Hedda, Jennifer Elaine. *His Kingdom Come: Orthodox Pastorship and Social Activism in Revolutionary Russia.* DeKalb: Northern Illinois University Press, 2008.

Herrlinger, Page. *Working Souls: Russian Orthodoxy and Factory Labor in St. Petersburg, 1881–1917.* Allan K. Wildman Group Historical Series 2. Bloomington: Slavica, 2007.

Hobsbawm, Eric, and Terence Ranger, eds. *The Invention of Tradition.* Cambridge: Cambridge University Press, 1983.

Howard-Johnston, James, and Paul Antony Hayward, eds. *The Cult of Saints in Late Antiquity: Essays on the Contribution of Peter Brown.* Oxford: Oxford University Press, 1999.

Husband, William. "Godless Communists": Atheism and Society in Soviet Russia, 1917–1932. DeKalb: Northern Illinois University Press, 2000.

Hussey, Joan Mervyn. *The Orthodox Church in the Byzantine Empire.* Oxford: Clarendon Press, 1986.

Iatsmirskii, A. I. *Slavianskie i russkie rukopisi rumynskikh bibliotek.* St. Petersburg: Izd. Imperatorskoi akademii nauk, 1905.

———."Vizantiiskii religioznyi mistitsizm XIV veka pered perekhodom ego k slavianam." *Strannik* 10 (1908): 55–140, 167–219.

———. *Vozrozhdenie vizantiisko-bolgarskogo religioznogo mistitsizma i slavianskoi asketicheskoi literatury v XVIII veke.* Kharkov, 1905.

Il'in, V. N. *Prepodobnyi Serafim Sarovskii.* Paris: YMCA Press, 1925.

Ipatova, S. A. "Otkrovennye rasskazy strannika dukhovnomu svoemu ottsu: paradigmy siuzheta." In *Khristianstvo i russkaia literatura,* edited by V. A. Kotel'nikov, 4:300–35. St. Petersburg: Nauka, 2002.

Ivanov, S. A. *Blazhennye pokhaby: Kul'turnaia istoriia iurodstva.* Moscow: Iazyki slavianskikh kul'tur, 2005.

Kääriainen, Kimmo, and D. E. Furman. "Veruiushchie, ateisty, i prochie (evoliutsiia rossiiskoi religioznosti)." *Voprosy filosofii* 6 (1997): 35–52.

Kahla, Elina. "Art as Glorious Deed: Creating the Community of Martha and Mary in Moscow." *The Russian Review* 66 (January 2007): 73–94.

Kalitin, P. V., ed. *Vysokopreosviashchennyi Gavriil Petrov: Vopreki veku prosveshcheniia.* Moscow: Palomnik, 1999.

[Kavelin, L]. "Poslednie russkie pravoslavnye pustynnozhiteli." *Domashniaia beseda,* no. 21 (1862): 487–90; no. 22 (1862): 507–17; no. 23 (1862): 539–47; no. 24 (1862): 563–70; no. 25 (1862): 595–601; no. 26 (1862): 619–27.

Kenworthy, Scott. "The Revival of Monasticism in Modern Russia: the Trinity-Sergius Lavra, 1825-1921." PhD diss., Brandeis University, 2002.

———. "Monasticism in Russian History." *Kritika: Explorations in Russian and Eurasian History* 10, no. 2 (2009): 307–31.

———."To Save the World or to Renounce It: Modes of Moral Action in Russian Orthodoxy." In *Reclaiming the Sacred: Morality, Community, and Religion after Communism,* edited by Mark Steinberg and Catherine Wanner, 21–54. Washington, DC: Woodrow Wilson Center Press and Bloomington IN: Indiana University Press, 2008.

(Kern), Kiprian. *Pravoslavnoe pastorskoe sluzhenie.* Paris: Zhurnal "Vechnoe", 1957.

Khoruzhii, S. S. "Fenomen russkogo starchestva v ego dukhovnykh i antropologicheskikh osnovaniiakh." *Tserkov' i vremia* 21 (2001): 208–26.

Kilpeläinen, Hannu. *Valamo-karjalaisten luostari? Luostarin ja yhteistkunnan interaktio maailmansotien välisenä aikana*. Helsinki: Suomalaisen kirjallisuuden seura, 2000.
Kirichenko, O. "Znachenie pravednika-startsa dlia sela." *Nauchnyi pravoslavnyi zhurnal: Traditsii i sovremennost'* 1, no. 1 (2002): 61–76.
Kiseleva, M. S., ed. *Chelovek mezhdu tsarstvom i imperiei: sbornik materialov mezdunarodnoi konferentsii*. Moscow: Institut cheloveka RAN, 2003.
Kitch, Faith C. M. *The Literary Style of Epifanii Premudryi 'Pletenije Sloves'*." Munich: Verlag Otto Sagner, 1976.
Kizenko, Nadiezda. *A Prodigal Saint: Father John of Kronstadt and the Russian People*. University Park: Pennsylvania State University Press, 2000.
Klibanov, A. I. *Istoriia religioznogo sektanstva v Rossii: 60-e gody XIX v.–1917 g.* Moscow: Nauka, 1965.
Knox, Zoe. *Russian Society and the Orthodox Church: Religion in Russia after communism*. London: Routledge Curzon, 2005.
Komissarenko, A. I. *Russkii absolutism i dukhoventsvo v XVIII veke: ocherki istorii sekulariazatsionnoi reformy 1764 g.* Moscow: Izd-vo Vses. zaochnogo politekhnicheskogo instituta, 1990.
Kondakov, Iu. *Dukhovno-religioznaia politika Aleksandra I i Russkaia pravoslavnaia oppozitsiia, 1801–1825*. St. Petersburg: Nestor, 1998.
Konstantinovsky, Julia. *Evagrius Ponticus: The Making of a Gnostic*. Farnham and Burlington: Ashgate, 2008.
Kontsevich, I. M. *Stiazhanie sviatogo dukha v putiakh Drevnei Rusi*. Paris: YMCA Press, 1952. Reprint, Moscow: Lepta, 2002.
Kontsevich, I. M. *Optina pustyn' i ee vremia*. Zagorsk: Sviato-Troitskaia Sergieva Lavra, 1995.
Kotel'nikov, V. *Pravoslavnaia asketika i russkaia literature: na puti k Optinoi*. St. Petersburg: Prizma-15, 1994.
Kovalenko, Z. P. "Lev Nagolkin i Belobrezhskaia pustyn'." In *Stranitsy istorii Karacheva*, edited by V. V. Krasheninnikov, 18–24. Briansk: Brian. obl. nauch. b-ka, 1996.
Kovalevskii, Ioann. *Iurodstvo o Khriste i Khrista radi Iurodivye Vostochnoi i Russkoi tserkvi: istoricheskie ocherk i zhitiia sikh podvizhnikov*. Moscow: Pech. A. I. Snegirovoi, 1895.
Krueger, Derek. *Symeon the Holy Fool: Leontius's Life and the Late Antique City*. Berkeley: University of California Press, 1996.
Krushel'nitskaia, E. V. *Martirii Zelenetskii i osnovannyi im Troitskii monastyr'*. St. Petersburg: Aleteiia, 1998.
Lavrov, A. S. *Koldovstvo i religiia v Rossii, 1700–1740 gg.* Moscow: Drevlekhranilishche, 2000.
Levin, Eve. "Dvoeverie and Popular Religion." In *Seeking God: the Recovery of Religious Identity in Orthodox Russia, Ukraine, and Georgia*, edited by Stephen K. Batalden, 31–52. DeKalb: Northern Illinois University Press, 1993.
———. "From Corpse to Cult in Early Modern Russia." In *Orthodox Russia: Belief and Practice under the Tsars*, edited by Valerie. A. Kivelson and Robert H. Green, 81–103. University Park: Pennsylvania State University Press, 2003.
Levitskii, A. V. *Svidetel' istiny: pamiati protopresvitera Ioanna Meiendorfa*. Ekaterinburg: Ekaterinburgskaia eparkhiia, 2003.
Lindholm, Charles. *Charisma*. Cambridge: Blackwell, 1990.
Lindquist, Galina. *Conjuring Hope: Magic and Healing in Contemporary Russia*. New York: Berghahn Books, 2005.
Linnér, Sven. *Starets Zosima in The Brothers Karamazov: A Study in the Mimesis of Virtue*.

Stockholm: Almqvist & Wiksell, 1975.

Lisovoi, N. N. "Dve epokhi, dva dobrotoliubiia (prepodobnyi Paisii Velichkovskii i sviatitel' Feofan Zatvornik)." In *Tserkov' v istorii Rossii,* edited by Iaroslav Shcharov and Pavel Zyrianov, 2:108–78. Moscow: Institut Rossiiskoi istorii Rossiiskoi Akademii Nauk, 1998.

———. "Vosemnadtsatyi vek v istorii russkogo monashestva." *Monashestvo i monastyri v Rossii*, edited by N. Sinitsyna, 186–222. Moscow: Nauka, 2002.

Liubomudrov, A. M. *Dukhovnyi realizm v literature russkogo zarubezh'ia: B. K. Zaitsev, I. S. Shmelev*. St. Petersburg: Dmitrii Bulanin, 2003.

Lotman, Iu. M. *Istoriia i tipologiia russkoi kul'tury*. St. Petersburg: Iskusstvo-SPb, 2002.

Le Maître spirituel dans les grandes traditions d'Occident et d'Orient. Hermes: Recherches sur l'expérience spirituelle 4. Paris: Tournai, 1967.

Maiorova, O. E. "Mitropolit Moskovskii Filaret v obshchestvennom soznanii kontsa XIX v." *Lotmanovskii sbornik* 2 (1997): 615–38.

Makarii, Metropolitan, I. K. Smolitsch, and Vladislav Tsypin. *Istoriia russkoi tserkvi*. 9 vols. Moscow: Izdatel'stvo Spaso-Preobrazhenskogo Valaamskogo monastyria, 1994–1997.

(Makhanov), Onufrii. *Prichal molitv uedinennykh: Valaamskii monastyr' i ego nebesnye pokroviteli prepodobnye Sergii i German*. St. Petersburg: Tsarskoe delo, 2005.

Maloney, George A. *Russian Hesychasm: The Spirituality of Nil Sorskii*. The Hague: Mouton, 1973.

Mansurov, Sergii. *Ocherki iz istorii tserkvi*. Klin: Khristianskaia zhizn', 2002.

(Maslov), Ioann. *Glinskaia Pustyn': Istoriia obiteli i ee dukhovno-prosvetitel'skaia deiatel'nost' v XVI-XX vekakh*. Moscow: Izdatel'skii otdel Moskovskogo patriarkhata, 1994.

Mauss, Marcel. *The Gift: the Form and Reason for Exchange in Archaic Societies*. London: Routledge, 1990.

Marrese, Michelle Lamarche. *A Woman's Kingdom: Noblewomen and the Control of Property in Russia, 1700–1861*. Ithaca: Cornell University Press, 2002.

Maylunas, Andrei, and Sergei Mironenko, eds. *A Lifelong Passion: Nicholas and Alexandra, Their Own Story*. New York: Doubleday, 1997.

McGuckin, John A. "Symeon the New Theologian (d. 1022) and Byzantine monasticism." In *Mount Athos and Byzantine Monasticism: Papers from the Twenty-eighth Spring Symposium of Byzantine Studies, Birmingham March 1994*, edited by Anthony Bryer and Mary Cunningham, 19–32. Society for the Promotion of Byzantine Studies Publications 4. Aldershot: Variorum, 1996.

McLeod, Hugh. *Secularization in Western Europe 1848–1914*. Basingstoke: Macmillan, 2000.

Meehan-Waters, Brenda. "Metropolitan Filaret (Drozdov) and the Reform of Russian Women's Monastic Communities." *The Russian Review* 50 (1991): 310–23.

———. "Popular Piety, Local Initiative, and the Founding of Women's Religious Communities in Russia, 1764–1904." *St. Vladimir's Theological Quarterly* 30 (1986): 117–42.

Meyendorff, John. "O bozhestvennom dostoinstve sviatogo dukha." In *Svidetel' istiny: pamiati protopresvitera Ioanna Meiendorfa*, edited by A. V. Levitskii, 103–13. Ekaterinburg: Ekaterinburgskaia eparkhiia, 2003.

———. *Zhizn' i trudy sviatitelia Grigoriia Palamy: vvedenie i izuchenie*. Translated by G. Nachinkin. St. Petersburg: Vizantinorossika, 1997.

Milbank, John. *Theology and Social Theory: Beyond Secular Reason*. London: Blackwell, 1993.

Miller, Liubov'. *Grand Duchess Elizabeth of Russia: New Martyr of the Communist Yoke.* Redding, CA: Nikodemos Orthodox Publication Society, 1990.

Mitrokhin, N. *Russkaia pravoslavnaia tserkov': sovremennoe sostoianie i aktual'nye problemy.* Moscow: Novoe literaturnoe obozrenie, 2004.

Nechaeva, M. Iu. *Monastyri i vlasti: upravlenie obiteliami Vostochnogo Urala v XVIII v.* Ekaterinburg: UrO RAN, 1998.

Nichols, Robert. "The Friends of God: Nicholas II and Alexandra at the Canonization of Serafim of Sarov, July 1903." In *Religious and Secular Forces in Late Tsarist Russia: Essays in Honor of Donald Treadgold,* edited by Charles E. Timberlake, 206–29. Seattle: University of Washington Press, 1992.

———. "The Orthodox Elders of Imperial Russia." *Modern Greek Studies Yearbook* 1 (1985): 1–30.

Nichols, Robert, and Theofanis Stavrou, eds. *Russian Orthodoxy under the Old Regime.* Minneapolis: University of Minnesota Press, 1978.

Nikolinkin, Aleksandr, and V. V. Rozanov. *Okolo tserkovnykh sten.* Moscow: Respublika, 1995.

Ozerov D. A. "Otets Ioann Kronshtadtskii." *Pravoslavnaia zhizn'*, no. 11 (1964): 14–21; no. 12 (1964): 8–14.

The Oxford Dictionary of the Christian Church. Edited by F. L. Cross and E. A. Livingstone. 3rd ed. Oxford: Oxford University Press, 1997.

Paert, Irina. *Old Believers, Religious Dissent and Gender in Russia, 1760–1850.* Manchester: Manchester University Press, 2003.

———. "'An Unmercenary Bishop': Ignatii Brianchaninov (1807–1867) and the Making of Modern Russian Orthodoxy." *Slavonica* 9, no. 2 (2003): 99–112.

Panchenko, A. *Khristovshchina i skopchestvo: fol'klor i traditsionnaia kul'tura russkikh misticheskikh sekt.* Moscow: Ob"edinennoe gumantarinoe izdatel'stvo, 2002.

Papoulidis, C. *Nicodème l'Hagiorite: 1749–1809.* Athens, 1967.

———. "Portée oecuménique du renouveau monastique au XVIII siécle dans l'église Orthodoxe," *Balkan Studies* 10, no. 1 (1969): 111–12.

Pascal, Pierre. *The Religion of the Russian People.* London: Mowbrays, 1976.

Pelikan, Jaroslav. *The Spirit of Eastern Christendom (600–1700).* Chicago: The University of Chicago Press, 1974.

———. *The Vindication of Tradition.* New Haven: Yale University Press, 1984.

Pentkovskii, A. "'Ot iskatelia neprestannoi molitvy' do 'Otkrovennykh rasskazov strannika' (k voprosu ob istorii teksta)," *Simvol*, no. 27 (1992): 137–66.

Pokrovskii, N. N. *Antifeodal'nyi protest uralo-sibirskikh krest'ian-staroobriadtsev v XVIII veka.* Novosibirsk: Nauka, 1974.

(Poliakov), Leonid. "Literaturnoe nasledstvo Paisiia Velichkovskogo." *Zhurnal Moskovskoi Patriarkhii* 4 (1957): 57–61.

Polunov, A. Iu. *Pod vlast'iu ober-prokurora: Gosudarstvo i tserkov' v epokhu Alexandra III.* Moscow: AIRO XX, 1996.

Popov, I. V. "Ideiia obozheniia v drevne-vostochnoi tserkvi." *Voprosy filosofii i psikhologii* 2, no. 97 (1909): 165–213.

———. *Misticheskoe opravdanie asketizma v tvoreniiakh prep. Makariia Egipetskogo.* Kozel'sk, 1905.

Popov, M. S. *Arsenii Matsieevich i ego delo.* St. Petersburg: Tip. M. Frolovoi, 1912.

Poselianin, E. *Russiaia tserkov' i russkie podvizhniki XVIII veka.* St. Petersburg: Izd. I. L. Tuzova, 1905.

———.*Prepodobnyi Serafim Sarovskii chudotvorets i russkie podvizhniki XIX veka*. Moscow: Aksios, 2003.

Pozov, A. *Logos-meditatsiia drevnei tserkvi: umnoe delanie*. Munich: Tovarishchestvo zarubezhnykh pisatelei, 1964.

Pravoslavnaia Entsiklopediia. Moscow: Pravoslavnaia entsiklopediia, 2000.

Price, Richard. "Informal Penance in Early Medieval Christendom." In *Retribution, Repentance, and Reconciliation: Papers Read at the 2002 Summer Meeting and the 2003 Winter Meeting of the Ecclesiastical History Society*, edited by Kate Cooper and Jeremy Gregory, 29–38. Woodbridge, Suffolk: Boydell Press, 2004.

Prokhorov, G. M. "Keleinaia isikhastskaia literatura v biblioteke Kirillo-Belozerskogo monastyria s XIV po XVII v." In *Monastyrskaia kul'tura: Vostok i Zapad*, edited by E. Vodolazkin, 44–58. St. Petersburg: Pushkinskii Dom, 1999.

———. "O vizantiiskoi bogoslovsko-filosofskoi literature v kul'ture Rusi XIV-XVI vv." In *Svidetel' istiny: pamiati protopresvitera Ioanna Meiendorfa*, edited by A.V. Levitskii, 426–34. Ekaterinburg: Informatsionnyi Otdel Ekaterinburgskoi eparkhii, 2003.

Put' k sovershennoi zhizni: o russkom starchestve. Moscow: Pravoslavnyi Sviato-Tikhonovskii Gumanitarnyi Universitet, 2006.

(Puzik), Ignatiia. *Starchestvo na Rusi*. Moscow: Izd-vo Moskovskogo Podvor'ia Sviato-Troitskoi Sergievoi Lavry, 1999.

———.*Starchestvo v gody gonenii: prepodobnomuchenik Ignatii (Lebedev) i ego dukhovnaia sem'ia*. Moscow: Moskovskoe Podvor'e Sviato-Troitskoi Sergievoi Lavry, 2001.

Raeff, Mark. *Russia Abroad: A Cultural History of the Russian Emigration, 1919–1939*. New York: Oxford University Press, 1990.

Rimskii, S. V. *Rossiiskaia tserkov v epokhu velikikh reform: tserkovnoe reformy v Rossii 1860–1870-kh godov*. Moscow: Krutitskoe patriarsh'e podvor'e, Obshchestvo liubitelei tserkovnoi istorii, 1999.

Robson, Roy R. *Solovki: The Story of Russia Told Through its Most Remarkable Islands*. New Haven: Yale University Press, 2004.

Rock, Stella. *Popular Religion in Russia: "Double Belief" and the Making of an Academic Myth*. London: Routledge, 2007.

Romanchuk, Robert. *Byzantine Hermeneutics and Pedagogy in the Russian North: Monks and Masters at the Kirillo-Belozerskii Monastery, 1397–1501*. Toronto: University of Toronto Press, 2007.

Roshko, Vsevolod. *Prepodobnyi Serafim: Sarov i Diveevo; Issledovaniia i materialy*. Moscow: Sam & Sam, 1997.

Roslof, Edward E. *Red Priests: Renovationism, Russian Orthodoxy, and Revolution, 1905–1946*. Bloomington: Indiana University Press, 2002.

Rousseau, Philip. "Ascetics as Mediators and as Teachers." In *The Cult of Saints in Late Antiquity and the Middle Ages: Essays on the Contribution of Peter Brown*, edited by James Howard-Johnston and Paul Antony Hayward, 45–59. Oxford: Oxford University Press, 1999.

Rudi, T.V. "Rannie zhitiia Serafima Sarovskogo: voprosy literaturnoi istorii." *Trudy otdela drevnerusskoi literatury* 51 (1999): 427–34.

Runciman, Steven. *The Great Church in Captivity: A Study of the Patriarchate of Constantinople from the Eve of the Turkish Conquest to the Greek War of Independence*. London: Cambridge University Press, 1968.

Sanders, Jack T. *Charisma, Converts, Competitors: Societal and Sociological Factors in the*

Success of Early Christianity. London: SCM Press, 2000.

Sakharov, Nicholas. *I Love, Therefore I Am: The Theological Legacy of Archimandrite Sophrony*. New York: St. Vladimir Seminary Press, 2002.

Sayings of the Desert Fathers. Translated by Benedicta Ward. London: Mowbray, 1975.

[Semenov-Tian-Shan'skii], Aleksandr. *Otets Ioann Kronshtadtskii*. New York: Izdatel'stvo im. Chekhova, 1955.

Shabalin, N. V. *Russkaia pravoslavnaia tserkov' i sovetskoe gosudarstvo v seredine 40–50-e gg. XX v.: na materialakh Kirovskoi oblasti*. Kirov, 2004.

Shevzov, Vera. "Letting the People into Church." In *Orthodox Russia: Belief and Practice Under the Tsars*, edited by Valerie Kivelson and Robert Green, 59–80. University Park: Pennsylvania State University Press, 2003.

———. "Popular Orthodoxy in Imperial Rural Russia." PhD diss., Yale University, 1994.

———. *Russian Orthodoxy on the Eve of Revolution*. New York: Oxford University Press, 2004.

Shkarovskii, M. V. *Iosiflianstvo: techenie v Russkoi Pravoslavnoi Tserkvi*. St. Petersburg: Memorial, 1999.

———. *Tserkov' zovet k zashchite rodiny: religioznaia zhizn' Leningrada i Severo-Zapada v gody Velikoi Otechestvennoi voiny*. St. Petersburg: Satis, 2005.

Silber, Ilana. *Virtuosity, Charisma, and Social Order: A Comparative Sociological Study of Monasticism in Theravada Buddhism and Medieval Catholicism*. Cambridge Cultural and Social Studies. Cambridge: Cambridge University Press, 1995.

Sinitsyna, N. V. "Tipy monastyrei i russkii asketicheskii ideal (XV–XVI vv.)." In *Monashestvo i monastyri v Rossii XI–XX vv.*, edited by N.V. Sinitsyna, et. al., 116–49. Moscow: Nauka, 2002.

———,ed. *Monashestvo i monastyri v Rossii XI–XX vv.* Moscow: Nauka, 2002.

Smilianskaia, E. *Volshebniki, bogokhul'niki, eretiki: narodnaia religioznost' i "dukhovnye prestupleniia" v Rossii XVIII v*. Moscow: Indrik, 2003.

Smirnov, P. I. *Drevne-russkii dukhovnik: issledovanie po istorii tserkovnogo byta*. Moscow: Sinodal'naia Tipografiia, 1913.

———. *Dukhovnyi otets v drevnei Vostochnoi tserkvi*. Sergiev Posad, 1906. Reprint, Moscow: Pravoslavnyi Sviato-Tikhonovskii Bogoslovskii Institut, 2003.

Smolitsch I. K. *Russisches Mönchtum: Entstehung, Entwicklung, und Wesen, 988–1917*. Würzburg: Augustins-Verlag, 1953.

———. *Russkoe monashestvo, 988–1917: Zhizn' i uchenie startsev; prilozheniie k "Istorii Russkoi Tserkvi."* Moscow: Pravoslavnaia entsiklopediia, 1997.

———. "Sviataia Gora Afonskaia." *Vestnik RKhD* 70–71 (1963): 40.

Stanton, Leonard J. *The Optina Pustyn Monastery in the Russian Literary Imagination: Iconic Vision in Works by Dostoevsky, Gogol, Tolstoy, and Others*. Middlebury Studies in Russian Language and Literature 3. New York: Peter Lang, 1995.

Stefanovich, P. S. *Prikhod i prikhodskoe dukhovenstvo v Rossii v XVI-XVII vekakh*. Moscow: Indrik, 2002.

Stepashkin, V. *Prepodobnyi Serafim Sarovskii: predaniia i fakty*. Sarov, 2002.

Syrku, Polikhronii. *K istorii ispravleniia knig v Bolgarii v XIV veke*. St. Petersburg: Tip. Impteratorskoi akademii nauk, 1890.

Tarabukina, A. V. "Fol'klor i kul'tura protserkovnogo kruga." Kand. diss., St. Petersburg University, 2000.

(Tertyshnikov), Georgii. "Zhitie ieromonakha Varnavy (Merkulova), startsa Gefsimanskogo skita pri Sviato Troitse-Sergievoi Lavre." *Zhurnal Moskovskoi Patriarkhii*, no. 9/10 (1994): 41–59.

Theodor of Sanaxar, *Saint Theodore of Sanaxar*. Vol. 5, *Little Russian Philokalia*. Platina, CA: St. Herman of Alaska Brotherhood, 2000.

Thompson, Ewa. *Understanding Russia: The Holy Fool in Russian Culture*. Lanham, MD: University Press of America, 1987.

Titlinov, B. V. *Gavriil Petrov, Mitropolit Novgorodskii i Sankt-Peterburgskii: Ego zhizn' i deiatel'nost' v sviazi s tserkovnymi delami togo vremeni*. Petrograd: Tip. M. Melkusheva, 1916.

(Trubachev), Andronik. *Prepodobnyi Amvrosii Optinskii: Zhizn' i tvoreniia*. Kiev: Obshchestvo liubitelei pravoslavnoi literatury, 2003.

(Trubachev), Andronik, A. A. Bovkalo, and V. A. Fedorov. "Monastyri i monashestvo." In *Pravoslavnaia entsiklopedia Rossiiskoi Pravoslavnoi Tserkvi*, 325–345. Moscow: Rossiiskaia pravoslavnaia entsiklopediia, 2000.

Tserkov' v istorii Rossii. 8 vols. Moscow: Institut Rossiiskoi istorii Rossiiskoi Akademii nauk, 1997–2009.

Turner, Victor. *The Ritual Process: Structure and Anti-Structure*. Chicago: Aldine de Gruyter, 1969.

(Turkestanov), Trifon. *Drevnekhristianskie i Optinskie startsy*. Moscow: Martis, 1997.

(Uspenskii), Porfirii. *Istoriia Afona*. 4 vols. Kiev: Tip. V. L. Frontskevicha, 1877–1892.

Valliere, Paul. *Modern Russian Theology: Bukharev, Solov'ev, Bulgakov; Orthodox Theology in a New Key*. Grand Rapids: Eerdmans, 2000.

Vasil'eva, O. Iu. *Russkaia pravoslavnaia tserkov' v politike sovetskogo gosudarstva v 1943–1948 gg*. Moscow: Institut rossiisskoi istorii RAN, 1999.

Vernitski, Anat. "The Way of a Pilgrim: Literary Reading of a Religious Text." *Slavonica* 4, no. 12 (2003): 113–22.

Viise, Michelle. "Filaret Drozdov and the Language of Official Proclamations in Nineteenth-Century Russia." *The Slavic and East European Journal* 44, no. 4 (2000): 553–82.

Vishlenkova, E. *Zabotias' o dushakh poddannykh: religioznaia politika v Rossii pervoi chetverti XIX veka*. Saratov: Izdatel'stvo Saratovskogo universiteta, 2002.

Wagner, William. "'Orthodox Domesticity': Creating a Social Role for Women in Late Imperial Russia." In *Sacred Stories: Religion and Spirituality in Modern Russia*, edited by Mark D. Steinberg and Heather J. Coleman, 119–45. Indiana-Michigan Series in Russian and East European Studies. Bloomington: Indiana University Press, 2007.

———. "Paradoxes of Piety: The Nizhegorod Convent of the Exaltation of the Cross, 1807–1935." In *Orthodox Russia: Belief and Practice Under the Tsars*, edited by Valerie Kivelson and Robert Green, 211–38. University Park: Pennsylvania State University Press, 2004.

———. "The Transformation of Female Orthodox Monasticism in Nizhnii Novgorod Diocese, 1764–1929, in Comparative Perspective." *Journal of Modern History* 78, no. 12 (2006): 793–845.

Walker, Carolyn Bynum. *Jesus as Mother: Studies in the Spirituality of the High Middle Ages*. Berkeley: University of California Press, 1982.

Wallis, Roy. "Charisma, Commitment, and Control in a New Religious Movement." In *Millennialism and Charisma*, 167–79. Belfast: Queen's University, 1982.

(Ware), Kallistos. "The Spiritual Guide in Orthodox Christianity." In *The Inner Kingdom*. Vol. 1, *The Collected Works*. Crestwood, NY: St. Vladimir's Seminary Press, 2001.

Weber, Max. *Economy and Society: An Outline of Interpretive Sociology*. Vol. 3. New York: Bedminster Press, 1968.

Wigzell, Faith. *Reading Russian Fortunes: Print Culture, Gender, and Divination in Russia from 1765*. Cambridge: Cambridge University Press, 1998.

Wilson, Bryan R. *Magic and Millennium: A Sociological Study of Religious Movements of Protest among Tribal and Third-World Peoples*. St. Albans: Paladin, 1975.

———. *The Noble Savages: the Primitive Origins of Charisma and its Contemporary Survival*. Berkeley: University of California Press, 1975.

Wimbush, Vincent. L. and Richard Valantasis, eds. *Asceticism*. New York: Oxford University Press, 2002.

Worobec, Christine. *Possessed: Women, Witches, and Demons in Imperial Russia*. DeKalb: Northern Illinois University Press, 2001.

Wortman, Richard. *Scenarios of Power: Myth and Ceremony in Russian Monarchy*. 2 vols. Princeton: Princeton University Press, 1995–2000.

Wuthnow, Robert. *After Heaven: Spirituality in America since the 1950s*. Berkeley: University of California Press, 1998.

Wynot, Jennifer. *Keeping the Faith: Russian Orthodox Monasticism in the Soviet Union, 1917–1939*. College Station, TX: Texas A&M University Press, 2004.

Young, Glennys. *Power and the Sacred in Revolutionary Russia: Religious Activists in the Village*. University Park: Pennsylvania State University Press, 1997.

Zapal'skii, G. M. *Optina Pustyn' i ee vospitanniki v 1825–1917 godakh*. Moscow: Rukopisnye pamiatniki drevnei Rusi, 2009.

Zelnik, Reginald. "'To the Unaccustomed Eye': Religion and Irreligion in the Experience of St. Petersburg Workers in the 1870s." *Russian History* 16, nos. 2–4 (1989): 214–36.

Zernov, Nicholas. *The Russian Religious Renaissance of the Twentieth Century*. London: Dartmon, Longman, & Todd, 1963.

Zhivov, V. M. *Iazyk i kul'tura v Rossii XVIII v*. Moscow: Iazyki russkoi kul'tury, 1996.

Ziff, Bruce and Pratima V. Rao, eds. *Borrowed Power: Essays on Cultural Appropriation*. New Brunswick: Rutgers University Press, 1997.

Ziolkowski, Margaret. *Hagiography and Modern Russian Literature*. Princeton: Princeton University Press, 1988.

Znamenskii, P. *Prikhodskoe dukhovenstvo v Rossii so vremeni reformy Petra*. Kazan, 1873.

Zorin, A. *Kormia dvuglavogo orla . . . Literatura i gosudarstvennaia ideologiia v Rossii v poslednei treti XVIII–pervoi treti XIX veka*. Moscow: Novoe literaturnoe obozrenie, 2001.

Zyrianov, P. N. *Pravoslavnaia tserkov' v bor'be s revoliutsiei 1905–1907 gg*. Moscow: Nauka, 1984.

———. *Russkie monastyri i monashestvo v XIX i nachale XX veka*. Moscow: Russkoe slovo, 1999.

———. "Russkie monastyri i monashestvo v XIX–nachale XX veka." In *Monashestvo i monastyri v Rossii*, edited by N. Sinitsyna, 302–31. Moscow: Nauka, 2002.

Index